Early Cyprus

Vassos Karageorghis

Early Cyprus
Crossroads of the Mediterranean

The J. Paul Getty Museum
Los Angeles

Acknowledgments

The book owes much to a large number of people: to all museum curators and collectors who have provided photographs and given permission for their publication. They are listed in a separate section, on page 230.
To Alison South, who not only edited the text and prepared the maps but also helped substantially with suggestions for its improvement. G.R.H. Wright and Ian Todd assisted with the captions for the illustrations. Kapon Editions made important improvements to the layout of the book.

First published in the United States of America
in 2002 by the J. Paul Getty Museum

Getty Publications
1200 Getty Center Drive
Suite 500
Los Angeles, California 90049-1682
www.getty.edu

At Getty Publications:
Christopher Hudson, Publisher
Mark Greenberg, Editor in Chief

Mollie Holtman, Editor
Robert Swanson, Indexer

Library of Congress Control Number: 2002115191

ISBN: 0-89236-679-6

Printed and bound in Italy

Contents

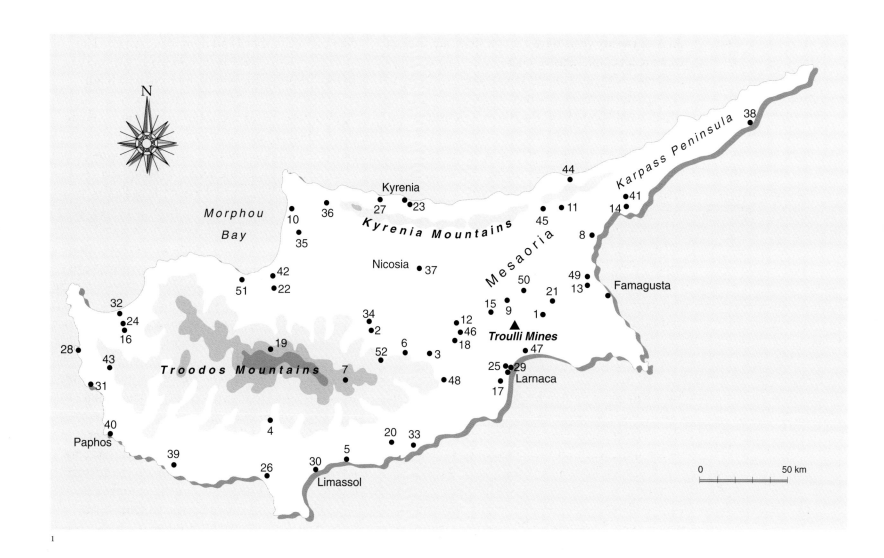

Morphou Bay

N

Kyrenia

Kyrenia Mountains

Mesaoria

Karpass Peninsula

Nicosia

Troodos Mountains

Troulli Mines

Larnaca

Famagusta

Paphos

Limassol

0   50 km

1

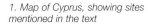

1. Map of Cyprus, showing sites mentioned in the text

1. Achna
2. Akhera
3. Alambra
4. Alassa-*Paliotaverna*
5. Amathus
6. Analiondas
7. Apliki
8. Arnadhi
9. Arsos
10. Ayia Irini-*Palaeokastro*
11. Ayios Iakovos
12. Ayios Sozomenos-*Nikolidhes*

13. Enkomi
14. Gastria-*Alaas* and *Grotirin*
15. Golgoi
16. Goudhi
17. Hala Sultan Tekke
18. Idalion
19. Kakopetria
20. Kalavassos-*Ayios Dhimitrios*
21. Kalopsidha
22. Katydhata
23. Kazaphani
24. Khrysochou
25. Kition
26. Kourion/Episkopi
27. Lapithos

28. Lara
29. Larnaca
30. Limassol
31. Maa-*Palaeokastro*
32. Marion
33. Maroni-*Vournes*
34. Meniko
35. Morphou-*Toumba tou Skourou*
36. Myrtou-*Stephania*
37. Nicosia-*Ayia Paraskevi*
38. Nitovikla
39. Palaepaphos/Kouklia
40. Paphos
41. Patriki
42. Pendayia

43. Peyia
44. Phlamoudhi
45. Platani
46. Potamia
47. Pyla-*Kokkinokremos*
48. Pyrga
49. Salamis
50. Sinda
51. Soloi
52. Tamassos

Preface

Almost twenty years have elapsed since my attempt to write a comprehensive book on the archaeology of Cyprus, *Cyprus from the Stone Age to the Romans* (Karageorghis 1982). The need for a new book, which would include all the discoveries made since then and the new theories proposed by various scholars about the place of Cyprus within the Mediterranean region, has become more and more apparent.

Young scholars entering the field of Cypriote archaeology often find themselves at a loss in trying to gain an overview of Cypriote archaeology within which to place their own narrower field of research. In recent years, excavations both in Cyprus and in the whole of the Mediterranean region have yielded vast quantities of material relevant to all periods of Cypriote archaeology. The student needs to look around very carefully, almost on a daily basis, in order to be informed about new discoveries from the Near East, Egypt, Anatolia, and the Mediterranean as far as the Iberian peninsula. He or she must also become familiar with current theories and be aware of the results of the application of science to archaeology. These are not easy tasks. Therefore, to write a comprehensive book on all periods of Cypriote archaeology is a gigantic undertaking, which might more efficiently have been entrusted to a team of experts. For this reason I declined the idea of undertaking it by myself.

Three periods of Cypriote archaeology have attracted much attention during the last twenty years or so. First, the Neolithic, Chalcolithic, Early and Middle Bronze Ages (circa ninth millennium to circa 1600 B.C.). Second, the Late Bronze Age (circa 1600–1050 B.C.). The third period, covering the Geometric and Archaic periods (circa 1050–500 B.C.), has been in the spotlight as a result of the renewed interest in the study of Phoenician civilization and the Phoenician expansion to the west, in which Cyprus played a leading role.

The fact that I have undertaken to write a comprehensive study covering the second and third areas of study, that is, the period from about 1600–500 B.C.,
does not mean that I can do it exhaustively. The bibliography has increased enormously since 1982 and so have the discoveries, many of which are unpublished, causing major difficulty and a great disadvantage for research. However, I am fortunate to have had the opportunity to follow most of the archaeological discoveries in Cyprus very closely, as Director of the Department of Antiquities of Cyprus until 1989, and subsequently as Professor of Archaeology in the University of Cyprus until 1996; I have also been able to maintain close contacts with the major practitioners of Cypriote archaeology, and with many colleagues working in Mediterranean archaeology, including those from the Levant, the Aegean, and the Central Mediterranean. Thus I ventured to accept the invitation by Professor Paolo Matthiae to write the present book for the Electa publishers.

Most of my archaeological research over the last fifty years or so has been concentrated on the period covered by this book, which is one of supreme importance for the development of the ancient civilization of Cyprus. I attach great importance to interconnections in the Mediterranean in order to explain the phenomena of Cypriote culture; this is apparent throughout the various chapters of this book. The study of such interconnections has gained more and more ground in recent years, and my colleagues and myself have been instrumental in promoting several international symposia in order to study the particular role of Cyprus.

This book is intended for the general public, but that does not imply that it offers imprecise or superficially treated information. A lengthy and up-to-date bibliography has been included, so that specialists and students may satisfy their scholarly curiosity by further reading.

Vassos Karageorghis

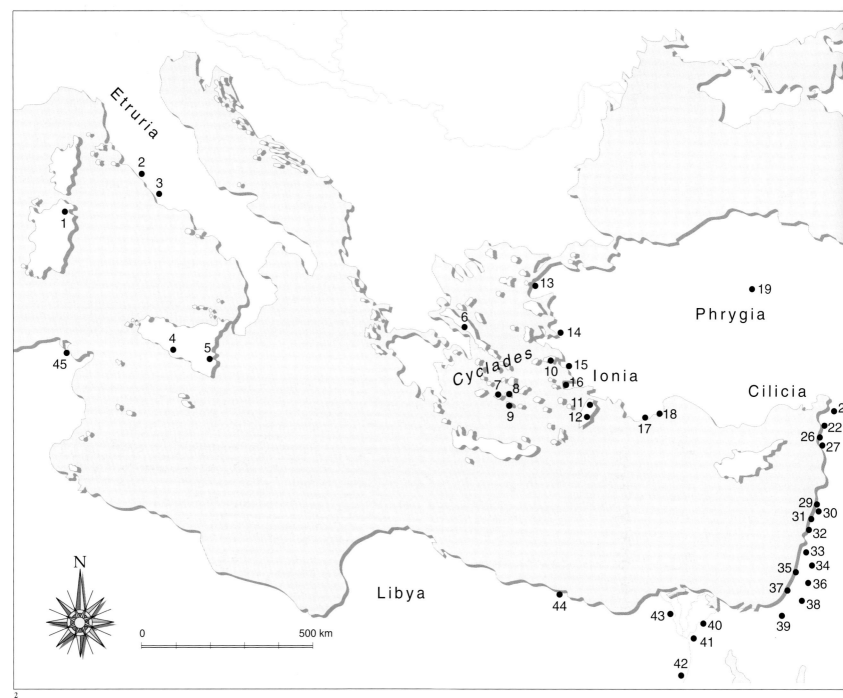

2. Map of the East Mediterranean, showing sites mentioned in the text

Italy
1. Golfo di Cugnana, Olbia (Sassari)
2. Cerveteri
3. Praeneste
4. Thapsos (Sicily)
5. Cannatello

Greece
6. Lefkandi-Toumba
7. Paros-Koukounaries
8. Naxos
9. Thera
10. Heraion (Samos)
11. Trianda (Rhodes)
12. Lindos (Rhodes)

Turkey
13. Troy
14. Old Smyrna
15. Miletus
16. Knidos
17. Uluburun
18. Cape Gelidonya
19. Gordion
20. Altintepe
21. Toprakkale
22. Al Mina
23. Alalakh

Iraq
24. Nineveh
25. Nimrud

Syria
26. Ugarit
27. Ras Ibn Hani
28. Mari

Lebanon
29. Sidon
30. Sarepta
31. Tyre

Israel/Palestine
32. Kabri
33. Megiddo
34. Samaria
35. Tell Qasile
36. Tel Miqne-Ekron
37. Ashkelon
38. Lachish
39. Tell el-Farah

Egypt
40. Tell el-Dab'a
41. Tell el-Yahudiyeh
42. El-Lisht
43. Naukratis
44. Marsa Matruh

Tunisia
45. Carthage

3. Map of Crete, showing sites mentioned in the text

1. Arkadhes
2. Ayia Triadha
3. Eleutherna
4. Gortys
5. Kastelli Pediada
6. Kastrokephala-Almyros
7. Kavousi
8. Khania
9. Knossos
10. Kommos
11. Malia
12. Palaeokastro-Kastri
13. Pandanassa Amariou
14. Zapher Papoura

Kydonia

Bay of
Herakleion

● 8

● 3

● 6

● 13

● 11

● 9

● 5

● 12

● 7

● 4

● 2

● 1

● 10

● 14

0   50 km

3

● 20

● 21

Lake Van

Urartu

Tigris

● 24

Mesopotamia

● 25

Euphrates

● 28

Babylonia

● 1

● 2

Boeotia

● 3

● 15

Attica

● 6

● 5

● 7

● 9

● 4

Arcadia

● 8 ●● 10

● 11

● 12

● 13

● 14

N

0   100 km

Crete

4

The Late Bronze Age

I. The Late Cypriote I Period (circa 1600–1450 B.C.)

1. Cyprus between the Aegean and the Near East

The relative isolation of Cyprus during the Early Bronze Age and the first part of the Middle Bronze Age had already been broken in the eighteenth century B.C., with the development of lively interconnections among the various countries of the Eastern Mediterranean. If we identify the name Alashiya of the Babylonian texts with Cyprus, as the vast majority of scholars now do (Catling 1980, 9; Knapp [ed.] 1996, 3–11), we learn that Cypriote copper was exported to Mari in Mesopotamia at the very beginning of the eighteenth century B.C. (Knapp [ed.] 1996, 17–19). During the same period, in the cosmopolitan city of Ugarit on the Syrian coast opposite Cyprus, there were Cretan traders headed by a chief who had a recognized status and regulated trade between Crete and Ugarit. Cretan goods of all kinds were forwarded from Ugarit to the rest of the Near East. Among the goods that were traded we read about finished products, such as Cretan weapons used by the king of Mari, Cretan vases, textiles, even a pair of sandals (Heltzer 1989, 13–14; see also Knapp 1991, 37–38). Ugarit was the entrepôt through which goods had to pass both to and from Crete and Cyprus (Heltzer 1989, 14, 24–25).

Its privileged position must have lasted throughout the seventeenth century and later, until urban trade centers developed along the east and south coasts of Cyprus, and the rulers of these centers and other entrepreneurs were able to take over much of the entrepôt trade with the neighboring countries (cf. Knapp 1991, 47–50). The wealth of Cyprus in copper and the island's strategic position between the Aegean, Egypt, and the Near East no doubt conferred a leading role in these interconnections, a position that was to be maintained throughout the Late Bronze Age. It was toward the end of the Middle Cypriote period that urban sites emerged near the coast, as a result of increased foreign contacts, e.g., at Enkomi on the east coast; in the area around Morphou Bay, near the northern coast; in the area of Myrtou-*Stephania* further inland; and at Palaepaphos, near the west coast. At all these sites imported objects have been found, illustrating relations with Syria, Palestine, Crete, and Egypt. For the first time in Cyprus, a stratified society appeared in these coastal centers.

The close commercial and cultural ties between Cyprus and the Syro-Palestinian coast, especially Ugarit, are universally recognized (Catling 1980, 16) and continued uninterrupted from the Middle Cypriote III period and throughout the period under review (sixteenth century B.C.).

It is within the framework of these interconnections that we should place the sudden appearance in Cyprus of various ceramic innovations, namely, the so-called Bichrome Wheelmade ware and the Red Lustrous Wheelmade ware, about which many theories have already been proposed. Although a local Cypriote manufacture for all of them has been suggested, based on scientific analysis of the clay (in the case of Bichrome Wheelmade ware), the tendency now is to believe that the origin of these fabrics is Syrian/Anatolian and that they were imitated in Cyprus. This is particularly the case with the pictorial style of the Bichrome Wheelmade ware, where the motifs are of Levantine origin (Karageorghis 2001b). Eriksson suggested a Cypriote origin for Red Lustrous Wheelmade ware, which appeared in LC IA:2 (1550/40–1525/1500 B.C.) and continued for three hundred years. It also occurs in Egypt, Palestine, Syria, Anatolia, Crete, and Rhodes. Whether it was produced in some of these places or was all exported from Cyprus is difficult to determine without clay analyses. It reached Egypt in large quantities during the reign of Tuthmosis III. In Anatolia the ware appears later, in the fourteenth century B.C. In a recently published article, however, it is proposed that Cilicia may be the production area of Red Lustrous Wheelmade ware (Knappett 2000).

2. Relations with Egypt

Copper was not the only commodity that Cyprus exported to the neighboring countries. To Egypt in particular the island probably exported timber and

5. Jug of White Painted V ware, from Morphou-*Toumba tou Skourou* (excavations of Harvard University), Tomb I. 245. On the shoulder, opposite the handle, is the flat protome of a human figure with caricature face. This style of pottery is characteristic of the Morphou Bay region. Apart from *Toumba tou Skourou* we encountered it at the necropolis of Akhera, also dating to the Late Cypriote I period. The plastic decoration on the shoulder manifests also protomes of birds and quadrupeds.

6. Two craters of Bichrome Wheelmade ware.
Left: crater with two vertical loop handles on the shoulder, from Ayia Irini (Italian Mission, 1971), Tomb IX.N.243. Height: 26.6cm.; mouth diam.: 33.3cm. Cyprus Museum, Nicosia. The shoulder zone between the handles is decorated on one side with a fish and a bird, each within a rectangular panel; on the other side are a bird and a cross within a circle, each within a rectangular panel. These panels are flanked by narrow vertical panels containing "union jack" motifs.
Right: crater without handles from Morphou-*Toumba tou Skourou* (excavation by Harvard University), Tomb II, no. 79. Height: 31cm.; mouth diam.: 30.6cm. Cyprus Museum, Nicosia. The fabric and decoration are much inferior to those of the crater to the left. It is possible that it was made by local potters. The main decoration consists of groups of vertical/oblique parallel bands around the shoulder zone.

7. Two jugs of Painted Wheelmade ware, from Ayia Irini (Italian Mission).
Left: from Tomb 21, no. 144. Height: 18.1cm. Cyprus Museum, Nicosia. Decorated with linear motifs on neck and shoulder.
Right: from Tomb 21, no. 64. Height: 17.2cm. Cyprus Museum, Nicosia. Decorated in the same style as the jug on the left. On the rim there are incised strokes, transverse and oblique, probably indicating the capacity of the jug.

6

7

oils of all kinds. Egypt could offer in exchange gold and other objects that have not left traces in the archaeological record. The earliest relations were with the Hyksos, already at the close of the Middle Cypriote period (for a general survey see Karageorghis 1995b). Recent excavations at Tell el-Dab'a, the capital of the Hyksos in Egypt, have brought to light fragments from over five hundred Cypriote vessels, dating from the second half of the seventeenth century B.C. (from circa 1640 to 1500 B.C.; see Merrillees 1968 and most recently Bietak 2000). Most of this ceramic material consists of jugs and juglets with long narrow necks and narrow spouts, which probably contained perfumed oils. They include White Painted V–VI wares, White Slip I, and Base-Ring I, as well as Red Lustrous Wheelmade. Such vessels, suitable for the export of perfumed oils, circulated widely in the Levant, Cyprus, and the Aegean. In Cyprus we find the Egyptian variety of the so-called Tell el-Yahudiyeh ware, which also occurs on the Cycladic island of Thera. Syria produced its own White Painted "eyelet style" version (Karageorghis 1995b, 73–75; Swiny 1997, 228–231). Apart from Egyptian Tell el-Yahudiyeh and el-Lisht ware pottery found in Cyprus

and dated to circa 1600 B.C., we should also mention a scarab found in a tomb at Akhera, which may date to the end of the Hyksos period or the beginning of the XVIIIth Dynasty (Karageorghis 1995b, 74, with bibliography). Important discoveries suggesting relations between Cyprus and Egypt during the early part of the XVIIIth Dynasty are the two bronze hooked razors of an Egyptian type, found in two Cypriote tombs at Morphou-*Toumba tou Skourou* and Ayia Irini. These are *Toumba tou Skourou* Tomb V, Chamber 1, which also yielded Tell el-Yahudiyeh ware and Late Minoan IA pottery; and the Ayia Irini tomb at *Paleokastro*, which contained Late Minoan IA and Late Helladic IA cups (see Eriksson 2001, 34).

Relations with Egypt not only continued after the establishment of the XVIIIth Dynasty, but they were also enhanced. Cypriote pottery, particularly jugs and juglets of Base-Ring I and Red Lustrous Wheelmade ware, continued to be exported to Egypt for their contents, which may have been perfumed oils or opium, a substance that was used as a painkiller or as an agent for the creation of ecstatic conditions. Scientific analysis (gas chromatography) leaves no doubt about the substance that some of these flasks

8. Spindle bottle of Red Lustrous Wheelmade ware. Severis Collection, Nicosia, Inv. no. LS 1521. Height: 27.3 cm. Late Cypriote I-IIA.

9. Jug of Bichrome Wheelmade ware from Enkomi (British excavations), the British Museum, London, Inv. no. 1897.4–1.1144. Height: 18.7cm. The neck is decorated with four human figures, warriors and boxers (?), in a rather crude style. Late Cypriote I period.

10. Jug of Bichrome Wheelmade ware, from Dromolaxia-*Trypes*, Tomb 1, no. 58. Height: 24cm. Larnaca District Museum. The neck and shoulder are decorated with linear patterns. In two rectangular panels on the neck there is an armed warrior, brandishing a spear and holding a sword; there are traces of another human figure in a second panel. Pictorial decoration on such jugs is usually confined to birds and fish.

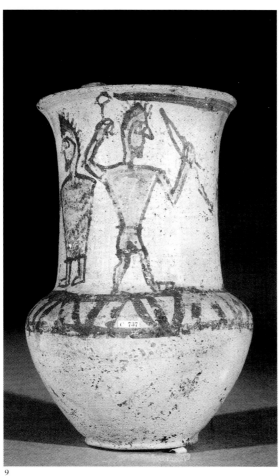

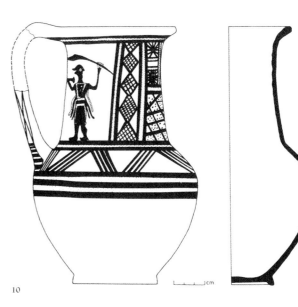

8

9

10

11. Crater of Bichrome Wheel-made ware, from Enkomi. Medelhavsmuseet, Stockholm, no. 672. Base missing. Diam. of body: 49cm. Three vertical loop handles around shoulder. The shoulder zone between handles is decorated with rectangular panels filled with pictorial motifs, including a bull figure and a bird. Late Cypriote I period.

12–13. Fragment from the neck and shoulder of a large crater of Bichrome Wheelmade ware, from Palaepaphos-*Teratsoudhia* (excavations of the Cyprus Department of Antiquities), Tomb 105, Chamber B, Well, no. 52. Preserved height: 25cm.; restored diam.: 36.2cm. Kouklia Site Museum. The shoulder zone is decorated with a bull being led to the sacrifice (?) by a human figure. Below the shoulder zone is a horizontal frieze of running spirals. The theme and the style of the pictorial composition recall Near Eastern prototypes. Late Cypriote I–II period.

contained, which may also have been exported to other parts of the Mediterranean (Merrillees 1989, with previous bibliography).

One of the most important Egyptian objects dating to the early XVIIIth Dynasty that has been found in Cyprus is a fragment of a serpentine vase with an engraved hieroglyphic inscription, unfortunately incomplete and worn. On the surviving part can be seen two royal cartouches that Gisèle Clerc (Clerc 1990) has identified, though with some reservations, as belonging to the founder of the XVIIIth Dynasty, Ahmosis I. The fragment was found in the fill of the dromos of a tomb complex at Palaepaphos-*Teratsoudhia* that was used throughout the Late Bronze Age. If the attribution of the cartouches is correct, this is the earliest occurrence of a royal cartouche in Cyprus. The discovery in Cyprus of an object associated with Ahmosis I is of particular importance, considering that the beginning of his reign is now placed between 1552 and 1539 B.C., and that he is the one who

expelled the Hyksos from Egypt. It may strengthen the hypothesis that after the expulsion of the Hyksos from Avaris, Egypt began a new era of liberal policies and connections with the outside world, which included Cyprus. But unfortunately we cannot be certain when the vase to which this fragment belonged reached Cyprus, nor do we know whether it was traded directly from Egypt or reached Cyprus indirectly from the Levantine coast.

The expulsion of the Hyksos from Egypt marked a new era of relations between the land of the Pharaohs and Cyprus. The Egyptians were now the undisputed dominant power in the East Mediterranean. Their ambition was to conquer Syria, but in this they met with opposition from the Hittites. The army of the Pharaoh Tuthmosis I reached the Euphrates around 1523 B.C. (cf. Baurain 1984, 115–118). There are several written documents that record events in the East Mediterranean during this period. Cyprus, under the name of Isy or Alashiya, is mentioned both directly

11

12

13

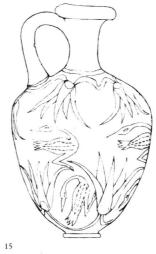

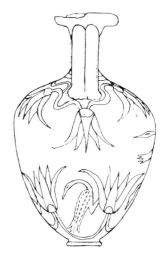

14

15

and indirectly (cf. Baurain 1984, 115–140). When, in 1470 B.C., in the ninth year of his reign, Tuthmosis III undertook an expedition against Syria, the inhabitants of Cyprus (Isy) offered gifts to the Pharaoh as a tribute for his maintaining peace in the region.

In the great temple of Amon at Karnak there is a list of the tributes from Isy in the Hall of the Annals of Tuthmosis III; they include copper, lead, horses, timber, ivory, and lapis lazuli (Clerc 1990, 96–97, for references). Obviously ivory and lapis lazuli were goods that Cyprus did not produce, but could provide through trade. Though these products are mentioned in the customary way as a tribute, it is doubtful whether the island really depended in any way on Egypt. It was an independent, prosperous country, but in view of Egypt's influence on the Levantine coast the king of Cyprus made it his policy to have good relations with a powerful neighbor by exchanging gifts (cf. Clerc 1990, 97; Eriksson 1993, 152).

Several scarabs with the cartouches of pharaohs of the XVIIIth Dynasty have been found in Cyprus, but in later contexts and/or of uncertain date since they do not always belong to the period of the pharaoh whose name they mention (Clerc 1990, 97). Better evidence is provided by a gold ring found in the LC I sanctuary of Ayios Iakovos, now in the Cyprus Museum, which bears the cartouche of Tuthmosis III, flanked by two scarabs (Gjerstad *et al.* 1934, 357, no. 2, pl. LXVII).

In fact it was during the reign of Tuthmosis III (1479–1425 B.C.) that Cypriote exports to Egypt increased considerably. These included mainly pottery, Base-Ring I, White Slip I, and Red Lustrous Wheelmade (cf. Eriksson 2001, 21–26). During the military campaigns undertaken by this pharaoh to Syria-Palestine, trade must have developed considerably along the routes used to supply his army. The list of "Aegyptiaca" found in Cyprus is quite long (Clerc 1990; see also idem 1983 and Jacobsson 1994), but some of them may have been kept as heirlooms, and their importance as evidence for relations with Egypt is considerably diminished.

3. Relations with Minoan Crete

The Minoan connections with the Eastern Mediterranean are manifested in various forms (for references see Karageorghis 1997c). Late Minoan pottery has been found in sizable quantities in tombs excavated at Morphou-*Toumba tou Skourou* and Ayia Irini-*Paleokastro*, both situated in the northwestern part of Cyprus. There are also LM IA cup sherds from Tombs 104 and 105 at Palaepaphos-*Teratsoudhia*; although these tombs were used for a long time, it is safer to relate the LM IA sherds and pottery with the LC IB period (sixteenth century B.C.) (for references see Eriksson 2001, 31–33). This pottery dates to circa 1525–1475 B.C. and includes mainly drinking cups. It

14. Two jugs of Tell el-Yahudiyeh ware in the Cyprus Museum, Nicosia. On the left, no. A 1432, height: 14.5 cm. On the right, no. 1430, from Hala Sultan Tekke, height: 15cm. The first has a punctured surface; the second is plain, stroke polished. Such jugs, imported to Cyprus from Egypt during the Late Cypriote I period, most probably contained perfumed oils, hence their narrow spout.

15. Juglet of Tell el-Yahudiyeh ware, from Morphou-*Toumba tou Skourou* (excavations of Harvard University), Tomb V, no. 24. Height: 13.4cm. Lost after the Turkish invasion of 1974. The body is decorated all over with engraved "nilotic" motifs consisting of birds and lotus flowers.

16

is true that some of this material may be identified as Mycenaean (Pecorella 1977, 247–248), but this is not a major obstacle, in view of the fact that trade relations with the Aegean during this early period were dominated by Minoan Crete. In the same way we may explain the occurrence in Cyprus (unfortunately in a private collection, without provenance) of a short bronze sword of a type known as Class B (Catling 1980, 4). It is known to have been found in the island together with other Cypriote bronze weapons of ordinary type of the Middle and Late Cypriote periods. It may be of a Late Minoan I or a Late Helladic I type and is the earliest Aegean weapon found so far in Late Bronze Age Cyprus (Karageorghis 1999e, 165, no. 124).

Up to now Cypriote pottery of the Middle Bronze Age and Late Cypriote I has been found on Crete in very limited quantities, but the situation may change when the ceramic material found in the harbor town of Kommos, on the south coast of Crete, is published. It is not easy to explain the relations between Cyprus and Crete during the sixteenth century B.C. These relations are more clearly evidenced with the east and south coast of Cyprus (Enkomi, Maroni, Hala Sultan Tekke) than with Morphou Bay, where contacts with the West, namely Crete, seem rather ephemeral. In an effort to explain the occurrence of Minoan ceramic material in the Morphou Bay area (*Toumba tou Skourou* and Ayia Irini), Catling suggested that some Theran refugees, who left Thera after the eruption of the volcano at the end of the sixteenth century, established themselves at Trianda on Rhodes; others may have continued their journey to the east and settled at Morphou Bay. "Their arrival there has no connection with the copper trade, and no economic significance. Unlike the Trianda settlement, they established no permanent hold on their landfall, and either were quickly assimilated into the local population or lived out the remainder of their lives in an enclave of their own in the Toumba tou Skourou settlement" (Catling 1980, 12). This is an attractive theory, but not entirely convincing. Is it a coincidence that the Morphou Bay area, where they settled, is rich in copper? Should we offer the same explanation for the nearby site of Ayia Irini? It is true that the importance of the Morphou Bay area as a copper trading center declined in the fifteenth–fourteenth centuries B.C., in favor of the eastern and southern centers, but there may have been other reasons for this decline. It is unfortunate that this area cannot be further investigated archaeologically at present.

After the expulsion of the Hyksos from Egypt circa 1550 B.C. (?) and the establishment of the XVIIIth Dynasty by Pharaoh Ahmosis I (for a comprehensive recent report see Bietak and Marinatos 2000), the Minoan influence in Egypt and the Levant became more important. Genuine Minoan fresco paintings have been found in dumps belonging to a palatial fortress at Tell el-Dab'a (Avaris). More or less contemporary with the Avaris Minoan wall paintings are those found at Alalakh by the river Orontes and at Kabri, in northern Israel. Several theories have been put forward to explain this phenomenon, but one thing is certain: the frescoes could only have been made by Minoan artists, though the presence of a

Minoan colony in Egypt or the Levant cannot be archaeologically substantiated. At Miletus, however, recent excavations have proved the existence of a real Minoan colony on the west coast of Anatolia, a fact that demonstrates the importance of Cretan power that expanded beyond the Aegean (cf. Bietak and Marinatos 1995, 42, with bibliography; also Caubet 1982, who also describes the relations between Ugarit and Minoan Crete in even later periods).

4. The Cypro-Minoan Script

Toward the end of the sixteenth century B.C. there appeared in Cyprus a system of writing, known as Cypro-Minoan since it was so termed by Sir Arthur Evans, that resembles the Linear A script of Crete. How it came to be transmitted to Cyprus is uncertain. One theory is that it was borrowed by the Cypriots from the Cretans at Ugarit, where both these peoples had commercial interests and could meet frequently. It is true that not enough has survived in the archaeological record to justify a suggestion that there were very close and direct contacts between Cyprus and Crete during this period, but we must always bear in mind that the nature of the relations between these two large islands has always been elusive and may have been much more elaborate than we may envision.

Very few documents have survived from the earliest form of Cypro-Minoan writing. They include a fragmentary baked tablet from Enkomi with three horizontal rows of signs engraved on one side, a clay loomweight and a cylinder seal from the same site, and a plain ware vase from Katydhata with several signs engraved on the outer part of its handle. All attempts to decipher this script have failed, but its appearance circa 1500 B.C. is of great importance: it demonstrates that the urban centers that had begun to emerge, especially along the east and south coasts, needed a script for administrative and other purposes. It should be noted that the Enkomi tablet of circa 1500 B.C. has caused quite a lot of embarrassment to scholars. Although the affinities of its script with Minoan Linear A have been recognized by all specialists, there is a consensus that the two scripts are not the same, but may have had a common parentage, as has been suggested (cf. Catling 1980, 4, 8, with bibliography).

Far more written documents have survived from the fourteenth and thirteenth centuries B.C. Though most of them have been found at Enkomi, on the east coast of Cyprus, they are now known from other sites as well, especially from Kalavassos-*Ayios Dhimitrios*, where one complete and four fragmentary inscribed clay cylinders have been found in an administrative

17

19

18

20-21. Two jugs of Base-Ring ware I. Late Cypriote I-IIA. Left: Juglet, Severis Collection, Nicosia, Inv. no. LS 1433. Height (restored): 12.2 cm. Funnel spout; decoration in relief. On either side of the body, two wavy bands in relief terminate in snake heads. Right: Jug, Severis Collection, Nicosia, Inv. no. LS 833. Height: 22.2 cm. It has a funnel spout, and simple decoration in relief.

22. Tentative restitution of the cartouche of Ahmosis I (?) on a stone vase fragment from Tomb 104, Palaepaphos-*Teratsoudhia* (after Gisèle Clerc in Karageorghis 1990, 95, fig. 1).

23. Fragment from the shoulder of a vase of serpentine, with a faintly preserved engraved cartouche of a Pharaoh (Ahmosis I?). From Palaepaphos-*Teratsoudhia,* (excavations of the Cyprus Department of Antiquities, 1984), Tomb 104, Chamber K, Dromos L, 1. Preserved height: 10.1cm.; thickness: 1.5cm. Kouklia Site Museum. If the identification of the cartouche is correct, this may constitute the earliest occurrence of the cartouche of an Egyptian Pharaoh in Cyprus. Ahmosis I was the founder of the XVIIIth Dynasty. It is not certain when this stone vase was brought to Cyprus.

24. Gold finger ring from Ayios Iakovos (Swedish Cyprus Expedition), the Bronze Age sanctuary, no. 2. Cyprus Museum, Nicosia. Elliptical flat bezel with an engraved cartouche of Tuthmosis III flanked by two beetles. This is one of the earliest cartouches of a Pharaoh found in Cyprus.

25. Bronze dagger with bent blade, in the Severis Collection, Nicosia. Length: 30cm. This object, dating to the Late Helladic I or Late Minoan I period, may be considered the earliest Aegean weapon found in Late Bronze Age Cyprus.

26. A fragmentary tablet of baked clay, from Enkomi (excavations of the Cyprus Department of Antiquities, 1955). Preserved height: 5.5cm.; width: 7.5cm. One side of the tablet is engraved with signs of the Cypro-Minoan script in three rows, separated by horizontal lines. The signs were engraved before firing, unlike on the inscribed tablets from the Aegean, which were engraved on unbaked clay, which was hardened accidentally as a result of a fire. This tablet, dated stratigraphically to circa 1500 B.C., is the earliest evidence for the use of a script in Cyprus, which was borrowed from the Aegean, namely from Crete (Linear A script of Crete). Up to now this script, known as Cypro-Minoan, has not been deciphered; the language is unknown.

20

21

building (Masson 1983). The complete cylinder comprises more than one hundred signs. There is a similar but larger, complete cylinder from Enkomi.

Although the Aegean character of the Cypro-Minoan script is undisputed, we should note several Near Eastern peculiarities that differentiate the Cypriote documents from the Aegean tablets found on Crete and on the Greek mainland, which are usually oblong and unbaked. The large fragmentary tablets from Enkomi are rectangular, cushion-shaped, measuring around 20 x 19cm; they are divided into two equal vertical columns and are engraved on both sides. The signs have a cuneiform appearance that was achieved by pressing a pointed bone stylus into the clay surface before firing.

In spite of various attempts, no one has so far succeeded in providing a convincing decipherment of the Cypro-Minoan documents, no doubt because the language of their text is not known to us, and the only

hope for a decipherment is the discovery of bilingual texts. Though three groups of signs of the Cypro-Minoan script have been identified (Masson 1974), one of them, named "Cypro-Minoan 1," is common to the whole island, from the fourteenth to the twelfth centuries B.C. Specialists confirm that there was a linguistic uniformity throughout the island. Toward the end of the thirteenth century B.C. "Cypro-Minoan 2" made its appearance on the large clay tablets from Enkomi. It comprises sixty signs, and the language that it represents may differ from that of the documents in the Cypro-Minoan 1 script. There is a "Cypro-Minoan 3" script that appears on a baked clay tablet found at Ugarit. The text comprises a list of twenty-five proper names, all Semitic. Emilia Masson has been able to decipher twenty of these, but the language of the script is still unknown (Masson 1974).

Apart from the administrative documents mentioned

22

23

24

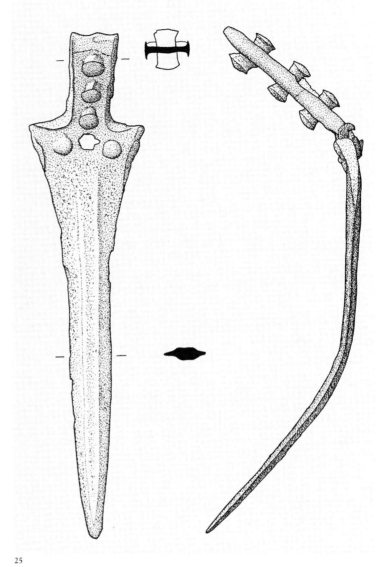

25

above (clay cushion-shaped tablets) the script appears also on a variety of documents of everyday use or of a votive character: cylinder seals, clay balls probably used in sanctuaries, copper miniature ingots, metal bowls, clay vessels (see below), etc. This suggests that literacy was rather more widespread than in the Aegean, where it was confined to the palaces.

5. Internal Unrest

The early part of the Late Bronze Age (Late Cypriote I, circa 1600–1450 b.c.) was not a peaceful period for Cyprus. Troubled political conditions, which were already evident in the Middle Cypriote III period (cf. Åström 1972, 763–768; Merrillees 1971), continued into the beginning of Late Cypriote I, a phenomenon that is also seen in other parts of the Near East (Åström 1972, 763). A fortress built in the northernmost part of the town of Enkomi, on the east coast of the island, was destroyed a few years after its construc-

26

27. Bone styli from Kition, Area II (excavations of the Cyprus Department of Antiquities), Larnaca District Museum. Such styli, made from animal ribs, were used for engraving signs on clay tablets, on vases, or on small clay balls, before firing. They were pressed into the clay surface, thus giving a cuneiform aspect to the signs. Bone styli have been found in fairly large quantities at practically all Late Bronze Age sites, suggesting a widespread use of writing.

28. Inscribed clay cylinder from Kalavassos-*Ayios Dhimitrios*, no. 389. Cyprus Museum, Nicosia. Length: 3cm.; diam.: 2cm.

29. Baked clay ball with five (?) signs of the Cypro-Minoan script engraved before firing. From Enkomi (French Mission), no. 1905. Cyprus Museum, Nicosia. Diam.: 2.7cm. Such clay balls have been found in the major urban centers of the island and are dated to the Late Cypriote II–III periods. They probably designate proper names. Their function is not certain (games of marbles? Ration tokens? Vows in sanctuaries?).

30. Inscribed handle of a Plain White Wheelmade I ware jug, from Katydhata, Tomb 11, no. 11 (excavated by M. Markides for the Cyprus Museum in the years around the First World War). Cyprus Museum, Nicosia, A 1496. There are three engraved signs of the Cypro-Minoan script on the handle, in an early form of this script.

31. Loomweight of baked clay, with one line of six signs of the Cypro-Minoan script engraved before firing at the base (to be held upside down). From Enkomi (French Mission, 1967), no. 19.3. Height: 7.2cm. This is one of the earliest documents that we possess of the Cypro-Minoan script (sixteenth–fifteenth century B.C.). Another document of the same date is the inscribed handle of a jug from Katydhata (see above).

27

28

29

30

31

32

tion in LC IA but was soon rebuilt, obviously in the face of an imminent danger. A similar need was felt elsewhere in the easternmost part of the island, at Nitovikla in the Karpass peninsula, where a fortress, built in MC III and destroyed at the end of the period, was rebuilt in LC IA. In the central part of Cyprus the fortress of Nikolidhes was reconstructed and destroyed by the end of LC IA.

At the same time, there were mass burials in tombs at Pendayia and Myrtou-*Stephania* in the northwestern part of Cyprus, and at Ayios Iakovos, in the northeastern part. Evidence for destruction is also observed at Kalopsidha and Episkopi-*Phaneromeni*. Are we to attribute the mass burials to epidemic, or military conflict between the eastern and western parts of the island? The western part of the island includes most of the copper mines, while the eastern part has the best arable land, and conflicts may have arisen for control of the resources.

There is also a theory that the enhancement of trade in copper was organized by the Syro-Palestinians, who built the fortresses for their own protection, to give them safe access to the mines, with the consent of the local population (cf. Baurain 1984, 80–87). It is unlikely that the island was invaded by foreigners (such as the Hyksos); at least, there is no such evidence in the archaeological record (cf. also Eriksson 2001, 15–18).

6. Fortresses

The architecture of the various fortresses of LC I varies considerably. We describe here very briefly the fortress of *Nikolidhes*, in the central part of the island, near the village of Ayios Sozomenos. It occupies an area of about 150 square meters. All around the fortress were dwellings for the soldiers. The fortress is square, about 6m high, and closed on all four sides by defensive ramparts. There were two gates in the eastern rampart and a storeroom on the west side of the fortress (for a fuller description see Gjerstad 1926, 37–47; Åström 1972, 30–32).

The fortress of Enkomi, built in the northern part of the town, is larger than that of *Nikolidhes*. It is rectangular in plan, measuring 34 x 12m., and has massive external walls. On its southwest there was a gate, protected by a rectangular tower. Access to the roof was possible through a staircase in the interior of the rooms of the fortress, which led also to an upper story. Most features of the fortress may have had Syro-Palestinian prototypes.

32. Fragment from a baked clay tablet from Enkomi (excavations of the Cyprus Department of Antiquities, 1953), no. 1687. Preserved height:10cm.; width: 9cm. This is about a quarter of the complete cushion-shaped tablet. Both sides of the tablet were engraved with signs of the Cypro-Minoan script in horizontal rows, in two vertical columns. The ending of each line is not always on the same vertical axis, and this induced Michael Ventris, the decipherer of the Aegean Linear B script, to suggest that the text might represent a poem. As for all other inscriptions in this script, the text (the longest so far) remains undeciphered. This was the first lengthy inscribed document to be discovered, and several attempts at its decipherment have been made, but so far unsuccessfully.

33. Tables showing the three classes of Cypro-Minoan script (Cypro-Minoan 1, 2, and 3). This script was introduced to Cyprus circa 1500 B.C. It is still undeciphered (after E. Masson 1974, figs. 2–4).

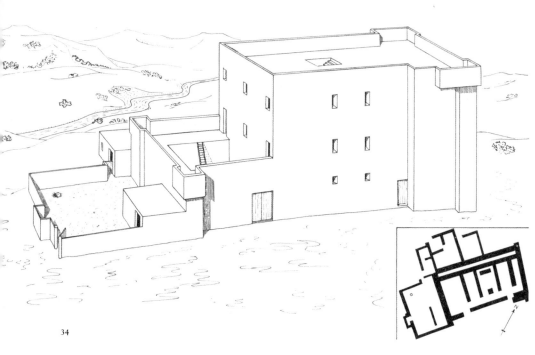

7. Economic Growth and Development

In spite of the internal unrest, the economic and cultural growth of the island during the sixteenth century is indisputable. Whereas in the Middle Bronze Age the important centers were situated inland (e.g., Kalopsidha, Alambra), new coastal centers now emerged, no doubt as a result of trade relations with the outside world. Such centers include Enkomi, Hala Sultan Tekke, Maroni, Palaepaphos, Morphou, Ayia Irini, and Kazaphani-*Ayios Andronikos*. Most of these are known from tombs with rich finds, which illustrate relations with the Aegean, particularly Crete, as well as Anatolia, the Near East, and Egypt (cf. Dikaios 1969–71; Pecorella 1977; Nicolaou and Nicolaou 1989; Quilici 1990; Vermeule and Wolsky 1990; Karageorghis 1990a). New evidence for the external relations of Cyprus with both Crete and Anatolia has been brought to light from the tombs at Ayia Irini, Morphou, and Kazaphani. It is regrettable that all these sites are in the now-occupied part of Cyprus and therefore inaccessible for research (cf. Courtois

34. Reconstructed sketch and ground plan of the fortress at *Nikolidhes*, in the central part of the island. It was constructed at the very beginning of the Late Cypriote I period (after Åström 1972, 31, fig. 17).

35. Reconstructed sketch of the fortress at *Nitovikla*, in the northeastern part of Cyprus. It was constructed at the end of the Middle Bronze Age and was restored at the beginning of the Late Bronze Age. This was a period of internal turmoil on the island (after Sjöqvist 1940, 92, fig. 37).

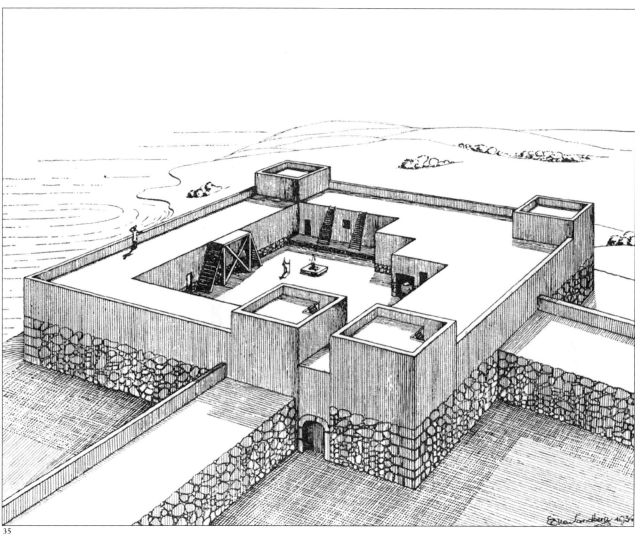

36

36. Footed bowl of Painted Red Slip I ware, from Kazaphani, Tomb 2B, no. 177. Height: 16.5cm.; diam.: 28cm. Cyprus Museum, Nicosia.

37. Juglet of White Slip I ware. Giabra Pierides Collection, Bank of Cyprus Cultural Foundation Museum, Nicosia. Height: 15.5cm. Decoration in light, dark and orange matt paint. The shape imitates a Base-Ring I ware juglet.

38. Bowl of Base-Ring I ware, with conical body and raised wishbone handle. Height: 13.2cm.; diam.: 16cm. Cyprus Museum, Nicosia, Inv. no. 1933 /IV–14/2. The surface is dark brown and has a lustrous appearance, recalling metallic vessels that may have served as prototypes. This fabric, together with White Slip ware, has an impermeable surface, and bowls like this may have been used for hot liquids. They were popular not only in Cyprus but were exported widely to the Eastern and Central Mediterranean regions as well as to Egypt.

38

39. Bowl of Proto White Slip ware. Severis Collection, Nicosia, Inv. no. LS 843. Height: 11 cm.; mouth diam. (including handle): 17 cm. Late Cypriote I.

39

40. Jug of White Slip I ware, from Palaepaphos-*Teratsoudhia* (excavations of the Cyprus Department of Antiquities, 1984), Tomb 104, Chamber K, no. 41. Height: 22.4cm. Kouklia Site Museum. The mouth forms a funnel with a strainer at the bottom, where one could put herbs or other substances, over which water was poured and filtered into the jug. The fine quality of the fabric and decoration demonstrates the excellence White Slip ware potters attained during the Late Cypriote I period in the area of Palaepaphos.

37

40

23

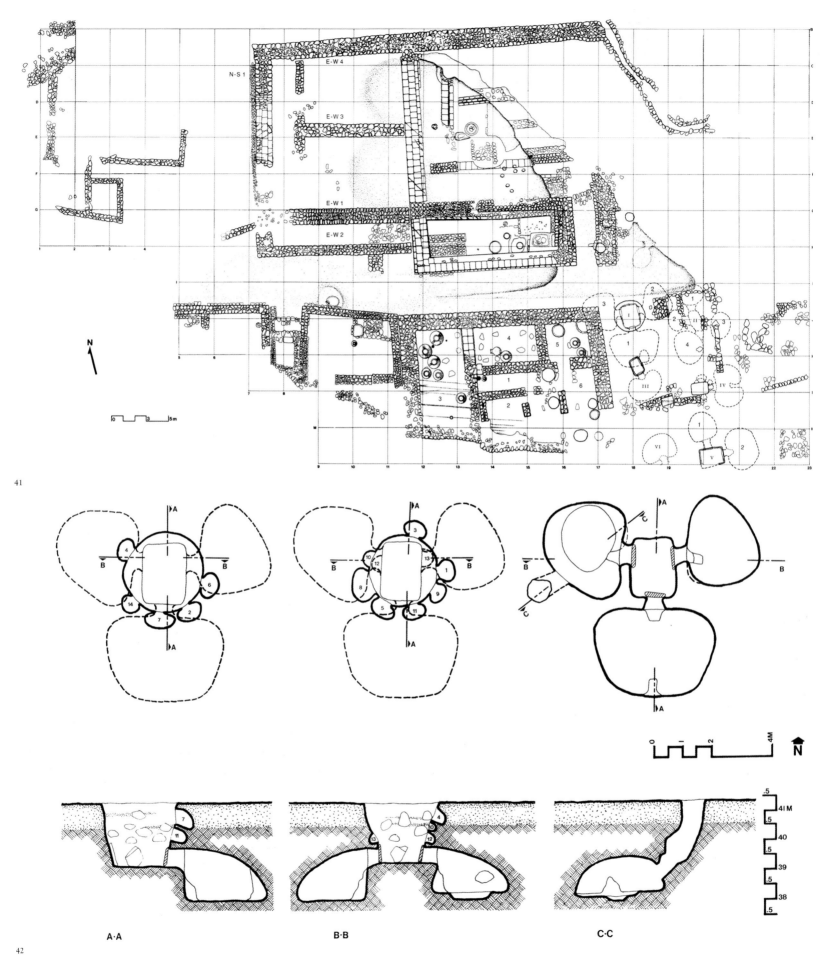

A·A B·B C·C

in Nicolaou and Nicolaou 1989, 94; Karageorghis 2001b, with previous bibliography).

Apart from the foreign imports to Cyprus, mentioned above, the rich tombs of LC I yielded a wealth of locally made pottery. Some ceramic types were inspired from Anatolia and Syria (Bichrome Wheelmade, Red Lustrous Wheelmade, and White Painted Wheelmade I wares), but others are the products of the inventive spirit of the Cypriote potters. Particularly popular were the White Slip and Base-Ring wares that appeared at the beginning of the LC I period and became dominant in the ceramic art of Cyprus for about four hundred years. They were popular not only in Cyprus, but also had a great appeal in most of the Mediterranean regions, including Egypt, the Aegean, and the Central Mediterranean. It has been proposed that the reason for their popularity was the fact that their impermeable surface and hard clay could resist hot liquids and were also suitable for the export of other liquid commodities such as perfumed oils (Karageorghis 2001a).

Copper, which as we have already seen was the main export of Cyprus from the Middle Cypriote III period onward, must have been a major factor in the development of the coastal urban centers. It is still uncertain how the various centers obtained their share of the ore from the copper mines. Was there a central authority, regulating this distribution, with well organized transportation routes to the coastal center? Was some of the smelting, as might be expected, taking place on the spot, near the mining areas in the central part of the island? (cf. Kassianidou 1999; Knapp et al. 1999). No doubt the routes for the dispatch of ore from the mining area to the harbor towns must have somehow been guarded, as a result of an arrangement with all concerned.

The disturbed conditions referred to above must have lasted only for a short time at the beginning of the LC I period or were considerably eased, because soon afterward there was a perfect homogeneity in the material production (e.g. pottery, bronzework) and considerable prosperity in all coastal centers. The interior of the island, however, was not neglected. Agricultural centers or centers near the copper mines or the transport routes were quite plentiful, such as Ayios Sozomenos, Katydhata, and Akhera.

8. Domestic and Funerary Architecture

Of the domestic architecture of LC I we know very little. Although Enkomi did exist in this period as a small town, the architectural remains that survived date to the later parts of the LC period. Part of a settlement of the early part of the period was excavated in the 1970s at Episkopi-*Phaneromeni* (Carpenter 1981), but it has not been fully published.

It is unfortunate that the architectural remains of a potters' quarter excavated at Morphou-*Toumba tou Skourou* suffered severely through modern leveling. The buildings were constructed on an artificial oblong mound around 1600 B.C. They consisted of several workshops built against a terrace wall. These early workshops were destroyed circa 1550 B.C., but were soon reconstructed. They included kilns, basins, and benches. Basins with plastered ridges and pithoi buried up to their rims in the floor suggest a workshop for refining clay, and indeed three sacks of clay were found on the floor. Houses were located in the lower area on the outer side of the ramp, and southeast of them were chamber tombs.

A large number of specimens of tomb architecture are known, at sites throughout the island. They are mostly chamber tombs with a circular or oval chamber and a rectangular stepped dromos with narrow stomion, sealed with a slab, rubble, or mud bricks. In several cases there are side chambers.

A chamber tomb excavated at Morphou-*Toumba tou Skourou* is unusual: it consists of a circular shaft with thirteen niches all around it, in superimposed rows; there were also three chambers around the shaft. The tomb was used for about one hundred years, the earliest burials having taken place around 1550–1525 B.C.

Quite exceptional are three built tombs, or tholoi, at Enkomi, one excavated by the Swedish Cyprus Expedition, Tomb 21, dated to LC IA, and the other two excavated by the French Mission, dating to a slightly later period. Enkomi Tomb 21 has a rectangular rock-cut dromos; a slab blocked the entrance. The chamber has a beehive shape with a circular floor, with a large circular basin in the middle. The sides of the chamber are lined with irregular masonry without mortar, forming a corbeled vault. A large flat slab covered the roof. The chamber measures 2.38m. in diameter and 2.43m. in height. There was probably a mound of earth above this built tomb. Although the tholoi of Enkomi may have some similarities with the tholoi of the Aegean, they are more likely a local creation, probably with an inspiration from the Levant (Pelon 1976, 427–432; Wright 1992, 343–344).

41. General view of the excavated remains at Morphou-*Toumba tou Skourou*, near the northern coast of Cyprus (excavations of Harvard University). On an artificial oblong mound a potters' quarter was established circa 1600 B.C. It included workshops with basins, kilns, and benches; sacks of clay were found on the floor. On the southeastern part of the mound rich chamber tombs were found. The area of Morphou Bay was quite important during the Late Cypriote I period, no doubt because of its proximity to the copper mines of Skouriotissa.

42. Plan and sections of Morphou-*Toumba tou Skourou* Tomb I (excavations of Harvard University). Second half of the sixteenth century B.C. The tomb contained thirteen niches all around it for infant burials. It yielded a large amount of pottery, some imported from Minoan Crete and the Near East (after Vermeule and Wolsky 1990, fig. 30).

The Late Bronze Age

ii. The Late Cypriote ii Period (circa 1450–1200 B.C.)

1. External Relations

The relations between Cyprus and Egypt must have reached their peak during the reign of Amenophis iii, whose external policies propagated Egyptian influence in Asia (Clerc 1990, 98); the same policies were continued in the reign of Akhenaton until Tutankhamon. It is from this time that we have detailed information about these relations, as they appear in the so-called Amarna letters, representing the correspondence between the pharaoh and the king of Alashiya and various small city-states in the Levant. The exchange of gifts between heads of state was a common practice, but real trade should not be excluded (cf. Peltenburg 1991, 166–168), especially since we now know that Cyprus exported large quantities of copper, as attested by the recently excavated shipwreck at Uluburun off the southwestern coast of Anatolia, where 354 oxhide copper ingots, weighing ten tons, have been found (see below).

From the reign of Amenophis iii comes a large scarab of a series that commemorates the exploits of the Pharaoh in lion-hunting during the first ten years of his reign. It may have been carefully kept as an heirloom for three hundred years by the same family before it was buried in a tomb of the eleventh century B.C. at Palaepaphos (Clerc 1983, 389–392). Fourteenth-century tombs in Cyprus have revealed a variety of items either certainly or probably imported from Egypt, such as the two flasks of variegated glass found in the early-fourteenth-century-B.C. Tomb 11 at Kalavassos-*Ayios Dhimitrios* (South 1994, 190–191). Other exotic materials, such as gold and ivory, may have been imported from Egypt (though much ivory may have come from Syria; cf. Caubet and Poplin 1987) and were used for the manufacture of objects by Cypriote craftsmen.

The excavations at Enkomi have brought to light evidence for two successive destructions (levels iA and iB). Whether these destructions were the result of physical phenomena (such as earthquakes) or invasions from outside is not easy to determine. It is possible that the second destruction was caused by an invasion by vassals of the Hittites. These raids are mentioned in Hittite documents and aroused the wrath of the Hittite king, who boasted that Alashiya was his own territory, although there is no proof of this in the archaeological record (cf. Baurain 1984, 157–164). During the same period, circa 1420 B.C., there were abandonments or destructions at other sites in Cyprus, such as the fortress of *Nitovikla* and the sanctuary at Phlamoudhi.

Relations with the Syro-Palestinian coast continued uninterrupted (cf. Catling 1980, 16–17). Though the evidence from Ugarit is rather obscure, this town, with which Cyprus was to have direct and lively relations from the fourteenth century B.C., underwent a period of decline during the fifteenth century B.C. (Yon 1997, 28).

43. Mycenaean IIIA:1 crater (Early Pictorial I, circa 1410–1390 B.C.), from Enkomi (Swedish Cyprus Expedition), Tomb 17, no. 1. Height: 37.5cm. Cyprus Museum, Nicosia. It is decorated all over the largest part of the body with two pictorial scenes; one side of the vase is decorated with a large octopus; the other with a chariot composition, with two human figures, a bull, and a bird in the field. One of the human figures, wearing a long robe, has been associated by Martin Nielsson with the well-known scene in the *Iliad* where Zeus holds the scales of destiny in front of the warriors before they depart for battle. Others have proposed that the long-robed figure is weighing copper ingots. If Nielsson's identification is correct, then we have here one of the earliest depictions of a scene that later became popular in Homeric epic. The small human figure carries on his shoulders what has been identified as a campstool, provided for important persons to sit on during cult activities and athletic games (Rystedt 1987).

44. View of the shipwreck of Uluburun, off the SW coast of Anatolia. The ship was loaded mainly with copper ingots, of which 354 have been discovered.

44

45

46

47

45. Goblet of faience with a green surface, decorated with abstract and floral motifs in black paint. Louvre Museum, Inv. no. S 575. Height: 24.5cm. Though the form of the vase is of Egyptian inspiration, certain anomalies betray a non-Egyptian provenance; it may have been made in Cyprus. Kition has yielded a number of similar vases of faience, manufactured locally.

46-47. Kalavassos-*Ayios Dhimitrios*, Tomb 11. Ivory disc and duck. Cyprus Museum, Nicosia. The rich offerings in Tomb 11 at Kalavassos-*Ayios Dhimitrios* included many ivory objects, mostly decorated discs that formed the lids of small cylindrical boxes (*pyxides*) (diam. of disc: 7.9cm.), rods with decorative heads, and duck-shaped vessels (length of duck: 12.8cm.). There were also two small glass bottles imported from Egypt.

The fifteenth century B.C. was a troubled period in the Aegean as well. By 1450 B.C. the power of Minoan Crete had collapsed, and the establishment of Mycenaean rule is apparent at Knossos (for a recent survey see Driessen 1994). The Minoan exports to Cyprus were very few (Catling 1980, 12), but by the second half of the fifteenth century the situation had changed; Late Helladic II pottery began to make its appearance in Cypriote tombs, though in relatively small quantities (Catling 1980, 12).

2. The Amarna Letters

The establishment of peaceful conditions in the East Mediterranean by Egypt (the *pax aegyptiaca*) promoted trade not only in this region but also throughout the Mediterranean. This favored Cyprus in particular because the island could now export its copper safely over long distances, in fairly large ships. Egypt was a major partner, as we learn from written sources, particularly in the correspondence between Pharaoh Akhenaton of Egypt and the king of Alashiya. The letters date to the second quarter of the fourteenth century B.C.

The king of Alashiya refers to the Pharaoh as his "brother," and, as an ally of Egypt, he advises the Pharaoh not to conclude a treaty with the Hittites, who were the enemies of Alashiya.

Below, we reproduce some characteristic texts of the Amarna letters (taken from Knapp [ed.] 1996, 21–23).

EA 34 (royal letter);

1–6 Message of the king of Alashiya to the king of Egypt, my brother: be informed that I prosper and my country prospers. And as to your own prosperity, may your prosperity and the prosperity of your household, your sons, your wives, your horses, your chariots, your country, be very great.

16–25 And behold, I (also) send to you with my messen{g}er 100 talents of copper. Moreover, may your messengers now bring some goods: one ebony bed, gold-(trimmed),…; and a chariot, *šuhitu*, with gold; two pieces of linen; fifty linen shawls; two linen robes; 14 (beams of) ebony; 77 *habannatu*-jars of "sweet oil." [And] as to *byssos*, four pieces and four shawls.

26–31 {And as} to goods that are not available [in your country], I am sending [in the charge of] my [mess]enger a donkey-hide […] of a bed, and [hab]annatu-jars that are not available […]

42–49 So an alliance should [be ma]de between the two of us, and my messen{g}ers should go to you and your messengers should come to me.

Moreover, why have you not sent me oil and linen? As far as I am [concer]ned, what you yourself request I will give.

50–53 I herewith send a *habannatu*-jar [that] is full of "sweet oil" to be poured on your head, seeing that you have sat down on your royal throne.

EA 35

10–15 I herewith send to you 500 (?) of copper. As my brother's greeting-gift I send it to you. My brother, do not be concerned that the amount of copper is small. Behold, the hand of Nergal is now in my country; he has slain all the men of my country, and there is not a single copper-worker. So, my brother, do not be concerned.

16–18 Send your messenger with my messenger

48

immediately, and I will send you whatever copper you, my brother, request.

19–22 You are my brother. May he send me silver in very great quantities. My brother, give me the very best silver, and then I will send you, my brother, whatever you, my brother, request.

49–53 You have not been put (on the same level) with the king of Hatti or the king of Shankhar. Whatever greeting-gift he (my bother) sends me, I for my part send back to you double.

EA 38

Say to the king of Egypt, my brother: message of the king of Alashiya, your brother.

7–12 Why, my brother, do you say such a thing to me, "Does my brother not know this?" As far as I am concerned, I have done nothing of the sort. Indeed, men of Lukki, year by year, seize villages in my own country.

49

50

Copper was the main commodity that the Pharaoh demanded from the king of Alashiya. Recent excavations have demonstrated that copper was produced, and/or processed, during the fourteenth–thirteenth centuries B.C., not only at Enkomi but also at Kalavassos-*Ayios-Dhimitrios*, Maroni, Kition, Hala Sultan Tekke, and Alassa-*Paliotaverna*. Thus, as Knapp rightly argues, not just the site of Enkomi (as originally proposed by its excavator, C. F. A. Schaeffer), but rather the whole island should be identified with Alashiya (Knapp [ed.] 1996, 8, with previous bibliography).

Refuting the suggestion that Alashiya might have been located somewhere in North Syria, Lebanon, or Cilicia, Knapp remarks that there is no evidence of copper deposits at these places; the best evidence for Bronze Age metallurgy in Syria, the oxhide ingot mold found at Ras Ibn Hani, near Ugarit, is not a valid argument, since the lead isotope analysis of copper prills from this mold points to an ore from Cyprus (Knapp [ed.] 1996, 9).

Frequent reference is made in the Amarna letters of commodities, demanded by the Pharaoh, that are not produced in Cyprus, such as ivory. This is not surprising, since it was the habit in all commercial centers in the East Mediterranean to store such luxury goods (ivory, gold, silver, lapis lazuli, perfumed oils) as a symbol of economic strength.

The reference to invasions by the Lucca or Lukki (as mentioned in one of the Amarna letters that was quoted above) has been associated by Dikaios with a destruction at Enkomi at the beginning of Level IIA. However, this destruction, and the reference to Nergal, the god of war, cannot safely be associated with certainty with any particular destructions in the archaeological record (cf. Baurain 1984, 194–198). Physical phenomena or epidemics are other possible causes of such catastrophes.

3. The Uluburun Shipwreck

From the Amarna letters we can see very clearly how wealthy the king of Alashiya was and the luxury in which he lived, like other reputable rulers of his time. We also get an idea of the commodities that were circulating in the East Mediterranean. The information from the Amarna letters is substantiated by archaeological evidence, especially by the cargo of an ancient ship that was wrecked at Uluburun off the southwestern coast of Turkey at the end of the fourteenth century B.C. (for general accounts see Bass *et al.* 1989; Pulak 1991; Cline 1994, 100–105; Pulak 2001).

The ship was about 15m. long and carried a cargo of about 15 tons (not counting the ship's anchors, ballast, and cargo that perished). The main commodity carried on the Uluburun ship was copper, in the form of 354 ingots, representing about ten tons of copper. Lead isotope analysis suggests that the copper ingots,

51

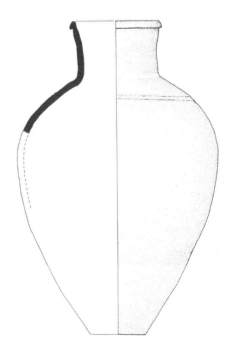

52

54. Cypriote wall bracket from the Uluburun shipwreck. Height: about 40cm. Ten such objects were carried on the ship (after Pulak 2001, fig. 4).

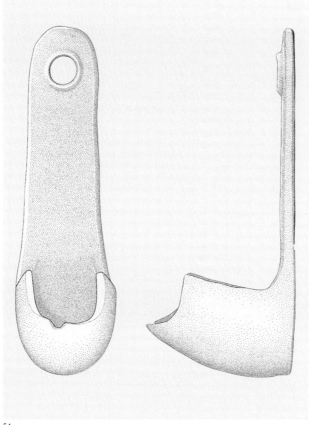

54

most of them of the oxhide type, are of Cypriote copper. A number of tin ingots were also found, illustrating the importance of metals in overseas trade during this period. Glass ingots were also present.

Other raw materials included hippopotamus and elephant tusks. Among the luxury goods were objects of gold, faience, bronze, Mycenaean pottery, and a considerable number of Cypriote vases of fine ware that were contained in three large pithoi (storage jars), also of Cypriote provenance. Ten such pithoi were on the ship, some of them containing agricultural products. This is the first time that evidence has been found for the methods by which fine export ware was transported from Cyprus. The vessels include White Slip, Base-Ring, Bucchero, and particularly White-Shaved ware juglets, of a type found also in other parts of the Aegean and the Central Mediterranean. Ten Cypriote wall brackets or incense burners were carried by the ship; it seems that this was a Cypriote ceramic product that was appreciated also outside Cyprus; several examples have been found in the Levant and in the Aegean (Cline 1994, 221–223). Another Cypriote association with the cargo of the ship is offered by the twenty-four stone anchors of Cypriote type that were found lying in rows.

Agricultural goods must have formed a substantial part of overseas trade. Large quantities of terebinth resin were contained in nearly 150 "Canaanite jars" (Haldane 1991, 11).

It has been suggested that terebinth resin was brought to the Aegean from the Levant for the production of resin-scented wine (which appeals to the Greeks even today) (Negbi and Negbi 1993, 325).

Another organic commodity was coriander. About one hundred grains were found in association with the Uluburun shipwreck, which must have formed part of a cargo stored in baskets or woven bags (Haldane 1990, 57–58; idem 1993, 356; Karageorghis 1996b). Coriander was used extensively in the Cretan palaces in the perfume industry and as a spice. It may have also been used in religious ritual.

Although coriander is known in the Aegean and possibly Crete, it has been one of the traditional spices of Cyprus and is widely used today in Cypriote cuisine.

The Knossian tablet Ga676 includes the words *Tu-wi-no-no ku-pi-ri-jo ko-ri-ja-do-no*. It seems unlikely that the recipients of goods of various kinds issued from the Palace of Knossos were Cypriots in as many as sexteen cases, and that Cypriots were again involved four times with the issue of goods in the Palace of Pylos. Mentioned in the Mycenaean documents are 720 liters of coriander seeds; they were mixed with wine, honey, and other spices in the perfume industry. Coriander was also used to hold the scent of a perfume with an olive oil base. Even Gallavotti, who in other cases favors the ethnic interpretation of Κύπριος (a Cypriot), in the case of *ku-pi-ri-jo ko-ri-ja-do-no* is prepared to accept that *ku-pi-ri-jo* refers to the Cypriote origin of coriander, Cyprus being an island on which, as he says, coriander is still very widely cultivated and used. The possibility that the coriander on the Knossian tablet was destined for export to Cyprus is remote, if not absurd (for further discussion and references see Karageorghis 1996b, 64).

The examples of terebinth resin and coriander are indicative of the importance of agricultural, organic goods in overseas trade during the Late Bronze Age. This may perhaps explain some of the lacunae in our knowledge about the kinds of goods that were exchanged, other than those that have left their traces in the archaeological record.

The problem of the country of origin of the Uluburun ship has been discussed several times and is still being discussed (for references see Pulak 2001).

55

Whether the ship was Cypriote or Levantine, perhaps we will never be able to know. The commodities that she contained, even the personal items, could have formed part of the international goods that could be found throughout the Mediterranean during the fourteenth and thirteenth centuries B.C. It cannot be denied, however, that the ship called at a Cypriote harbor on her westward journey, where she was loaded with the main body of her cargo, copper. We argued elsewhere (Karageorghis 1995b, 76), that ten tons of copper represent an enormous quantity, which only a king could afford to assemble for export, and on this argument we suggested that the ship was on a "royal trade mission" on behalf of the king of Alashiya.

This raises the problem of the political system prevailing on the island (also referred to above). It must have been based on a centralized administration and an elaborate but efficient "international" exchange system (cf. Knapp 1986). The connection of the ship with Cyprus is further strengthened by the evidence of the stone anchors, the fine Cypriote pottery, the ten large pithoi, the wall brackets, and perhaps coriander.

Cemal Pulak, who succeeded George Bass in the direction of the excavation of the Uluburun shipwreck, though not committing himself as to the ethnicity of the ship, makes some very pertinent remarks about the character of the cargo:

"The ship and its cargo appear to represent an offi-

55. Cypriote pottery recovered from the Uluburun shipwreck. One large Cypriote pithos contained five White Slip II ware bowls, three White-Shaved ware juglets, three Bucchero jugs, and four clay lamps. The jug with the trefoil mouth was found just outside the pithos (after Pulak 2001, fig. 3).

56

4. Relations with Anatolia

Relations with Anatolia are not as well documented as with other lands of the Mediterranean (for short surveys see Åström 1989; Todd 2001) for the late thirteenth century B.C. There are Hittite texts that speak of a Hittite conquest of Alashiya, the capture of its king, and the imposition of a tribute, consisting of copper and grain. The two enemies faced each other in a naval battle, and the ships of Alashiya were captured and burned at sea. In a letter sent to the king of Alashiya by the king of Ugarit, the latter says that enemy ships had already set fire to towns and created havoc in the countryside around Ugarit, and that the infantry of the Ugaritic king was in Hit-tite land, his ships in *Lukka*-land (for references see Knapp et al. 1996, 10).

It is difficult to relate these texts to the archaeological facts. The archaeological evidence for connections between Cyprus and Anatolia is rather sparse, though it has increased during recent years, with the discovery of more Cypriote pottery in Anatolia and Anatolian pottery (or pottery inspired from Anatolia) in Cyprus. A notable addition to Anatolian objects found in Cyprus is a silver statuette representing a Hittite god standing on the back of a deer (South 1997, 163, pl. xv.1) discovered in a tomb at Kalavassos-*Ayios Dhimitrios*. There is also a gold ring with a Hittite hieroglyphic inscription from Tamas-sos, and a silver ring from a shaft grave at Hala Sul-tan Tekke decorated with a winged disc of Hittite style; however, it dates to a later period (early twelfth century B.C.) (see Åström 1989).

Another notable addition to the few Hittite objects found in Cyprus is the "rediscovery" in the Pergamon Museum, Berlin, of a terra-cotta head of a bull of Anatolian provenance, found in a Late Cypriote II tomb at Nicosia-*Ayia Paraskevi* (Ohnefalsch-Richter 1893, 247). It belonged to a bull figurine of a fairly large size (Karageorghis 1999a). The tomb in which it was found must have belonged to an important person, in view of the Mycenaean crater that was also found in it. It is not certain whether the tomb was found intact or partly looted. The discovery of the head in a Late Cypriote II tomb poses some questions that are not easy to answer. Was this object imported by a Hittite visitor to the island or a Cypriote who visited Anatolia? Why did he choose such a large object? No doubt the bull figure had the same symbolic meaning both for an Anatolian and for a Cypriot.

cial dispatch of an enormously rich and valuable cargo of raw materials and manufactured goods largely intended for a specific destination. The presence of utilitarian objects and raw materials aside, the prestige goods on the ship would appear to indicate that Late Bronze Age Aegean was not so far removed from the international trade based on royal gift-giving of the Near East that is reflected so clearly in the Amarna letters. As was the practice in such ventures, the ship's cargo probably was placed in the care of an official or a semi-official who represented the king's interest, was entrusted with a contingent of prestige goods that he would present personally to the royalty receiving the cargo and who also may have engaged in some private trade of his own on the side" (Pulak 1998, 220).

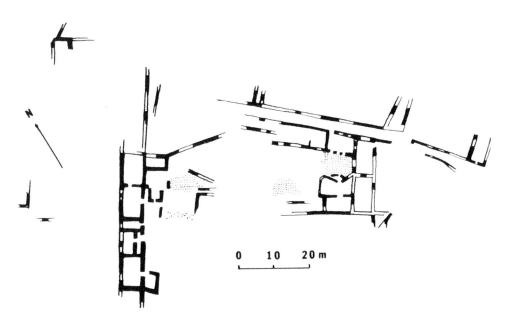

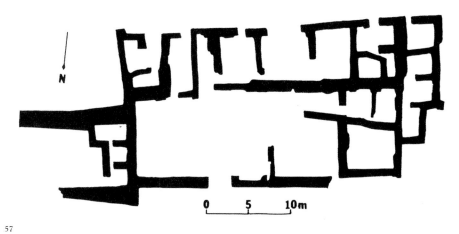

57

59

58

57. Thapsos, plan of excavated buildings (above), compared with the plan of a building from Enkomi (below) (after Ross Holloway 1981, fig. 52).

58. Fragment from the shoulder of a large Cypriote pithos found at Cannatello, near Agrigento, in Sicily. Such storage jars have been found at several sites in the Aegean and the Central Mediterranean and were probably used as containers for Cypriote pottery or other goods.

59. Composite stone anchor of a Late Bronze Age Cypriote type from Golfo di Cugnana, Olbia (Sassari). Archaeological Museum, Sassari. Height: 62.5cm.; weight: 74kg. It is made of local granite and is decorated with horizontal parallel grooves. Similar stone anchors have been found at other sites all along the Sardinian coast, which were used as landing places for the maritime trade between Cyprus and Sardinia, which must have been quite brisk from the thirteenth century B.C. onward.

35

60

60. Seven Mycenaean vessels
were among the grave gifts
provided for three young women
whose skeletons were found
on the rock-cut benches in
Kalavassos-*Ayios Dhimitrios* Tomb
11 (circa 1375 B.C.). Cyprus
Museum, Nicosia. The two open
craters (heights 33.2cm. and
27.4cm.) are decorated with
painted dolphins or fish and lilies,
and each was found with a Base-
Ring ware cup inside, probably
for serving wine as part of the
funerary ritual. The kylix (goblet)
was also for drinking, while the set
of three piriform jars and the flask
may have held perfumed oils.

61. A gold necklace from
Kalavassos-*Ayios Dhimitrios*,
Tomb 11. Preserved length:
15.5cm. Cyprus Museum, Nicosia.
Flat beads with embossed "sacral
ivy" decoration. The type of the
beads is Aegean.

5. Relations with the Central Mediterranean

During the last two decades important discoveries have been made outside Cyprus, namely in North Africa and the Central Mediterranean area, that throw light on the overseas relations of Cyprus. The Cypriots, probably in collaboration with others (Mycenaeans?), soon discovered the westward trade route, beyond the Aegean. Cypriote pottery dating to the fourteenth–thirteenth centuries B.C. has been found in tombs on the east coast of Sicily and particularly on the promontory of Thapsos (for references see Karageorghis 1998d, 31–34; idem 1999d). What is even more important is the discovery at Thapsos of pottery of non-Cypriote fabric, most likely local, imi-

tating shapes of Cypriote pottery (Base-Ring ware juglets) (cf. also Karageorghis 1995a, where a number of bowls are published that were found in earlier excavations of Thapsian tombs that are made of local gray clay but imitate the characteristic shapes of Cypriote Base-Ring ware bowls). The tombs of Thapsos also yielded Mycenaean pottery as well as a cylinder seal probably of Cypriote origin. A change in architecture is also noted at this time: whereas the houses of the local population traditionally were round, new types of houses with rectangular rooms were introduced in the fourteenth–thirteenth centuries B.C. Thus, on the basis of imports, local imitations, and changes in architectural styles, it has been

61

suggested that a commercial colony of Cypriots and Mycenaeans established themselves on the island of Thapsos. Furthermore, it has even been suggested that the ground plan of these new houses resembles that of houses of Enkomi in Cyprus (Ross Holloway 1981, 85; idem 2000, 34–35; Vagnetti 1996, 152–153).

More Cypriote pottery, along with Mycenaean, has been found in recent years at the site of Cannatello, near Agrigento, on the south coast of Sicily. Particularly interesting among the Cypriote pottery are large storage jars (pithoi) (Karageorghis 1993b, 584, fig. 3) of the type found on the Uluburun shipwreck, at Kommos in Crete, and, as we shall see later, in Sardinia and Cape Iria (in the Argolid). The use of these large pithoi in the Uluburun shipwreck as containers for other goods suggests a similar use for those found in other foreign contexts. The finer Cypriote pottery found in Sicily includes White Slip II and Base-Ring II ware sherds.

In the preliminary publication of some of the Mycenaean and Cypriote ceramic material found at Cannatello, Ernesto de Miro proposes that this ceramic material—including the Mycenaean—was imported to Cannatello from Cyprus (De Miro 1996, 999). He bases this argument on the fact that the Mycenaean material resembles very strikingly that found in Cyprus and that real Cypriote material (including large pithoi) was also found. Of particular importance are three handles of amphorae with incised signs of the "Cypro-Minoan" script, which implies a trading connection with Cyprus.

The problem of relations with Sardinia is more complex. Evidence for close relations with Sardinia, especially in the twelfth century B.C., is increasing. This includes the discovery of a fragment from the shoulder of a large pithos of the same type as those found at Cannatello; analysis has shown that this fragment is of the same origin as the large pithoi of the end of the thirteenth century B.C. found in the storerooms of the palatial building at Kalavassos-*Ayios Dhimitrios* in Cyprus. There are also sherds of fine Cypriote fabrics. Finally we should mention the discovery of a stone anchor in the Golfo di Cugnana, Olbia (Sassari), of Cypriote type, like those found in the shipwreck of Uluburun and at Kommos (Lo Schiavo 1995, 54–55).

What were the Cypriots exchanging their copper for in the west? Very little has been preserved in the archaeological record for the fourteenth–thirteenth

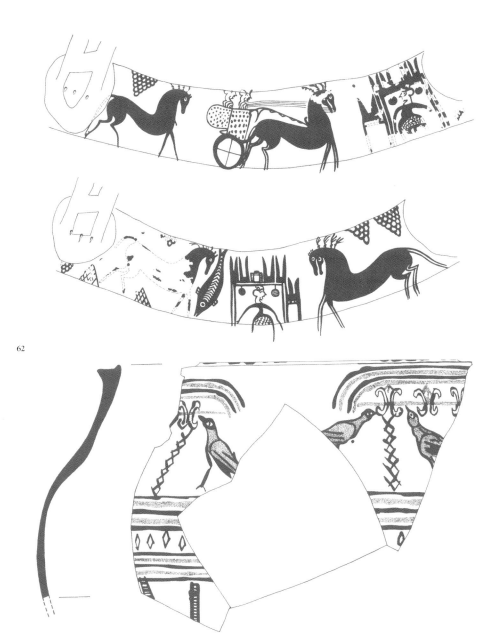

62

63

centuries B.C. An ivory comb of Italian type was found in a LC IIIB tomb at Enkomi (Vagnetti 1986, 210–213); also a bronze dagger of possibly Italian type was among the material in the Uluburun shipwreck (Vagnetti 1996, 163, with references). We may suggest that agricultural or other perishable products traveled eastward. Jones and Vagnetti (1991, 141) suggested alum as a possible commodity for exchange (an important mineral in leather working, textile dyeing, pharmacy, and wood construction) and even slaves (for a general discussion see Vagnetti and Lo Schiavo 1989; Vagnetti 1996; for a general survey see Castellana 2000, 236–237). Relations with the Central Mediterranean around 1200 B.C. and later will be discussed in a later chapter.

Further evidence for Cypriote trade with areas far-

62. The decoration of a Mycenaean IIIA:2 amphoroid crater from Kalavassos-*Ayios Dhimitrios*, Tomb 13. Height: 37.4cm.; mouth diam.: 28.7cm. Cyprus Museum, Nicosia (after Steel 1994, 206, fig. 4).

63. Fragment from a White Slip II crater from Kalavassos-*Ayios Dhimitrios*, Tomb 14, no. 2062, decorated with an unusual pictorial composition (after Steel 1997, pl. VIIa).

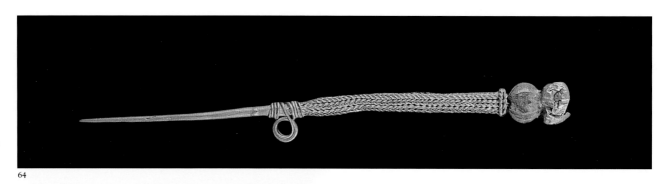

64

65

66

ther to the west is provided by the excavation of a small trading outpost near Marsa Matruh, near the border between Egypt and Libya (White 1985). This excavation yielded Aegean (Mycenaean and Minoan) as well as Cypriote pottery dating to the fourteenth–thirteenth centuries B.C. Most likely this trading post (or Egyptian garrison frontier post) was used by mariners primarily for the supply of provisions on their westward voyages, but it seems that some degree of trade with the local population was also carried out. The discovery of fragments of ostrich eggs at the site may suggest that this commodity was part of the trade; we know how very much these exotic objects were liked by both Mycenaeans and Cypriots. The exact nature and meaning of the Cypriote and Mycenaean material from this site will not be easy to define until the final publication of the results of the excavation. It is still not clear who was in charge of the trade, but a Cypro-Mycenaean involvement is plausible (cf. Watrous 1992, 176–177).

6. **The Age of Prosperity: Evidence from the Tombs**
Metallurgical activity during the fourteenth and thirteenth centuries B.C. is evident, as already stated above, at a number of urban centers in Cyprus. Kalavassos-*Ayios Dhimitrios* and Enkomi seem to be among the most prominent. The wealth of both is reflected in the spectacular richness of the tomb offerings that accompanied their dead.

Tomb 11 at Kalavassos (South 2000, 349–353) is one of the richest tombs ever excavated from Late Bronze Age Cyprus. It is a chamber tomb 4.2m in width, divided into two compartments by a buttress projecting from the wall opposite the stomion, and it had a rock-cut bench on either side. On the benches the skeletons of three young women were found; the skeleton of a child, as well as remains of three newborn infants, were lying on the floor. The tomb-gifts comprised local Cypriote fabrics as well as Myce-

67

naean pottery, including two open craters, one of them decorated with large dolphins; there were also two Base-Ring ware bull-shaped rhyta. The gold jewelry found in this tomb is exceptionally rich: there were bracelets, one with ivory inlay; earrings; several kinds of fine beads, including one decorated with the typical Mycenaean "sacral ivy" pattern. There were several finger rings, one with an Egyptian inscription and two with a Cypro-Minoan inscription. The jewelry of solid gold found in this tomb weighs about 432 grams (15 ounces). There were also objects of ivory: rods with decorated heads, cylindrical boxes,

and two cosmetic boxes in the shape of a duck. There were two flasks of Egyptian glass, beads of glass, and faience. Of exceptional beauty is one small cylindrical box of glass and gold. It is interesting that many objects were found in pairs or in sets of three. The tomb was found completely intact. Its ceramic material dates it to about 1375 B.C.

Close to Tomb 11 there were several other chamber tombs, partly looted, but they all yielded rich ceramic material and other tomb-gifts (ibid., 353–361). Tomb 12, the tomb of a child and several infants, yielded the small silver Hittite figurine, 6.2cm. high,

67. The painted decoration of a Mycenaean IIIA:1 open crater (Early Pictorial I style, circa 1410–1390 B.C.), decorated on both sides with a chariot scene. From Enkomi (French Mission), Tomb 7, no. 4787. Height: 33cm.; diam.: 34.1cm. Cyprus Museum, Nicosia. This is one of the earliest Mycenaean craters of the pictorial style found in Cyprus. The theme was probably inspired by Near Eastern mythology: a large bird chases the occupants of the chariot over a rocky landscape. One of them raises his arms in despair. On the other side one of the warriors is whipping the team on to greater speed. In Old Babylonian mythology there is such a story of a monstrous bird, Enzu or Anzu. On a Mycenaean crater found at Ugarit the sequel of the same myth is depicted, namely, the capture of the bird.

68. A silver bowl with a hemispherical body and a wishbone handle. From Enkomi (French Mission), Tomb 2, no. 4207. Height: 6cm.; diam.: 15.7cm. Cyprus Museum, Nicosia. The decoration of the exterior surface is inlaid with gold and a black substance known as niello. It consists of a horizontal row of bulls' heads with two stylized flowers between them. Below is a frieze of rosettes, each within a semicircle. This inlaid technique is known in Mycenaean art. An almost identical bowl was found at Dendra in the Peloponnese. Although the wishbone handle may recall Cypriote bowls of the same period (fourteenth century B.C.), this form of handle was also known in the Aegean.

68

69. Large Late Minoan III stirrup jar decorated with a stylized octopus. Height: 44cm. Cyprus Museum, Nicosia, A1504. Several such vases have been found in Cyprus; they date from the Late Cypriote II–IIIA periods, i.e., from the fourteenth to the early twelfth century B.C. They may have contained liquids (wine or olive oil). Such jars have also been found in the Cape Iria wreck (circa 1200 B.C.), which occurred on her return voyage from the Aegean (see below). They usually have engraved signs of the Cypro-Minoan script on the handles, like this one, perhaps suggesting a Cypriote involvement in the trade of the liquid it contained.

70. Small Late Minoan III B stirrup jar in the Bank of Cyprus Cultural Foundation Museum, Nicosia. Height: 12cm.

71. Bull-shaped rhyton of Base-Ring II painted ware, from Kazaphani, Tomb 2B, no. 220. Height: 12.9cm. Cyprus Museum, Nicosia. Such rhytons were very common during the Late Cypriote II period.

72. Late Minoan IIIA amphoroid crater from Pyla-*Verghi* (excavations of the Cyprus Department of Antiquities), Tomb 1, no. 37. Height 43cm.; mouth diam.: 34.5cm. Cyprus Museum, Nicosia, Inv. no. 1952/IV–12/1. Decorated with vertical narrow bands filled with abstract motifs. This vase (erroneously identified before as Mycenaean) is one of two Late Minoan craters found in the same tomb. Similar vases were found in the region of Larnaca.

69

70

71

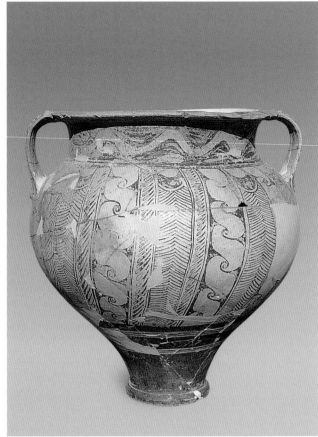

72

referred to above. It represents a kilted male divinity wearing the usual high conical Hittite headdress and shoes with upturned ends, holding a crook and standing on the back of a deer. The tomb dates to the end of the thirteenth century B.C. Tomb 13, though previously looted, yielded an impressive quantity of Mycenaean pottery, including three amphoroid craters decorated in the pictorial style: two are decorated with octopus motifs and the other (Steel 1994) with a very unusual composition: on one side there is a chariot group followed by a simple horse, turned toward a structure, obviously a sanctuary, inside which is a female figure, probably a goddess or a priestess. The building is topped by several "horns of consecration," a symbol of Minoan-Mycenaean religion. On the other side there is, in the center, a similar structure with a female figure inside; on either side there is a horse; a vertical fish is placed next to the building. This is a most unusual composition. Probably the Cypriots understood such religious scenes, which they identified with sanctuaries known to them from their own island (ibid., 211). However, such vases "were appropriated by the elite as status symbols to define their own exclusivity" (Steel 1998, 296). The tomb was in use in the four-

73. Pottery of Base-Ring I and II ware in the Cesnola Collection, the Metropolitan Museum of Art, New York. From left to right: (1) Bowl, no. 74.51.1255. Height: 10.6cm.; diam.: 16.8cm. (2) Jug, no. 74.51.1171. Height: 12.5cm. (3) Jug, no. 74.51.1135. Height: 22.7cm. (4) Double bil-bil, no. 74.51.1185. Height: 10.6cm. (5) Conical footed bowl, no. 74.51.1142. Height: 10.2cm.; diam.: 15.6cm. Jug no. (2) is decorated with two confronted coiling serpents. Vases (1)–(4) are of Base-Ring I ware, bowl (5) of Base-Ring II ware. Jugs like no. (3) were used for the export of opium and are often found abroad, particularly in Egypt. If looked at upside down they have the form of a capsule of opium.

74. Vases of White Slip I–II ware in the Cesnola Collection, the Metropolitan Museum of Art, New York. From left to right: (1) Jug, White Slip I–II, no. 74.51.1365. Height: 21.5cm. It imitates a Base-Ring ware shape. (2) Bowl of White Slip I ware, no. 74.51.1348. Height: 6.2cm.; diam.: 15.4cm. It is decorated in two colors, dark brown and dilute brown. (3) Small bowl, White Slip I ware, no. 74.51.1115, of a rather unusual shape, decorated in two colors, dark brown and orange. Height: 7.5cm.; diam.: 8.1cm. (4) Conical bowl, White Slip II ware, no. 74.51.1022. Height: 7cm.; diam.: 11.9cm.

75. Mycenaean IIIA:2 crater (Middle Pictorial II, circa 1345–1325 B.C.) from Enkomi (excavations of the Cyprus Department of Antiquities), Tomb 10, no. 200. Height: 43.5cm.; mouth diam.: 31.7cm. Cyprus Museum, Nicosia. One side of the shoulder zone between the handles is decorated with three leaping bulls and one human figure. On the other side there are two bulls and a human figure between them. The background on both sides is filled with parallel chevrons, seashell motifs, and concentric semicircles, indicating a rocky landscape. Filling ornaments, usually floral, against the background of pictorial compositions become very common in the second half of the fourteenth century, thus diminishing the vigor of the pictorial scenes themselves. The themes on this crater, with bulls both in a peaceful scene and in a scene of action, recall those on the well-known gold cups from Vapheio in the Peloponnese.

teenth–thirteenth centuries B.C. It also contained objects of gold and ivory.

Tomb 14 was also exceptionally rich. It yielded an amphoroid crater decorated with two large antithetic birds and a fragment from a large White Slip II ware crater with a unique bichrome decoration, consisting of naturalistically rendered birds (Steel 1997). There were also objects of gold, ivory, and glass. Tomb 14 dates to the fourteenth century B.C.

The tombs so far excavated at Kavassos-*Ayios Dhimitrios* reveal the exceptional wealth of an elite society that, no doubt, was in control of the economy of the town, namely the copper trade (the copper mines of Kalavassos are within a short distance from the site) and oil production (see below). The fact that they show continuity in use and orientation, and respect for earlier burials (Tomb 11), prompted their excavator, Alison South, to suggest that they indicate strong political/social continuity at Kalavassos from the fourteenth to the late thirteenth century B.C. She further suggests that Building x, an administrative palatial building that we shall discuss later, had been deliberately placed next to the elite tombs of

the ancestors of its builders (South 1997, 171). A glance at the tomb-groups excavated by the Swedish Cyprus Expedition at Enkomi reveals the fabulous wealth of its inhabitants. We mention in particular Tomb 3, which yielded about one dozen Mycenaean amphoroid craters (one Minoan) and other Mycenaean vases, as well as gold, silver, ivory, glass, and faience objects; Tomb 17 yielded a bowl of solid gold. Exceptionally rich was Side Chamber 18, dating to the thirteenth century B.C. It produced a phenomenal number of large Mycenaean vases, including craters decorated in the pictorial style and dinner sets, objects of gold, silver, ivory, glass, and faience. We note in particular a necklace with beads in the form of the figure-of-eight shield (an Aegean motif) and a gold-plated finger ring, the bezel of which is engraved with a naturalistically rendered lion in an Aegean style.

Equally rich are some of the tombs excavated by the French Mission at Enkomi. Among the numerous Mycenaean craters brought to light is an open crater of the early fourteenth century B.C. that is decorated with a chariot scene with probable Near Eastern connections. Depicted on both sides of the crater are chariot groups with a large bird chasing the figures in the chariot over a mountainous area. This scene has been associated with the chase and final capture of the monstrous bird Enzu. (For the excavations of the Swedish Cyprus Expedition see Gjerstad *et al.* 1934; for a detailed study of the Mycenaean vases of the pictorial style found at Enkomi and elsewhere in Cyprus see Vermeule and Karageorghis 1982; for the Enkomi tombs in general, with references to previous literature, including the tombs excavated at Enkomi and elsewhere by a mission from the British Museum, see Courtois, Lagarce, and Lagarce 1986.

A remarkable object that was found in a tomb at Enkomi by the French Mission is a hemispherical silver bowl with a wishbone handle, decorated with bulls' heads and lotus flowers, inlaid with gold and niello. Its striking similarity with a bowl from Dendra in the Peloponnese may suggest an Aegean origin for this bowl. The possibility need not be excluded, however, that such objects may have been made also in Cyprus, by Cypriote or foreign artists. It is a fine example of the "international" art that prevailed in the East Mediterranean and the Aegean during the Late Bronze Age. It is dated to the beginning of the fourteenth century B.C. (for a bibliography see Courtois, Lagarce, and Lagarce 1986, 100–107).

75

7. Mycenaean and Minoan Pottery Found in Cyprus

We have already referred to the large quantities of Mycenaean vases, particularly those of the pictorial style, during the fourteenth and thirteenth centuries B.C. Other ceramic imports from the Aegean were the Late Minoan IIIA–B vases, including amphoroid craters and stirrup jars, but also cups of various types. There are a number of LM IIIB large stirrup jars, almost all of them bearing engraved signs in the Cypro-Minoan script on their handles; no doubt they were used for the trade of liquid products (oil, wine) (Benson 1961). Crete during this period must have been under Mycenaean domination, but it continued its own cultural traditions and some of its special commercial relations with the East Mediterranean, particularly Cyprus. Late Minoan III pottery has been recorded at several Levantine sites, mainly Ugarit. In Cyprus the numbers of Late Minoan IIIA–B imports have increased considerably during recent years (Karageorghis 1979c, 199; Åström 1978, 62; Popham 1979; Kopcke 2001, 244). Late Minoan IIIB pottery from the Kydonia region of Crete was discovered on Cyprus (at Kition and Hala Sultan Tekke) in the early explorations of the island; it is in this particular region of Crete that most of the Cypriote pottery of the fourteenth–thirteenth centuries B.C. has been found, a phenomenon that suggests particular trade relations between southeastern Cyprus and Kydonia (Karageorghis 1979c, 201–203). It would be interesting to investigate the nature of this trade, in relation to the discoveries at Kommos as well as the information provided by the Linear B tablets (for references see Karageorghis 1996b).

The large quantities of Mycenaean pottery found in Cyprus have been interpreted in various ways by scholars over the last fifty years or so. Was it because of the fascination exercised by these luxury vases on the Cypriots and the Levantines that they bought most of them for their own sake, not as containers? Were they status symbols of the elite society as we mentioned above? I believe that the latter hypothesis may be correct and that the Cypriots at least exchanged art for copper; but other organic materials may have also been involved in this exchange.

It has been suggested, no doubt rightly, by Louise Steel (1998) that the influx of Mycenaean pottery to Cyprus in the fourteenth and thirteenth centuries B.C. may be associated with social changes and new habits among an elite society in the main urban centers of Cyprus, like Enkomi, Kalavassos, Kition, and

76

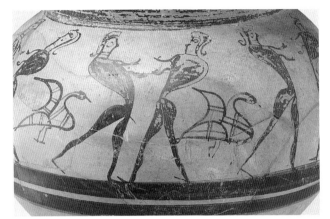

77

78

76. Mycenaean IIIA:1 amphoroid crater (Early Pictorial III, circa 1375–1360 B.C.), probably from Maroni. The Cesnola Collection, the Metropolitan Museum of Art, New York, no. 74.51.964. Height: 36.7cm.; mouth diam.: 27.2cm. Second quarter of the fourteenth century B.C. The two zones between the handles are decorated with two chariot groups to the right; usually there is only one group on each side of amphoroid craters.

77-78. Mycenaean IIIB (early) amphoroid crater. Bank of Cyprus Cultural Foundation Museum, Nicosia. Height: 44.5cm.; mouth diam.: 31cm. The two zones between the handles are decorated on one side with three pairs of confronted human figures (boxers) and birds, on the other side with two pairs of confronted human figures and a pair of runners.

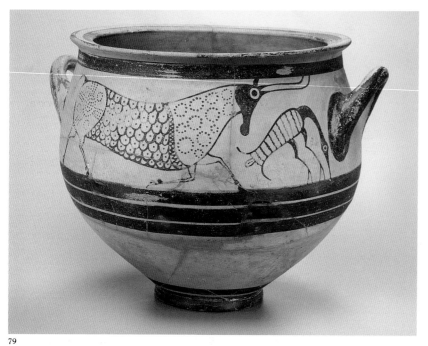

79

81

80

82

83

84

elsewhere. These involved elaborate mortuary display, a vehicle through which the emergent elite group could express its new identity and differentiate itself from other social groups. In the same spirit luxury goods from the Near East and elsewhere were included among funerary furniture. There must have been elaborate drinking rituals, symposia, or ceremonies equivalent to the Near Eastern marzeah, often with funerary connotations (for references see Steel 1998, 290, n. 34). During such drinking rituals, drinking sets were used, including craters for mixing wine, jugs, and cups. Though the local Cypriote pottery (White Slip and Base-Ring) continued in use, the most elegant and elaborate forms were now in Mycenaean fabric. Very often the craters are decorated with elaborate pictorial compositions (chariot groups, hunting scenes, etc.), indicating the high status of their owner. Thus, Mycenaean pottery was incorporated within a preexisting system of social behavior of an aristocratic society, in whose possession they became status symbols, hence their great popularity (see Karageorghis 1999c, 47–51).

On many of the Mycenaean vases found in Cyprus and on the Syro-Palestinian coast there are engraved or painted signs in the Cypro-Minoan script. These signs were incised or painted on the vessels after firing, and current research tends to suggest the involvement of Cypriote merchants in the selection of these vases and their diffusion in the Eastern Mediterranean (cf. Hirschfeld 1993; eadem 1996; eadem 2000, 163–184).

Based on the fact that large quantities of Mycenaean vases have also been found in the Levant, particularly at Ugarit (these numbers have now increased considerably: see Yon *et al.* 2000), Catling proposed that some, at least, of those vases "went directly from ports in the Aegean to certain major near Eastern clearing houses, Ras Shamra is the most obvious candidate, but it certainly need not be the only one. It would then be these towns that acted as major centers of distribution for the whole area." Following the same thinking, Catling refuses to allow any initiative to Cypriote merchants. He goes on to suggest that Cypriote copper, too, may have been handled by Levantine merchants as middlemen, and the amount of direct contact between Cyprus and the West may, in this phase, have been substantially less than we have hitherto supposed (Catling 1980, 18). I am unable to follow this theory, not only because it is now weakened by the interpretation of the occurrence of Cypro-Minoan signs on Mycenaean pottery found both in Cyprus and in the Levant (some also in the Argolid), but also taking into account the impact of Mycenaean art on Cypriote art as a whole, which presupposes close and direct contacts between Cyprus and the Aegean in the fourteenth–thirteenth centuries B.C. Mycenaean pottery from Cyprus could easily be exported to the Levant, together with the large quantities of Cypriote pottery of the same period found there. The influence (through Cyprus) of Mycenaean IIIC:1b on the ceramic production of the Levant in the twelfth century offers a useful model.

45

85

87

86

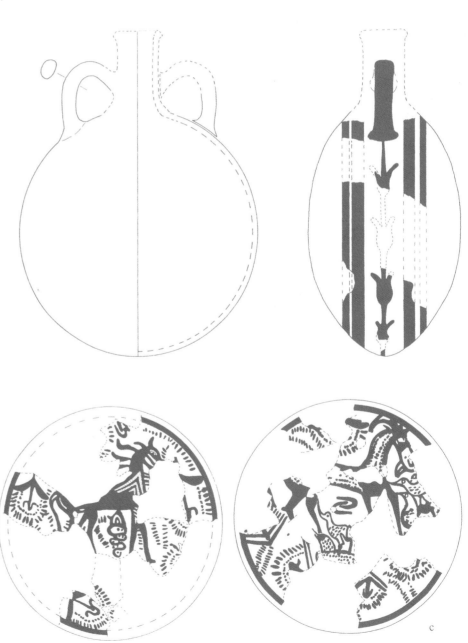

c

88

The explanation that has hitherto been proposed for the Mycenaean vases found in Cyprus is that they were created in the Peloponnese with the Cypriote market in mind. I do not find this explanation convincing. One should not exclude the possibility that Mycenaean-type pottery was produced in other centers on the periphery of the Mycenaean world. Artists, and in this case potters, could travel and produce their works of art elsewhere.

There are several forms of Mycenaean pottery that have been labeled "Levanto-Helladic" because their form recalls Cypriote and Levantine shapes; one of these forms is the lentoid flask. Mycenaean IIIB lentoid flasks, at present, appear exclusively in the Levant (on the appearance of Mycenaean lentoid flasks with two handles in the Levant see Leonard 1994, 81–83, where thirty-two examples are listed). Similar, but not identical, lentoid flasks appear in the Aegean (Furumark 1992: FS 186, pls. 107–108). Those in the Aegean have a high base or one vertical handle from the neck to the broad side of the body. This form had a long tradition in the Near East and Egypt. On Cyprus it occurred as early as the Middle Bronze Age in White Painted ware. Its popularity in the Levant is demonstrated particularly in Lebanon, where in one single tomb at Sarepta three Mycenaean IIIB examples have been found along with ten others made of local clay (Baramki 1958, Mycenaean IIIB: 1135–1137, pls. XV.26A–B, XVI.23–24, figs. 23, 24, 26, nos. 24, 26–27; local clay: 136–138, pls. XVI.27, 34, figs. 27–36, nos. 28–37; "oriental imitation": 136, fig. 25, no. 25; see also Baramki 1973: 193–196 and legends for pls. XIII.2–4). The most important of the three Mycenaean IIIB flasks from this tomb (Baramki 1958, no. 27) is very fragmentary, and the pictorial decoration on both sides is very worn (for new photos and drawings of this object see Karageorghis 1999b). On Cyprus, the form was quite popular. In addition to specimens discussed previously (Karageorghis 1965, 214–217), there are also fragments of lentoid flasks from Kition and Enkomi.

Although the application of scientific methods may suggest the Argolid as the place of manufacture of the bulk of Mycenaean pottery found in various places in the Mediterranean area, other possibilities cannot be ignored. It may be suggested that some local workshops for making Mycenaean-type pottery may have been established outside the Argolid, especially toward the end of the thirteenth century B.C.,

when the conditions of trade traffic in the Mediterranean became difficult. Instead of arguing that the Mycenaean lentoid flasks, indeed all other forms known only in Cyprus and the Levant, were made exclusively in the Argolid with the Eastern Mediterranean in mind, the possibility should be considered that some Mycenaean vases, particularly of forms favored in the Levant, such as the lentoid flasks, were made by Mycenaean potters using imported clay. It is known that some craftsmen traveled during the Late Bronze Age, and the potters may have done the same. Some of them could have taken their own clay with them from the Argolid and continued to import such clay afterward for the manufacture of luxury Mycenaean pottery, so much favored in the Eastern Mediterranean by the local elite. The suggestion of clay trade in antiquity is now substantiated by written evidence. As pointed out already, the writer no longer doubts that the bulk of Mycenaean pottery must have been made in the Argolid (a fact that was also established by the discovery of a potter's kiln at Berbati in the Peloponnese), but allowance should be made for exceptions. The fact that it is often uncertain whether a Mycenaean type vase is of Mycenaean or local clay (this is true of at least one of the lentoid flasks from Sarepta which was slightly deformed during firing) should induce students of Mycenaean ceramics to have a more open mind.

In an attempt to show how much clay would be needed to produce a Mycenaean vase that would sell at a high price in the Levant, the author asked a qualified potter, Valentinos Charalambous, to undertake a practical experiment that showed that with a bag of clay a potter could produce enough Mycenaean pottery to make its import from the Argolid to the Eastern Mediterranean more than worthwhile. If the cargo ships that were crossing the Mediterranean could carry organic goods like terebinth resin, oils, or even coriander, a bag of clay could have been accommodated among the rest of their cargo. The problem is that such evidence could not easily survive in the archaeological record (Karageorghis 1999b, 400).

8. Art of the Fourteenth–Thirteenth Centuries B.C.

A number of works of art dating to the fourteenth–thirteenth centuries have already been mentioned, e.g., the silver bowl from Enkomi with inlaid decoration and several pieces of jewelry with an Aegean inspiration. One of the most outstanding gold neck-

85. Mycenaean IIIB bowl with S-shaped sides and wishbone handle, from Kition Area II (excavations of the Cyprus Department of Antiquities), Tomb 9, lower burial, no. 12. Height: 8cm.; diam.: 12.5cm. Larnaca District Museum. The shape clearly imitates a Cypriote form (Base-Ring ware bowls). Whether this bowl was made in Cyprus by Mycenaean potters using Greek Mainland clay or was made in the Peloponnese with the Cypriote market in mind is not easy to determine.

86. Mycenaean IIIB "pilgrim" flask with a lentoid body, decorated with concentric bands on either side. Height: 17cm. Cyprus Museum, Nicosia, Inv. no. 1933/V-6/5. Such forms, known in Cyprus and the Eastern Mediterranean since the beginning of the Late Bronze Age in faience and clay, may have had metallic prototypes. All the examples so far known in Mycenaean ware (fourteenth–thirteenth centuries B.C.) have been found in Cyprus and the Levant. They were either made in the Aegean with the Cypriote and Levantine markets in mind or made in the Levant by Mycenaean potters using imported clay. In several cases they are also made of local clay.

87. Two Mycenaean IIIB bowls imitating Cypriote shapes. Left: Cyprus Museum, Nicosia, Inv. no. 1951/III-7/5. Height: 7cm.; diam.: 12.6cm. Decorated inside and outside with thick horizontal bands. It has a carinated profile and a wishbone handle, recalling the shape of Cypriote Base-Ring ware bowls. Right: Cyprus Museum, Nicosia, Inv. no. 1955/IV-14/3. Height: 9.3cm.; diam.: 14.6cm. Only the exterior surface is decorated with a horizontal frieze of parallel chevrons. Hemispherical body, wishbone handle. It imitates the form and style of decoration of Cypriote White Slip ware bowls.

88. Mycenaean IIIB pilgrim flask from Sarepta, Museum of the American University of Beirut. Restored height: 32cm. (after Karageorghis 1999b, pl. LXXXV).

89. Gold diadem or pectoral from Enkomi (Swedish Cyprus Expedition), Tomb 18, no. 95. Cyprus Museum, Nicosia. It consists of a thin sheet of gold, rectangular in shape with rounded corners, perforated at the ends. It is decorated in repoussé with two horizontal rows of Mycenaean-type winged sphinxes, framed within rectangular panels. Late Cypriote II period.

90. Thin sheet of gold decorated in repoussé with two winged sphinxes confronted on either side of a "sacred tree." Length: 20.3cm. From Enkomi, Tomb 2. Louvre Museum, Paris. Such objects were used as funerary gifts. They are usually oblong (diadems), but occasionally they are elliptical and may have been used as mouth-pieces or pectorals. The sphinx is a common decorative motif for such objects, either of the Near Eastern type or of the Aegean type, with a flat headdress. They date to the Late Cypriote II period (fourteenth century–circa 1200 B.C.).

91. Gold necklace from Ayios Iakovos (Swedish Cyprus Expedition), nos. 3+4+27. Cyprus Museum, Nicosia. It consists of seven hollow beads in the shape of pomegranates and six large and two small hollow beads in the shape of dates. In the middle is a large hematite Babylonian cylinder seal with gold caps, used as a pendant. Length of necklace: 19.8cm.; length of cylinder seal: 3.7cm. Pomegranates symbolize fertility and constitute a favorite motif in both Aegean and Levantine art. Late Cypriote II period.

92. Gold pendant in the form of a pomegranate, with a ring at the top for suspension. From Enkomi. Height: 4.7cm. Cyprus Museum, Nicosia, Inv. no. 1954/III–24/1. The whole surface is decorated with twelve horizontal rows of granulated triangles. Thirteenth century B.C. There is an identical object from Enkomi, now in the British Museum.

93. A gold earring. Bank of Cyprus Cultural Foundation Museum, Nicosia. Length: 3.2cm. Circular ring of thin wire and hollow pendant in the form of a stylized bull's head. Both sides are decorated with granules and antithetic spirals of filigree. Late Cypriote I–III periods. Pendants with granulation are known also from the Aegean. The commoner type in Cyprus is decorated in repoussé.

89

90

91

92

93

laces from Enkomi is the one found in Tomb 93 by the British Museum expedition in 1896. It is composed of sixteen large beads in the form of two superimposed figure-of-eight shields. They are perforated horizontally four times and are separated from one another by means of four spacers in the form of small globular or cylindrical beads of gold wire. The central part of the necklace (if the restoration is correct) consists of six large amygdaloid beads of carnelian and smaller gold globular beads. The length of the large beads is 3.5cm. Another remarkable necklace, from Ayios Iakovos, consists of gold beads in the form of pomegranates and dates, also of Aegean inspiration. A hematite Babylonian seal, used as a pendant, adds an exotic character to the necklace, at the same time illustrating the mixed origins of the art of Cyprus and the "international" taste of the Cypriots. We have already referred to the extraordinary jewelry found in Kalavassos-*Ayios Dhimitrios* Tomb 11. From Enkomi comes a pendant in the form of a pomegranate, the surface of which is covered entirely by rows of small granulated triangles.

The rich tombs of the fourteenth–thirteenth centuries B.C. throughout the island yielded a large number of gold oblong-rectangular diadems or pectorals of an elliptical shape that are decorated with embossed motifs. Some of the dies used were no doubt imported from the Aegean; others were local or of Levantine inspiration. This art is well illustrated by diadems and pectorals from Enkomi; some are decorated with seated sphinxes of a well-known Mycenaean type, others with sphinxes of a Levantine type, confronted on either side of a "sacred tree." There is a great variety of earrings: loop shaped, elegant, and simple, or crescent shaped, composed of plaited wire terminating in plain overlapping ends. But the commonest shape is that of the earrings consisting of a ring of plain wire with overlapping ends and a pendant in the shape of a bull's head composed of two embossed pieces of gold with two holes for suspension from the gold ring. The surface is adorned with either embossed or granulated decoration (for a general discussion see Buchholz 1986, 133-143).

One of the most remarkable works of art from Late Bronze Age Cyprus is a faience rhyton found in a thirteenth century B.C. tomb at Kition. The handle and lower tip are missing; its preserved height is 26.8cm. The surface is covered with a thick layer of blue glaze and the decoration, in three registers, consists of human, animal, floral, and abstract motifs,

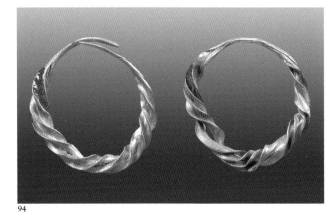

94

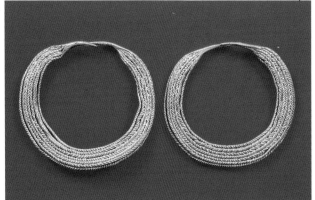

95

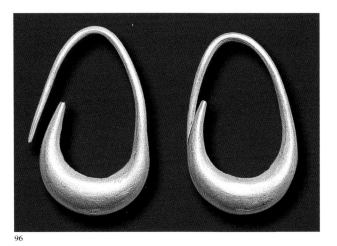

96

97

94. Pair of gold earrings from Ayios Iakovos-*Dima* (Swedish Cyprus Expedition), no. 5. They are flat and crescent shaped and consist of twisted interwoven wire; thin terminals are of plain wire. Cyprus Museum, Nicosia. Diam.: 4.7cm. Late Cypriote II period.

95. Pair of crescent-shaped gold earrings. Cyprus Museum, Nicosia, no. J.67. Diam.: 3cm. They consist of twisted bands with thinly hammered overlapping ends. Late Cypriote II period.

96-97. Two pairs of gold earrings, from Kition, Area I (excavations of the Cyprus Department of Antiquities), Tomb 9, upper burial. Larnaca District Museum. Above: solid, leech shaped, with overlapping ends. Length: 2.2cm. Below: circular ring of thin wire and pendant in the shape of a bull's head. Total length: 3cm. Both pairs are of types that were very popular in Cyprus during the Late Cypriote II period (fourteenth–thirteenth centuries B.C.).

98. Fragmentary rhyton of faience from Kition, Area II (excavations of the Cyprus Department of Antiquities), probably belonging to Tombs 4 and 5, special series no. 1. Preserved height: 26.8cm. Cyprus Museum, Nicosia. It is made of hard faience, covered with a thick layer of blue glaze. It is decorated in three registers (painted and inlaid), with running animals (above), hunting of animals (in the middle), and running spirals (below). The style of the decoration is mixed (Aegean and Near Eastern). Thirteenth century B.C.

99. Impression of a cylinder seal of hematite, from Enkomi (French Mission, 1934), Trial Trench 37, no. 2. Cyprus Museum, Nicosia. Length: 3.5cm. The central figure is a youth wearing a kilt; he stretches his arms to hold two lions by the ear. To his left and right are genies holding jugs. Above are birds and griffins. This cylinder belongs to the Levanto-Aegean group, which is represented by a fair number of examples. Late Cypriote II period.

100. Impression of a cylinder seal from Idalion. Cyprus Museum, no. 69. Length: 1.5cm. The representation consists of a procession of human figures holding vases. Two wear a long robe; one wears a kilt. In the field there are also vases, tree motifs, and chrysalides. The scene is of a processional character, and two of the figures wear hieratic garments. The style of the rendering of the figures and also the vase forms are of a distinct Minoan character. There is a whole series of such seals found in Cyprus, which show strong Aegean influence. Late Cypriote II period.

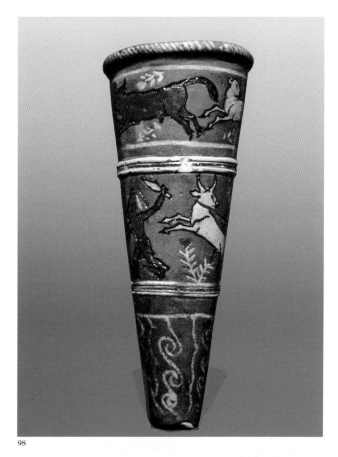

98

either shown in yellow with a black outline or inlaid in red faience. The upper register is decorated with galloping animals, recalling the styles of Egyptian art. The middle register, representing hunters of bulls, is of purely Egyptian inspiration (note in particular the magic knives on the sandals of the hunters), whereas the lower register is decorated with vertical rows of running spirals, a motif that is well known from Mycenaean but also Egyptian art. The shape of the vase itself, a conical rhyton, is an imitation of a Mycenaean form. This object is a good example of the successful result of the amalgam of Aegean, Levantine, and Egyptian elements in art at the end of the Late Bronze Age, of which Cyprus may have been the chief instigator (although this rhyton itself may have been manufactured in the Levant) (for further discussion of faience objects from Cyprus during this period see Peltenburg 1974). Aegean elements mixed with local or Levantine motifs are quite conspicuous in a class of seals. A good example is a hematite cylinder seal from Enkomi; the design represents a standing male figure wearing a short kilt, with outstretched arms holding

99

100

101. Impression of a cylinder seal from Enkomi (surface find). Cyprus Museum, Nicosia, Inv. no. 1957/V-4/1. Preserved length: 1.6cm. It is decorated with a frieze of figures, rendered in a Minoanizing style. The subject matter (a cult or an offering scene) is also strongly Minoan in character. A devotee wearing a mask of a bull offers an animal to a god and goddess. He is assisted by the Minoan genius holding aloft a libation vessel. The goddess holds a bird by the leg in her right hand as an emblem; the god also holds an emblem in his right hand (obliterated by the fracture). Between the goddess and the god there is a bucranium. Late Cypriote II period.

102. Cylinder seal of hematite in a private collection. Length: 2.7cm. The central part represents two genies holding jugs with a bull's head between them. Below them are two lions and a goat's head; above are a winged disc and four signs of the Cypro-Minoan script with a central rosette. There are also other human figures and animals. This is a typical Late Cypriote II (early fourteenth century B.C.) cylinder seal, combining Aegean, Near Eastern and Cypriote elements.

two lions by the ears; to his left and right are genies holding jugs; birds and griffins fly above them. The motifs of the composition are of an Aegean type, particularly the rendering of the kilted "master of animals." On another hematite cylinder seal from Idalion there is a procession of male human figures, one wearing a short kilt and two others a long robe (Karageorghis 1982, 66, fig. 47). They hold vases, and more vases are in the field, in a vertical row. Both the human figures and the vase forms are of Aegean inspiration. Finally, another hematite seal now in a private collection shows confronted genies holding jugs. The other motifs (human figures wearing bulls' masks and a winged disc) are of Near Eastern inspiration. At the top there are engraved signs of the Cypro-Minoan script. The seal has been dated to the early fourteenth century B.C. (for further discussion of the glyptic art of Cyprus during the fourteenth–thirteenth centuries B.C. see Boardman 1970, 65, 106, pls. 203–206; Pini 1979, 121–127).

Similar phenomena are observed on sealings on pithoi of the thirteenth century B.C. A pithos

103. Impressed fragment from the shoulder of a large pithos, from Analiondas-*Pareklisha*. Cyprus Museum, Nicosia, Inv. no. 1953/IX-3/6. Height of impressed decoration: 3cm. The representation consists of a hunting scene, with a hunter shooting at two bulls who run in front of the horses; behind the chariot there are two runners. The chariot and the hunter may recall Egyptian prototypes, but the rest is of Aegean inspiration, particularly the runners with their kilts. The impression may have been made with a wooden cylinder seal. There are several other examples of impressed pithoi, mainly from Alassa-*Paliotaverna*, Maa-*Palaeokastro*, Enkomi, and Palaepaphos, all of the Late Cypriote IIC–IIIA period.

104-105. Alassa-*Paliotaverna* (excavations of the Cyprus Department of Antiquities). Fragments of pithoi with an impression of bull-hunting scenes. Cyprus Museum, Nicosia. This decoration was achieved by rolling a cylinder seal on the wet surface of the pithos (often on a band of finer clay).

106. Base-Ring ware nude female figurine holding an infant. The National Museum of Denmark, Copenhagen, Inv. no. 3713. Height: 8.1cm. This is one of the very rare cases of a seated "Kourotrophos." Late Cypriote II period.

107. Terra-cotta group in Base-Ring ware, representing a nude male attendant and a bull, probably led to the sacrifice, from Kazaphani. Cyprus Museum, CS1829, no. 136. Height: 12cm. Similar compositions from the Late Cypriote II period are also known in bronze; the bull and the attendant are usually standing on wheeled vehicles.

108. Horse and rider figurine of Base-Ring ware. The horse is hollow, handmade. Details on the body of the horse and the rider are rendered with black and purple paint. Cyprus Museum, Nicosia, Inv. no. 1979/XII-8/2. Height: 15.8cm. Horse riding in Cyprus may have started already during the Middle Bronze Age, as seen on some rare representations on vases, but it received a new impetus during the Late Bronze Age. Riding sidesaddle (*en amazone*) may have an Aegean origin. Such figurines have been found in Attica and Crete, but this type is not unknown in the Near East. None of the few known figurines of this type have been found in a datable context, but the fabric suggests a fourteenth–thirteenth century B.C. date.

103

104

105

107

106

108

109

fragment from Analiondas shows a hunter in a war chariot drawing his bow in an Egyptian fashion, preceded by fleeing bulls and followed by two runners in an Aegean style (Buchholz and Karageorghis 1973, no. 1758).

In coroplastic art the local Cypriote types prevail. These include mainly the representation of the nude female figure, either holding her breasts or bending her arms to touch her body below the breasts; there are also many representations of a nude female figure holding an infant. The figures are handmade and hollow, but there is also a variation with a solid body. They are in a fabric that resembles that of Base-Ring ware. They have a bird-like face, following Syrian prototypes of an earlier period, but there are also female figures with a more normally shaped head, occasionally betraying Aegean features (Karageorghis 1996a, 1051–1052). There is also a preference for the rendering of the bull figure, the symbol

of male fertility. Apart from the Base-Ring ware bull-shaped rhyta there are also terra-cotta bull figurines in the same ware as the nude female figures. In one case a human figure is represented holding a bull by the horns, recalling figurines in bronze; others show horses, in some cases with a rider who is seated sideways on a saddle. Similar figurines of the same period are known also from Attica and from Crete (Karageorghis 1980a, 128–132; idem 1993a, 24). Apart from the locally produced terra-cotta figurines, a few Mycenaean figurines of humans and animals were imported.

Bronzework must have been flourishing, no doubt, in view of the profusion of copper on the island, but very few bronzes from this period have survived. There is more evidence from the Late Cypriote III period. This may be either due to the fact that bronze vessels, for example, easily decay or, more probably, because of the recycling of metals. The

109. Five terra-cotta female figurines of Base-Ring ware. The Cesnola Collection, the Metropolitan Museum of Art, New York. They were probably found in tombs in Nicosia-*Ayia Paraskevi*. From left to right: (1) Bird face, solid, with both hands on the stomach, no. 74.51.1541. Height: 15.6cm. (2) Bird face, solid, holding an infant, no. 74.51.1545. Height: 13.2cm. (3) Bird face, hollow, holding an infant, no. 74.51.1542. Height: 20.8cm. (4) Bird face, hollow, with arms on the hips, no. 74.51.1547. Height: 15.7cm. (5) Normal face, hollow, with arms bent and hands below the breasts, no. 74.51.1549. Height: 21.8cm. Painted decoration on face, around neck, and on pubic triangle. The types represented above are usually dated to the Late Cypriote II period.

110

111

112

110. Bronze weight in the form of the head of an African, filled with lead. From Kalavassos-*Ayios Dhimitrios*, no. 545. Height: 3.2cm.; weight: 94g. Several zoomorphic weights have been found at the same site.

111. Bronze statuette of a lion seated on its hind legs. From Ayios Iakovos (Swedish Cyprus Expedition), sanctuary site, no. 36. Height: 5.5cm. Medelhavsmuseet, Stockholm. It betrays influence from Aegean art.

112. A conical rhyton of Base-Ring I-II (?) ware. Louvre Museum, Paris, Inv. no. AO 18335. Height: 24.5 cm. The spout, opposite the handle, is in the form of a bull's protome. Vertical "rope" patterns in relief around body. Similar vessels have also been found at Ugarit and may have been used for pouring libations. They imitate the form of Aegean conical rhyta, of which several examples have been found in Cyprus and in the Levant.

113

type of bronze vessel that survived in fairly large numbers is the small hemispherical bowl, found mainly in tombs of the thirteenth century B.C. (cf. Catling 1964, 147–148). Other shapes, e.g. handled bowls and jugs, are more safely dated to the twelfth century B.C.

A few bronze statuettes have survived that demonstrate the same tendencies as the coroplastic art, mentioned above, namely, influence from the Aegean, as may be seen in a statuette of a squatting lion, found in the sanctuary of Ayios Iakovos (Buchholz and Karageorghis 1973, no. 1735). A statuette, probably from Enkomi, in the attitude of the smiting god is clearly of Near Eastern style; remains of gilding survive on the chest and head (Buchholz and Karageorghis 1973, no. 1732). The imaginative spirit of Cypriote bronzework during the thirteenth century B.C. is illustrated by a large number of bronze weights found in Building III at Kalavassos. They were probably used for weighing a valuable commodity, most likely metal. One of them represents the head of an African. It was probably imported from Egypt or made in Cyprus. A comparable weight in the form of a female head was found at Palaepaphos (for further discussion see Courtois 1983).

Pottery production continued to be plentiful but somehow lacks the imaginative spirit of the pottery of the Late Cypriote I period. The predominant fine fabrics are Base-Ring II and White Slip II, which persist, either as tableware (suitable for hot liquids) or for export, sometimes as containers for opium, as already mentioned. Other wares in use included Monochrome cooking wares, Plain White utilitarian vessels, and both imported and locally made "Canaanite" jars. The influx of Mycenaean tableware had, no doubt, a detrimental effect on local ceramic production. It is indicative of the predilection of the Cypriots for Mycenaean pottery that some potters emulated in Base-Ring fabric shapes of Mycenaean vases, e.g. three-handled jars, pyxides, and even conical rhyta. The latter were also exported to Ugarit, where they were probably used for ritual (cf. Yon 1980b; also Åström 1972, pls. LI.4–6).

9. **Architecture**

The architectural remains that survive from the fourteenth century are very scanty. We know more about the architecture of circa 1300–1200 B.C., which is discussed in a later chapter.

No doubt there were cult places during the LC I

period, but of these we have no remains; they may have been simple open-air enclosures. The earliest remains of a sanctuary that have been brought to light so far are those at Ayios Iakovos, Famagusta District, near the slopes of the Kyrenia mountain range. The structure consists of a circular enclosure that probably had a wooden peribolos. A low structure divided the enclosure into two compartments, which communicated with each other. One of the enclosures comprised two altars, one large and the other smaller, probably dedicated to the two divinities that were worshiped in the sanctuary—perhaps a female mother goddess and her consort. On the floor of the courtyard there was a clay basin in the shape of a bathtub that was found filled with ashes and burned bones (Åström 1972, 1).

There is ample evidence for domestic architecture among the excavated remains of Enkomi. The standard plan of a house consisted of a rectangular courtyard with the rooms arranged on all three sides, a plan no doubt dictated by climatic conditions that survived in the Cypriote countryside down to the middle of the twentieth century.

A "tholos" tomb at Enkomi with its possible Near Eastern inspiration has already been mentioned. There are also remains of seven built tombs at Enkomi, probably dating to the fourteenth century B.C. (see Courtois, Lagarce, and Lagarce 1986, 24). One of these, discovered in 1896 by the British Museum expedition, is the best preserved. It was constructed entirely of ashlar blocks and had a corbeled roof that was covered with large flat slabs. The stomion was in the center of one of the sides. A similar tomb had a stepped dromos. The Levantine inspiration for these structures is obvious. Similar tombs, also within the settlement, were found at Ugarit (for discussion see also Wright 1992, 344).

The commonest tomb type during the fourteenth and thirteenth centuries B.C. was the rock-cut chamber tomb, which had a long tradition in Cyprus, as we saw already in the LC I period. We previously referred to the shape of Kalavassos-*Ayios Dhimitrios* Tomb 11; many tombs were oval, circular, or subrectangular in shape. In many cases older tombs were reused for burials (for a further discussion see Åström 1972, 48–50).

114

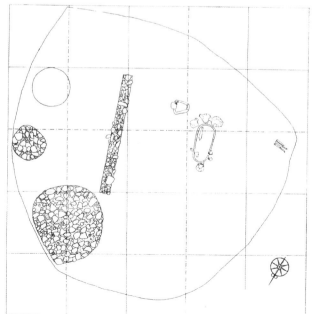

115

113. Base-Ring II ware three-handled jar. Cyprus Museum, Nicosia, Inv. no. 1954/VII-24/12. Height: 9cm. From Lithrangomi-*Arkades*. The surface is decorated with bands and dots of white paint. The form imitates the well-known Mycenaean IIIA–B three-handled jar, of which many examples have been found in Cypriote tombs of the Late Cypriote II period.

114. Built tomb at Enkomi, excavated by the French Mission, Tomb 1322. Seven built tombs have been found within the boundaries of the city. They consist of a rectangular chamber and a stepped dromos. They date to the Late Cypriote II period.

115. Plan of the Late Bronze Age sanctuary at Ayios Iakovos (after Åström 1972, fig. 1).

The Late Bronze Age

III. The Late Cypriote IIC Period (circa 1320–1200 B.C.)

1. The Major Settlements

Although the period from the middle of the thirteenth to the early twelfth century B.C. falls within the Late Cypriote II period, it is worthwhile to examine it separately, as it presents specific problems that are linked with the development of Cyprus, both cultural and political, in the twelfth century, the period known as Late Cypriote IIIA. After a short account of some of the main sites of the Late Cypriote IIC period and the problems related with them, a short "historical" survey of the period is attempted.

The sites of Enkomi and Kition are the most extensively excavated, but as they are already well documented in archaeological literature we give a brief review here, paying equal attention to other sites where new evidence has been found in recent years. There are some other sites that started in LC IIC but continued into the LC IIIA period; these will be discussed in a later chapter.

i. Enkomi

Enkomi, on the east coast of Cyprus, is the most extensively excavated site of all the Late Bronze Age towns of Cyprus. It had an inner harbor, communicating with the sea through a navigable channel and was situated in a rich plain that was probably better irrigated in antiquity than today.

Though the site of Enkomi was inhabited at the end of the Middle Bronze Age, it was during the Late Cypriote II period that the town attained its floruit, together with the rest of Cyprus, with the economic growth that resulted from the copper trade. The domestic architecture and the rich tombs of Enkomi in the LCIIA–B period have already been mentioned.

Level IIB at Enkomi represents a period of brisk trade relations with the Aegean and the Levant that resulted in the accumulation of considerable wealth, as is evident from the rich gifts that were deposited in tombs. Metallurgical activity had already started in the early stages in the life of this harbor town and must have played an important role in its development and prosperity.

Level IIB at Enkomi was destroyed at the very end of LC IIC, circa 1200 B.C., and was succeeded by Level IIIA, which will be discussed later. One of the most imposing buildings of the site is Building 18, which was constructed with ashlar blocks. Below the floor of Building 18 a tomb was found that could be dated to the very end of Level IIC, i.e., circa 1200 B.C. If this is true (there is considerable discussion about their association), then we have useful chronological evidence from the contents of the upper burial in this tomb; it was probably that of a foreign warrior, who was provided with a Naue II-type bronze sword, bronze greaves of Mycenaean type, and a bronze helmet (Catling 1955). It also contained pottery, mainly shallow conical bowls decorated with horizontal bands of matt paint, which are characteristic of the end of the LC IIC period, when trade links with the Aegean were few. There is strong evidence concerning the identity of the warrior: he was most likely an Aegean. But did he (and others) reach Cyprus before the destruction of Level IIB, or was he one of those who were responsible for this destruction and was buried in Tomb 18 before the erection of Building 18? (for further discussion see Schaeffer 1952 and idem 1971; Dikaios 1969–1971; Courtois, Lagarce, and Lagarce 1986).

ii. Kition-*Kathari*

Kition-*Kathari*, on the southeast coast, was already a flourishing urban center in the LC IIC period. Workshops in Area I yielded ample evidence for smelting during this period. It was a prosperous harbor town, with an inner harbor like Enkomi's, and had international links with the Aegean, Egypt, and the Levant. LC IIC is represented in both excavated Areas I and II by Floor IV, by workshops and sanctuaries in Area II, and by workshops, private houses, and tombs in Area I. The tombs in Area I have yielded rich material, including Mycenaean pottery, faience objects, alabaster vases, scarabs, and other seals, gold jewelry, bronze objects, etc. (Karageorghis 1974).

The wealth of this harbor town may be due to the proximity of Kition to Syro-Palestine and Egypt, with which trade relations were intense. The town was

116. Vases from the cargo of the ship that sank off Cape Iria in the Gulf of Argos, circa 1200 B.C. They include three large storage jars and a large jug of Cypriote origin, a stone anchor of Cypriote type, and Late Minoan IIIB stirrup jars. The ship must have been on her return voyage to Cyprus. This trade mission between Cyprus and the Aegean may have been one of the last, circa 1200 B.C., effected just before the political turmoil caused the discontinuation of trade between the two regions. The material from the Cape Iria wreck is now in the museum on the island of Spetses, near Attica.

117. An ingot of copper, in the form of an oxhide, with horns at each corner. There is an impressed sign on its surface. Length: 72cm.; weight: 39.18kg. From Enkomi. Cyprus Museum, Nicosia, Inv. no. 1939/VI-20/4. Cyprus exported her copper in the form of such ingots, many of which have been found in shipwrecks (Cape Gelidonya, dated to circa 1200 B.C.; Uluburun, dated to the end of the fourteenth century B.C.). Fragments of copper ingots have also been found in the Aegean, in Anatolia and Egypt, and also in the Central Mediterranean (Sardinia). Lead isotope analysis suggests that most of these ingots are of Cypriote copper, although this method of analysis is considered unreliable by some scholars. The fact remains, however, that Cyprus was the main producer of copper ingots, which constituted the main commodity of her export trade. The oxhide shape is the commonest, but there are also other forms, e.g., the bun ingot.

118. A miniature copper ingot, probably from Enkomi. Length: 9.5cm. Cyprus Museum, Nicosia, Inv. no. 1936/VI-19/1. It is engraved with two signs of the Cypro-Minoan script. Such inscribed miniature ingots were probably dedicated in sanctuaries as prayers for the increase of copper production. References to the export of ingots are to be found in the correspondence between the Pharaoh of Egypt and the king of Alashiya (Tell el-Amarna letters).

119. Miniature copper oxhide ingot from Enkomi (French Mission), no. 53.2. Length: 8.5cm.; thickness 1cm.; weight: 162.95gr. Cyprus Museum, Nicosia. On one side of it there is an engraved inscription in the Cypro-Minoan script in two lines, two signs in the upper line and five in the lower.

120. The façade of Enkomi Building 18, excavated by the French Mission. This is the largest and most imposing building at Enkomi and may be the official residence of a "prince." It is dated to the end of the Late Cypriote IIC period (circa 1200 B.C.).

121. Ivory pyxis from Kition (excavations of the Cyprus Department of Antiquities), Tomb 9, upper burial, no. 354. Length: 32cm.; height: 5cm. Larnaca District Museum. It certainly had a lid (see dowel hole at one end) and was used as a "toilet box." It has the form of a miniature bathtub with four vertical handles. Miniature bathtubs of similar form in stone have also been found in tombs of the Late Cypriote IIIA period.

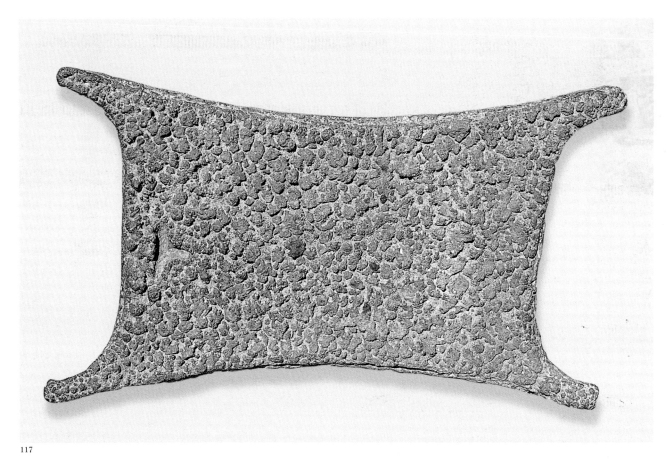

117

118

119

also near the copper mines of Troulli and Kalavassos. Kition was fortified from the very beginning of its foundation (for a detailed account of the excavation and the architectural remains of Kition see Karageorghis and Demas 1985). Its defensive wall followed the outline of a slightly elevated area on which the town was built. Only very few parts of this early wall have been traced. It was built of mud bricks on a low foundation of rubble. Two large solid rectangular bastions have been found against the northern façade of the wall, at a distance of 24m. from one another. The wall and bastions were washed by the waters of

the marshes in antiquity, which offered an extra element of defense.

Kition had an inner harbor, which, as has hitherto been believed, communicated with the open sea through a direct east–west channel. This hypothesis has recently been challenged. Sedimentological, paleontological analyses and c14 results from seventeen cores obtained in the vicinity of the Phoenician military harbor (eighth–fourth centuries B.C.) at Kition-*Bamboula* provide new paleoenvironmental information for the reconstruction of ancient shoreline changes for Kition and Larnaca Bay over the last

120

four thousand years. It has been proposed that a communication existed between the inner harbor of *Bamboula* (which is now 400m. inland) and the northern district of *Lichines*, which was a marine embayment. A spit of coarse material isolated the lagoon from the open sea from 2600 to 1600 B.C. Two inlets across the spit provided communication between the lagoon and the open sea (Morhange *et al.* 2000).

The two small sanctuaries, Temples 2 and 3, excavated in Area II are of a Levantine type, with a courtyard and a narrow holy-of-holies, separated from the courtyard by a parallel wall, not unlike the sanctuar-

121

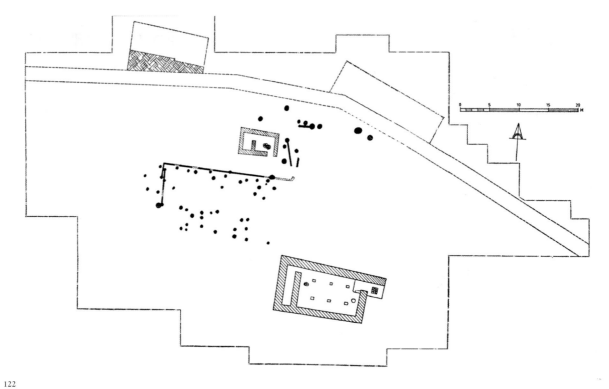

122. Plan of Kition, Area II, at floor IV, showing Temples 2 and 3, with pits for "sacred gardens." Beginning of the thirteenth century B.C.

123. Aerial view. Kition, Area II. Temple 5 (below) and Temple 4 (above).

122

123

124

124. Kition, Area II, Tower A, view from the west (excavations of the Cyprus Department of Antiquities). The foundation of the tower was of stone blocks and gypsum slabs. Against it ran a street, on the surface of which one may still see the tracks of the wheels of chariots.

125. Kition, Area II, Tower B, view from the northeast (excavations of the Cyprus Department of Antiquities). Against the northern part of the Kition fortification wall two rectangular towers were found, the lower parts of which were constructed of stones. They were washed by a marsh.

125

126

ies excavated at Lachish, Tell el-Farah, Tell Qasile, and elsewhere. Inside the courtyard, near the parapet wall, there was an altar. Temple 2 is the largest, measuring 14.5 x 9m. It had a side entrance to the courtyard and a side entrance to the holy-of-holies. Two rows of pillars supported the roof of the courtyard. These must have been of wood, resting on stone bases. The opening of the roof allowed an outlet for the smoke from the altar.

There was a "sacred garden" between the two temples; about fifty small pits were found, dug in the soft rock, communicating with one another with channels for watering plants. Similar sacred gardens were known in the East and in Egypt, during the xviiith and xixth Dynasties. This is the first time that such sacred gardens have been found in Cyprus, but there may have been others in the sanctuary of Aphrodite in Palaepaphos. According to Strabo, Aphrodite was worshiped at a site called "Ierokepis," the "Sacred Garden." Sacred trees, as we know, existed during the Late Cypriote period in the sanctuary of Ayia Irini, near the northwestern coast.

iii. Kalavassos-*Ayios Dhimitrios*

Kalavassos-*Ayios Dhimitrios* and nearby Maroni-*Vournes* are located in major river valleys near the south coast, about 30km west of Kition.

Although the architectural remains that have been brought to light at *Ayios Dhimitrios* in recent years date mainly to the Late Cypriote iic period, there is evidence for substantial architectural remains dating to an earlier period (South 1997, 152–154), perhaps the period of Tomb 11 described earlier. We reiterate that, as in Ugarit, tombs during the fourteenth and thirteenth centuries b.c. were constructed within the courtyards of houses or under streets, as also at Enkomi and Kition (Courtois, Lagarce, and Lagarce 1986, 40–50). The site was particularly rich from the fourteenth century b.c. down to its abandonment around 1200 b.c. because of its proximity to the copper mines, situated about 8km to the north, and the rich arable land all around it. The settlement of about eleven to twelve hectares is situated on gently sloping ground near a river. The town seems to have been well organized, with long straight streets, 2.5–6m. wide, frequently with drains. No definite traces of any fortification wall have been found so far. The excavators estimate that the population of the site may have been two to three thousand (South 1994, 192).

The most important part of the settlement is situated in the northeast area of the site, where a large ashlar building and walls of other buildings, also built of ashlars, have been found. Building x, the main ashlar building, is one of the largest "palatial" buildings that have been discovered in Cyprus until now and deserves a special discussion. It occupies an area of

30.5×30.5m. and consists of a rectangular courtyard, with rooms arranged symmetrically all around it, and a main entrance to the south. There are indications of an upper story, reached by a staircase in the southwest corner of the courtyard.

The most imposing part of the building is a large hall along the western side, measuring 19.5×7.25m., that was used for storing large pithoi. Forty-seven of these were found placed in four rows, standing on slabs on the lime-cemented floor of the hall; six were sunk in pits. Six monolithic pillars at least 2.6m. high were arranged in a row along the central part of the hall to support the ceiling. There is a smaller storeroom in the northwest corner of the building. In it there were two rows of large pithoi, standing on flat stones, and a large pithos sunk below the floor (South 1991, 133). Gas chromatog-

127. Kalavassos-*Ayios Dhimitrios*, Building X, Pithos Hall. In the large administrative building (Building X, thirteenth century B.C.) at Kalavassos-*Ayios Dhimitrios*, the largest room was the Pithos Hall (19.5 x 7.25m.), where at least forty-seven huge pithoi (storage jars) stood in rows, some on flat stone plinths on the floor, while others were sunk in pits below floor level. Each pithos (empty) weighs about 300kg and when full would contain at least 600 liters, or over 1,000 liters for the largest ones. Analyses have shown that they probably contained olive oil (at least 33,000 liters altogether), which could have been made in the olive press just outside the building. The Pithos Hall was built of fine ashlar masonry with blocks up to 3.2m. long, and six solid stone pillars supported the ceiling.

127

128. Kalavassos-*Ayios Dhimitrios*, olive press room in Building XI. An olive press installation was located just to the west of the large administrative building (Building X). A large room or workshop had a pebbled floor with a paved area in one corner, where the press may have stood. The floor sloped down to a huge stone tank (1.91 x 1.67 x 1.6m.) cut from a solid block of calcareous sandstone and weighing about 3.5 tons. This was probably the collecting basin for the olive oil; if full to the brim, it would hold about two thousand liters.

129. General view of the excavated remains at Maroni-*Vournes* (excavations of the University of Cincinnati and the British School at Athens). The administrative building, east wing, view from the northeast. The walls were built partly with ashlars and partly with mud bricks. Evidence for metallurgical activity and olive-oil production has been found inside the building, which closely resembles that of Kalavassos-*Ayios Dhimitrios*. The building was remodeled in the Late Cypriote IIC period and was abandoned just before 1200 B.C.

raphy analyses have shown that most of the pithoi contained olive oil. It has been calculated that fifty thousand liters of olive oil could be stored in the pithoi, no doubt not all for the use of the occupants of the building, but perhaps for export.

This shows the importance of olive oil in the economy of the area and also explains the administrative character of the building. This is also suggested by the discovery of five small cylinders of clay, each bearing an engraved multiline Cypro-Minoan inscription (Masson 1983).

Several other buildings were dependent on the palatial Building x. To its west, separated by a street, is Building xi, which was an olive press. In it a very large rectangular tank was found, cut from a monolith, which had a capacity of two thousand liters and was sunk in the pebble floor that sloped toward the tank. There was a circular depression in the middle of the floor of the tank, probably to collect the last drops of oil, and this contained pieces of pumice for cleaning the tank. Carbonized olive pits from floors adjacent to this building, as well as gas chromatography, strengthen the identification of this building as an olive press in the service of Building x, where the

128

129

130. Kalavassos-*Ayios Dhimitrios*. Mycenaean bowls from a "well" in Area 173 (Building X). Larnaca District Museum. A large quantity of table wares (bowls, cups, and jugs) was found in a stone-lined shaft (perhaps a well reused as a rubbish pit) in the large administrative building (Building X). More than half of these vessels were Mycenaean imports, a far higher proportion than occurs in the pottery in use in other buildings in the town, showing that the inhabitants of Building X had access to, and a taste for, imported goods. Some of the bowls are decorated with painted birds, fish, nautilus patterns, and other motifs (diams.: 22–17cm.).

130

oil was stored in the pithoi of the storerooms described above.

Building x itself has not yielded any spectacular objects; probably before its abandonment its occupants had the time to collect them and take them away. But in a built well or deep shaft, in a room of the east wing of the building, a large group of pottery (dishes and drinking cups) was found, together with large quantities of animal bones and well-preserved seeds. The excavators suggest that these may be the debris from elite dinner parties (South 1988, 228). About ninety such vases were found, of which about sixty percent are Mycenaean. This shows the high status of the occupants of Building x, who not only controlled the economy of the area but also enjoyed a high standard of living (cf. South 1994).

Other activities within the site include metallurgy. In Building ix, to the southeast of Building x, metallurgical evidence suggesting small-scale activity (a small furnace, ash, slag, and fragments of furnace lining, ingot fragments, and a group of bronze tools) was found (South 1982, 64–66). Perhaps large-scale smelting took place in the mining area.

The site of Kalavassos-*Ayios Dhimitrios* was aban-doned very suddenly and was subsequently partly destroyed by fire around 1200 B.C. Those enemies who caused the fire may have reached the area after the local inhabitants had fled, obviously taking with them all their valuables, unlike those of Pyla-*Kokkinokremos* (see below), who, like modern refugees, had confidence that they would return to reoccupy their homes. The debris found in the deep shaft in the east wing of Building x may represent the last "dinner party" of its occupants. The ceramics are mostly Mycenaean (Late Helladic iiib), but there are also locally made dishes, a fact that is very useful for dating the abandonment of the building sometime around 1200 B.C., before the appearance of Mycenaean iiic:1b-type pottery (see below).

iv. Maroni-*Vournes*

At Maroni-*Vournes* (Cadogan 1992), situated about 7km to the southeast of Kalavassos, we have a situation in many ways similar to that of Kalavassos-*Ayios Dhimitrios*. Although the site had been inhabited at the beginning of the lc i period, as we know from tombs in the area, its floruit was the lc iic period. On a prominent part of the site a large ashlar building

131. Schematic plan of the excavated area at Maroni-*Vournes* (after Cadogan 1992, 55, fig. 2).

132. Maroni-*Vournes*. The olive press in the administrative building. Evidence for olive oil production also appears on a very large scale in the administrative building at Kalavassos-*Ayios Dhimitrios*.

was constructed, comparable to Building X at Kalavassos, but a little smaller.

The Maroni ashlar building must also have been of a palatial and administrative character, associated with the industrial activities of olive oil production and metallurgy; pieces of oxhide ingots, metal slag, casting spillage, furnaces, etc., have been found in the building (Muhly, Maddin, and Stech 1988, 292; Cadogan 1988, 203–204). There were also large pithoi for storage. The excavator suggests that the occupants of this ashlar building, like those of Kalavassos Building X, supervised, stored, and doubtless taxed food production in the region (Cadogan 1988, 230). The ashlar building at Maroni was abandoned at about the same time as Kalavassos Building X. The reasons for its construction, as in the case of Kalavassos Building X, according to its excavator, must be linked with the creation of new conditions in the region resulting from the expansion of the metal

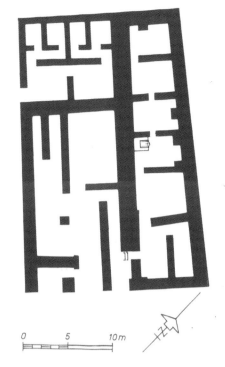

0   5   10m

131

132

133. The sanctuary at Myrtou-*Pigadhes*, constructed circa 1200 B.C., with a monumental built altar at the top of which were "horns of consecration," a symbol of Aegean religion. Similar "horns of consecration" of stone have been found at other Late Cypriote IIIA sites, namely at Kition and Palaepaphos.

134

134. Stirrup jars of Late Minoan III type from the cargo of the Cape Iria shipwreck. The ship was on the way back to Cyprus, having first visited Crete, hence these storage jars, which probably contained oil. Similar stirrup jars have been found in various parts of Cyprus and date to the late thirteenth century B.C. Spetses Museum (see Catling 1997, 404–414).

industry in the Kalavassos area, which demanded supervision and food (Cadogan 1988, 231).

v. Myrtou-*Pigadhes*
Myrtou-*Pigadhes*, situated in the northwest of the island, on a plain some distance from the north coast, is known mainly from its sanctuary within the settlement area (Taylor 1957). Though the cult had started here earlier (Period III, LC IIA:2), it was from circa 1300 B.C. onward (Period V, LC IIC:1) that the sanctuary really flourished. Its important feature, unique in Late Cypriote architecture, is an altar, over 2m high (as reconstructed), which was topped by "horns of consecration." The sanctuary was destroyed at the end of LC IIC. Though some pottery (skyphoi) may be assigned typologically to the very beginning of LC IIIA:1, it would be incorrect, we believe, to consider Myrtou-*Pigadhes* as belonging to a period beyond the cultural phase of LC IIC, if we take into account the overall picture provided by the ceramic material. The

fact that the LC IIC period may have lasted longer in some areas should not be forgotten in the discussion of the transition from LC IIC to LC IIIA:1.

vi. Apliki
Similar observations may be made in the case of Apliki, another settlement site in the northwest of the island (Taylor 1952) that was associated with the mining and smelting of copper. It was abandoned at the end of LC IIC.

2. Shipwrecks
In considering the LC IIC period, it is important to take into account two shipwrecks with strong Cypriote associations, which may be dated to the very end of LC IIC.

i. Cape Gelidonya
A ship that was wrecked at Cape Gelidonya, off the southwestern coast of Anatolia, about 1200 B.C. con-

tained as part of her cargo a number of copper oxhide ingots and bronze tools of Cypriote type. George Bass, the excavator, suggested that the ship was of Syrian origin (Bass 1967), based on a single object, a Syrian cylinder seal found on the ship. As in the case of the earlier Uluburun shipwreck (mentioned above), however, identifying the country of origin is not easy; similar cylinder seals were widely used in both Cyprus and the rest of the Levant.

ii. Cape Iria

Also of considerable relevance is another ship that sank at about the same time in the Gulf of Argos, off Cape Iria (see reports in Phelps *et al.* [eds.] 1999). This ship was probably on her return voyage to Cyprus, having visited ports in Crete and then sailed north to the Gulf of Argos to unload part of her cargo at the main Mycenaean centers along the gulf. The existence of such a trade route is suggested by the fact that several objects of Cypriote origin have been found at Mycenae (including a copper ingot) and Tiryns (which yielded wall brackets of Cypriote origin of the same type as those found in the shipwreck of Uluburun). The Cape Iria ship-wreck was loaded mainly with pottery: large stirrup jars of Cretan type (they may have contained a liquid commodity), some Mycenaean vases, and a number of large Cypriote pithoi, which may have been used as containers for ceramic or other goods, as mentioned above (see also Vagnetti 1999, 189–190). There were also two Plain White ware Cypriote jugs, possibly used by the crew for fresh water (?). The vessel also contained two stone anchors of Cypriote type (see discussion in Vagnetti 1999, 188–189).

The ship has been identified as Cypriote or Cypro-Mycenaean and, together with the Cape Gelidonya ship, may be regarded as among the last to sail westward for the export of Cypriote goods before the major upheavals in the Aegean that rendered sailing in the eastern Mediterranean hazardous (for a general account of the Iria shipwreck see Vichos and Lolos 1997; Lolos 1999).

3. The Evidence of the Tablets

Important new information about the relations between Cyprus and Syria and the nature of the officials of Late Bronze Age Cyprus has come from the recent discovery in Syria of five tablets sent from the kingdom of Alashiya to Ugarit, which were found

135. Stone anchor of Cypriote type from the shipwreck at Cape Iria in the Gulf of Argos. Spetses Museum. Though the ethnicity of the ship cannot be determined with certainty, the Cypriote connection of her cargo is undoubted. Such anchors have been found elsewhere in the Mediterranean (e.g., at Kommos on Crete, in Sardinia, and in the Uluburun wreck, off the southwestern coast of Anatolia).

135

among approximately 240 Akkadian texts uncovered at the site in 1994. These texts date to circa 1200 B.C. and augment the already ample archaeological and epigraphical information about contacts between Cyprus and its neighbors to the east (for relations between Cyprus and Ugarit at the end of the Late Bronze Age see Yon 1999b).

Texts from Ugarit make it clear that the kingdom of Alashiya was considered an esteemed and powerful neighbor. Among the new texts from the site, we read that the king of Alashiya addressed the king of Ugarit as "son." The new epigraphical discoveries provide exciting new details about the authorities of Alashiya who wrote to the king of Ugarit. In particular, we learn, for the first time, the name of the king of Alashiya: Kušmešuša, who sent two of the five tablets. The remaining three tablets were sent by officials called "chief superintendents" and a scribe. The scribe, we learn, is from Ugarit; he dispatches a message from Alashiya requesting that his master send him five chairs and one beautiful table, perhaps of ebony (Yon, Bordreuil, and Malbran-Labat 1995, 445; Malbran-Labat 1999).

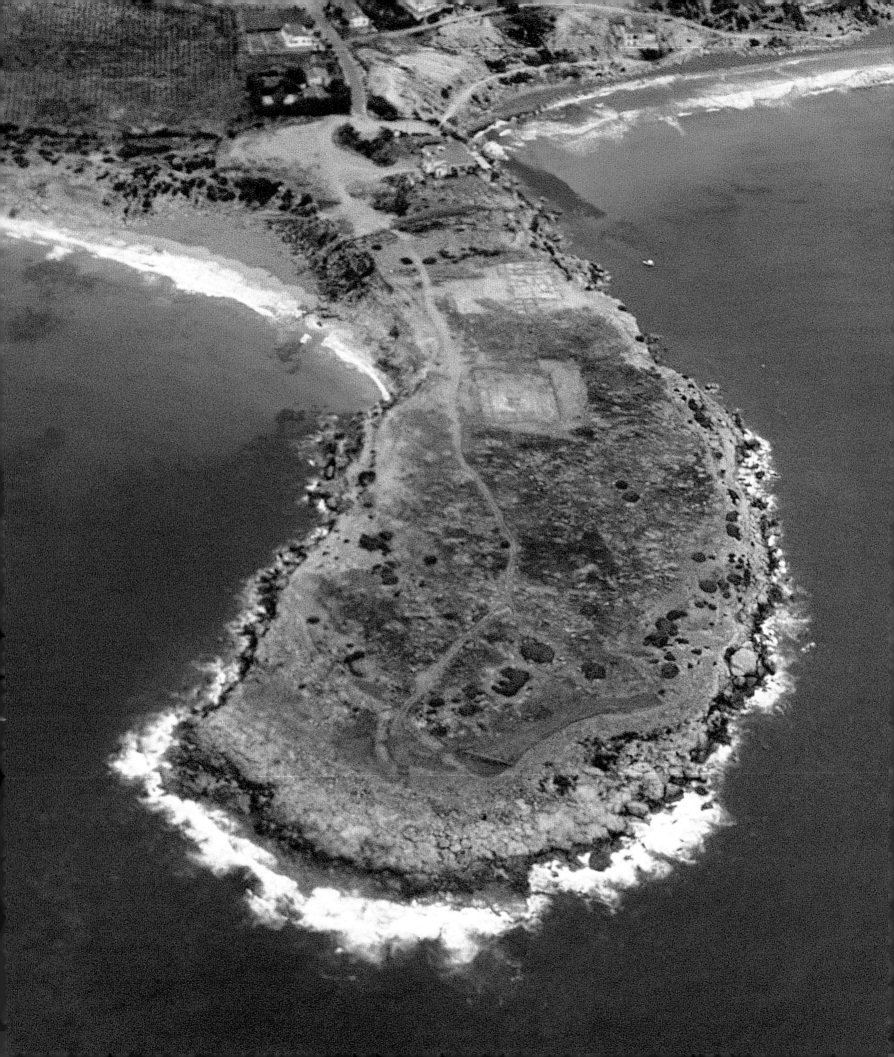

The Late Bronze Age

IV. The Late Cypriote IIIA Period (circa 1200–1100 B.C.)

1. The "Sea Peoples" in the Eastern Mediterranean
This period has received particular attention during the last two decades or so by scholars dealing with the problem of destructions, emigrations, and political turmoil in the Eastern Mediterranean and the Aegean (e.g., Deger-Jalkotzy 1994). Several international conferences have been organized in order to examine particular aspects of the problems involved (see especially Ward and Joukowsky [eds.] 1992; Gitin *et al.* [eds.] 1998; Oren [ed.] 2000). Many theories have been put forward, and various controversies have arisen. The problems are still being discussed, and no doubt they will continue to occupy an important place in international scholarship for several years to come. What happened in Cyprus circa 1200 B.C. is related directly to events in the Aegean and the Levant.

In the Aegean a series of events, concerning the nature of which there is still no consensus among scholars, caused the destruction of the palaces and the collapse of the central system of government, and as a result a large number of the population of the Mycenaean mainland became refugees (for a recent attempt to provide a survey of these events see Nowicki 2000, 256–265, with bibliography). During the second half of the thirteenth century B.C. the main Mycenaean centers in the Peloponnese were destroyed, including Mycenae, Tiryns, and Pylos, as well as Troy (Level VIIA) in Asia Minor. This caused anarchy and piracy in the Aegean and the East Mediterranean. Those who survived the catastrophes emigrated in search of a different life, having lost the political, social, and economic security offered by the palaces (cf. Rutter 1992). Egyptian historical sources indicate that waves of adventurers, under the collective name "Peoples of the Sea" (seven races are mentioned), caused havoc in the Eastern Mediterranean and quite a lot of turmoil in Cyprus. This manifested itself in various ways. The intervention of the "Sea Peoples" in Egypt is usually placed chronologically in the eighth year of the reign of Rameses III, but their impact in the Mediterranean should not be fixed at one particular moment.

In a recently published article it is proposed that the activities of the "Sea Peoples" in the Levant were not confined to one particular episode during the eighth year of the reign of Ramses III, as is conventionally accepted, when they were defeated and repelled, but "it must have been a matter of several small episodes, the recurrence of which brought about the continuous infiltration of the new elements, so that their entrenchment became increasingly difficult to reverse" (Cifola 1994, 20). It is further proposed that the "Sea Peoples appeared already in the fourteenth century and persisted throughout the eleventh" (ibid.). This scenario conforms perfectly to the archaeological evidence in Cyprus, as described below.

In another recently published article Israel Finkelstein proposed that "the migration of the Sea Peoples was a process that spanned at least half a century and comprised several phases" (Finkelstein 1995, 229). Destructions of sites in northern Philistia took place in the late thirteenth or early twelfth century B.C., and these destructions may not have taken place contemporaneously (ibid., 229–230).

For a considerable period some scholars rejected completely the view that the "Sea Peoples" were migrating people from the Aegean who eventually settled in Cyprus and on the Levantine coast. It is true that other scholars based their argument for a Mycenaean settlement in the Eastern Mediterranean mainly on the appearance in this region (Cyprus and the Levant) of a locally made pottery of Mycenaean IIIC:1b type. Those who opposed the theory of a Mycenaean settlement (Sherratt 1992, 1994, 1998) argued that this was because of a socioeconomic process, according to which a loose confederation of maritime merchants based in Cyprus was responsible for a massive distribution of Mycenaean-style pottery in the Eastern Mediterranean at the beginning of the twelfth century B.C. This theory was recently refuted by Barako, who, based on other significant cultural changes in various coastal regions of the Levant (including Philistia, the Akko Plain, and Phoenicia), argues that *trade* in Mycenaean pottery is completely lacking and that their material culture lacks the uni-

136. Aerial view of the promontory of Maa-*Palaeokastro*, north of Paphos, on the western coast of Cyprus, where a defensive settlement of refugees from the Aegean was established around 1200 B.C. The steep sides of the promontory offered an ideal site for the establishment of such a settlement. The sandy bays on either side provided safe anchorage for their ships.

137

137. The defensive settlement of Pyla-*Kokkinokremos* was established on the top of a rocky plateau, about 800m. from the coast of the northern part of Larnaca Bay. The highest point of the plateau is 63m. above sea level. It is heart shaped at the top, circa 600m. long and circa 450m. at its widest part, with a deep ravine to the southeast, forming the bay of the heart. It seems that the entire plateau was inhabited. With its abrupt sides, it offered a natural fortification, and the settlement dominated the bay of Larnaca; it also controlled the pass connecting the Mesaoria plain with that of Larnaca.

138. Ground plan of the excavated area at Pyla-*Kokkinokremos* (excavations of the Cyprus Department of Antiquities, 1981–82) (after Karageorghis and Demas 1984, 25, fig. 4).

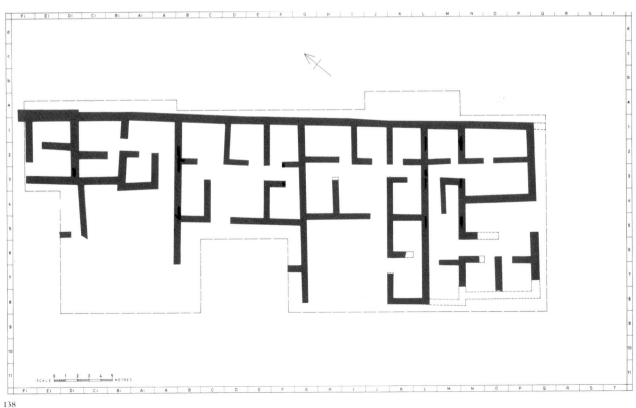

138

139

formity of the previous Canaanite period. There was use of force in the destruction of the Bronze Age layers and no traces at all of a smooth operation of mercantile communications (Barako 2000).

The main result of the upheavals described above as the activities of the "Sea Peoples" was the dissolution of empires and the creation of small kingdoms, which enjoyed prosperity and experienced new cultural, social, and political institutions.

2. Turmoil and Changes in Cyprus

In Cyprus, a series of phenomena have been observed during the period before and after 1200 B.C. that are relevant to the activities of the "Sea Peoples." The most important may be summarized as follows.

i. At Kalavassos-*Ayios Dhimitrios* and Maroni-*Vournes*, two urban centers that had flourished since the early part of the thirteenth century B.C., as seen above, two large "administrative buildings" were suddenly abandoned, and that of Kalavassos was destroyed by fire.

ii. Similar destructions may be observed at other LC IIC centers, namely at Hala Sultan Tekke, Sinda, Palaepaphos, Myrtou-*Pigadhes*, and Apliki.

iii. Enkomi Level IIB was violently destroyed and a major rebuilding followed.

iv. At Kition the buildings of Floor IV were replaced by imposing new buildings, and the grid of the town was changed, but there was no violent destruction.

v. At Alassa-*Paliotaverna* a large palatial building constructed during the LC IIC period was remodeled during the transitional period from LC IIC to LC IIIA; an extra wing was added in order to accommodate a large megaron with a central hearth, and a bathroom (see below).

vi. Two new settlements of a defensive character were established in remote places, Pyla-*Kokkinokremos* on the southeast coast, east of Kition, and Maa-*Palaeokastro*, on the west coast, north of Paphos. Both these settlements, built in places where there was no water supply or arable land in

139. The excavated area at the northeastern edge of the plateau of Pyla-*Kokkinokremos*. The house complexes are contiguous units built along the ridge of the plateau, following its contour. Each unit had a courtyard in front, while the back wall of every complex formed a continuous heavy defensive wall. This wall, together with the flat roof of the houses, is close in conception to medieval fortified villages built on elevated ground.

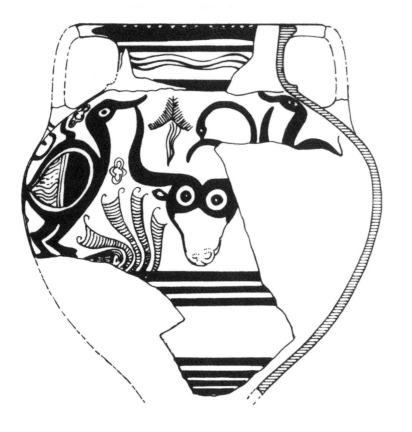

140

141

140. In 1953 a considerable quantity of Late Minoan III pottery, mainly storage jars, was collected from the surface at Pyla-*Kokkinokremos*. It included a large Late Minoan III pithos (restored), decorated with large confronted birds on either side of a bucranium. Restored (wrongly) height: 81cm.; mouth diam.: 30cm. Inv. no. 1953/ III-9/1. Now in the Larnaca District Museum. It is doubtful whether such large vases were traded for their own sake; they were probably brought to the island by their owners when they settled at Pyla-*Kokkinokremos* at the end of the thirteenth century B.C.

141. Large amphora of Late Minoan III ware, from Pyla-*Kokkinokremos* (excavations of the Cyprus Department of Antiquities, 1981–82), no. 20. Height: 57.3cm.; mouth diam.: 34.3cm. Larnaca District Museum. Both sides of the vase are decorated with a stylized octopus. This is one of several Late Minoan III vases found at the site.

the immediate vicinity, were short-lived and should be related to the activities of the "Sea Peoples," as will be suggested below.

From the above enumeration of the various events that occurred in Cyprus around 1200 B.C. it becomes clear that these did not affect the island in exactly the same way and at precisely the same moment; rather, they span a significant period of time. In addition, a number of cultural innovations can be observed, and all these factors taken together give the picture of Cyprus during what has been called "the Crisis Years."

In a recently published article Sturt Manning and collaborators tried to establish absolute dates for the chronology of the LC IIC period based on radiocarbon data. The result of this scientific approach was to confirm more or less traditional dates based on archaeological criteria (Manning *et al.* 2001). Although I do not doubt the validity of the method for establishing absolute dates, I believe that many more data are needed from as many sites as possible that fall within the chronological range of LC IIC–LC IIIA.

The two new settlements, Pyla-*Kokkinokremos* (Karageorghis and Demas 1984) and Maa-*Palaeokastro* (Karageorghis and Demas 1988), were built on virgin soil and were not immediately preceded by any earlier occupation, though in the case of Pyla-*Kokkinokremos* we should note that there were other settlements in the vicinity; but it is doubtful whether they existed at the time of its founding. The locations that were chosen for the establishment of these two sites are remote, and they could exist independently, without any direct communication or relation with the other communities in their neighborhood.

i. Pyla-*Kokkinokremos*

The defensive character of Pyla-*Kokkinokremos* is obvious. The settlement is built on a rocky plateau, situated about 800m. from the coast on the northern part of Larnaca Bay. The plateau has been largely denuded of topsoil and traces of architectural remains may be seen on the surface over a wide area, a fact that attracted looters to the site quite early. The plateau is 63m. above sea level at its highest point; it is heart shaped at the top, around 600m. long and around 450m. at its widest part, with a deep ravine to the southeast, forming the bay of the heart and a narrow point to the northwest, where the *Kokkinokremos* plateau connects to a much larger plateau. Although excavation was confined to the northeastern portion of the "heart," a surface survey has shown that the entire plateau was inhabited. This suggests that the settlement was of considerable size. The site was not chosen for settlement by accident. It is surrounded by low-lying land that has all the characteristics of a marsh and was perhaps a land-locked harbor in antiquity. The plateau rises steeply from this low land, dominating not only the whole plain on three sides but also Larnaca Bay. It more-over controls the pass connecting the Mesaoria plain with that of Larnaca. This strategic position was cer-tainly one reason why it was chosen for settlement and turned into a fortified site.

One problem that is still unclarified is that of water supply. According to the view of geologists it would have been totally impossible to have an adequate water supply from wells on the plateau. Indeed, no well has been found among the excavated remains. The water supply must have been located outside the settlement area in the plain, where wells exist even today (Karageorghis and Demas 1984, 3–5).

In summary, the following are the characteristics of this settlement:

- It was a new settlement that did not succeed a pre-existing occupation.
- It was relatively remote and independent from other existing settlements.
- The site chosen is naturally fortified because of its height and the abruptness of the slopes of the plateau.
- It was close to the coast, and the plateau was quite conspicuous and almost inviting to anyone who landed on the nearby sandy beaches; people could easily walk to it. The sandy beach provided safe anchorage for their ships.
- A marshy area provided an extra defensive ele-ment to the site on top of the plateau, providing inaccessibility from that side.
- An abundant supply of building stone was avail-able, which could easily be collected from the top and the edges of the plateau, and the flat plateau would make building an easy task for both the houses and the fortification wall.
- Water was not available right on the plateau but could be found in the plain very nearby. This

necessitated the storage of water in large pithoi, which have been found in large numbers within the houses.

Some scholars have doubted the interpretation that we gave to the settlement, preferring the idea that it was established by local people who were seeking protection, rather than by a foreign population. Arguments in favor of our suggestion that this was a settlement of newcomers who arrived from abroad are the following:

- The local population, if seeking protection from pirates or invaders who came from the sea, would

142

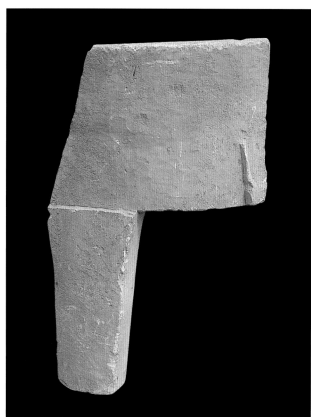

143

142. Fragment from a large Coarse ware Late Minoan III pithos from Pyla-*Kokkinokremos*. Cyprus Museum, Nicosia, Inv. no. 1959/IV-30/1. Decoration with "pie crust" ornament. Such pithoi, sometimes over one meter high, were not objects of trade, but must have been used as containers by those who first settled at the site.

143. Fragment from a circular limestone trough, supported on three legs. Surface find from Pyla-*Kokkinokremos*. Height: 61.5cm. Larnaca District Museum, no. 431. On the side of the trough one may distinguish part of the symbol of "horns of consecration" in relief. The use of the trough may have been cultic. It should be mentioned that a high percentage of Late Minoan III vases have been found at the site. It has been suggested that among the refugees who settled at this defensive outpost there must have been Cretans who knew the meaning of this religious symbol.

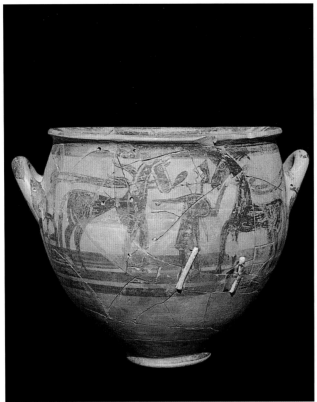

144

146

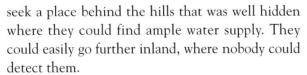
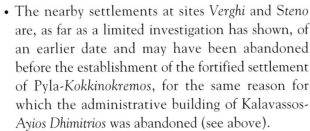

145

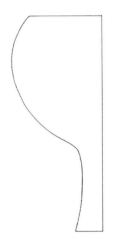
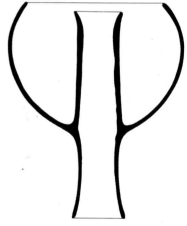

147

seek a place behind the hills that was well hidden where they could find ample water supply. They could easily go further inland, where nobody could detect them.

- The nearby settlements at sites *Verghi* and *Steno* are, as far as a limited investigation has shown, of an earlier date and may have been abandoned before the establishment of the fortified settlement of Pyla-*Kokkinokremos*, for the same reason for which the administrative building of Kalavassos-*Ayios Dhimitrios* was abandoned (see above).
- The nature of the material found at the site, such as the very high proportion of Late Minoan IIIB pottery including large pithoi, a limestone trough with "horns of consecration" in relief, and a Mycenaean IIIB chariot crater that was in actual use in the settlement rather than being a gift to the dead (it was even repaired in antiquity, after having been broken, perhaps during transportation) all point of the foreign character of the inhabitants. The fact that local types of pottery and other artifacts were also found need not be surprising, because there is no reason that the inhabitants should not have had dealings and exchanges with the neighboring native

148. Maa-*Palaeokastro*. Aerial photograph showing the peninsula of Maa in the middle, with a sandy bay on either side.

communities. They did not come as invaders, but as refugees looking for a place to settle after the collapse of the urban centers in the Aegean, and they chose to keep a low profile, not knowing the intentions of the local population. Mention may also be made of yet another interesting element in the material that they used: torches for signaling, in order to communicate with other incoming people from the seashore (for a detailed discussion on torches see Karageorghis 1999f). Similar objects have been found at Enkomi and Palaepaphos.

ii. Maa-*Palaeokastro*

The fortified settlement of Maa-*Palaeokastro* presents features similar to those of Pyla-*Kokkinokremos:*

- It was a new settlement.
- The site is remote, yet the peninsula and its bays are the most conspicuous landmark for people arriving by sea from the west.
- The peninsula has superb natural defenses, with steep cliffs around the plateau, and can easily be fortified even further.
- It is on the coast, with two bays on either side with sandy beaches.
- There is an ample supply of stone in the vicinity

for the construction of the Cyclopean defensive wall and the houses.

- A water supply was not available right on the plateau but just outside, and water was stored in large pithoi, many of which were found in the settlement (for a detailed discussion see Karageorghis and Demas 1988, 255–266).

At both settlements there was limited metallurgical activity for the manufacture of tools, weapons, and sling bullets. At Maa-*Palaeokastro* there is evidence that the population used horses and perhaps chariots. One of the residences at Maa was of a distinctly higher quality than the others. Both at Maa and at Pyla-*Kokkinokremos* there is evidence that the population used bathtubs, an element that was introduced to Cyprus from the Aegean in the period around 1200 B.C. Among the pottery types found at Maa is Handmade Burnished ware (or "Barbarian" ware), which was newly introduced to the island by settlers from the Aegean. There were also fibulae and gold rivets for a sword, of Aegean type (see below).

Another very significant feature at Maa-*Palaeokastro* is the occurrence of central hearths in communal halls, an element that, like the bathtubs, did not have a predecessor in Cyprus before circa 1200 B.C.

149

150

151

153

152

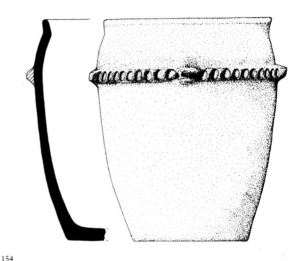

154

155

156

150. Three bronze arrowheads from Maa-*Palaeokastro* (excavations of the Cyprus Department of Antiquities). Length (from left to right): no. 152: 10cm.; no. 180: 9.7cm.; no. 178: 11cm. Paphos District Museum. Such objects, as well as spearheads, sling bullets, etc., demonstrate the military character of the settlement.

151. Bronze sling bullet from Maa-*Palaeokastro* (excavations of the Cyprus Department of Antiquities), no. 1987.712. Length: 4.8cm. Paphos District Museum. Amygdaloid sling bullets, mostly in lead but also in bronze, appear at several sites of the Late Cypriote IIIA period, particularly at Enkomi. They also illustrate the military character of the settlement.

152. Fragmentary clay bathtub from Pyla-*Kokkinokremos* (excavations of the Cyprus Department of Antiquities, 1981–82). Height: 57.5cm.; length: 74cm. Larnaca District Museum. It has four vertical handles near the rim and a perforation in the middle of one of the short sides, near the bottom. Such bathtubs (of clay or limestone) have been found on the island in settlements (e.g., Maa-*Palaeokastro,* Enkomi, Kalavassos-*Ayios Dhimitrios,* Alassa-*Paliotaverna*), in sanctuaries, (Palaepaphos), and also in tombs (e.g., Kourion, Palaepaphos-*Skales*). Bathtubs and bathrooms were previously unknown in Cyprus and must have been introduced, together

with other cultural novelties, circa 1200 B.C., by the first Achaean settlers.

153. Bronze buckle from the gear of a horse, from Maa-*Palaeokastro* (excavations of the Cyprus Department of Antiquities), no. 219. Length: 7.1cm. Paphos District Museum. Such objects have been found also at Enkomi and may have been part of the harnesses of horses.

154. Jar of Handmade Burnished ware (also known as "Barbarian ware"), found at Maa-*Palaeokastro,* (excavations of the Cyprus Department of Antiquities, 1985), no. 255. Height: 20cm.; mouth diam.: 15.7cm. "Pie crust" decoration between the handles.

This jar and others found at various sites in Cyprus and dating after circa 1200 B.C. were certainly not imported for their own beauty, but as kitchen vessels, suitable for the preparation of a certain kind of food. This fabric, known in Mycenaean Greece and Crete from the thirteenth century B.C. onward, was no doubt introduced to Cyprus by the early Achaean settlers circa 1200 B.C.

155. Fragmentary bronze fiddle-bow fibula from Maa-*Palaeokastro* (excavations of the Cyprus Department of Antiquities), no. 2. Preserved length: 6.3cm. Paphos District Museum. This type of fibula was introduced to Cyprus from the Aegean.

156. Heads of two bronze rivets, covered with a thin sheet of gold from Maa-*Palaeokastro* (excavations of the Cyprus Department of Antiquities), no. 108. Height: .5cm.; diam.: 1.15cm. Paphos District Museum. Rivets of this type were used in the Aegean for fixing the handle to the hilt of a sword or dagger.

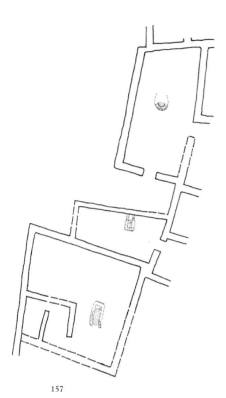

157

157. Central hearths at Maa-*Palaeokastro* (excavations of the Cyprus Department of Antiquities) (after Karageorghis 2000a, 269, fig. 13.15).

158. Plan of the peninsula of Maa-*Palaeokastro,* with excavated areas (I, II, III) and the northern and southern fortifications (after Karageorghis and Demas 1988, pl. 2).

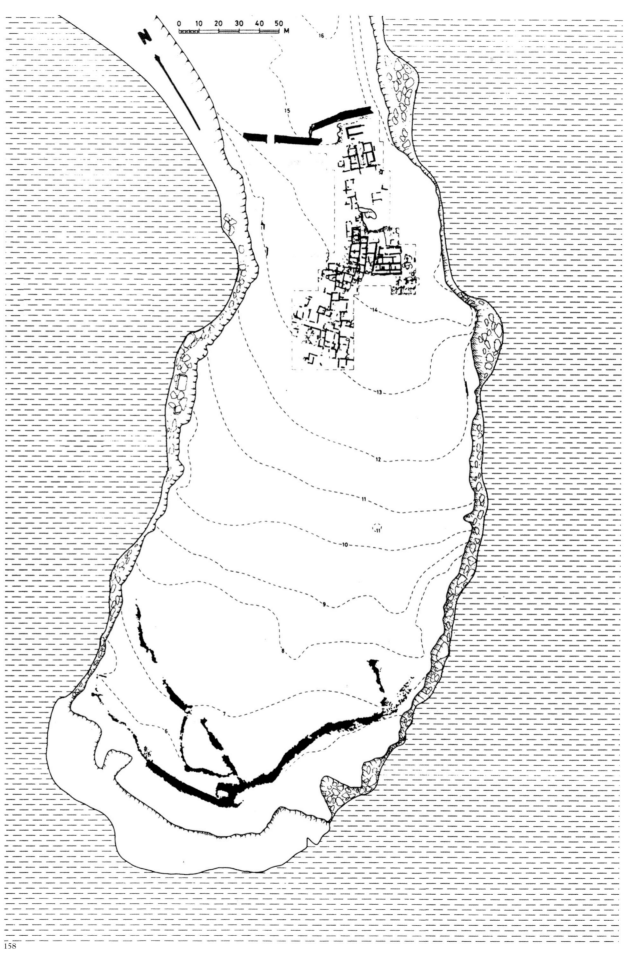

158

159

160

(see below). Other architectural features pointing to a foreign population are the Cyclopean fortification walls and the dog-leg gate. There must be other fortified settlements in Cyprus of the same period, such as Lara, a rocky plateau with sandy bays on either side, north of Maa, but the evidence here is too scanty for any worthwhile discussion (Fortin 1978).

3. Fortified Settlements in the Aegean
In two articles (Karageorghis 1998b and 2001c) I have proposed that there is a similarity between the defensive settlements of Pyla-*Kokkinokremos* and Maa-*Palaeokastro* on the one hand and those of the Aegean on the other. In a recently published book Nowicki endorses this proposal (Nowicki 2000, 251–254) and also our comparison with defensible sites in Crete, particularly Kastrokephala Almyrou, near Herakleion, a short distance from the sea, which is more or less of the same extent as Maa-*Palaeokastro* (42,000 square meters).

i. Koukounaries on Paros
A comparison with a fortified settlement on the Cycladic island of Paros, at the site of Koukounaries,

161

161. General view of the hill of
Paros-*Koukounaries*, on top of
which a fortified acropolis was
built circa 1200 B.C.

will give a clearer understanding of the situation in
Cyprus that prompted the building of the two above-
mentioned fortified settlements (cf. Nowicki 2000,
249–250). At the top of the hill of Koukounaries, a
palatial building and a Cyclopean fortification wall
were constructed early in the twelfth century B.C., i.e.,
after the destruction of the Mycenaean palaces of the
Peloponnese. According to the excavator (Schilardi
1984, 1992, and 1995), it was a well-organized group
of Mycenaean refugees who fortified and built their
residence on this hill. No doubt they were under the
leadership of powerful Mycenaeans who could com-
mandeer ships for their transportation to the periphery of the Mycenaean world. The pottery recovered
from Koukounaries is standard Mycenaean IIIC and
points to the Greek mainland as the origin of the
occupants of the site.

The excavator points out that the people who built
the outpost at Koukounaries wished to create a specially fortified refuge on the top of a hill that was not
easily accessible (Schilardi 1995, 487). Only those

parts of the hill that were vulnerable were fortified.
The same is true on Cyprus at Maa-*Palaeokastro*,
where those who built the Cyclopean wall did not
construct it to encircle the entire plateau, but only
those parts that were easily penetrable.

A large part of the residential area at Koukounaries
was occupied by storerooms and workshops, as at
Maa-*Palaeokastro* and Pyla-*Kokkinokremos*. Several
luxury objects were found in the Koukounaries storerooms (cf. the alabaster vases found at Pyla-*Kokkinokremos*, the objects of gold, and two silver
ingots), as well as weapons, recalling those found at
Maa-*Palaeokastro*. There is evidence that there were
horses at Koukounaries, a symbol of military power,
recalling a similar situation at Maa-*Palaeokastro*.

The fortified settlement of Koukounaries had a short
life span, of less than fifty years, and in circa 1150
B.C. it was destroyed by violent action followed by
fire. The excavator describes this destruction very
dramatically: "the walls collapsed and the first floor
of the buildings tumbled down. The invaders with-

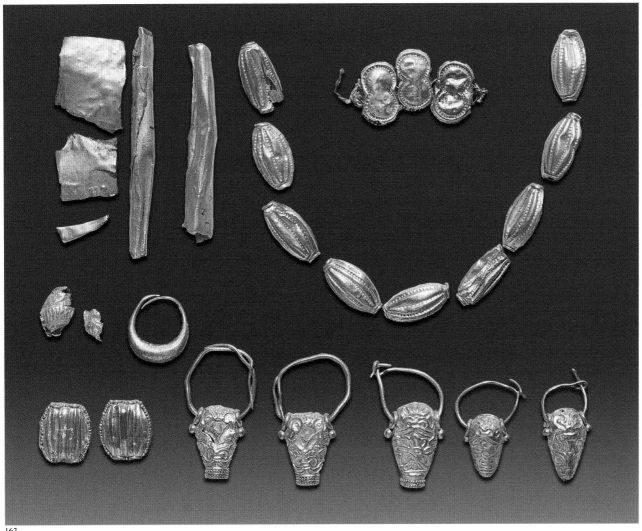

162

drew immediately after the destruction. Very few of the inhabitants survived and returned to Koukounaries after the departure of the enemy to settle among the ruins in poverty" (Schilardi 1992, 634–635). Who were the invaders? Mycenaeans from Naxos or some of the "Sea Peoples"? No doubt they were adventurers, pirates. Those who have read the description of the destruction and rehabitation of Maa-*Palaeokastro* or the abandonment of Pyla-*Kokkinokremos* in Cyprus will no doubt be struck by the similarities.

The reason for the description at length of a site outside Cyprus is that Koukounaries offers a perfect "model" that helps in the understanding of the two major Cypriote sites that were built circa 1200 B.C., in fact the only new settlements known in the whole of the island during this period. At all other sites the older settlements were either destroyed circa 1200 B.C., abandoned, or rebuilt. Pyla-*Kokkinokremos* and Maa-*Palaeokastro* were the only new foundations, and they had a number of common character-

istics: they were both fortified outposts, away from major urban centers, built at sites that by themselves could provide safety. They were inhabited for a short time. Pyla-*Kokkinokremos* was abandoned only a few decades after its establishment, whereas Maa-*Palaeokastro* was destroyed, rebuilt on a smaller scale by the survivors of the destruction, and then abandoned circa 1150 B.C.

ii. Kastrokephala Almyrou

Kastrokephala Almyrou was a Cretan fortified settlement situated on an abrupt hill, 355m above see level, west of Herakleion Bay (cf. Nowicki 2000, 42–44, with bibliography). It was erected toward the end of LM IIIB and continued through early LM IIIC. To the north lies the Bay of Herakleion and the plain, whereas on the southeast side there is a deep gorge and marshy land with a spring; this marshy land may have served as an additional element of fortification, and it may have been one of the reasons for the choice of the location for a fortified site (cf.

Pyla-*Kokkinokremos*). The survival of the toponymic *Linoperamata* (lake ford) may recall the marshy land at the estuary of the river Almyros. The site of Kastrokephala with its steep gorge along the southeast side is clearly visible to those entering the Bay of Herakleion, and the choice of the site for a fortress was easy to make. The gorge and the outcrop of Kastrokephala impressed the cartographer Basilicata, who produced a panoramic view of it. Nowicki also recognized its Mycenaean character and described it as "resembling rather Mycenaean citadels than Minoan refuge settlements." Kastrokephala has a large, roughly triangular plateau on the top that was protected by a wall, visible along one of the sides of the triangle; it is preserved for a length of about 480m., approximately 2.1–2.2m. in thickness and with a height of 2–3.5m. It is constructed with large boulders. At the highest point of the site the walls of an oblong building are preserved: described by Alexiou as a garrison, it may well be part of an official residence (for references see Karageorghis 1998b, 133–134; Nowicki 2000, 42–44).

Kastrokephala, together with other fortified sites on Crete, like Palaikastro Kastri (for other Cretan sites see Nowicki 2000), may show the extent and the character of the Mycenaean migration to Crete after the fall of the Mycenaean palaces. This migration probably explains the strong Cretan elements in the material culture of Cyprus of the twelfth and eleventh centuries B.C., since we believe that some of

these Mycenaean refugees later migrated from Crete to Cyprus.

There are a number of comparable fortified settlements, illustrating the magnitude of the phenomena that followed the destruction and abandonment of the Mycenaean palaces (the evidence was recently discussed at a conference on fortified settlements in the Aegean and the Levant (Karageorghis and Morris [eds.] 2001; see also Nowicki 2000, 249–255). These settlements are scattered over a wide area in the Aegean (the Cyclades, the island of Salamis, Dymaion Teichos, 40km west of Patras).

4. Cultural Changes in Cyprus

These developments, which had such a profound effect on the major urban centers of the island, were not confined to destructions, abandonments, and rebuildings. Since a sizable number of refugees, apparently coming from the Aegean, established themselves permanently on the island, they caused a number of cultural changes, which we shall enumerate below (for a general survey see Karageorghis 1994; idem 2000a). Similar changes have also been observed in the Levant, in places that were affected by the activities of the "Sea Peoples" (see Barako 2000). The cultural scenario of the twelfth century B.C. in Cyprus or the Levant did not undergo a complete change, and it would be illogical to expect that such a phenomenon should occur overnight, especially if we consider that the newcomers were faced with highly developed cultures in their new homes. Some significant cultural changes may be enumerated, as follows:

i. Pottery

Toward the end of LC IIC the supply of Mycenaean pottery in Cyprus became difficult, no doubt as a result of the upheavals in the Eastern Mediterranean and the Aegean, which curtailed overseas trade. As a result the Cypriots began to imitate Mycenaean pottery, especially the "dinner sets" that were used for elite dinner parties. The evidence from Kalavassos-*Ayios Dhimitrios* is an eloquent example, where the vast majority of the vases found in a pit or well (already mentioned above) are plates and drinking cups, both imported Mycenaean and local imitations. A large quantity of locally made bowls, dishes, and drinking cups, including some rare examples of skyphoi (deep bowls with two handles), was found in deposits at Kouklia-*Mantissa* (for a general discussion

163

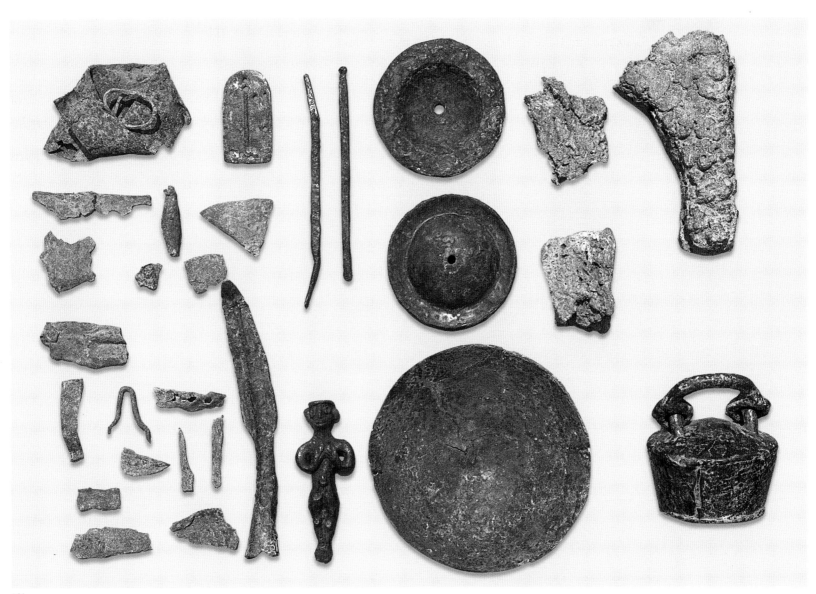

164

and previous bibliography see Karageorghis 2000a, 256–257; also idem 1965, 157–184). Amphoroid and open craters, used for mixing wine, became very rare. There is only one Mycenaean IIIB chariot crater found at Pyla-*Kokkinokremos*, which was probably brought by newcomers to the island. It was broken during transportation and mended locally. As a result the Cypriots started producing craters with local clay, imitating Mycenaean shapes and decorating them in a style known as the "Pastoral style," with pictorial motifs (bulls, goats, birds, fish, and more rarely chariot groups and lions, but also spirals and tree motifs). This style, which appeared circa 1200 B.C., was short-lived (for a general discussion see Vermeule and Karageorghis 1982, 59–67).

Some types of local pottery still lingered on, e.g., White Slip and Base-Ring ware bowls, as well as Plain White ware vessels, but a style of decorated pottery now became fashionable and predominated among the local Cypriote ceramics. It consisted mainly of deep bowls (skyphoi), decorated with abstract and occasionally pictorial motifs; there were also some craters. Both in shape and style of decoration these vessels are Aegean, but it is not easy to pinpoint to what region of the Aegean they may be related; the clay is in all cases local. There are very few examples that may be identified as their imported predecessors, of Late Helladic IIIB:2 (for a survey with bibliography see Karageorghis 2000a, 256–257).

A similar phenomenon may be observed in the Levant (Stager 1995, 334–336). I propose that they were made by newcomers from the Aegean who were familiar with the shapes and decoration of pottery prevailing in their homeland during this period.

The change in pottery style as a sole criterion for the arrival of a new ethnic population has been very

164. During the excavations by the Cyprus Department of Antiquities at Pyla-*Kokkinokremos* in 1981–82, a "foundry hoard" was discovered in a shallow cavity in the courtyard of a house; it is now in the Larnaca District Museum. It was well hidden by stones and pithos fragments. It may have been concealed in the same way as the hoard of gold objects and the two silver ingots (nos. 162 and 163, above). This foundry hoard includes a statuette of a nude male (?) figure, with arms bent against the chest (no. 62, height: 10.3cm.), a weight of almost cylindrical form with a loop handle (no. 60, total height: 10.6cm.), a pair of "cymbals" (no. 68, diam.: 8.8cm.), a spearhead (no. 61, length: 17.7cm.), a bronze scale from a piece of "scale-armor" (no. 67A, length: 6.1cm.), and a fragment from an oxhide ingot and some scrap metal.

165

165. View of the fortification wall on the plateau of Kastrokephala Almyrou, west of Herakleion Bay (Crete). It was constructed circa 1200 B.C.

166. Part of the fortification of the Acropolis of Dymaion Teichos, situated at Araxos Point, about 40km west of Patras, at the extreme northwest corner of the Peloponnese. It is dated to circa 1200 B.C. and was built on a plateau that is almost surrounded by a marsh, affording extra protection. This is one of several fortified Mycenaean acropolises where the occupants of the Mycenaean palaces took refuge after the collapse of the Mycenaean system circa 1200 B.C. We find them also on Crete, on some islands of the Cyclades, on the island of Salamis, and also in Cyprus.

166

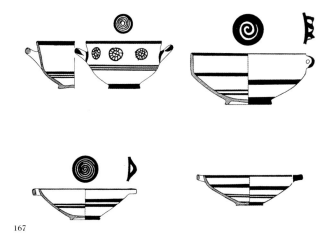

167

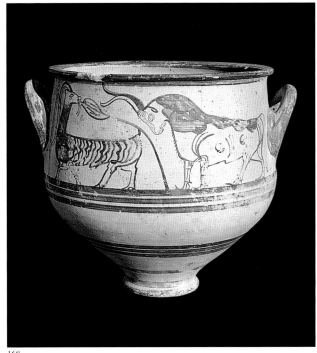

168

169

170

much criticized by various scholars, especially Sherratt and others, who attempted to interpret the new style in terms of the activity of a loose confederation of maritime merchants based in Cyprus (see above). The appearance of a predominant new style of pottery is significant only if viewed in the context of all the other cultural innovations that appeared in Cyprus circa 1200 B.C., rather than as an isolated ceramic phenomenon.

Another significant ceramic novelty is the appearance in Cyprus soon after 1200 B.C. of the so-called Handmade Burnished ware, or "Barbarian ware" (Pilides 1992 and 1994). It is a coarse, handmade ware that could not have been imported for its own beauty but was favored by the Mycenaean newcomers for some reason that is not easy to specify (e.g., perhaps the preparation of a certain kind of food). It appears at several sites, e.g., Enkomi, Maa-*Palaeokastro*, Hala Sultan Tekke, and Sinda. Some of it is imported, but it was also made locally. It continued to be made on the island down to the early Cypro-Geometric period. The appearance of Trojan Grey ware in Cyprus and the Levant at various Late Bronze Age sites as late as the early twelfth century B.C. has been associated by Allen with refugees from Troy Level VIIa, victors, or possibly groups of marauding "Sea Peoples." She has proposed that a few individuals may have brought this pottery to the Levant, having fled Troy after its destruction (Allen 1994, 44–45).

ii. Central hearths

The appearance of the central hearth in the architecture of Cyprus early in the LC IIIA period is quite significant. This new element appears not only in "palatial" complexes, such as Alassa-*Paliotaverna* (Hadjisavvas 1994, 112), but also in ordinary domes-

tic architecture. Such hearths appeared at Enkomi, occupying a prominent place in large rooms, occasionally in association with benches where people could sit. At Maa-*Palaeokastro* they occupy the center of communal or assembly halls in which people gathered for eating and drinking. Similar hearths appear also at Hala Sultan Tekke during the same period. A similar phenomenon is observed in the Levant, at places that are related to the activities of the "Sea Peoples." We propose that this architectural phenomenon, with a deeply rooted social significance in the Mycenaean mainland and Crete, was introduced to Cyprus by Aegean newcomers (for a detailed discussion and bibliography see Karageorghis 1998c).

171

171. Fragment of a crater of the Pastoral Style, from Morphou-*Gnaftia*. Cyprus Museum, Nicosia, CS5103. This fragment belonged to a chariot scene. What is important about it is the fact that by the beginning of LCIIIA the Cypriote vase painter knew about the existence of the light, rail-type chariot, which replaced the heavy Late Helladic IIIA–B chariot with a solid breast.

172. Pyla-*Kokkinokremos*: two skyphoi of Mycenaean IIIC:1 style, nos. 1952/23 (left) and 1952/22 (right) (after Karageorghis and Demas 1984, pl. xxxv).

173. Two vases of locally made clay, in the Mycenaean IIIC:1b style. On the left: jug with side spout and strainer, Cyprus Museum, A 1749A. Height: 26.2cm. On the right: a skyphos from Sinda (Swedish Mission, 1948). Height: 11.5cm.; diam.: 14.5cm. Cyprus Museum.

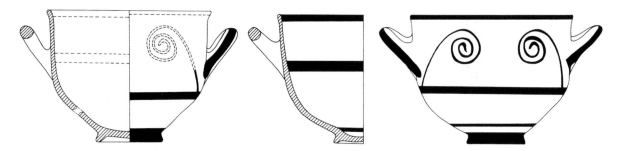

172

173

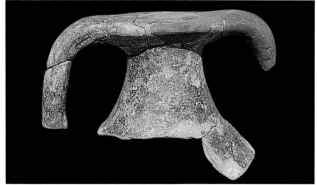

176

177

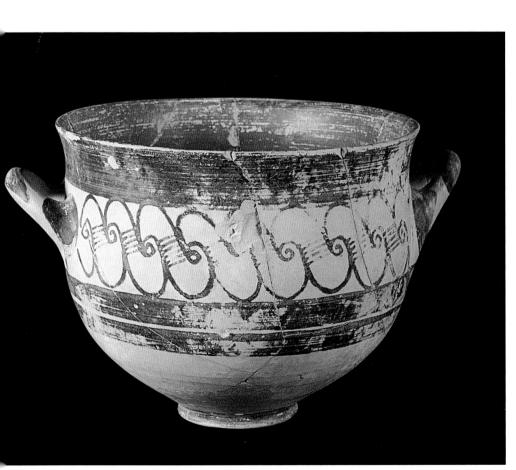

174. Bell crater of Mycenaean IIIC:1b style, from Enkomi. Medelhavsmuseet, Stockholm, no. 164. Height: 23cm. Carinated body, two opposed horizontal loop handles on shoulder. The shoulder zone between the handles is decorated on both sides with a rectangular checkered panel in the middle and a bird on either side. The vase is locally made, like many others of the Late Cypriote IIIA period.

175. An imported Mycenaean IIIB:2 skyphos from Enkomi (Swedish Cyprus Expedition), Tomb 6, no. 52. Height: 15.7cm; diam.: 19.2cm. The zone between the handles is decorated with a guilloche pattern. The interior is painted red. This is one of the rare cases of a Mycenaean IIIB:2 skyphos found in Cyprus. It is dated circa 1200 B.C., a time when imported Mycenaean ware became rare but was soon to be replaced by locally made pottery (at the beginning of the twelfth century B.C.), in imitation of the Mycenaean IIIC:1b style).

176. The upper part of a stirrup jar of Anatolian Grey Polished ware, from Pyla-*Kokkinokremos* (excavations of the Cyprus Department of Antiquities, 1981–82). Preserved height: 8cm. Larnaca District Museum. Anatolian Grey Polished ware is not unknown in Cyprus. The usual form imported into the island was the open crater with horizontal loop handles. The fact that imports from Anatolia as well as Late Minoan and Mycenaean pottery were found at the site is an indication that it was established shortly before trade in pottery ceased in the Eastern Mediterranean circa 1200 B.C.

177. Fragment from a locally made crater of Mycenaean IIIC:1b style, from Sinda (Swedish Mission, 1948). The vase was decorated with a horse (and a rider?), a motif that is rare in pottery of this style.

89

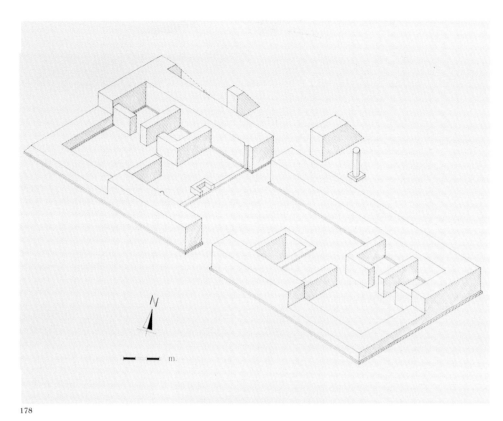

iii. Baths and bathtubs

Another innovation with social significance is the appearance of baths and bathtubs in domestic architecture at LC IIIA sites; there are many examples at Enkomi. They also occur in "palatial" buildings, e.g., at Alassa-*Paliotaverna* (Hadjisavvas 1994, 112, pl. XIX.2). There is also a bathtub from a private house within the "palatial" complex of Building 18 at Enkomi (Courtois 1992). Bathtubs found at Enkomi are either in limestone or in clay. In Room 40 at Enkomi, a bathtub and a toilet were found; the floor of the room was covered with concrete. This demonstrates a high degree of progress in hygienic installations in the houses of the elite. Bathtubs dating from the end of LC IIC to the Early Geometric period have been found not only in domestic architecture but also in sanctuaries and in tombs, where they were intended for purification purposes (for a detailed discussion see Karageorghis 1998c, 266–274). At Hala Sultan Tekke a room with a stone slab floor and with walls revetted with regular plaques of limestone, dating to the LC IIIA

178. Isometric plan of the southwestern wing of Alassa-*Paliotaverna,* Building II (after Hadjisavvas and Hadjisavva 1997, 144, fig. 1). Across the large central hall there was a central hearth, on the right a bathroom.

179. Aerial view of the excavated remains at Alassa-*Paliotaverna*. In the foreground is the south wing, with the hearth-room and the bathroom.

period, has been identified as a bathroom (Åström *et al.* 1977, 78–79, figs. 73–77). At one end of this room a "well" was found, covered by a slab with a hole in the middle; this was obviously used as a latrine. The identification as a bathroom is probable, in view of the comparison of this example with Minoan bathrooms or lustral basins (cf. Graham 1987, 255–269). If this is correct, it is yet another example of influence from Crete, which adds to the other cultural elements of a Cretan nature (e.g., pottery and religious symbolism) mentioned above.

iv. Military architecture

It has previously been suggested that the appearance of the Cyclopean-type fortification wall and the characteristic dog-leg gate in LC IIIA settlements demonstrates influence from the Aegean (Karageorghis and Demas 1988, 63–64). Such fortification walls have been found at Enkomi, Sinda, Kition, and Maa-*Palaeokastro*. It is true that the prototype for this type of fortification may be Anatolian. In any case, it is a novelty for the military architecture of Cyprus, and the inspiration may have reached Cyprus either directly or via the Aegean, where these types of Cyclopean walls and dog-leg gates also existed.

v. Religious symbols

As discussed below, the religious architecture of Cyprus was deeply rooted in the Levantine tradition and continued to be so even during the LC IIIA period. At Kition, Enkomi, Hala Sultan Tekke, and elsewhere there were a number of sanctuaries, the ground plan of which was purely Levantine. However, an important innovation appeared connected with the sanctuaries: large-scale "horns of consecration" of stone, a symbol of Minoan religion. Such symbols appear at Palaepaphos, Kition, and Myrtou-*Pigadhes*. The same symbol appears in relief on the exterior of a cult trough of limestone from Pyla-*Kokkinokremos*. This implies that those who were involved in the cult were aware of the significance of this new religious symbol, which could not have been used as a meaningless ornament. It is very probable that this symbol was introduced to Cyprus from Crete, where it appeared not only in architectural complexes but also on sarcophagi and vases. In Cyprus it appeared, together with the double axe, another symbol of Minoan religion, on a locally made LC IIIA crater from Hala Sultan Tekke (for references see Karageorghis 2000a, 261).

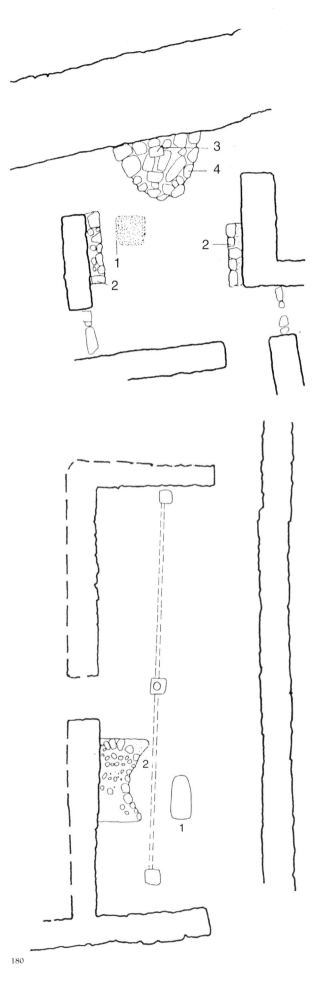

180. Central hearths at Enkomi (after Karageorghis 2000a, 268, fig. 13.14).
Legend
1. hearth; 2. bench; 3. cubical seat; 4. paved area.

180

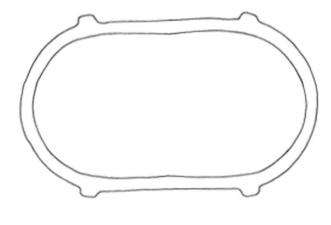

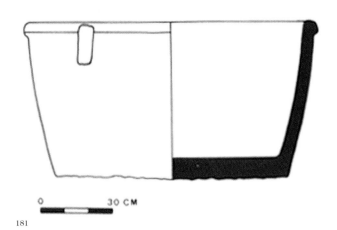

0   30 CM

181

181. Limestone bathtub from Enkomi (French Mission, 1959). Length: 123cm.; height: 64cm. (after J. Courtois 1992, 153, fig. 2).

182. A "bathroom" at Hala Sultan Tekke (Swedish Mission). It has a stone slab floor and walls faced with regular slabs of limestone. Late Cypriote IIIA.

182

vi. Coroplastic art

The terra-cotta figurines in Base-Ring ware showing nude female figures holding their breasts or an infant, which dominated the coroplastic art of Cyprus during the LC II period, suddenly gave way to different types of anthropomorphic figurines at the beginning of the LC IIIA period. These new types were very much influenced by the coroplastic art of the Aegean, especially some of the male figurines, which now appear more frequently than previously. Two female figurines, made of Cypriote clay, copy types of Mycenaean terra-cottas, several of which have been found in Cyprus.

The real novelty, however, was the appearance of bull figures with a hollow, wheelmade body and painted decoration, of a type known in Crete and on the Mycenaean mainland. These have been found in sanctuaries and may be evidence of new religious concepts that were associated with the ambitions of a new economic elite (for a further discussion see Karageorghis 1993a, 40; idem 1996a; idem 2000a, 258–259; see also idem 2001d).

vii. Bronzework and miscellanea

Although Cyprus had a long tradition in bronzework from as early as the Early Bronze Age, there were a few innovations at the beginning of LC IIIA that are important to note, particularly the appearance of weapons of an Aegean type, namely the Naue II-type swords and the bronze greaves from Enkomi (already mentioned above, in connection with Tomb 18 [chamber] below the floor of Building 18). The type is known in Cyprus from a number of examples dating to the early twelfth century B.C. (Catling 1964, 113–117, 140–142; see also Matthäus 1985, 362–366). The two bronze statues from Enkomi, the Horned God and the Ingot God, have been discussed by various scholars and their Aegean and Near Eastern influences have been pointed out; the same applies to a number of other bronze figurines, human and animal, of the same period (Catling 1964, 253–258). Many of them are associated with religious practices (cf. Catling 1971, 29).

In Catling's early researches into Cypriote bronzework the Aegean element was perhaps overemphasized, but considerable Aegean influence is nevertheless undeniable and fits perfectly within the general cultural atmosphere prevailing in Cyprus at the dawn of the twelfth century B.C. Catling himself summarized the situation as follows:

Of the very rich series found in Cyprus from "the latter years of the thirteenth century B.C., most particularly in sanctuary deposits, melting hoards and tombs, a significant proportion has strong Aegean elements, whether in form, style or technique. That proportion, though, no longer seems as high as I once thought, while the Near Eastern and Egyptian elements are more pervasive than I allowed. These are not, I think, symptoms of commercial activity, but of the mobility of partly destabilised individuals, families or communities whose interaction in the final stages of the Late Bronze Age and the early Dark Age produced that amalgam of Cypriot, Near Eastern and Aegean features that is so much easier to sense than to understand and explain" (Catling 1986, 99).

One of the finest expressions of Cypriote bronzework is the group of rod and cast tripods and four-sided stands supporting a ring at the top. The four-sided stands, some of them with four wheels, are decorated either in relief or in the ajouré technique and demonstrate the remarkable degree of technical and artistic excellence attained by Cypriote craftsmen. The four sides of the stands bear pictorial composi-

tions, such as the well-known scene of a standing Cypriot, carrying a copper ingot on his shoulders in front of a sacred tree; a recently illustrated fragmentary stand of the same group also represents an ingot bearer, together with human figures and sphinxes. There is yet a third fragment with an ingot bearer from Cyprus, now in the Royal Ontario Museum (Karageorghis and Papasavvas 2001). Other scenes include a lyre-player, chariot scenes, running animals, antithetic sphinxes, and bulls fighting with lions and griffins. Their style often reflects a combination of Aegean and Levantine elements (for a general discussion see Catling 1984; idem 1986).

Among the miscellaneous bronzes we should also add the violin-shaped fibulae, which appear at Enkomi, Kition, Maa-*Palaeokastro*, and elsewhere (Karageorghis and Demas 1988, 227; Giesen 2001, 40–55). The site of Enkomi has yielded other important works of art, namely in ivory carving and glyphics.

The attention of scholars has only recently been drawn to loomweights or "reels," usually of unbaked clay. These have direct relations with the Aegean. They appear at Enkomi, Kition, and Maa-*Palaeokastro*. In the Levant they are also recorded in large numbers at Ashkelon and Tel Mikne-Ekron in Philistia. Their Aegean connection has been emphasized by Stager (1991, 36–37; idem 1995, 346).

183. Enkomi (French Mission). The northern section of the Cyclopean wall: it consists of two parallel rows of large boulders at the foundation. The upper part was made of mud bricks. There are similar defensive walls at Kition, Maa-*Palaeokastro*, and Sinda.

183

184. Stepped capital and fragment from "horns of consecration" of limestone, from the site of the sanctuary of Aphrodite at Palaepaphos. Stepped capitals may have adorned the tops of pillars in the courtyard of the sanctuary; some pillars are still preserved. Similar capitals have been found at Enkomi, Kition, and Myrtou-*Pigadhes*, all associated with sanctuaries. Limestone "horns of consecration" have been found at Kition and Myrtou-*Pigadhes*. They were introduced from the Aegean circa 1200 B.C., the date when the sanctuary of Aphrodite was constructed at Palaepaphos.

185. Kition, Area II (excavations of the Cyprus Department of Antiquities). Built altar in Temenos A with "horns of consecration" at its base (fallen from the top). This must have been an altar for bloodless offerings. A second altar, for animal sacrifices, was found nearby, on the floor of the same temenos. A monumental altar crowned by "horns of consecration" was found in the sanctuary of Myrtou-*Pigadhes*.

184

185

viii. Monumental architecture

Some examples of monumental architecture, dating to the period circa 1200 B.C. or soon after, are described below in order to illustrate the significant changes that occurred at a number of urban centers.

a. Alassa-*Paliotaverna*

We have already referred to this site and its ashlar building, which was constructed in the LC IIC period and was contemporary with the large administrative Building X at Kalavassos-*Ayios Dhimitrios*. Alassa is situated in the Kouris valley, not far from the copper mines of the foothills of Troodos. Its Building II (Hadjisavvas 1994; Hadjisavvas and Hadjisavva 1997) is Π shaped, with an inner courtyard and a portico at the inner side. Its southern wall is 37.7m. long and runs parallel to a street 4.3m. wide. It is entirely constructed with large hewn blocks (ashlar), with bosses and drafted edges. The south wing communicates with the street through an entrance

2.65m. wide. The wing measures 29.5 × 6.8m. and is divided by thinner walls into a large central and other smaller spaces. This subdivision is later than the original structure, and there are indications that it dates to the LC IIIA period (cf. Hadjisavvas and Hadjisavva 1997, 145). The easternmost room was used as a bathroom, and a clay bathtub was found in it. The central large space constitutes the largest room in Building II, measuring 16.7 × 6.8m. There was a free-standing square hearth in the middle of a plinth or stylobate that ran across the width of the room. Bricks with traces of fire were found on the three sides of the hearth. Fragments of pillars, semicircular in section, have been found near the hearth, recalling those around hearths in the Aegean, e.g., in the Palace of Mallia in Crete (Driessen 1994, 72). The evidence for the changes effected in the south

wing of Building II in LC IIIA, with a central hearth and bathroom, offers valuable evidence for the cultural novelties referred to above.

b. Enkomi

The richness of the tombs of Enkomi during the fourteenth and thirteenth centuries B.C. has already been mentioned. About 1200 B.C. the town experienced a severe catastrophe by fire, after which there was a major rebuilding. The town was now provided with a Cyclopean wall, monumental sanctuaries, and a palatial building. Almost the whole of the Cyclopean wall of Enkomi has been uncovered; it ran along the south, west, and north sides of the town and was 2.5–3.5m. thick. The foundation consisted of two parallel rows of large unhewn blocks, the height of which reached 1.5–2m. Those of the inner

186. Fragment from a bell crater of Painted Wheelmade ware, of Late Cypriote IIIA date, from Hala Sultan Tekke (Swedish Excavations), N1566. Larnaca District Museum. The two zones between the handles are decorated with vertical panels filled with abstract motifs, but also with "horns of consecration" and double axes, which are Minoan religious symbols. These motifs may not be simply decorative; they probably had a meaning for those who painted them or used the crater.

187-188. Terra-cotta head of a male(?) figure from Enkomi (French Mission, 1949), no. 4006. Cyprus Museum, Nicosia. Height: 4cm. Flat head, long pointed nose, recalling some heads of Mycenaean terra-cottas. Late Cypriote IIIB period.

189. Terra-cotta wheelmade bull figurine from Enkomi (French Mission, 1946), no. 2210. Height: 22.6cm.; length: 25.5cm. Musée du Louvre, Paris. Hollow wheelmade body, with painted decoration. Wheelmade bull figurines appear frequently during the Late Cypriote IIIA period, replacing the Base-Ring ware rhyta. They recall the style of similar bull figurines in the Aegean.

190. Terra-cotta female (?) figurine with arms bent against the chest. From Hala Sultan Tekke (Swedish Excavations), N2000. Part of head and base chipped off. Preserved height: 8.3cm. Larnaca District Museum. Traces of red paint on body. This figurine imitates Mycenaean *Psi*-shaped figurines.

191. Female figurine from Cyprus in the Musée du Louvre, Paris, AM159. Height: 8.9cm. The right arm is raised; the other was bent forward (forearm missing). Decoration in brown matt paint. Both the facial characteristics and the attitude recall the Mycenaean *Psi*-shaped figurines that obviously were the prototypes for the Cypriote coroplast who made this figurine.

186

189

187

188

190

191

192. Bronze statue of a bearded god, cast solid, found in the cella of the sanctuary of the Ingot God at Enkomi (French Mission, 1963), no. 16.15. Height: 35cm. Cyprus Museum, Nicosia. The god is fully armed, carrying a spear and a small round shield. He wears a horned helmet and his legs are protected by greaves. He stands on a base in the form of an oxhide ingot and has been identified as the protector of the copper mines of Cyprus, which constituted the backbone of the island's economy. Ample evidence for metallurgical activity (smelting of copper) has been found during the excavations at the site of Enkomi. Copper ore must have been transported from the mines of the Troodos region, having undergone preliminary smelting on the spot, where timber was readily available. The statue is dated to the beginning of the twelfth century B.C. and may have served as a cult statue in the sanctuary.

193. Bronze statuette of a nude standing female figure, probably from Cyprus. The figure stands frontally on an oxhide ingot. The arms are missing; the hands are placed below the prominent breasts. She has long tresses and wears a long necklace. The pubic area is prominently indicated. The statuette may represent a goddess, symbolizing the fertility of the copper mines of Cyprus. Twelfth century B.C. The Ashmolean Museum, Oxford (Bomford collection). Height: 9.9cm.

194. Bronze statuette of a female figure, from Palaepaphos-*Teratsoudhia* (excavations of the Cyprus Department of Antiquities, 1984), Tomb 104, Chamber K, no. 5. Height: 9.5cm. Kouklia Site Museum. The figurine is shown with both arms bent, holding her breasts. She has long locks of hair and her pubic triangle is accentuated with punctures, recalling the clay figurines of the same period (thirteenth century B.C.). She wears a long necklace with a pendant falling between her breasts. Her feet are missing, so one may not determine on what she was standing. A similar figurine (no. 193), stands on a base in the form of a copper ingot. There is another, similar figurine (but without the feet), from Nicosia, now in the Cyprus Museum.

192

193

194

195

row were smaller, and the space between them was filled with rubble. The superstructure was of mud bricks. Several towers were built at irregular intervals against the city wall. A gate opened on each of the four sides of the town. Ten straight parallel streets crossed the town from one side to the other, east to west, with a perpendicular central street from north to south, exactly in the middle of the town; there was also a circular road running inside along the walls on all three sides. At the point where the north–south street intersects with Street 5 a "public square" measuring 15.5 × 7.5m. was created, paved with stone slabs. The whole inhabited area of the town may easily be calculated; it measures around 400m. from north to south and 350m. from east to west. East of the north gate, abutting against the wall, there is a rectangular structure that its excavator, P. Dikaios, identified as a tower, but it may well be a sanctuary, where ceremonies may have been carried out when the patron gods and goddesses were admitted into the town. A similar phenomenon was observed at Kition (see below).

Three important sanctuaries have been uncovered at Enkomi, all dating to the twelfth century B.C. The largest is the Sanctuary of the Horned God, so called because of the bronze statue of a god wearing a horned helmet that was found there. It is constructed of ashlar blocks and consists of a hall and two cult rooms to the east, in one of which the cult statue of the Horned God was found. The hall, whose roof was supported on two rectangular pillars, was where sacrifices and other rituals took place. There was an altar, around which a large number of skulls of oxen, goats, and deer were found. Numerous clay bowls may have been used for libations during sacrificial ritual. Adjacent and to the east of the main Sanctuary of the Horned God there was a smaller sanctuary,

195. Four bronze swords of the so-called Naue II-type. From Enkomi (French Mission), excavated from Well 212. Length: 59.2–62.1cm. Such swords appear in Cyprus circa 1200 B.C. and were brought by the first Aegean settlers to Cyprus. One such sword was found in a tomb of a warrior (with greaves) in Building 18, which is dated to circa 1200 B.C. or soon after.

196. Bronze statue of a youthful god, cast solid, found in the Sanctuary of the Horned God at Enkomi (excavations of the Cyprus Department of Antiquities, 1948), no. 19. Height: 54.2cm. Cyprus Museum, Nicosia. The figure is represented in a strictly frontal attitude, with the left arm bent toward the chest; the right arm is bent forward in an attitude of blessing. He wears a headdress with horns, recalling the horned helmets of Mycenaean warriors, and a short kilt. He has been identified with Apollo *Alasiotas* (the god of Alashiya, the Late Bronze Age name for Cyprus) or Apollo *Keraeatas* (Horned Apollo), after inscriptions of a much later period found on the island. If Apollo, he may be a god of cattle and fertility. This is one of the finest works of Cypriote bronzework of the end of the thirteenth century B.C. found in Cyprus, and certainly the largest bronze statue of this period found on the island so far.

197. Fragment from the ajouré decoration of a four-sided stand, the Royal Ontario Museum, Toronto, Inv. no. 995.144.1. Preserved height: 3.9cm.; width: 6.2cm. It represents a flat draped human figure, head in profile, holding an oxhide ingot on his shoulders. The body is shown *en face*. He has long hair falling on his shoulders.

196

197

198

199

200

where a small bronze statuette of a double-headed female divinity was found. She may have been the consort of the male god. In contrast to earlier periods when the female divinities were predominant and played a major role in an agrarian society, now the predominant divinity in an "industrial" society was a male, who also symbolized fertility. The bronze statue of the Horned God, cast solid, measures 54.2cm. in height and is by far the largest bronze statue found in Late Bronze Age Cyprus. The god wears a short kilt and a horned helmet, not unlike Mycenaean warriors as they were depicted in Mycenaean vase painting. His youthful facial characteristics recall Aegean prototypes, but his attitude, with the left arm bent against the chest and the right bent forward, suggests Near Eastern influence. He has been identified as Apollo *Keraeatas* (horned), after a Hellenistic inscription found at Pyla in Cyprus. Apollo *Keraeatas* was also worshiped in Arcadia, in the Peloponnese, from where Mycenaean colonists reached Cyprus, as

is attested by the dialect that was introduced to the island and that survived down to later times. This god was the protector of shepherds and cattle, and he no doubt replaced the Cypriote divinity of fertility of earlier periods. Another inscription found at Tamassos, however, dating to the fourth century B.C., refers to an Apollo or Reshef *Alasiotas* (of Alashiya), which was the name of Cyprus in the Late Bronze Age. Some scholars identify the Horned God with this one (for a general discussion on the identification of this god see Hadjioannou 1971; also Karageorghis 1998f, 30–33).

Another sanctuary excavated at Enkomi, also built of ashlar blocks, consists of a porch and a main shrine (cella). In the central part of the cella, near a well, there was a large stone base for a pillar. A capital with a stepped profile was found nearby, like those found at Kition, Palaepaphos, and Myrtou-*Pigadhes*. This building has been compared with sanctuaries in the Aegean associated with the pillar

201   202

203

204

cult. The monumental character of its architecture and the objects found on its floor (animal horns, carved ivory) leave no doubt about its identification as a sanctuary. The date proposed by Schaeffer for this building is the end of the thirteenth century B.C.; its use lasted throughout the twelfth century.

The third sanctuary of Enkomi is that of the Ingot God, so called because of the bronze statue found in it of a god standing on a base in the form of an oxhide ingot. This sanctuary, dated to the twelfth century, was also in use in the eleventh century B.C. Unlike the other two sanctuaries, which were constructed with ashlar blocks, the walls of this sanctuary were of rubble and mud bricks. It consisted of a rectangular courtyard in which there was a hearth altar and two stone blocks 80 and 72cm. in height. One of them was pierced in the upper part, perhaps for tethering the animals that were destined to be sacrificed on the altar and that were slaughtered on the other block. Along the northern part of the

201-202. Bronze four-sided stand, probably from Episkopi (Kourion). The British Museum, London, Inv. no. 1920.12-20.1. Height: 11cm.; diam. of ring: 8.5cm. It consists of a ring placed on top of a four-sided rectangular stand. The four sides form rectangular frames decorated with human figures in the ajouré technique. We illustrate two of the four frames, one showing a draped human figure standing in front of a stylized "sacred tree" and carrying an oxhide ingot on his shoulders; he is one of three known similar representations (see nos. 197 and 203); the other frame is decorated with a figure seated on a stool in front of a stylized tree; he is playing a harp. The remaining two scenes also represent human figures in front of a stylized tree. Probably of Late Cypriote IIC–IIIA date.

203. Bronze four-sided stand on wheels. Provenance unknown. Bible Lands Museum, Jerusalem, no. 862. Maximum height of preserved side: 28cm. Ajouré decoration on two surviving sides, in two registers. On one side, at the upper register, there are four long-robed human figures carrying gifts; one of them carries an oxhide ingot. Late Cypriote IIIA period.

204. Bronze stand supported on four wheels. The British Museum, London, Inv. no. 1946.10-17.1. Height: 31cm.; diam. of ring: 15cm. It consists of a ring at the top and four framed sides decorated in the ajouré technique, all cast. The ring is decorated in relief with a frieze of animals. The four panels are richly decorated; we illustrate one decorated with a biga. On the other three sides there are a lion, a sphinx, and two people approaching a seated figure, respectively. At the lower part of each side there is a narrow horizontal frame with birds and fish in the ajouré technique. This is one of the most monumental four-sided wheeled stands from Cyprus. Late Cypriote IIIA period.

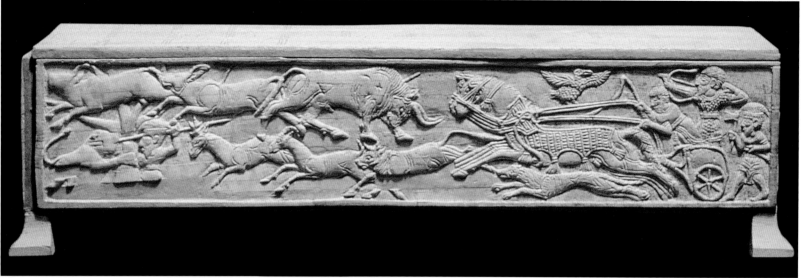

205

206

207

205. An ivory gaming box from Enkomi (British Excavations), Tomb 58. The British Museum, London, Inv. no.1894.4-1.996. Length: 29cm.; width: 7.5cm.; height: 8.5cm. The upper part of the lid is divided by carved lines to serve as a gaming table. The four sides are decorated in relief. On the best preserved side there is a scene of bull hunting from a chariot. The other long side is similarly decorated. One of the short sides is decorated with two couchant bulls under an olive tree, very naturalistically rendered, in an Aegean style. The other short side is decorated with two antithetic goats on either side of a tree. The style of the figure drawing shows Aegean and Near Eastern influences, and the box was probably carved in Cyprus in the twelfth century B.C.

206. Impression of a domed seal of black serpentine, from Enkomi (excavations of the Cyprus Department of Antiquities, 1950), no. 184. Cyprus Museum, Nicosia. The oval base measures 1.6 x 1.1cm.; height: 1.3cm. It is carved with a warrior protecting

himself with his large shield; he wears a headdress of feathers, recalling that of the Philistines at the time of Rameses III (1195–1164 B.C.). A similar headdress appears on other works of art from Cyprus, e.g., the ivory gaming box from Enkomi. Enkomi level IIIB, circa 1190–1180 B.C.

207. Reels of unbaked clay have been found in large quantities at the site of Maa-*Palaeokastro* as well as at Kition, Enkomi, and other Late Cypriote IIC–IIIA sites. They are also known in the Levant, e.g., at Ashkelon, and may be related to weaving. They are about 6–8 cm. in length. Such reels are known also from Crete, and it has been suggested that their introduction to Cyprus and the Levant formed part of the novelties in the material culture of the region that existed circa 1200 B.C.

208. Site plan of Enkomi (after Schaeffer 1971, folded plan).

209. Plan of the Sanctuary of the Horned God at Enkomi (after Dikaios 1969-1971, vol. IIIB, pl. 275).

210. Aerial view of Enkomi, a Late Bronze Age urban center on the east coast of Cyprus. It was established as a small rural settlement at the end of the Middle Bronze Age, but flourished considerably during the Late Bronze Age as a harbor town (it had an inner harbor). It was abandoned and succeeded by the city of Salamis in the eleventh century B.C., which had a natural harbor. Enkomi was one of the largest urban centers in Cyprus, if not the largest. Extensive excavations by the French Mission and the Cyprus Department of Antiquities, which started early in the 1930s and continued, with interruptions, until 1974, revealed imposing public buildings and a Cyclopean fortification wall. Previously the Swedish Cyprus Expedition (1929–32) excavated richly furnished tombs at the same site, considering the buildings above them to belong to a later period. Enkomi has a "modern" regular grid with straight streets crossing at right angles.

courtyard there was a portico, the roof of which was supported by wooden pillars. Against the walls there were benches for the deposit of offerings, a feature known from the sanctuaries of Kition and others in the Levant. On the floor of the courtyard there were numerous foreparts of skulls of oxen and deer that were probably worn as masks by priests and worshipers during ritual performances, as is also evidenced in the sanctuary of the Horned God, at Kition and at Myrtou-*Pigadhes* (see below). Also significant are about a dozen notched scapulae (shoulder bones of oxen), which were probably used to provide rhythmic music for ritual dances during ceremonies in the sanctuary. Similar scapulae were found at Kition and other places in the Levant (see Caubet 1987, 735–737). At the northeastern corner of the sanctuary there was a small rectangular annex in which the statue of the Ingot God was found. It represents a bearded male, cast solid, 35cm. in height, wearing a kilt and a close-fitting vest. Like the Horned God, he wears a horned helmet and is fully armed: in his left hand he holds a round shield and in his right hand he brandishes a spear. His legs are protected by greaves. He stands on a base in the form of an oxhide ingot. A bronze female statuette of the same period, probably found in Cyprus and now in the Ashmolean Museum, Oxford, stands on a similar base. The Ingot God has been identified with the protector of the metallurgists and the copper mines of Enkomi, whereas the female divinity may symbolize the fertility of the mines (cf. Catling 1974). Thus, we have here an eloquent example of the connection between metallurgy and religion, a phenomenon that is even more explicit in the sacred area of

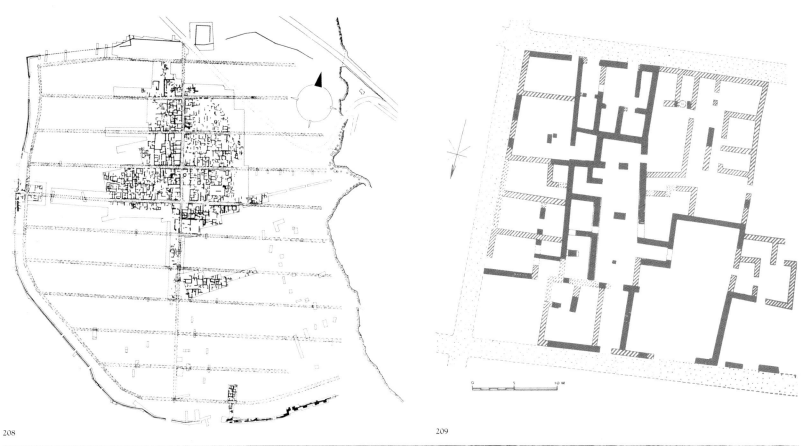

208

209

210

211. Plan of the Sanctuary of the Ingot God, Enkomi (excavations of the French Mission). On the floor of the courtyard were found skulls of oxen. In the cella the bronze statue of the Ingot God was found (after Courtois in Schaeffer 1971, folded plan).

Legend
1. enter; 2. south courtyard; 3. north hall; 4. cell.

212. The Sanctuary of the Horned God at Enkomi was excavated by the Cyprus Department of Antiquities. It was built circa 1200 B.C. and is one of the most monumental public buildings on the site. In this general view one can see the fine construction of the walls with well-hewn large stones (known as ashlar blocks), a style of building introduced to the island in the thirteenth century B.C., as we now know from the administrative building at Kalavassos-*Ayios Dhimitrios*. This style was well known in Ugarit, in Syria, from where it may have been introduced to Cyprus. In the sanctuary, near the altar, large quantities of bowls were found, as well as skulls of oxen, worn as masks during ritual performances.

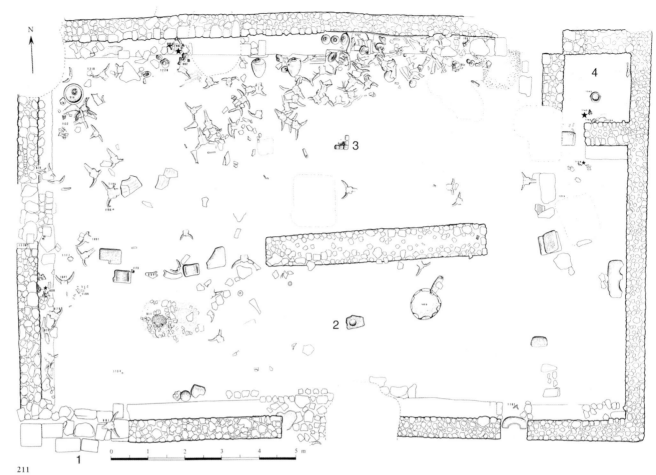

211

212

213

213. View of Kition, Area II (excavations of the Cyprus Department of Antiquities), showing the Cyclopean city wall and Temples 1, 4, and 5.

214. Kition, Area II (excavation of the Cyprus Department of Antiquities), viewed from the west. Temple 1 is in the foreground.

214

215. Kition, Area II (excavations of the Cyprus Department of Antiquities). Temples 5 (left) and 4 (right).

Kition (see below). Metallurgy was the backbone of the economy of Cyprus, and those who controlled it searched to find divine symbolism for this control.

The type of the Ingot God of Enkomi has a parallel at Megiddo in Palestine, where a similar bronze statuette of a god holding a shield and brandishing a spear was found (Guy and Engberg 1938, pl. 153.8). The real name of the Ingot God is not known, but the fact that he is the god of metallurgists has induced some scholars to identify him as the predecessor of the Greek smith-god Hephaestos, whose spouse was Aphrodite. The sanctuary of the Ingot God continued to function until about the middle of the eleventh century B.C. (see below).

Finally, further mention should be made of Building 18, a palatial building excavated by the French Mission, referred to above. Situated in a central part of the town, this building occupied an area of 1,800 square meters. Its extraordinarily well-built façade is more than 40m. long; the width of the building is 33m. Some of the blocks of the façade measure 3×1.4m. Its floors were made of thick, hard "concrete," recalling the floors of Kalavassos-*Ayios Dhim-itrios* Building X. The excavator, C. F. A. Schaeffer, proposed a construction date late in the thirteenth century B.C. and suggested that the building was violently destroyed by fire soon after its completion and suffered several changes and repairs. The fire left its traces on the large ashlar blocks; this happened at a time when Mycenaean IIIC:1b pottery (local) was widely in use, i.e., early in the twelfth century B.C. After that the building was divided into smaller compartments and used for metallurgical activity (for a short account see Courtois in Courtois, Lagarce, and Lagarce 1986, 18–20; for other buildings of a domestic or industrial character see also ibid., 22–23, 26–27).

c. Kition

At Kition, on the southeast coast, there was a flourishing harbor town from the beginning of the thirteenth century B.C., as seen above. The rebuilding of the beginning of the twelfth century B.C. (LC IIIA) gave a completely new aspect to the town, as seen in the two areas, I and II, that have been excavated by the Cyprus Department of Antiquities (Karageorghis

215

and Demas 1985). Prominent among the various buildings excavated in Area II, in the northernmost part of the town, along the fortification wall, are the metallurgical installations that had a direct relation with a cult, as will be discussed below.

The Cyclopean wall of Kition, which succeeded the mud brick wall of LC IIC date described above, was very much like that of Enkomi and followed the edge of the low plateau on which the town was built.

As already mentioned above, there was no violent destruction of the buildings of the LC IIC period, but a rebuilding. We described this change as follows: "There was a deliberate decision to expand and remodel the temple precinct using a new type of masonry which has become fashionable in Cyprus. What lay behind this decision is clearly of crucial importance, and in this regard the use of ashlar masonry for the construction of the new temples may be of particular significance. The very clear association of ashlar masonry with wealth and power must have made it a desirable attribute to the rulers of any city. One might even suggest that ashlar masonry had become one of the principal, and certainly the most visible, prestige symbols that a ruler could employ. Its absence at Kition in LC IIC cannot be simply a matter of local architectural tastes or traditions. Rather it would seem to imply that Kition had not yet achieved sufficient stature to erect such a grand public façade.

If this is a correct diagnosis, we must look for the source of Kition's new wealth and prestige in LC IIIA which allowed for this architectural transformation. The coincidence of certain events at the transitional period from LC IIC to LC IIIA may provide us, if not with the answers, at least with some probable directions in which to look for them" (Karageorghis and Demas 1985, 92–93).

The northern part of the town, along the Cyclopean wall, was occupied by four temples (1, 2, 4, and 5). The largest is Temple 1, which replaced Temple 3 of the LC IIC period. Temple 2 succeeded an LC IIC structure, which was remodeled. This imposing sacred area was conceived to include a series of open spaces for sacrifices (Temenos A and Temenos B), and also a complex of workshops for metallurgical work. Thus again, as at Enkomi, there is evidence for the close association between metallurgy and religion. This northernmost point of the town, near the city wall, was intentionally chosen, so that the fumes from the workshops, which must have been unroofed, would

216

217

216. Detail from the south wall of Temple 1 at Kition, Area II (excavations by the Cyprus Department of Antiquities). The large ashlar blocks are engraved with stylized ships, of a type characteristic of the "Sea Peoples'" ships. Kition was a harbor town, and no doubt these ships were engraved on the wall of its main temple of circa 1200 B.C. so that the divinity might protect the city's fleet.

217. Kition, Area II, Temple 4 (excavations of the Cyprus Department of Antiquities). Graffiti of ships on the blocks used for the built altar. Cf. similar graffiti occurred on the south façade of Temple 1.

be blown away by the prevailing southern winds and thus avoid pollution. It is significant that the main Temple 1 could communicate at its northwestern corner with the workshops and vice-versa. Furnaces, as well as ample quantities of copper slag, crucibles, and tuyères, were found on the floor of the workshops (Karageorghis and Kassianidou 1998).

Temple 1 was an imposing rectangular structure, measuring 35m. in length (east–west) and 22m. in width (north–south). It comprised a large courtyard and a tripartite holy-of-holies on the west, copying Levantine prototypes. The courtyard was accessible either from the street on the south side through a monumental side entrance, or through another monumental entrance on the east, from Temenos B. The temple was constructed of large ashlar blocks, some of them measuring 3m. in length and 1m in height. On the south façade of the temple there are engravings on the ashlars, representing a fleet of ships. These have been identified as "Sea Peoples'" ships, with an inwardly curved fan on the stem; this is how they are represented on the walls of the temple of Medinet Habu in Egypt, in a scene showing their defeat by Rameses III (Basch and Artzy 1985; Wachsmann 1997).

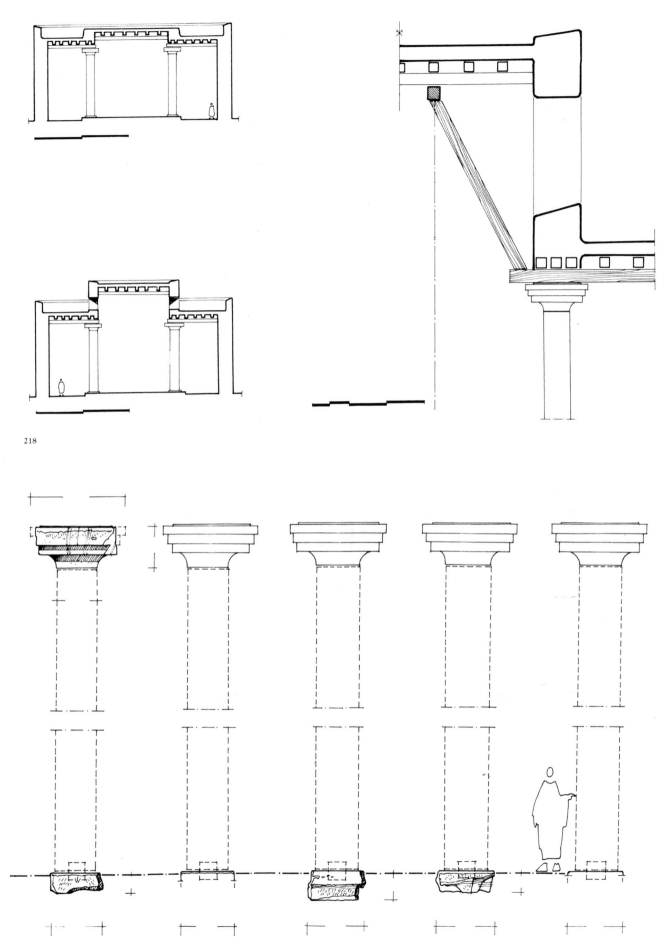

218. Kition, Area II, Temple 1 (excavations of the Cyprus Department of Antiquities). Suggested roofing of the temple (after O. Callot in Karageorghis and Demas 1985, 223, figs. 39–40).

219. Kition, Area II, Temple 1. Reconstructed stone pillars and capitals (after O. Callot in Karageorghis 1985, 220, fig. 36).

218

219

The ship carvings must have been intended as a prayer to the divinity to protect the sailors on their voyages. The roof of the courtyard was supported by two rows of five wooden pillars; thus there were three aisles, the central one being larger than the lateral ones. The pillars had stepped stone capitals; similar pillars and capitals also supported the roof in Temenos B, north of Temple 2.

Temples 2, 3, and 5 have more or less the same plan, with a courtyard in front of the holy-of-holies and benches along the walls for the deposit of offerings. Among the objects found in the holy-of-holies of Temple 4 was an ivory plaque in the ajouré technique, clearly intended originally to decorate a piece of furniture; on the lower part of the plaque there is an engraved inscription in the Cypro-Minoan script. Another ivory object is a pipe for smoking opium, also with a Cypro-Minoan inscription. This is the earliest known opium pipe. Opium, as mentioned earlier, was already exported from Cyprus during LC I, in Base-Ring ware juglets. It was used as a painkiller in antiquity.

Another important object found in the courtyard was a cylindrical clay vase that had two antithetic openings in its lower part and may have been used for inhaling opium, which was placed on charcoal at the bottom of the vase. Terra-cotta figurines found in this temple suggest that it was dedicated to a female divinity. In the northwestern courtyard of the temple, below the floor, two unfinished bronze tools and a large bronze peg were discovered, probably part of a foundation deposit. The bronze peg has parallels in inscribed clay examples from the Near East.

An interesting feature in Temple 5 is the large rectangular altar built against the holy-of-holies. A stone anchor was found leaning against this altar, obviously dedicated by a sailor to Baal, the god of voyagers, for a safe journey. Stone anchors built into the foundations of Temple 4 may be of religious significance (cf. Frost 1985, 293–295).

The two temene were open spaces for sacrifices. In Temenos A there was an altar constructed with small ashlar blocks and topped by stone "horns of consecration," recalling the more monumental altar of the sanctuary at Myrtou-*Pigadhes* (mentioned earlier), and a low altar for burnt sacrifices. A second pair of stone "horns of consecration" was found reused in a later wall in Temenos B. From Temenos A there was direct access to the metallurgical workshops.

220

221

222

220. Stepped stone capital from Kition, Area II (excavations of the Cyprus Department of Antiquities), found in Temenos B. Such capitals were placed on top of structural stone pillars that supported a roof. Several have been found at Kition, inside and outside Temple 1, and they are also known from Palaepaphos, Enkomi, and Myrtou-*Pigadhes*. They are associated with sanctuary buildings of circa 1200 B.C.

221. Ivory pipe for smoking, found at Kition, Area II (excavations of the Cyprus Department of Antiquities). Found in the holy-of-holies of Temple 4, no. 4262. Length: 14cm. Larnaca District Museum. It is partly tubular, with an outlet to the side. It was most likely used for smoking opium, a substance often employed in antiquity as a painkiller. It is decorated with engraved abstract motifs and also with an inscription in the Cypro-Minoan script. This is probably the earliest known pipe for smoking (circa 1200 B.C.).

222. Ivory plaque from Kition, Area II (excavations of the Cyprus Department of Antiquities), no. 4252. Found in the holy-of-holies of Temple 4. Height: 22cm. Larnaca District Museum. It represents the Egyptian god Bes and is carved in the ajouré technique. Tenons above and below indicate that it was meant to decorate a piece of furniture. On the lower tenon there is an engraved inscription in the Cypro-Minoan script. The god Bes was very popular in Cyprus down to later periods, as a household god helping women during pregnancy.

d. Sinda

The site of Sinda, situated in the heart of the Mesaoria plain about 15km. west of Enkomi, was established in the LC II period and was destroyed by fire at the end of LC IIC. Only the massive fortification wall survived the catastrophe; it is of the Cyclopean type with a dog-leg gate, like that of Maa-*Palaeokastro*. An important hoard of bronzes was unearthed by looters at Sinda after the 1947–48 excavations and was acquired by a private collector (Karageorghis 1973b). The hoard, which comprises a sacrificial table, tweezers, a wall bracket, a situla, etc., was

223. Bronze portable hearth from Sinda. Hadjiprodromou Collection, Famagusta. Height: 20cm.; diam. of the tray at the top: 59.5cm. There is a sunken depression at the center of the tray and a raised border all around. The tray is supported on three loop legs. There is a similar bronze portable hearth from Enkomi, found in "La Maison des Bronzes" (French Mission), now in the Cyprus Museum. This hearth, together with a bronze wall bracket and other objects, formed part of a hoard found at Sinda in 1971. They probably belonged to a sanctuary. Other objects in the hoard include a shovel, tongs, and a situla.

224. Bronze wall bracket from Sinda. Hadjiprodromou Collection, Famagusta. Height: 30.7cm. The front of the shaft is decorated with four pairs of applied S-shaped spirals, with a triangular perforation between pairs. There are also two spirals on the upper part of the shaft, on either side of the suspension hole. Wall brackets are usually made of clay; an almost identical bronze wall bracket from Cyprus is in the Royal Ontario Museum, Toronto. There is a third bronze wall bracket in the Cyprus Museum, from Enkomi. Late Cypriote IIIA.

225-226. Ugaritic cuneiform inscription engraved on a silver bowl found at Hala Sultan Tekke (Swedish Excavations), no. 1450. It reads: "made by Aky, son of Yiptahaddou." Cyprus Museum, Nicosia. Height: 4.2cm.; diam.: 14.3–15.2cm.

227. General view of excavated remains at Athienou-*Pamboularin tis Koukkouninas* (excavations of Hebrew University of Jerusalem). The architectural remains uncovered may be associated with a combined cult and copper-working installation. The site lies on the transport route of copper ore from the mines of the Troodos mountains to Kition. This establishment was built in the Late Cypriote II period and continued in operation into Late Cypriote IIIA.

223

224

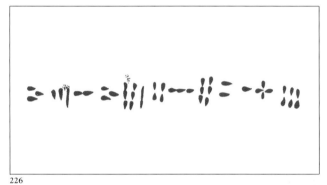

225

226

227

228

found in a pit covered with ashes, according to information supplied by the finders. We know that Sinda I was destroyed by fire. We may thus associate this hoard with Sinda I (LC IIC period). This would be in perfect harmony with recent theories that hoards of bronzes, especially "from Enkomi and Sinda, [were] buried in the ground in the face of impending disasters that were to overwhelm Bronze Age civilization in the Eastern Mediterranean. It is to these extraordinary events that we owe the existence of such hoards" (Muhly 1980, 159). This is an important piece of evidence, not only because it shows that metalworking was highly advanced at Sinda, as at other LC IIC sites, but also that the destruction of Sinda I occurred after the concealment of a hoard,

circa 1200 B.C. It is unfortunate that the results of the excavations at Sinda, carried out some fifty years ago, have not yet been published (see short preliminary report Furumark 1965). The proximity of Sinda to Enkomi may not be accidental: it may have been established and fortified in order to guard the route through which copper ore from the Troodos mountains reached Enkomi.

e. Athienou
Similar factors may account for the establishment of Athienou, where a sanctuary, connected with metallurgy was built. It is located on the route through which copper ore may have been transported to Kition. The site flourished at the very end of LC IIC

228. Hala Sultan Tekke. Aerial view of the excavated remains (Swedish Excavations). The site lies on the shore of one of the lakes/lagoons by the southeast coast of Cyprus (in antiquity they communicated with the sea as inlets). The site had an inner harbor. It may have been established during the Late Cypriote I period (evidence of tombs), but the actual architectural remains date to the Late Cypriote IIIA period. They include domestic as well as religious architecture.

229

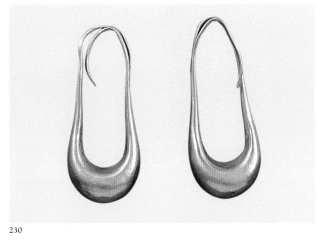

230

231

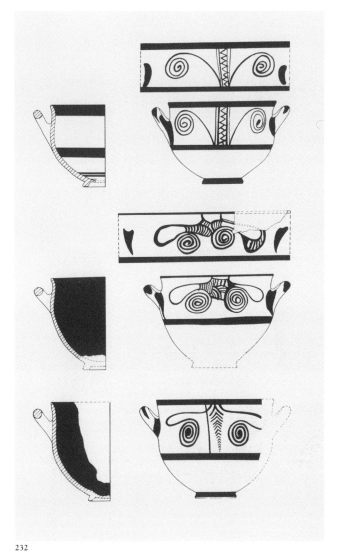

232

229. Gold finger ring with a cloisonné bezel, from Kouklia-*Evreti* (British Excavations, 1952), Tomb VIII. Diam.: 2.2cm. Cyprus Museum, Nicosia. Tomb VIII, dating to the twelfth century B.C., yielded the most sumptuous material: gold earrings, finger rings, a decorated ivory mirror handle, an iron spatula with an ivory handle, etc. The cloisonné technique of the six finger rings found in Tomb VIII represents the earliest true cloisonné enameling known from the Mycenaean world. Another object decorated in the same technique is the Kourion scepter head, but it dates to the eleventh century B.C.

230. Pair of gold earrings from Kouklia-*Evreti*, Tomb VIII, no. 33. Length: 4cm. Cyprus Museum, Nicosia. Late Cypriote III period. Solid, boat shaped, terminating in elongated wire with overlapping ends.

231. Scepter head in Egyptian blue decorated with white inlay. Height: 3.7cm. From Hala Sultan Tekke (Swedish Excavations, 1977), N.1188. Larnaca District Museum. It resembles a papyriform Egyptian capital. On its top it bears the cartouche of Egyptian Pharaoh Horemheb (1333–1306 or 1322–1295 B.C.); it was obviously kept as an heirloom, as it was found in a Late Cypriote IIIA context (circa 1190–1175 B.C.). The town near the mosque of Hala Sultan Tekke, close to the Larnaca Salt Lake, was a cosmopolitan harbor town during the whole of the Late Bronze Age, and excavations have yielded material illustrating its relations with neighboring countries and the Aegean.

232. Skyphoi of Mycenaean IIIC:1b style, from Palaepaphos: (a) from *Marcello* Tomb KAT I.37, (b) from *Evreti* Well TE III.50 and (c) from *Evreti* Well TE III.23. Kouklia Site Museum.

and the beginning of LC IIIA (Dothan and Ben Tor 1983, 140).

f. Hala Sultan Tekke

The existence of a prosperous town at this site as early as LC I–II is known only from tombs, mostly excavated at the end of the nineteenth century (Åström *et al.* 1976). The site is situated along the west shore of the Larnaca Salt Lake, near the southeast coast of Cyprus. At that time the lake was open to the sea, and the town had an inner harbor, near which stone anchors have been found. The settlement flourished particularly during the LC IIC–LC IIIA period, like several other sites that have been discussed above. Ample evidence for metallurgical activity has been uncovered dating to this period, including copper slag, tuyères, molds for casting, and various bronze objects, including a number of fine vessels. Its harbor must have been very lively, with many international trade links. Pottery and other goods from Egypt,

Anatolia, the Aegean and the Levant have been found in considerable quantities, both on the floors of the houses and in tombs. A fragmentary open crater (already mentioned above), locally made and dating to the LC IIIA:1 period, is decorated with motifs of Aegean (Cretan) origin: double axes and "horns of consecration." A silver bowl of LC IIIA:1 date is inscribed with letters in the Ugaritic cuneiform script (Åström and Masson 1982). The inscription reads: "made by Aky, son of Yiptahad-dou." It has been suggested that its maker, Aky, had a Hurrian name, and his father a Semitic name. This is indicative of the cosmopolitan character of the town. A silver ring was found in a tomb of LC IIIA:1 date; its bezel is decorated with a festive scene centered on an altar under a floating disc resting on wings of Hittite origin (Porada 1983). We should also mention a scepter-head of Egyptian blue, decorated with the cartouche of Pharaoh Horemheb and obviously an heirloom.

233. Ivory mirror handle from
Kouklia. Cyprus Museum, Nicosia.
Inv. no. K.T.E. T.8/34. Height:
22.3cm. The flat part of the handle
is decorated in relief on both sides
with a warrior fighting a lion.
12th century B.C.

234. Fragment from an ivory
mirror handle from Kition (French
Mission, 1976), no. KEF 141.
Height: 7.5cm.; thickness: 1.5cm.
Larnaca District Museum. It shows
a draped seated woman holding a
mirror. The bronze mirror itself was
fixed into the upper part of the
handle. Several such ivory mirror
handles have been found in tombs
at Enkomi and Palaepaphos. They
show influences from Aegean
ivory carving.

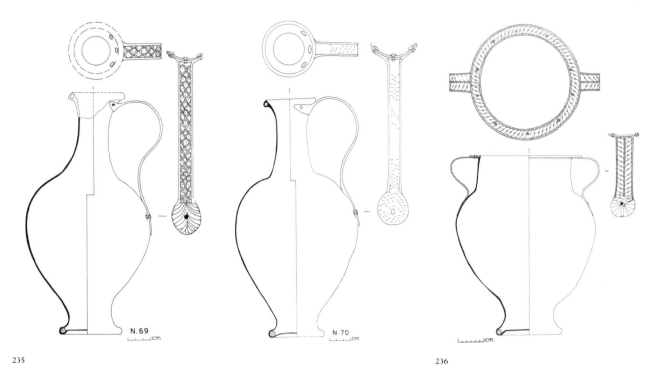

235

236

The "international" character of this town is no doubt owing to its geographical position and its important harbor. An important factor for its development may have been its proximity to the Kalavassos and Troulli mines, especially after the abandonment in LC IIC of Kalavassos-*Ayios Dhimitrios* and Maroni-*Vournes*.

g. Palaepaphos

The area of Palaepaphos was inhabited throughout the Late Cypriote period. For the LC I–II periods the evidence comes mainly from tombs (for a general discussion see Maier and Karageorghis 1984, 50–117; also Karageorghis 1990a), and we have evidence for the settlement itself only for the periods LC IIC–LC IIIA onward. Important ceramic material has been found in two wells at the *Evreti* location and also from tombs at the same site. *Evreti* Tomb VIII is one of the richest tombs ever found in Cyprus and is usually considered to date to the early part of the LC IIIA period on the evidence of the pottery that it contained (Catling 1968). Local craftsmen included highly skilled jewelers, who produced elegant earrings, finger rings decorated with cloisonné enameling, and ivory carvers who were versatile in the styles of the Aegean and the Levant. Similar ivory handles of mirrors have been found at Kition and Enkomi. Another series of excavated tombs at the site of *Teratsoudhia* provides further evidence for the ingenuity of Paphian metalworkers. In a tomb that may date to the early part of LC IIIA two large bronze jugs as well

as a bronze amphoroid crater were found. They are of fine workmanship, with handles decorated with engraved patterns, and bases and rims strengthened with solid bronze rings; this technique was previously unknown in Cypriote metalworking and may have been introduced from the Aegean, where it is well attested (Karageorghis 1990a, 61–65).

The most important building excavated at Palaepaphos is undoubtedly the sanctuary of Aphrodite and its monumental peribolos wall, of which only a small portion is now preserved. Its ashlar blocks are among the largest and finest in Cyprus. A few stone pillars with stepped capitals (like those found at Enkomi and Kition) have been found at the site. We have also mentioned the stone "horns of consecration" found at the site of the temple. Another feature that relates this sanctuary to the Aegean is a clay bathtub, clearly used for purification (for a general account see Maier 1985).

The discovery of copper slag in the vicinity of the sanctuary, as well as the various bronze objects found in tombs of LC IIIA and particularly LC IIIB/CG I, suggest that there was metallurgical activity at Palaepaphos, as in other towns described above. Recent survey suggests the existence of copper-mining areas that would have been easily accessible to the Palaepaphians during the LC period.

Though the name of the goddess who was worshiped in the newly erected temple is not known, it is quite possible that she is the goddess whom the Myce-

237

naean Greeks adopted and introduced to their own pantheon, where she was previously unknown, as Aphrodite. The Greeks must have been impressed by her strangeness, majesty, and power. Her cult was deeply rooted in Paphos; she protected the king and the state, and her high priest was the king himself. They built for her a majestic temple, following oriental styles in architecture, but they introduced ele-

ments of their own religion, the "horns of consecration." They gradually altered her character to suit their own religious traditions, and from a purely fertility goddess Aphrodite became a goddess of beauty and love. If this theory is correct, then Cyprus may have given Aphrodite as a gift to the Greeks, as early as the twelfth century B.C. (for a detailed discussion see Karageorghis and Karageorghis forthcoming).

237. General view of the sanctuary of Aphrodite at Palaepaphos. It was constructed with large ashlar blocks, and in its courtyard there were rectangular pillars crowned by stepped capitals. Its courtyard was surrounded by an impressive wall. The "image" of the goddess, probably a conical stone, a "baetyl," may have been preserved in a tripartite holy-of-holies. The exact arrangement of this is not known, but schematic representations of the sanctuary on Roman coins and medallions and also on late Hellenistic sealings may offer some hints.

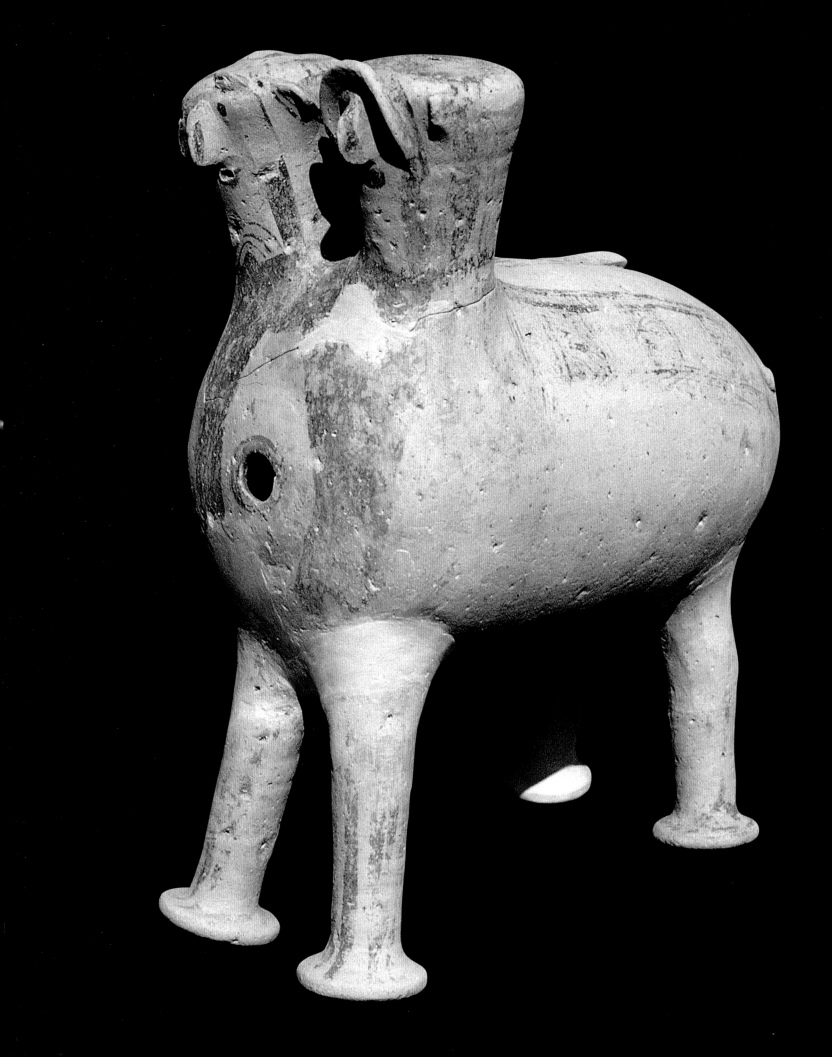

The Late Bronze Age

V. From the Late Cypriote IIIB to the End of the Cypro-Geometric I Period (1100–950/900 B.C.)

1. The Creation of Independent Kingdoms

The cultural changes that occurred at the beginning of the twelfth century B.C. had a profound effect on Cypriote society and prepared it for the next step of its evolution, which was realized in LC IIIB. The economic prosperity of Cyprus during the twelfth century B.C., with the development of metallurgy and other arts and crafts, has already been emphasized. The social field saw the emergence of an aristocratic elite that brought new and higher standards of living: new styles in architecture, the use of bathrooms and bathtubs, the use of painted pottery imitating Aegean prototypes, the introduction of new weapons and objects of personal use. In the meantime the Aegean was going through a period of social disruption and poverty, but Cyprus does not seem to have been affected in any way; rather, there was continuity and prosperity (Muhly 1999), and contacts with the Levantine coast were never broken.

This continuity, however, was disrupted around 1100 B.C., and a new era began, which we refer to as LC IIIB. Almost all the towns that had been rebuilt at the beginning of LC IIIA were abandoned. The population of Enkomi, near the east coast, shifted further to the east, where a town was built around a natural harbor on the bay of Salamis; Sinda, Alassa, and Hala Sultan Tekke were also abandoned. Maa-*Palaeokastro* was destroyed by fire soon after its establishment, about 1175 B.C.; it was rebuilt on a smaller scale and finally abandoned before the end of LC IIIA, circa 1150 B.C. Pyla-*Kokkinokremos*, built at the end of LC IIC, was abandoned soon after its establishment, at the very beginning of the twelfth century B.C. Its inhabitants fled suddenly, obviously in the face of an imminent danger, leaving behind them treasures that they hid but never returned to retrieve. Only Kition and Palaepaphos were unaffected by destruction, continuing their existence uninterrupted. Toward circa 1000 B.C., however, the northernmost part of the town of Kition (the Area II excavation area), which was in the vicinity of the inner harbor, was abandoned, and the town shifted to the south. This may have been instigated by the silting up of the navigable channel that connected the town with the sea, perhaps after a physical disaster (an earthquake?); the same phenomenon may have affected the inner harbor of Enkomi (see also pp. 58-59).

What caused the disruption of LC IIIA? Perhaps after almost a century of cohabitation, the new ethnic element that had arrived in Cyprus from the Aegean began to feel uneasy in their relations with the local population. As a result of the prosperous conditions on the island, more Greeks may have been tempted to emigrate to Cyprus circa 1100 B.C. to join the already existing Aegean population. This new wave of immigrants must have strengthened the Greek population considerably, to the extent that they felt confident of their political power and were encouraged to break from the native population and establish themselves in new towns (see Steel 1993). These were destined to become the ten kingdoms (independent city-states) of the island. Not only is there plentiful archaeological evidence about this new development, but there are also mythical traditions about the founding of cities in Cyprus by Greek heroes after the end of the Trojan War. Thus, for example, Teucer, the son of Telamon, the king of the island of Salamis, near Attica, was said to have built the city of Salamis, on the east coast near Enkomi; Agapenor, the king of Tegea, built Palaepaphos; Praxandros from Laconia built Lapithos; and so on. As well as the new sites of settlements there were also new burial grounds (cf. Catling 1994, Reyes 1994, 12, n. 7, 137; Iacovou 1999b, 148). The problem of the foundation legends and their interpretation has been discussed by many scholars. Some believe that these stories were put about for purposes of propaganda (see discussion by Catling 1975, 215–216; Iacovou 1999a, 9–10, with previous bibliography). Others have accepted, however, that behind each myth there is some "historical" reality, in some cases substantiated by the archaeological record, as for example in the cases of Salamis and Palaepaphos (see below).

There is further an allusion to a kind of separation among the two ethnic elements of the population of

238. A zoomorphic vase of Proto-White Painted ware, in the shape of a bicephalic "centaur." From Enkomi (French Mission, 1969), no. 40, "Centaur B" from the Sanctuary of the Ingot God. Height: 31cm.; length: 25.5cm. Cyprus Museum, Nicosia. This creature has been identified as a centaur, but others prefer to call it a sphinx. Similar monsters have been found on Crete, at Ayia Triadha. They may be associated with fertility. The body is decorated in the style of Proto-White Painted pottery. The influence no doubt derives from Crete. There were other influences (artistic and religious) from Crete circa 1100 B.C., the period to which this object is dated. A second, but fragmentary, "centaur" was found at the same spot.

239

240

239. Vase of Proto-White Painted ware, in the form of a warship. Cyprus Museum, Nicosia, Inv. no. 1943/V-29/1. Length: 28.2cm. The surface is covered with painted geometric patterns.

240. Vase of Proto-White Painted ware, in the form of a warship. From Lapithos, Tomb 74, no. 108. Cyprus Museum, Nicosia. Length: 27cm. The surface is covered with painted geometric patterns. Long and swift warships were no doubt used to bring the Achaean immigrants to Cyprus and other places where they settled at the end of the Late Bronze Age.

Cyprus in the myths about Agapenor and Kinyras, the former representing the Achaeans of Cyprus, the latter the indigenous population. In any case we believe that it was in the eleventh century B.C. that the new kingdoms were created in a political system based on Mycenaean kingship but adapted to local conditions and to the models of oriental principates (but cf. Petit 1991–92). To quote from a lecture given by Anthony Snodgrass in Nicosia in 1987 (Snodgrass 1988):

"As the Bronze Age drew to its close, successive waves of settlers from Mycenaean Greece (and probably Minoan Crete as well) came to Cyprus, establishing Greek as the dominant language of the island, and bringing certain other features of their culture with them as well. One of these features was certainly their political system: a network of warlike monarchies, each usually centered on a fortified

citadel, with the king called by the title of wanax, and performing a leading religious role as well as his political one. Modifications took place, as always happens when people transplant their culture to a new setting—just as modern Athenians emigrating to Cyprus must learn to drive to the left...For the Achaean kings, settlements in Cyprus offered some opportunities to enhance their wealth and self-glorification" (Snodgrass 1988, 12; cf. skepticism expressed by Maier 1999, 83).

Cyprus found itself in an extremely privileged position, which prescribed its historical destiny: the island became the guardian of Mycenaean civilization, which was threatened with dissolution and oblivion: "It fell to Cyprus to shelter the remains of Mycenaean civilization, including its political structure, aspects of its language, traces of its writing and much of its visual art, long after its complete disappearance from the Greek mainland" (Catling 1975, 213). Several scholars have tried to explain this new development in the political and social life of Cyprus. No doubt Iacovou is right when she says that "the coexistence of dissimilar ethnic elements in LC IIIA must have been a fragile affair and the destruction levels observed at LC IIIA sites...reflect a turbulent phase and an unstable political and economic substratum" (Iacovou 1989, 53; see also Karageorghis 1992). She concludes that "the Greek-speaking successors of the 'Mycenaeans' appear to be closely associated with the dissolution of the old political system and the foundation of new seats of power in the eleventh century B.C. Their supremacy over the indigenous population may have led some of the latter to withdraw to separate enclaves, like Amathus" (Iacovou 1989, 57; see also eadem 1999a, 6–7). Perhaps it is not quite correct to speak of supremacy. The Cypriots had a highly developed culture; they were rich and literate. It is more precise to speak about a different cultural background, a conscious feeling of common ethnicity and common language that united the Greeks who fled to Cyprus (cf. Iacovou 1999a, 2–3). They certainly profited economically from the possibilities that Cyprus offered, but in the cultural field they may have given more than they received.

Catling gives a dramatic account as to how the LC IIIA period ended and what led to the inauguration of LC IIIB, rightly stressing that those who were responsible for the transition were not exclusively Aegean based:

"I think we could explain the LC IIIA/LC IIIB transition as an extended period of urban breakdown during which Cyprus was the target of a series of uncoordinated attacks or incursions by bands of raiders whose ethnicity was largely, but not exclusively, Aegean-based. I suggest they plagued Cyprus on and off for half a century; individual groups descended on first one, then another of the old townships. In some cases such bands attempted to settle, usually, choosing a location distinct from but close to the old town. New burial grounds were opened. The lives of some of these new sites were of brief duration; either the community fell victim in its turn to violence, or chose to move on, even to return whence years before they had come. Finally, a number of these communities took root, handing on their language and, perhaps, their political structure to descendants who became rulers and ruled of some, at least, of the island's city-kingdoms" (Catling 1994, 137).

2. Cultural Changes

Some aspects of the material culture of eleventh-century-B.C. Cyprus, especially the pottery, demonstrate that Levantine elements should not be underestimated in the formation of this culture (cf. Bikai 1994). It is not easy to say whether there were already Levantines or "Proto-Phoenicians" in the eleventh century B.C. population of Cyprus. However, judging from the frequent occurrence of Levantine pottery on the island, it is certain that trade relations with Syro-Palestine never ceased.

It is often asked why we do not have any Greek imports during the eleventh century B.C. (cf., e.g., Maier 1999, 83). Some scholars have been reluctant to accept the arrival of Greeks in Cyprus at this time. In a recently published book the question is put rather bluntly, suggesting that the cultural innovations were due to an initiative of the Cypriots themselves:

"Whether or not the chamber tombs and the inscription (on the obelos of Opheltas) really testify to the arrival of a new population, it does seem fairly clear that they represent the active attempts on the part of a certain group on Cyprus to establish links with the Greek mainland. What is interesting, however, is that the scope of such signaling is not extended to the ceramic medium: the pottery deposited in the chamber tombs is decorated in the indigenous Proto-White Painted style of Cyprus" (Hall 1997, 136; cf. also skepticism expressed by Maier 1999, 83).

It is, therefore, necessary to analyze in detail the material culture of Cyprus during the eleventh century B.C. in order to elucidate this problem (for a general survey see Snodgrass 1994).

Whether the newcomers are called raiders or refugees seeking to settle in a new home, it is clear at any rate that those who came from the Aegean must have come to the island in organized groups, with aristocratic leaders who could afford to arrange their transport in warships during a period when piracy made traveling in the Mediterranean difficult. This may explain the scarcity of Aegean goods on the island in the eleventh century B.C. (and indeed the twelfth century B.C. as well). Not much could be loaded in the long, shallow warships, which were swift but quite unsuitable for heavy cargo. That such Aegean warships were known to the Cypriots and the Aegeans who settled on the island early in the eleventh century B.C. is evident from a number of askoi in the form of warships in Proto-White Painted ware found in Cyprus (Basch 1987, 148–149).

The settlement sites of the eleventh century B.C. are not very well known, but our information about the topography of this period is adequately supplemented with information from cemeteries (for a general survey see Iacovou 1994).

i. Funerary architecture

The largest LC IIIB cemetery excavated so far is that of Gastria-*Alaas*, northeast of Salamis, where the

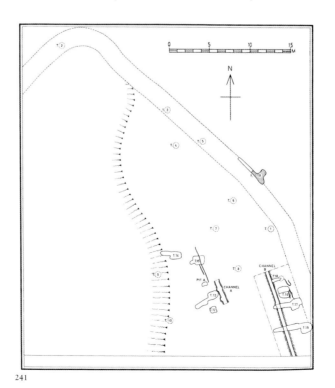

241

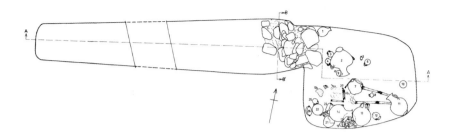

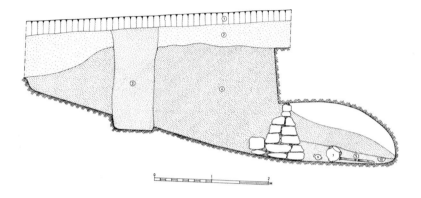

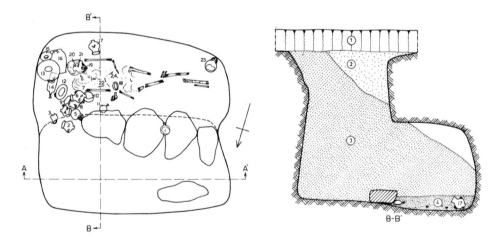

B-B'

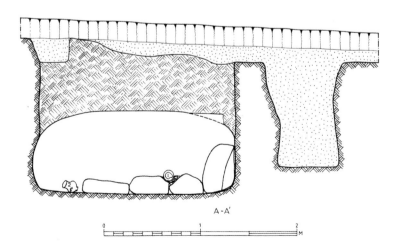

A-A'

present writer excavated nine tombs on behalf of the Cyprus Department of Antiquities in 1973–74. Material from other looted tombs was later detected in private collections and has already been published (Karageorghis 1975; idem 1977b). Apart from three tombs that were without a dromos, tombs excavated at *Alaas* had a small chamber and a long narrow dromos, very different from the traditional chamber tombs of the Late Bronze Age. Thus, not only are there new cemeteries in the eleventh century B.C. but also new types of tombs. It is significant that in the vicinity of *Alaas*, at the site of *Grotirin*, about 1km southeast of *Alaas*, a number of Late Cypriote II chamber rock-cut tombs of the traditional type were traced (they had all been looted). This means that prior to the use of the LC IIIB cemetery of *Alaas* there was an earlier cemetery and, obviously, an earlier town at *Grotirin*. Both town and cemetery shifted elsewhere, to *Alaas*, in the eleventh century, a phenomenon that may be paralleled by the move from Enkomi to Salamis, as we shall see below. The long narrow dromos slopes toward the chamber. At *Alaas* the walls of the dromos narrow upward, especially near the façade.

The stomion often has the same width as the dromos and is blocked with a pile of rubble. The dromos and the stomion usually do not have the same axis as the chamber. Similar tombs are found in the Aegean, at sites such as Perati, but particularly in Crete, from the beginning of the Late Minoan III period (for a recent discussion see Andreadaki-Vlasaki 1997, 495–498). This type of tomb was brought to Cyprus fully developed, as Catling pointed out (Catling 1994, 134).

The other type of tomb that appeared at *Alaas* (Tomb 16) and during the CGI–II period at Lapithos was the so-called pit-cave. The main characteristics of this tomb are a vertically cut rectangular shaft and an adjacent chamber along the side of the shaft. The shaft is separated from the chamber by a screening wall of rubble stones.

The same type also appeared in LM III Crete, in the cemeteries of Khania and Knossos. In the publication of the cemetery of *Alaas* we suggested that this type of tomb was probably an adaptation of local Cypriote traditions. Hallager and McGeorge (1992, 45), commenting on this type of tomb as it appears at Khania and Knossos, suggested a Cypriote origin, while Catling (1994, 135) recently proposed that this is an Aegean type of tomb, a suggestion to which

244

245

we now subscribe. At Zapher Papoura (Evans 1906, 15–21, figs. 11a, b, and c) this type appeared as early as the LM IIIA2 period. The pit-cave might also be compared with a type occurring at Perati in Greece in the twelfth century B.C. (Iakovides 1970, 24–25), for which, however, Catling proposes a different ancestry.

At Knossos, the pit-cave also appears in the eleventh century B.C. for the interment of cremated remains, which makes the connection with the *Alaas* tomb even more direct (Catling 1994, 135; for recently excavated pit-caves at Khania see Andreadaki-Vlasaki 1997, 498–499).

All the burials at *Alaas* were inhumations, with no traces of incineration. There was only one skeleton in each chamber, with one exception, Tomb 17, where there were two. The tomb-gifts were mainly pottery, but gold and bronze objects were also found in some tombs.

ii. Pottery

The largest proportion of the pottery of *Alaas* was of the Proto-White Painted and Proto-Bichrome wares (the latter with a decoration of black and red painted motifs on a light surface). The forms and decoration are predominantly Aegean, particularly Cretan, but there are also other examples that have Levantine affinities or follow local traditions. The new Aegean shapes include the straight-sided pyxis, the kalathos, the stirrup jar, and the kylix. The cylindrical bottle or jug, however, may have Levantine prototypes (cf. Karageorghis 1975, 51; Yon 1971, 32). The decorative motifs are predominantly geometric, of an Aegean character; there are occasional pictorial compositions of an Aegean-Minoan character (cf. Kanta 1998, 55–56; Karageorghis 1997a). An interesting ceramic form is the bird-shaped askos, which had an Aegean predecessor. Although it was also popular in Cypriote ceramics of the Bronze Age, in its new form it was influenced by the Aegean (cf. Lemos 1994). The same applies to a number of other zoomorphic askoi, which also appeared in the tombs of *Alaas*.

The Aegean connection, mainly with Crete and the Dodecanese, has recently been emphasized (Kourou 1997). The discovery of three lentoid flasks of Levantine type in the tombs of *Alaas* is significant (Karageorghis 1975, 57), especially because it is not only a local phenomenon at *Alaas* but also appeared a few years later at other sites such as Salamis, Kourion, and Palaepaphos (painted variety) in the CG IA period (Bikai 1983, 400).

242. Plan and section of *Alaas* Tomb 19 (after Karageorghis 1975, pl. LI).

243. Plan and section of pit-cave 16 from *Alaas* (after Karageorghis 1975, pl. XLVIII).

244. Zoomorphic askos of Proto-White Painted ware, from *Alaas*, Hadjiprodromou Collection, Famagusta. Height: 32cm. The biconical body rests on a high stem and is decorated all over with painted geometric patterns.

245. Pyxis of Proto-Bichrome ware, from *Alaas* Tomb 16, no. 16 (excavations of the Cyprus Department of Antiquities). Height: 23cm. Cyprus Museum, Nicosia. The surface is decorated in black and purple paint with horizontal zones filled with geometric motifs. There is also a stylized floral motif. The form of the vase imitates Cretan prototypes.

246

246. Female figurine from the waist upward, broken off from the rim of a kalathos (?) of Proto-White Painted ware, from *Alaas*, in the Hadjiprodromou Collection, Famagusta. Height: 13.2cm. Both arms are raised to the head in a mourning pose. Red paint for facial characteristics and breasts. This figurine closely resembles the so-called pleureuses (mourning women) from the Aegean. Imitations appear also in Palestine.

247. Two large stirrup jars of Proto-White Painted ware, from the necropolis of *Alaas* (excavations of the Cyprus Department of Antiquities), Tomb 15, no. 10 (on the left), height: 34.5cm. and Tomb 19, no. 13 (on the right), height: 40cm. Both the shape and decoration imitate Aegean pottery of the eleventh century B.C., a time when a number of cultural and political influences from the Aegean, particularly from Crete, are encountered in Cyprus. The tombs in which these vases were found have all the characteristics of Mycenaean funerary architecture.

248. Bird-shaped askos of Proto-White Painted ware, from Salamis (French Mission), Tomb 1, no. 107. Height: 9.5cm.; length: 24.9cm. Famagusta District Museum (this museum is now inaccessible since the occupation of Famagusta by the Turkish Army in 1974). The surface is decorated symmetrically with painted geometric patterns. Bird-shaped askoi of this type were of Aegean inspiration.

249. Lentoid flask of White Painted Levantine ware, from *Alaas* (excavations of the Cyprus Department of Antiquities), Tomb 15, no. 13. Cyprus Museum, Nicosia. Height: 16cm. Concentric circles of matt orange paint around body, vertically arranged on either side of body. Similar imported flasks have been found at Salamis, at Kourion, and elsewhere.

No doubt this is because of trade, which continued uninterrupted during the eleventh century B.C., as new evidence, particularly from Palaepaphos-*Skales*, demonstrates (see below).

The Late Cypriote IIIB material culture was homogeneous throughout Cyprus: tomb architecture, burial customs, pottery styles, and so on. This new cultural scenario common to the whole island tends to suggest that there was no geographical division of the two ethnic groups living on the island (immigrant Greeks and local Cypriots) (for the case of Amathus see below). The Greeks, however, as will be seen, not only preserved their own language but gradually imposed it on almost the whole island.

iii. The sites

We may now examine the case of a few of the eleventh century B.C. sites, especially those for which there are associated foundation legends, beginning with Salamis, on the east coast.

247

248

249

a. Salamis and Enkomi

Salamis, according to a number of Greek texts (see Chavane and Yon 1978) was founded by Teucer, son of Telamon, king of the island of Salamis, on his return from Troy at the end of the Trojan War. His ancestry is peculiar: he is recorded as Greek (son of Telamon) but at the same time as a "barbarian" (son of Laomedon, the king of Troy), related to the Teucrians of the Troad, who are related to the Tjekker of the "Sea Peoples." Thus, behind the legend of the foundation at Salamis may lie the distant memory of the arrival of the first Aegean settlers at the nearby town of Enkomi around 1200 B.C.

The French mission excavating at Salamis in 1965 revealed a tomb with a long narrow dromos and a rectangular chamber. It contained a rich variety of pottery of Proto-White Painted and Cypro-Geometric IA ware as well as jewelry and bronzes. Traces of the actual settlement of the same period (mid-eleventh century B.C.) were also found: in a trial trench that reached the bedrock was pottery of the eleventh century B.C., and elsewhere the course of the fortification wall of the new city was discovered. The earliest pottery from this trench includes Proto-White Painted ware, but since it has not been published in detail it is impossible to be sure of an exact date for this earliest phase of Salamis (see Yon 1980a, 75–77, where she suggests that the foundation of Salamis may date to the first half of the eleventh century B.C.; see also Yon 1999a for a mid-eleventh-century date. The writer would prefer the mid-eleventh century B.C. in view of the evidence from Tomb I). Thus it is certain that by the middle of the eleventh century B.C. a new town had been built around the natural harbor of the Bay of Salamis; it was fortified with a wall, and its cemetery was placed *extra muros*. From the richness of the tomb-gifts of the only tomb that has been excavated, it is clear that the population of the new town was wealthy and enjoyed a high standard of living. No doubt it was here that the Mycenaean aristocrats settled who had previously inhabited the nearby Late Bronze Age town of Enkomi, which was abandoned at about this time.

It is significant that, even after its abandonment, Enkomi did not disappear altogether. In one sanctuary, that of the Ingot God (described above), the cult lingered on for a few more decades. The offerings discovered in this sanctuary include anthropomorphic figurines of the well-known "Goddess with uplifted

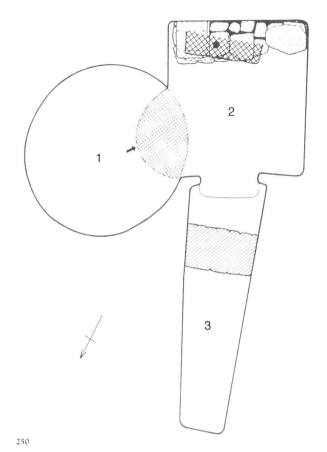

250. Salamis Tomb I (French Mission) (after Yon 1971, pl. 7).
Legend
1. trench ; 2. chamber; 3. *dromos*.

250

arms" type, wearing a tiara and decorated with spots on her cheeks. The most important discoveries of this late period in the life of the sanctuary are two fragmentary terra-cotta representations of bicephalic centaurs or sphinxes. They are hollow with wheel-made body and legs, and their surface is decorated with abstract motifs in the technique of Proto-White Painted ware; the best-preserved example is 31cm. high. The figurines have a striking similarity to ones found at Ayia Triadha on Crete (D'Agata 1997 and 1999, 69). The pottery that is associated with this last phase in the life of the sanctuary is the early phase of Proto-White Painted ware, dating before the establishment of a new town and a new cemetery at Salamis (Iacovou 1988, 1). I believe that Salamis was already a kingdom in the eleventh century B.C., like other towns that were inhabited in the eleventh century. It is no accident that these sites are mentioned in Near Eastern texts in later periods as the independent kingdoms of Cyprus (see below).

b. Palaepaphos

Palaepaphos (modern Kouklia) is no doubt the best-documented site of the eleventh century B.C. It is unfortunate that, as at many other sites of this period, our evidence comes solely from tombs. These were excavated as early as 1888 and 1889 by the British Museum and later by the British Mission of the University of St. Andrews and the Liverpool Museums (for references see Karageorghis 1967c, 2; Maier and Karageorghis 1984, 120–150; Maier 1999; notes on the more recent excavations appear in *BCH* 124 [2000], 673-675, 690-692). The tombs provide tangible proof for continuity at Palaepaphos from the Late Bronze Age to the Cypro-Geometric and later periods, though the topography of the cemeteries, occupying a large area east of the sanctuary of Aphrodite and also west of the village of Kouklia, at site *Plakes* (one mile from the village), raises questions concerning the exact location of the eleventh century B.C. town, and why the eleventh century occupation is so dispersed.

In 1967 the present writer published the contents of a tomb found by looters at the site of *Xerolimni*, northeast of the village of Kouklia. It yielded a rich variety of pottery of Proto-White Painted ware dating to the transition between LC IIIB and CG IA (Karageorghis 1967c; Iacovou 1988, 1), about the middle of the eleventh century B.C. The tomb yielded also a lentoid flask of Levantine origin (Karageorghis 1967c, 20, no. 17). But undoubtedly the most important vase in this tomb is a kalathos of Proto-White Painted ware (in fact Proto-Bichrome), decorated outside and inside with geometric and pictorial motifs. The latter include birds, a warrior lyre-player, a hunting scene, and "frogs" (for a discussion of the pictorial compositions see Iacovou 1988, 72, 81–82). In a recently published paper Kanta very ingeniously

251

252

253

252-253. Kalathos of Proto-White Painted ware, from Palaepaphos-Xerolimni, Tomb 1, no. 7. Height: 15cm.; diam.: 27cm. Kouklia Site Museum. The interior is decorated with pictorial compositions within rectangular panels. These include a lyre-player, a goat near an altar, and birds. The exterior is decorated with vertical narrow panels filled alternatingly with "human" figures (frogmen) and linear motifs. The influence of Cretan iconography in the decoration of the interior is very strong, illustrating the close cultural relations between the two islands during the eleventh century B.C.

compared the hunting scene on the Palaepaphos kalathos with a strikingly similar scene of Cretan iconography. On a pyxis or chest from Kastelli Pediada (Rethemiotakis 1997a and 1997b) there is a pictorial composition that very much recalls the hunting scene on the *Xerolimni* kalathos: the hunting of a goat and its subsequent sacrifice on an altar; the two episodes are depicted in the same composition. The scene is quite characteristic of the Cretan pictorial style of the Late Minoan III period (Kanta 1998, 55–56). We may now interpret the scene on the *Xerolimni* kalathos correctly as a goat standing on a sacrificial table. In front is a tree motif, as on the vase from Kastelli Pediada. Kanta rightly mentions yet another rare Proto-White Painted vase from Cyprus, decorated with a goat, a bird, and a human figure holding a kylix and a round shield, and stresses the goat-bird symbolism on Cretan larnakes depicting a sacred hunt. Birds also appear on the interior of the *Xerolimni* kalathos. It is not improbable that the lyre-player warrior, the goat, and the birds and the tree of the *Xerolimni* kalathos form part of the sacred hunt and that the painter placed them separately in four panels, the elements of which composed the sacred hunting scene: the hunter and the goat on the altar, the birds, the lyre-player (equivalent to the kylix holder on the pyxis mentioned above), and the tree motif. Kanta is no doubt right that instead of regarding the animals in silhouette appearing in the eleventh-century-B.C. pictorial vase painting in Cyprus as of Syrian origin, a Cretan parentage should be considered, as also shown by a number of

other elements in the eleventh century B.C. culture of Cyprus (cf. also Karageorghis 1997a).

There are two other vases with a pictorial decoration that are of interest and may have religious connotations. The first is a White Painted I (CG I) footed bowl in a private collection, undoubtedly from Palaepaphos (Iacovou 1988, cat. no. 24), decorated with two human figures and birds. One of the human figures wears what we interpret as a horned helmet, recalling the Horned God of Enkomi of the very end of the 13th century B.C. (Maier and Karageorghis 1984, 129, fig. 108). The other vase is a rhyton in the form of a horse with a rider, and snakes, most likely from Palaepaphos, now in the Ashmolean Museum, Oxford (Catling 1974). Catling interpreted the rhyton as representing "the dead man himself, setting out on his journey to the next world, with the snakes that remind us of immortality, accompanied by a pack horse that brings his sustenance for the journey" (ibid., 111).

Of all the cemetery sites of Palaepaphos, the best known and most fully published is that of *Skales*, to the southeast of the village of Kouklia. The Department of Antiquities conducted a major salvage excavation at this site in 1979–80 (Karageorghis 1983). Several of the tombs date to circa 1050 B.C. (Cypro-Geometric IA), although many were also used slightly later, in CG IB.

The eleventh century B.C. tombs are chamber tombs carved in soft calcareous or marly rock. They have a roughly rectangular chamber and a long narrow dromos of the type discussed above. There is consistency

254

255

254. Pyxis of Proto-White Painted
ware. Cyprus Museum, Nicosia,
Inv. no. 1968/V-30/113. Height:
13.4cm. It is decorated with a
human figure holding a kylix,
a goat, and a bird, probably
elements from a sacrificial scene.
Both the iconography and the
shape of the vase betray strong
Cretan influences.

255. Footed bowl of White
Painted I ware, from Palaepaphos-
Hassan Agha, now in a private
collection. Height: 17.9cm.; diam.:
21.1cm. The main body of the
vase between the handles on
both sides is divided by vertical
lines into rectangular panels
filled with pictorial motifs and
geometric patterns. Among the
pictorial motifs on one side we
see in the middle a nude (?) male
figure with raised arms, wearing a
horned headdress (a reminiscence
of the Horned God of Enkomi?), a
horned animal and its offspring (?),
and a long-legged bird. On the
other side there is only one human
figure in the middle; the other
panels are filled with geometric
patterns. This vase dates to the
late Cypro-Geometric I period,
when the pictorial style became
more firmly established.

256

in the orientation (northeast–southwest, with the dromos on the southwest), but this may not be significant; it was probably dictated by the inclination of the ground surface. The 3–4m. of collapsed soil and rock above the tomb floors saved their contents from the activities of looters.

The tombs are generally family tombs and were used for more than one burial. Whenever there was a new burial in a chamber, the skeletal remains of the previous burial would be swept aside or placed in a large amphora together with the associated small or valuable tomb-gifts. The dead were usually interred, but there are two instances of cremation, the incinerated remains having been placed in large amphorae. Cremation was very rare in eleventh century B.C. Cyprus, but it also occurred at the cemetery of Kourion-*Kaloriziki*. The practice may have been introduced by immigrants from the Aegean (Masson 1988).

The tomb-gifts usually included vases, with miniature vessels for infants. Weapons (swords, daggers, spearheads) were deposited for men, and fibulae, pins, and jewelry for women. The pottery was mostly of White Painted I ware, but there were also survivals of Proto-White Painted and Proto-Bichrome wares, mainly drinking cups but with various unusual forms also occurring. There was also an impressive amount of bronze vessels, bowls, and basins. These tomb-gifts are characteristic of a wealthy military aristocracy, enjoying the luxuries of life (eating and drinking) that their status allowed.

One of the most important tombs in the cemetery of *Skales* is Tomb 49; it was a family tomb of a Mycenaean aristocrat (cf. Coldstream 1989, 325–328) with remains of at least three individuals. It contained a bathtub of white chalk that was found filled with gravel, with pottery at the top. It is elliptical in shape, measuring 153cm. in total length with a maximum height of 73cm. The bottom is slightly raised at one end to provide a seat. Near the rim on the left-hand side of the raised seat is a half bowl-shaped projection carved out of the same block, which may have served to hold the "soap" or ointments of that time. The occurrence of a bathtub in a tomb is significant. This was not used as a sarcophagus, as the skeletons were lying on the floor; it may have been offered to the deceased as a luxury possession in which to take his or her bath in the next life, or it may have been connected with some purification ritual. A clay bathtub was found in a CG IA tomb excavated at Kourion-*Bamboula* (Christou 1994, 180), and two others

were uncovered in the recently excavated cemetery site at Palaepaphos-*Plakes* (see below).

The most important object found in Tomb 49 is undoubtedly one of three bronze obeloi (skewers) measuring 87.2cm. in length. On one side, near the socket, there is an engraved inscription of five signs in the Palaepaphian syllabic script, which represents a Greek proper name in the genitive: "(I am the obelos of) Ὀφέλτας." The genitive is given as O.pe.le.ta.u. In the common Mycenaean dialect the genitive would end in -o; the -u ending is a characteristic of the Arcadian dialect (Masson and Masson 1983). This is important, since the inscription on the obelos provides the earliest use not only of the Greek language in Cyprus but, more specifically, of the Arcadian dialect. We have already referred to legendary traditions, according to which Agapenor, King of Tegea, who came to the island after the end of the Trojan War, was regarded as the founder of Paphos. He and his fellow Greeks were no doubt responsible for the cultural innovations at Palaepaphos and formed part of the aristocratic elite who

256. Rhyton in the form of a horse with a rider, probably from Palaepaphos, of Proto-White Painted ware. Ashmolean Museum, Oxford. Inv. no. 1971.858. Height: 22.7cm.; length: 37.2cm.

257. Site plan of the excavated area at the necropolis of Palaepaphos-*Skales* (after Karageorghis 1983, pl. II).

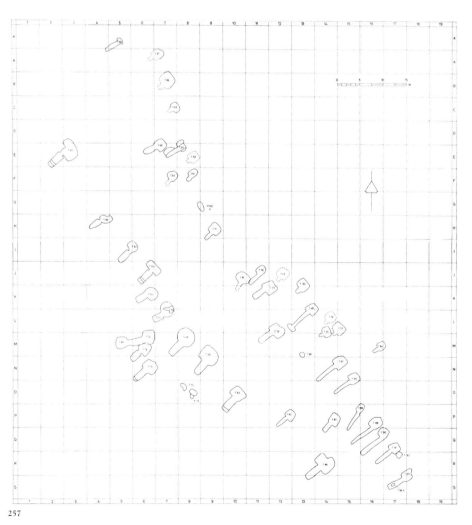

257

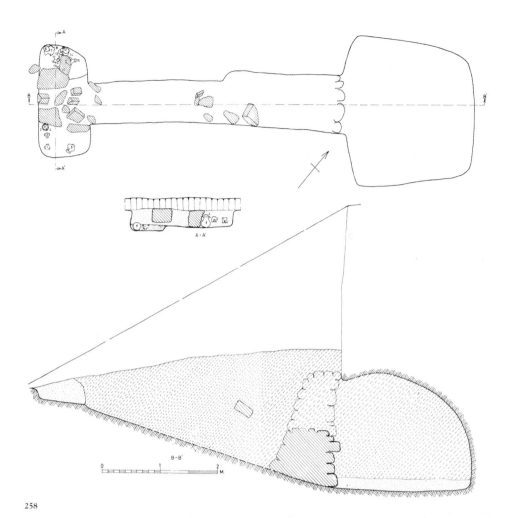

enjoyed a high standard of living, including "dinner parties" with eating and drinking.

The importance of the obelos of Opheltes is far-reaching. It helps to identify the eleventh century settlers of Palaepaphos and shows their loyalty to their own language and dialect, despite the fact that they found themselves in a non-Greek-speaking country. They adopted the Cypro-Minoan script to suit their Greek language, creating the beginnings of what was to survive down to the third century B.C. as the Cypriote syllabic script. It is interesting to note that the transition from the Cypro-Minoan script to the Cypriote syllabic script must have taken a few years to achieve and that this must have been the invention of one person among the aristocratic elite (cf. Hall 1997, 136; Iacovou 1999a, 11–13).

Several unique large bronze bowls were retrieved from Tomb 49. One is hemispherical with a rounded base and two opposed horizontal raised loop handles with a goat protome at the top, facing inward. Another large bronze bowl with a hemispherical body, rounded base, sharply angular shoulder, and upright collared rim has two opposed vertical ring handles. Also noteworthy are a silver fibula of the D-type with two gold bead bosses and numerous D-

258

258. Plan and section of Palaepaphos-*Skales,* Tomb 48 (after Karageorghis 1983, fig. IV).

259. Bathtub of white limestone from Palaepaphos-*Skales* (excavations of the Cyprus Department of Antiquities), Tomb 49, no. 198. Total length at the top, from rim to rim: 153cm.; height: 73cm. It was carved out of one single monolith. There are three pairs of projections, or "reel ornaments," along the upper part, below the rim. Near one of the short sides is a bowl-shaped projection, obviously for the substance that was used as "soap," perhaps ashes and oil. Inside, the floor is raised at one end to provide a seat. There are several bathtubs from Cyprus, found in tombs, sanctuaries, and houses, from the twelfth and eleventh centuries B.C., in both limestone and terra-cotta. This one did not serve as a sarcophagus but was placed in the tomb for purification purposes. It was found containing pottery.

259

260

262

261

263

260. Large bronze bowl from Palaepaphos-*Skales* (excavations of the Cyprus Department of Antiquities), Tomb 49, no. 1. Height: 20cm.; diam.: 37.1cm. Cyprus Museum, Nicosia. Hemispherical body. Two opposed horizontal upturned loop handles on body below rim, with a goat protome at the top facing inward. There were several bronze bowls of different sizes in the tombs from Palaepaphos-*Skales;* their handles are usually decorated with lotus flowers.

261. Large bronze bowl from Palaepaphos-*Skales* (excavations of the Cyprus Department of Antiquities), Tomb 49, no. 2. Height (without handles): 16.5cm.; diam.: 32.5cm. Two opposed vertical ring handles at the rim. Cyprus Museum, Nicosia.

262-263. The inscription on a bronze obelos from Palaepaphos-*Skales* (excavations of the Cyprus Department of Antiquities), Tomb 49, no. 16. The inscription, in the Cypriote syllabary, reads, from left to right, "of Opheltes," a genitive of a Greek proper name. This is the earliest evidence we have for the use of the Greek language in Cyprus (Cypro-Geometric I period). Two other bronze obeloi were found in the same tomb (nos. 17 and 18). The longest, no. 16, is 87.2cm. long. No. 17 measures 86.5cm. and no. 18 measures 76.5cm. Cyprus Museum, Nicosia. They are rectangular in section and have a tubular socket at one end for a wooden handle. In later periods obeloi are of iron (e.g., from Salamis Tomb 79).

shaped fibulae, the largest measuring 10.5cm. Fibulae of this type must have been introduced by the Greek settlers; previously Cypriote women used toggle pins to fasten their clothing. Two bronze strainers also come from this tomb; they formed part of drinking sets. The *Skales* tombs also yielded bronze rod tripod stands as well as imitations of them in clay and a bronze tripod cauldron.

The pottery found in Tomb 49 is extraordinary. It includes large amphorae of White Painted I ware; jugs, bowls, cups, and dishes of the same ware; and stemmed drinking cups (kylikes) of a form that had been more fashionable during the Mycenaean period. Remarkable is a jug of Proto-White Painted ware decorated with a human face at the top of the mouth. The chin is perforated, forming a strainer. A similar vase of White Painted I ware was found in another tomb and was obviously produced in the same workshop. Similar anthropomorphic vases have been found at Knossos and Arkadhes on Crete, but of a slightly later period (cf. Kanta 1998, 52).

Other remarkable vases found in other tombs at this site include some extraordinary askoi and a trick vase of a type also known from an eleventh century B.C.

tomb at Kition (this Kition tomb also contained bronze obeloi).

Finally, we should mention a White Painted I plate, from a rich family tomb of a Mycenaean aristocrat (Karageorghis 1998f, cat. no. 12), the base of which is decorated with an ambitious pictorial composition. It consists of two human figures trying to kill a large two-headed monster (a snake?) with arrows and daggers; there are other quadrupeds in the background. This is no doubt an effort by the vase painter to represent a specific theme, perhaps a myth. As Greek mythology must still have been fresh in the minds of these early inhabitants of Palaepaphos, it is permissible to recall the myth of Hercules and Iolaos killing the snake of Lerna. If this interpretation is correct, this is one of the first and most ambitious representations in the early Iron Age vase painting of Cyprus (cf. Hermary 1992, 131).

The appearance of Levantine imports at Palaepaphos from the eleventh century B.C. onward is significant (Bikai 1983). It shows that trade with the Levant, which had flourished during the Late Bronze Age, continued, and this may have been one of the causes of the wealth of Palaepaphos during this period. We

127

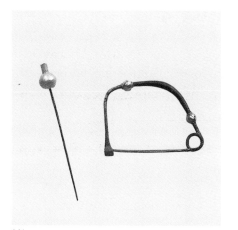

264. Jewelry from Palaepaphos-*Skales* (excavations of the Cyprus Department of Antiquities). On the left a silver pin with a pomegranate head made of a thin sheet of gold. Length: 10.8cm. From Tomb 79, no. 53. Cypro-Geometric II period. On the right a silver D-shaped fibula from Tomb 49, no. 13. Length: 7.5cm. It has a gold barrel-shaped bead boss on spring-arm and bow. The tomb dates to the Cypro-Geometric I period. Kouklia Site Museum.

265. Bronze strainer from Palaepaphos-*Skales* (excavations of the Cyprus Department of Antiquities), Tomb 49, no. 9. Height: 6.5cm.; diam.: 22cm. Kouklia Site Museum. It has a sunken hemispherical sieve and two opposed horizontal loop handles. Bronze strainers are not uncommon in the Cypro-Geometric I period; they formed parts of wine sets.

266. Bronze tripod cauldron, from Palaepaphos-*Skales* (excavations of the Cyprus Department of Antiquities), Tomb 58, no. 37. Height: 30.4cm.; diam.: 35cm. Cyprus Museum, Nicosia. Two opposed horizontal loop handles. Such cauldrons are very rare outside Greece, and only two have so far been recorded from Cyprus.

267. Bronze rod tripod from Palaepaphos-*Skales* (excavations of the Cyprus Department of Antiquities), Tomb 58, no. 31, Height: 30.3cm. diam. of ring: 21.4cm. Cyprus Museum, Nicosia. The ring is decorated with a frieze of thin, vertically arranged opposed spirals in relief. Bronze rod tripods were a Cypriote invention that was introduced from Cyprus to Crete. They must have been very popular at Palaepaphos during the Cypro-Geometric I period, considering the numerous imitations in clay that have been found in the *Skales* tombs. Cypro-Geometric I period.

264

265

266

267

should also mention a rich collection of gold jewelry, found in tombs of women.

Among the eleventh-century-B.C. tombs excavated at *Skales*, several must have been tombs of warriors. Tomb 76 contained two iron swords, one of which had been intentionally bent (or "killed"), so that it could no longer be used by its owner. Both swords are of a type known in the Aegean in bronze; in Cyprus this type was made in iron already in the eleventh century B.C. The "killed" sword must originally have been 70cm. in length. The shorter sword (41cm. long) had an ivory handle. Other weapons in this tomb include a bronze spearhead (length 39.7cm.), iron knives, and an iron axe (Karageorghis 1983, 249).

Desborough and Snodgrass had put forward the theory that Cyprus may have been the place from which the knowledge of the use of iron as a "working" metal was exported to Greece, and where weapons of an Aegean type, known on the mainland and in Crete in bronze, were tried in iron. The necropolis at *Skales* offers much supportive material for this theory. It is not easy to explain whether some of the Greek settlers went back to Greece in the course of the tenth century B.C. or whether Cypriots emigrated to Greece, taking there the new metallurgical technology in ironworking (cf. Snodgrass 1980). The fact, however, that certain CG pottery exercised an influence on the ceramic art of the Aegean of the same period supports the view that the two regions maintained a close connection, though it is surprising that so few genuine imports from either region have so far been found in the other.

In 1993 an important tomb was excavated at the site of *Xylinos*, 1km. northeast of the village of Kouklia, probably belonging to the same cemetery as the *Xerolimni* tomb mentioned above (Flourentzos 1997). The material that it yielded is of the CG IA period (second half of the eleventh century B.C.). It included a rich variety of pottery, bronze bowls, iron obeloi, objects of gold, ivory, and faience. Perhaps the most unusual object is a bronze thymiaterion (Flourentzos 2000). It may have a twelfth century B.C. antecedent from Palaepaphos (cf. Karageorghis 1990a, 64). The *Xylinos* thymiaterion is 43.5cm. in height, with drooping petals in two registers. Its type is Levantine, and, fits well within the kind of luxury material associated with symposia, e.g., bronze vessels, drinking cups, obeloi, all of which have been found in this tomb (for a further discussion see Matthäus 1999, 22–25).

Reference has already been made to the new cemetery site of Palaepaphos at the *Plakes* location, 1.6km west of the village of Kouklia, where excavation started in 1999. Most of the tombs had been disturbed during leveling operations, but they yielded large quantities of pottery, bronze, and iron objects, gold ornaments, and two bathtubs, one of limestone and the other of clay. Iron swords were found associated with male burials, gold ornaments with female burials. In one of the tombs the incinerated bones of the dead were found in a bronze amphora. Next to it were placed weapons; associated with it were a

268

269

270

271

273

272

274

271. Two anthropomorphic jugs from Palaepaphos-*Skales* (excavations of the Cyprus Department of Antiquities). The one on the left, from Tomb 49, no. 53, is of Proto-White Painted ware. Height: 26.6cm. Trefoil mouth covered with a human face at the top. The "chin" is perforated, forming a strainer. The almost identical jug on the right is of White Painted I ware, from Tomb 78, no. 23. Height: 24.5cm. Kouklia Site Museum.

272. Askos of White Painted I ware from Palaepaphos-*Skales* (excavations of the Cyprus Department of Antiquities), Tomb 76, no. 114. Height: 21.5cm. Kouklia Site Museum. The two opposed spouts are in the form of protomes of horned animals. False spout and tubular spout in the middle, with raised basket handle.

273. Zoomorphic askos of White Painted I ware from Palaepaphos-*Skales* (excavations of the Cyprus Department of Antiquities), Tomb 67, no. 26. Height: 28.8cm. Kouklia Site Museum. The askos represents a goat (?) resting on a high stem; it has a boat-shaped body and a long tail. This is one of a series of imaginative askoi from the *Skales* cemetery. Cypro-Geometric I period.

274. Composite stemmed kylix of Proto-White Painted ware from Palaepaphos-*Skales* (excavations of the Cyprus Department of Antiquities, 1980–81), Tomb 67, no. 53. Height: 15cm.; average diam. of bowls: 9.5cm. Kouklia Site Museum. All three bowls communicate with one another.

horse's head and horse's gear. Unfortunately, all had been dispersed by the bulldozer. Most of these tombs were used from the Cypro-Geometric I to the Cypro-Geometric III period.

Although it is not easy to estimate the population of a town the extent of which is uncertain, we may suggest that in view of the large extent of the cemeteries of the eleventh century B.C. (to which we may now add the cemetery at *Plakes*) it may have been one of the largest on the island.

As we have already mentioned, at Palaepaphos,

unlike anywhere else in Cyprus (with the exception of Kition), there was continuity of habitation from the Late Cypriote I period down to the Cypro-Classical period. There was no permanent destruction nor shifting to another site. This may be due to the importance of the sanctuary (Maier 1999, 82). There was, however, a change in the burial ground and burial customs from the beginning of the eleventh century B.C. The LC I–LC IIIA/B cemeteries of *Asproyi*, *Evreti*, and *Kaminia* that were located within the boundaries of the inhabited area were abandoned,

275

276

275-276. Stemmed kylix from Palaepaphos-*Skales* (excavations of the Cyprus Department of Antiquities), Tomb 58, no. 27. Height of bowl: 15.5cm.; diam.: 16.8cm. Kouklia Site Museum. This is a "trick vase." At its bottom there is a hollow frog, from the mouth of which the liquid in the bowl could flow into the tubular rim and from there be poured or drunk from the spout of a bull protome that communicates with the rim. Such drinking vessels may have been used during symposia. Cypro-Geometric I period.

277. Dish of White Painted I ware, from Palaepaphos-*Skales* (excavations of the Cyprus Department of Antiquities), Tomb 58, no. 104. Height: 5cm.; diam.: 28.3cm. Cyprus Museum, Nicosia. The base is decorated with an ambitious pictorial composition: two human figures trying to kill a large two-headed snake with arrows. In the field are three quadrupeds and a flying bird. No doubt this is a mythological theme, recalling the Greek myth of the slaying of the snake of Lerna by Hercules and his companion, Iolaos. There were similar Near Eastern myths. Cypro-Geometric I period.

and new ones were created at *Xerolimni/Xylinos*, north of Kouklia village, at *Kato Alonia* and *Hadji-abdullah*, and slightly later at *Skales*, *Lakkos tou Skarnou*, and *Plakes* (see Maier 1999, 80–82). These new tombs with a long narrow dromos replaced the traditional Late Cypriote IIIA tombs, and the ceramic material that they contained is Proto-White Painted and Cypro-Geometric (see more detailed discussion in Maier 1999, 80).

Maier, in his 1999 article quoted above, tried to approach the problem of ethnicity of the Palaepaphi-ans of the eleventh century B.C. He mentions the obe-los of Opheltes from *Skales* Tomb 49 and emphasizes the disparity between Phoenician and Greek imports, which relates to trade, but fails to consider the very important novelty that is the appearance of the new type of tomb, of Mycenaean origin (Maier 1999, 83; cf. Coldstream 1989, 325–328, where this novelty is underlined).

With regard to the Greek language of the obelos of Opheltes (whether of eleventh or tenth century B.C., cf. Maier 1999, 83, no. 18), it is not certain how many of the Palaepaphians spoke Greek in the eleventh or tenth centuries B.C., but we would agree with Board-man, who argues that if the Greek language were only used by an intrusive elite we would expect it to have been absorbed within a few generations—but the lan-guage survived. "So they were more than just an elite…, but they seem to have enjoyed some domi-

277

278. "Palm tree" storage jar from Palaepaphos-*Skales* (excavations of the Cyprus Department of Antiquities), Tomb 49, no. 80. Height: 39cm. Kouklia Site Museum. This is one of the earliest Levantine imports to Cyprus of the Cypro-Geometric I period. It is decorated with purple-red washy paint with linear motifs and stylized tree ornaments, hence the name of the group to which it belongs.

279. Lentoid flask of Phoenician Bichrome ware from Palaepaphos-*Skales* (excavations of the Cyprus Department of Antiquities), Tomb 76, no. 2. Height: 13.2cm. Kouklia Site Museum. The body on either side is decorated with concentric bands. Palaepaphos-*Skales* has yielded some of the earliest imports of Phoenician pottery. Cypro-Geometric I period.

280. Phoenician juglet from Palaepaphos-*Skales* (excavations of the Cyprus Department of Antiquities), Tomb 49, no. 184. Height: 18.5cm. Kouklia Site Museum. Dark red slip, matt black paint; horizontal bands around the middle of the body. Cypro-Geometric I period.

281. Imported storage jar of "Canaanite" type from Palae-paphos-*Skales* (excavations of the Cyprus Department of Antiquities), Tomb 49, no. 80. Height: 39.5cm. Kouklia Site Museum. This type had a long tradition during the Late Bronze Age. Its occurrence in the Cypro-Geometric I period demonstrates the continuation of trade relations between the island of Cyprus and the Levant.

282. Faience hemispherical bowl from Palaepaphos-*Skales* (excavations of the Cyprus Department of Antiquities), Tomb 58, no. 5. Height: 5.5cm.; diam.: 12.8cm. Kouklia Site Museum. The bottom is decorated with a painted eight-petalled rosette. The number of faience vases found in early Cypro-Geometric tombs shows a considerable decrease if compared with those imported during the Late Cypriote II period. Cypro-Geometric I period.

278

281

279   280

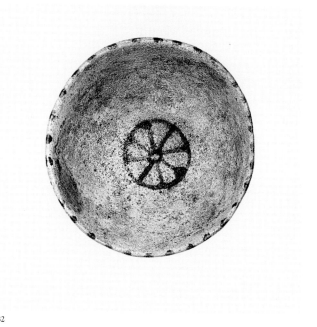

282

nance, and by the seventh century, when the Assyrian king names ten Cypriot kings, as many as eight of them may have Greek names" (Boardman 2001a, 11). If the Greeks did not take on this dominant role in the eleventh century B.C., we see no other period in the later history of the island when this could have happened.

In a recently published paper John Boardman (2001a, 22) commented on the story of Athena, disguised as Mentes and going to Temese (Tamassos) in Cyprus to fetch iron and exchange it for copper. Homer refers to the inhabitants of Temese as αλλόθροοι (speaking a foreign language), and rightly so, because we now have epigraphic evidence that as early as about 800 B.C. the Phoenicians acquired control of Tamassos, a copper-producing center. The Homeric heroes, as rightly pointed out by Boardman, expected the language of Temese to be normally Greek, but they knew about the Phoenician domination over this kingdom (*Odyssey* I, 183). Or was the word ἀλλόθροοι referring to the Cypriots speaking Greek with a strange accent?

283

284

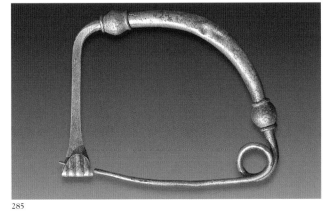

285   286

283-284. Gold objects from Palaepaphos-*Skales* (excavations of the Cyprus Department of Antiquities), Tomb 67. Kouklia Site Museum. They include plaques decorated in repoussé with a draped figure of Astarte holding flowers in both hands; she wears a tiara. There are also discs of gold foil, some decorated with embossed rosettes; they are perforated for sewing onto cloth. There are also earrings of various types. These gold ornaments may be associated with the second burial in the tomb, which is dated to the Cypro-Geometric II period.

285. Gold fibula from Palaepaphos, found in a looted tomb at *Hassan Agha*, now in a private collection. D-shaped, with two biconical bead bosses on spring-arm and bow. Hollow rounded bow. Solid forearm, coil, and pin. Triangular catchplate grooved vertically to create four "fingers." Length: 4.7cm. The ceramic material accompanying it dates to the Cypro-Geometric I period (cf. gold fibula in the Cesnola Collection, no. 286 below; also Csornay-Caprez 2000, 90, no. 154).

286. A bow-shaped gold fibula in the Cesnola Collection, the Metropolitan Museum of Art, New York, no. 74.51.3198. Length: 4.8cm.

287

288

287. Two iron swords from
Palaepaphos-*Skales* (excavations
of the Cyprus Department of
Antiquities), Tomb 76. Top:
no. 24, length: 41cm.; it had an
ivory handle. Bottom: no. 22,
intentionally bent ("killed"), restored
length: circa 70cm. They are both
of an Aegean type, but made in
Cyprus. Ironworking started quite
early in Cyprus, and it is believed
that knowledge of it was trans-
ferred from Cyprus to the Aegean.
Cypro-Geometric I period.

288. Bronze spearhead from
Palaepaphos-*Skales* (excavations
of the Cyprus Department of
Antiquities), Tomb 76, no. 65.
Kouklia Site Museum. Length:
39.7cm. Cypro-Geometric I period.

289. Bronze thymiaterion from
Palaepaphos-*Xylinos*, Tomb 132,
nos. 70 and 71 (excavations
of the Cyprus Department of
Antiquities). Height: 43.5cm.
Cyprus Museum, Nicosia. It
consists of four parts riveted
together. The bowl at the top is
shallow, with the lower part
splaying toward the base. The
middle part is decorated with two
registers of drooping petals. For
better stability the tubular stem
was reinforced with a wooden
insert. Thymiateria were used
during symposia in later periods,
as seen on Assyrian reliefs, and
this may have been one of the
privileges enjoyed by members
of the elite.

290. Two plaques of thin sheets
of gold, from Palaepaphos-*Plakes*,
Tomb 146, nos. 115, 116, 119.
Kouklia Site Museum. Average
dimensions: height: 8.8cm.; width:
6cm. They all have an identical
decoration with a draped human
figure in profile, holding a flower
in both hands, not unlike those
illustrated above, no. 284. Found
in a mixed context.

289

290

c. Kourion

Kourion, which according to Herodotus was a foundation of the Argives (Herodotus V, 113), was an
important eleventh century center, as far as we can
see from the evidence of tombs (see recently Buitron-
Oliver 1999). Much has been written about Tomb 40
at Episkopi-*Kaloriziki* (Episkopi is the modern village
nearest to the site of ancient Kourion).

This tomb, a spacious rectangular shaft without any
signs of a dromos, which was only partly excavated
scientifically (McFadden 1954), originally contained
the incinerated remains of a man in a bronze crater
and probably the buried remains of a woman (on the
analogy of the burial at Lefkandi-*Toumba*).

The tomb contained, apart from pottery, two bronze
tripod stands decorated with protomes of bulls and
three bronze phalara and bands that may have decorated a shield (Catling and Catling 1973). Similar
phalara were found in late CG I Tomb 21 at Amathus
(cf. Hermary 1999, 57, where a different identification is accepted), as well as in the newly excavated
tombs at Palaepaphos-*Plakes*, a bronze spearhead and
other bronze vases, a gold toggle pin, and the well-
known gold and cloisonné enamel scepter head. The
tomb is dated to the mid-eleventh century B.C. A
comparison of the material from Tomb 40 with the
material from Tiryns Tomb XXVIII and that of the
hero-burial from Lefkandi has already been made by
Catling (1995, 126–127).

With regard to the gold scepter, several views have
been put forward (Kourou 1994, 202–206), but there
is little doubt that here we have a scepter befitting a
king. It is 16cm. long and consists of a tubular socket,

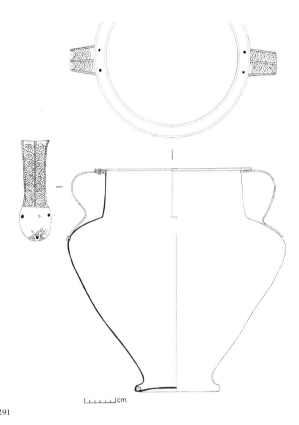

291

292

291. Bronze amphora from Episkopi-*Kaloriziki* (American Excavations), Tomb 40, no. 11. Height: circa 42cm. Episkopi Museum. It contained the incinerated remains of the dead, who was buried in Tomb 40 (after Karageorghis 1983, fig. 7).

292. A scepter from Episkopi-*Kaloriziki*, Tomb 40. Cyprus Museum, Nicosia, J.99. Height: 16.5cm. It consists of a plain gold tubular staff with a globe at the top, on which stand two falcons. The globe and the falcons are decorated in the cloisonné technique and are inlaid with white and blue enamel. This object was found by looters in a tomb that may have been that of a king whose remains were incinerated and placed in a bronze amphora. The scepter is considered to be a symbol of authority.

topped by a globe, decorated in cloisonné in blue and white enamel. It is unique in its kind. Whether it is of the same date as the pottery deposited in the tomb (mid-eleventh century) or earlier is debatable (Kourou 1994, 204–205). If it was placed in the tomb as an antique this should not be surprising, in view of the tendency to place heirlooms in "heroic burials" of this period. In any case, such scepters "were symbols of some form of exalted status, within the Cypriot political system" (Snodgrass 1988, 16–17). The shape of Tomb 40 (a shaft, not a chamber with a long dromos) induced Coldstream to suggest that "the chief incumbent in Tomb 40 was an indigenous Cypriot prince, who chose to ally himself with the new settlers from the Aegean. If so, this tomb will contain by far the richest Eteocypriot burials of the eleventh century" (Coldstream 1989, 333). This argument may not be valid because there are other tombs in the eleventh century in both the Aegean and Cyprus, the pit-caves, also of Aegean inspiration, that Tomb 40 may copy (see above). The eleventh century B.C. tombs of *Kaloriziki* have a long narrow dromos and a rectangular chamber, like the tombs of the other cemeteries mentioned above (Benson 1973, 19).

d. Amathus

The important kingdom of Amathus on the south coast does not have a foundation legend, unlike

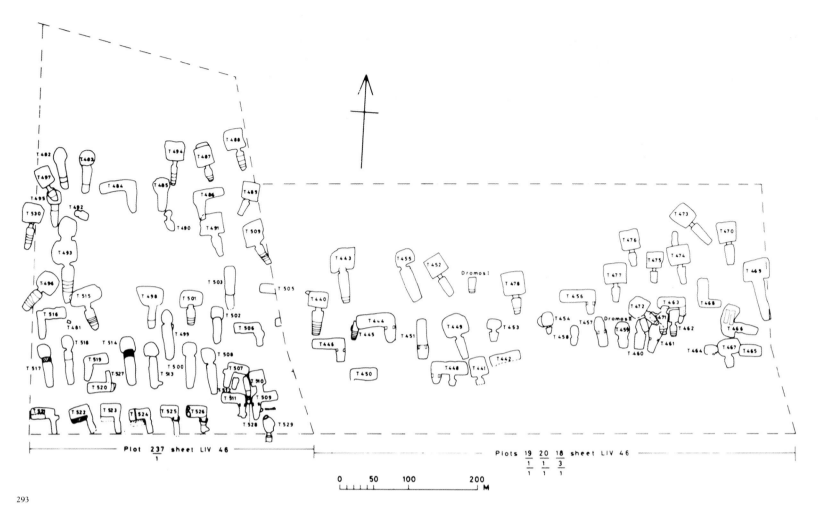

293

293. Site plan of the excavated area of the Western Necropolis of Amathus (after Karageorghis and Iacovou 1990, 75, fig. 1).

Salamis or Paphos. The historian Theopompus (350–300 B.C.) informs us that the Amathusians were the descendants of the companions of Kinyras, the mythical king of Cyprus, who were driven away by the Greeks who accompanied Agamemnon after the end of the Trojan War (for further references to Amathus by other Greek authors see Iacovou 1994, 156; Aupert *et al.* 1996, 18–19). The Amathusians are usually called Eteocypriots, descendants of the autochthonous race that allegedly assembled at Amathus after the domination of the Greeks elsewhere in Cyprus. Although some Amathusians spoke a language that was not Greek, as evidenced by three syllabic inscriptions, they nevertheless shared a culture that had been common to the rest of Cyprus since the eleventh century B.C. It is doubtful, therefore, that we can consider the whole population of Amathus as Eteocypriote (cf. Iacovou 1999a, 15–16, with references; see also recently Aupert 2001).

Although we know from the cemeteries of Amathus that the site was inhabited from the middle of the eleventh century B.C. onward, no actual remains have been found dating to this period (Hermary

1999). A deposit of sherds from the settlement is dated to the mid-eleventh century, as is one tomb excavated in 1942 and published recently (Hermary and Iacovou 1999).

The majority of tombs excavated in the Cypro-Geometric necropolis of Amathus date from the CG IB period. Some of the tombs are L-shaped, but there are others that follow the Mycenaean type of chamber with a long dromos (see plan published by Karageorghis and Iacovou 1990, fig. 1). One of the rich tombs of the Cypro-Geometric necropolis, Tomb 521, dated to the CG IB period (first half of the tenth century B.C.), yielded an extraordinary amount of ceramics, including zoomorphic and anthropomorphic askoi as well as box-pyxides and a high percentage of Levantine imports, which indicate the significance of the harbor of Amathus in trading connections with the Levantine coast. Tomb 523 in the same cemetery yielded a bronze obelos of a foreign type belonging to what is known as "Bronze final atlantique" of the Western Mediterranean. It is quite possible that this exceptional obelos came through Sardinia, for use in roasting meat by a rich aristocrat of Amathus (cf. the obeloi of Palaepaphos-*Skales*, Palaepaphos-*Xylinos*, and Kition, mentioned above). The date of this obelos has been discussed by various scholars (see Hermary 1999, 57).

In a recently published article Boardman suggests that exotic objects like the western obelos were the result of casual trade that was different from that of earlier periods, which was organized on a national basis. Merchants and sailors in the "Dark Ages" had no incentive to settle and develop regular trade on a large scale. We do not have trade establishments (cf. Boardman 2001b, 35).

We have already referred to Tomb 109, the earliest so far discovered tomb in the Western Necropolis of Amathus (CG IA). It yielded pottery of the CG IA period, as well as a miniature bronze tripod, two bronze bowls, and a bronze spearhead. The tripod is considered an heirloom from the thirteenth–twelfth centuries B.C. Such heirlooms are common in "heroic" burials, both in Cyprus and in the Aegean (Hermary and Iacovou 1999, with previous references).

The area of the modern town of Limassol has been inhabited almost uninterruptedly since the Early Bronze Age. Although excavations have necessarily been limited in this inhabited area, chance discoveries have brought to light enough material to justify this statement. Evidence of an eleventh century B.C. sanctuary was discovered in 1976, but the emergency character of the excavation did not allow a full investigation. Three terra-cotta figurines were found in a small built niche covered with a slab; they are of the type of the goddess with uplifted arms, dated to the eleventh century B.C. One of them is of Proto-White Painted ware. Two of them are bell shaped and wheelmade, recalling the Sub-Minoan type of the Cretan goddess, which also made its appearance in Cyprus in the eleventh century (Karageorghis 1993a, 58–59). Other objects include two wheelmade zoomorphic vases, probably representing sheep, a clay model of a ship, two Plain Wheelmade ware shallow bowls, and a miniature amphora of Plain White ware of the "Canaanite" type. Although there is very limited information about the structure with which these objects were associated, it may be suggested that this was a sanctuary or a favissa for a sanctuary of the eleventh century B.C. A thick layer of earth below the floor level of the niche contained Late Cypriote I and II sherd material. This is an important discovery and further investigations in the same area are warranted.

294

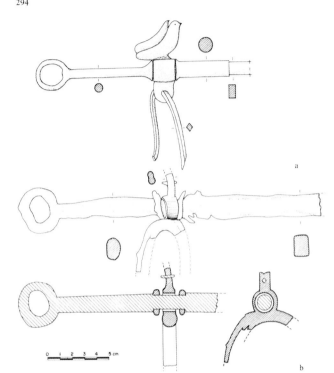

295

294-295. Bronze obelos from Amathus, Tomb 523, no. 40 (excavations of the Cyprus Department of Antiquities). Preserved length: 79.6cm. Limassol District Museum. This obelos, serving both as a firedog and a skewer, is of a western type and may have come to Cyprus via Sardinia. First half of the tenth century B.C.

296. Askos of Bichrome I ware, from Amathus (excavations of the Cyprus Department of Antiquities), Tomb 521, no. 83. Height: 24.2cm. Limassol District Museum. It is decorated with a horned animal's protome on one side and on the opposite side with the bust of a female figure carrying a miniature amphora on her head. Cypro-Geometric I period (first half of the tenth century B.C.).

296

e. Idalion

Idalion, one of the ten kingdoms of Cyprus and a city with a foundation legend (its founder was the Greek hero Chalkanor), was partly excavated by the Swedish Cyprus Expedition. On the Western Acropolis a fortified palace was found that was constructed in LC IIIA. Evidence for a settlement of the same period has come to light in the Lower City. There is also a tomb that was excavated at *Ayios Georghios* that yielded pottery of Proto-White Painted ware, dating typologically to the late phase of this ware (circa 1050 B.C.). Recent excavations have revealed evidence that there was a continuous habitation at Idalion from the LC IIC period down to the Cypro-Archaic period (Hadjicosti 1999).

f. Marion

Marion, on the northwestern coast of Cyprus, is yet another of the later ten kingdoms of Cyprus that may have been founded around 1000 B.C., as recent excavations have demonstrated (Childs 1997, 39).

g. Lapithos

Lapithos, on the north coast, has its own foundation legend: its founder was Praxandros from Laconia. Although no architectural remains from the Cypro-Geometric I period have yet been found, there is ample evidence from its cemeteries. It is interesting that during this period there were two distinct cemeteries at Lapithos, one at *Kastros* and the other at *Plakes*. The first, according to the excavator Einar Gjerstad, was used as a burial ground by the Greek community of Lapithos, whereas the second was for the autochthonous population (Gjerstad *et al.* 1934, 13–276; Pieridou 1964). In the first cemetery several tombs of Mycenaean architecture have been found, whereas at *Plakes* the burials were in traditional Cypriote chamber tombs. The tombs at *Kastros* have

297

298

138

299

300

301

299. A small stirrup jar of Proto-White Painted ware, from Idalion-*Ayios Georghios,* Tomb 2, no. 6 (height: 10.4cm.). Cyprus Museum, Nicosia. Airhole at neckline opposite spout. Decoration with geometric patterns on shoulder. The ceramic material from this tomb represents the last phase of Proto-White Painted ware.

300. Small jar of gray ware, handmade (Handmade Burnished or "Barbarian ware"). From Idalion-*Ayios Georghios,* Tomb 2, no. 16. Smooth surface. Two opposed projections on body, perforated vertically. Height: 6.4cm. Cyprus Museum, Nicosia. This fabric, alien to Cypriote ceramics of the Late Bronze Age, started to appear in Cyprus from the beginning of the twelfth century B.C. and may be related to the first Achaean settlers. It appears in the Aegean from the thirteenth century B.C. (see jar from Maa-*Palaeokastro,* no. 154).

301. Ring-kernos of Proto-White Painted ware, from Idalion-*Ayios Georghios,* Tomb 2, no. 1. Cyprus Museum, Nicosia. Height: 8.3cm.; diam.: 19.7cm. Painted linear decoration on body. An animal protome and a miniature vase are opposite it, on the upper part of the ring. There is a bar across the ring, with basket handle.

a small chamber and a long narrow dromos. An interesting burial custom observed in some of the tombs of *Kastros* is the sacrifice of humans in honor of the dead. In Tomb 417, dating to the eleventh century B.C., a human skeleton was found buried in the dromos when the door was closed; it "probably represents a slave burial, the door-keeper of the deceased, who was killed at the funeral in order to watch the door of the tomb and serve them in the life to come, as he had done previously" (Gjerstad *et al.* 1934, 228). Similar phenomena were observed in Tomb 422, of the Cypro-Geometric III period. In the Aegean there is evidence for the sacrifice of women during the burial of a prominent male; such customs have been observed at Tiryns and Lefkandi. The men were cremated and the women were buried. The Tiryns burial may be dated to the middle of the eleventh century B.C., that at Lefkandi to about 1000 B.C. (Catling 1995). Evidence for cremation at Palaepaphos-*Skales* and Kourion-*Kaloriziki* Tomb 40

302

302. Amphora of Proto-White Painted ware, probably from Lapithos. Hadjiprodromou Collection, Famagusta. Height: 40cm. It is decorated with a horizontal frieze of fish around the shoulder and a small boat with two sailors. The fish motifs are in outline, except one, which is in silhouette.

Painted ware show clear influences from the Levant (cf. Karageorghis 1975, 47–56), and Cypriote pottery was exported during the Cypro-Geometric I period to the Levant, where it influenced local ceramic styles (for references see Iacovou 1999b, 149; Gilboa 1999). Lentoid flasks from the Levant appeared in the eleventh century B.C. tombs of *Alaas* (Karageorghis 1975, 57) and were also imitated in local fabrics (ibid., 52). The same happened in the case of the "Canaanite" jars, which were both imported and imitated in Cyprus. One of the finest lentoid flasks with pictorial decoration, was found in Cyprus and is now in the Metropolitan Museum of Art, New York (Karageorghis *et al.* 2000, no. 125). A strong case for Phoenician influences in eleventh century B.C. Cyprus was made by Bikai (1994), as a natural reaction to the previously prevailing theories that the Cypriots and Levantines "were backward peoples who needed an infusion of presumably Greek 'Sea People' to teach them how to sail to the seas and how to work metal" (ibid., 35).

The role of the Phoenicians in the development of Cypriote culture, starting on a small scale as early as the eleventh century B.C. and reaching its apogee during the Cypro-Archaic I and II periods, should be neither overlooked nor overemphasized. Despite some views to the contrary that have been put forward from time to time, the Phoenicians never succeeded in occupying Cyprus. "If they had," says Bikai (1994, 35), "Cyprus would be speaking Phoenician rather than Greek today." Bikai is skeptical: "Either they never tried, or they tried and didn't succeed" (ibid.). She suggested in another paper published in 1992 that "there may have been a coalition between the Phoenicians and the 'Sea Peoples' when they participated in the Mediterranean network, a network that extended to the Aegean, Sicily, and Sardinia, and which seems to have found its most concrete expression in Cyprus" (eadem 1992, 137). At the end of Egyptian domination in Palestine in the mid-twelfth century B.C., the various peoples of that area (Canaanites, Phoenicians, "Sea Peoples," and others), finding themselves free from any outside powers, engaged in a struggle that resulted in the destruction of important centers in the area. Contacts with Cyprus were disrupted, and it was only after the mid-eleventh century B.C. that they resumed (cf. Mazar 1994, 54).

It is to this period (second half of the eleventh century B.C.) that we may date the Phoenician ceramic

has already been mentioned. The custom of cremation, as well as that of slave sacrifice, was no doubt introduced by the Greek colonists from the Greek mainland or even from Crete, as recent excavations in the cemetery of Pandanassa Amariou have demonstrated (Tegou in prep.).

iv. *Relations with the Levant*

The strong Greek character of Cypriote culture during the eleventh century B.C. has already been underlined. However, this does not mean at all that relations with and influences from the Levant ceased during this period. On the contrary, as already mentioned (e.g., the contents of the tombs of *Alaas* and of Palaepaphos-*Skales*; Bikai 1983), these relations were strong both commercially (as seen from the imports from the Levant) and culturally. Several types of vases of eleventh century B.C. Proto-White

material from the necropolis of Palaepaphos-*Skales* (Bikai 1994, 34; Mazar 1994, 51–55). During the early part of the eleventh century B.C. a similar situation may have prevailed in Cyprus. There was a relative isolation, with no evidence for direct trade between the island and the Aegean or the Levant (cf. Iacovou 1994, 159). This isolation came to an end at the close of the LC IIIB period (mid-eleventh century B.C.). Whatever was happening in the political field in Cyprus (and there was quite a lot of radical change), this was a Cypriote affair, involving the Eteocypriots and the Aegean immigrants (cf. eadem 1989). The scenario changed after the mid-eleventh century B.C.

There was no possibility of the Phoenicians being directly involved in the political affairs of Cyprus during the early part of the eleventh century B.C., and after the middle of the century there was enough political stability in the island not to allow such a development. The hostile reception of Wenamon, sailing to Alashiya in the eleventh century B.C. (1069–1043 B.C.) in a Canaanite/Phoenician ship, is indicative of the political situation prevailing on the island (cf. Bikai 1994, 34). Wenamon went from Egypt to Byblos to procure timber, but on his way back to Egypt the wind drove him to the land of Alashiya. Below he describes his adventure on the island, where the inhabitants understand neither his language (Egyptian) nor the language of his crew (Syrian): The wind drove me to the land of Alashiya. The inhabitants of the town came out to kill me. I pushed myself between them to the place where Hataba, the princess of the town was. I found her after she came forth from one house of hers and was entering into another. I greeted her and said to the people standing near her: "Is there no one amongst you who understands the language of Egypt?". One amongst them said: "I understand." I said to him: "Tell my mistress, I have heard as far (away) as Thebes, the place where Amun is, in every town wrong is done, (but) in the land of Alashiya right is done. Does one now do wrongly daily here?" She said: "Oh, what is that you've said?" I said to her: "If the sea rages and the wind drives me to the place in which you are, would you let them receive me so as to kill me, although I am the messenger of Amun? They will look for me to the end of days. As for the crew of the prince of Byblos which they seek to kill, will not its lord find ten crews with you and kill them himself?" She had the people summoned and

303

they were pulled up. She said to me: 'Be at ease.'" (Knapp [ed.] 1996, 49, text 88).

What was the reason for the economic expansion of the Phoenicians to the west after the middle of the eleventh century B.C.? Having become rich as a result of trade in timber, they became interested in the metals trade, and Cyprus was the logical destination.

303. Bichrome lentoid flask in the Cesnola Collection, the Metropolitan Museum of Art, New York, no. 74.51.431. Cypro-Geometric I period (1050–950 B.C.). Height: 27cm. Decorated in the Bichrome technique on both sides, with quadrupeds and birds. The fabric and form suggest that it is a Levantine import.

The Iron Age I. The Cypro-Geometric II–III Periods (950/900–750 B.C.)

The traditional date for the end of the Cypro-Geometric I period (the one suggested by Gjerstad [1948, 422]) is circa 950 B.C. Recent research by Coldstream, however, suggests as a terminal date for the period circa 900 B.C., thus allowing it fifty more years, making CG II start a little later. This proposal is supported by evidence from the Aegean (Coldstream 1999). If this new dating is accepted, then the end of the CG I period should include the earliest imported pottery from the Aegean to Cyprus, a Euboean Late Geometric skyphos and two cups found in a tomb at Amathus and dated to the late tenth century B.C. (Coldstream 1999, 112). It is within the tenth century B.C. that we may also date the early exchanges between the Euboeans and the Levantines, in which Amathus played an important role (Hermary 1999, 58). Euboean pottery has been found in Syria and Phoenicia, and Cypriote pottery and other oriental objects of faience, etc., have been found at Lefkandi in late-tenth century B.C. contexts. To the same period dates a bronze hemi-spherical bowl from the North Cemetery of Knossos in Crete, bearing an engraved Phoenician inscription; this bowl is of Cypriote type.

Although precise chronology is an important issue, in the case of the period circa 900 B.C., however, when the exchanges between the Aegeans (mainly Euboeans) and the Phoenicians began, the most important and controversial question is which of the two was the protagonist in these exchanges. There is a long tradition among Aegean scholars that the Euboeans were responsible for the trade between the Aegean and the Levant (e.g., Coldstream 1999; Boardman 2001a; and idem 2001b; cf. also Niemeier 2001).

Boardman stressed the fact that the initiative for export of Greek goods, mainly pottery, to the east was Euboean, not Phoenician. He brings as an argument the fact that there is nothing in the East from Crete, in spite of the close relations between Cyprus and the Levant with Crete from the ninth century B.C. onward. Furthermore, most of the innovations in

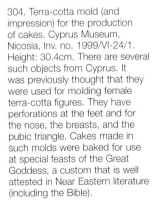

304. Terra-cotta mold (and impression) for the production of cakes. Cyprus Museum, Nicosia, Inv. no. 1999/VI-24/1. Height: 30.4cm. There are several such objects from Cyprus. It was previously thought that they were used for molding female terra-cotta figures. They have perforations at the feet and for the nose, the breasts, and the pubic triangle. Cakes made in such molds were baked for use at special feasts of the Great Goddess, a custom that is well attested in Near Eastern literature (including the Bible).

305. Two Euboean Late Protogeometric drinking cups from Amathus: on the left, a skyphos, Limassol Museum 46/3, height: 14cm.; on the right, a cup, Limassol Museum 46/4, height: 9.9cm. They are the earliest known Greek imports after the Mycenaean period and may date to circa 950–900 B.C.

305

306

306. The Phoenician temple of
Astarte at Kition, Area II (excavations of the Cyprus Department
of Antiquities). It was built on the
foundations of a Late Bronze
Age temple toward the end of
the ninth century B.C. It suffered
various alterations throughout
its history. It was abandoned in
312 B.C., when King Ptolemy I
killed the last Phoenician king of
Kition, Poumyathon, and put an
end to the Phoenician dynasty.

Crete were from Syria rather than Phoenicia (Boardman 2001b, 36). The current excavations at Kommos
and Eleutherna on Crete, however, may change this
picture.

Phoenician Settlement in Cyprus
Kition, on the southeast coast, was the first place the
Phoenicians set foot when they started their westward
expansion late in the ninth century B.C. (for a general
discussion and a bibliography see Reyes 1994, 18–21).
Not only were they acquainted with Cyprus from their
previous trade relations (see above), but the coast of
Kition is the first land to be seen when sailing westward from Sidon. Some reasons why the Phoenicians
chose Cyprus to settle may be the quest for natural
resources (metals and timber) and the fact that the
island was considered safe from the threat and pres-
sure of powerful neighbors (in this case the Assyrians,
a non-seafaring people), but, as Boardman rightly

observed, not for long (Boardman 2001b, 36). The
Phoenicians did not establish a real colony at Kition
as they did in the Central and Western Mediterranean but settled in an already inhabited town and
organized themselves as a commercial community, an
emporium, which gradually increased in size. One of
their first acts was to build a temple consecrated to
their "national" goddess, Astarte. In doing so, they
selected the site at the northernmost part of Kition,
which was the sacred quarter of the Late Bronze Age
town and which had been abandoned circa 1000 B.C.
as a result of the silting up of the inner harbor. The
remains of the Late Bronze Age temples, described
earlier, with their impressive walls, the lower parts of
which were built with ashlar blocks, were no doubt
still preserved up to a certain height. The Phoenicians
used these foundations to build their own temple,
naturally transforming the interior to suit their own
purposes and replacing a few orthostats of the Late

Bronze Age temple that had been damaged during the 150 years of abandonment.

The upper parts of the walls of the Late Bronze Age temple were constructed of bricks and wooden beams, but stratigraphic observations inside the temple did not show traces of such bricks, a fact that led us to believe that the Phoenicians used stones for the reconstruction of the walls. The northern gate, which led to workshops along the northern side of the temple, was blocked with small stones since these workshops ceased to function during the Phoenician period. The east gate with its porch, 3.5m. wide, remained the principal entrance to the temple, and the worshipers had direct access to the temple through this gate from the spacious open courtyard with the built altar in front of Temple 1. Only a few changes were carried out at the south gate with its staircase.

The holy-of-holies, in the western part of the temple, which during the Late Bronze Age had an elevated floor, was now emptied of its fill, and a long narrow compartment was created, measuring 2.5m. in width and 18.4m. in length. It was entered through two openings in the south and north, symmetrically arranged. Its floor was slightly higher than that of the rest of the temple.

The Phoenicians destroyed the Late Bronze Age floors of the temple and reached the natural rock (clay). The interior of the temple was divided by four rows of wooden pillars, of which the stone bases survive, into five aisles, of which the central one was widest (5.15m.). Each row consisted of seven pillars (total twenty-eight), the thickness of which is estimated at 60×40cm.; they were fixed by a dowel hole to their stone bases, on the surface of which they left traces. A low bench (20×65cm.) was constructed of mud bricks along the northern and southern walls of the temple, covering the roughly hewn bases of the orthostats.

Two rectangular pillars were constructed in front of the holy-of-holies, placed on the axis of the temple and measuring 2.1×1.75m.; the span between them is 1.2m. The two pillars were not destined to support a roof but were freestanding, supporting probably a capital or "horns of consecration" (not unlike those we see on either side of the central axis of the holy-of-holies on the later representations on coins, etc., of the temple of Aphrodite at Palaepaphos). O. Callot has ingeniously suggested another function, i.e., that these freestanding pillars flanked the base of a "statue," forming a structure like the naïskoi that are seen on the Hathoric capitals common in Cyprus and else-where in the Phoenician world. Thus, this structure could be the real holy-of-holies, comprising the cult statue. Comparable representations in the Near East appear on ivory plaques (Callot in Karageorghis forthcoming a). On the other hand, if the two pillars are accepted as simply supporting a capital or another symbol, as at Palaepaphos, they may be compared with the bronze pillars Jachin and Boaz of the Solomonic temple in Jerusalem (Karageorghis 1976, 98). Similar pillars appear on the representations of the temple of Melkarth at Tyre and on clay models of naïskoi found in Cyprus and elsewhere in the Levant (Karageorghis 1976, 98; idem 1996c, 57–67). In front of the two pillars (or the naïskos) the floor was covered with gypsum plaques, whereas elsewhere in the temple the floor was of beaten earth.

It is suggested that the twenty-eight wooden pillars (each consisting probably of two beams put together) were probably topped by capitals; their height is estimated at 5m., and they supported the roof. Several theories have been proposed by Callot regarding the roof. He suggests that the whole of the temple was roofed, except the western part, where the "naïskos" was much higher and therefore was open to the sky. Either light entered the temple through windows on the walls, or the central aisle had an elevated roof and therefore the possibility of higher windows. Callot also proposes a "second floor" above the central part of the long and narrow holy-of-holies, behind the

307

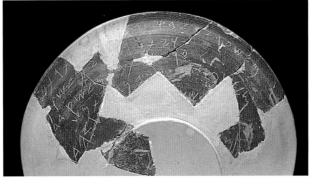

308

309

"naïskos," which functioned as a background to the "naïskos." In front of the east façade of the temple a large rectangular temenos replaced Temenos A of the Late Bronze Age. Its peribolos was constructed of small rectangular blocks of sandstone. Within the boundaries of the new temenos, in front of the entrance porch, there was a rectangular altar, and in the southeastern part a wall. The temenos was entered through the same east entrance that had also served the Late Bronze Age temenos.

The ceramic material found in association with the temple is quite rich. It consists of both local and Phoenician (Red Slip and Black Slip) fabrics, which date to the period circa 800 B.C. or slightly later (Bikai in press). The evidence of the Greek pottery found at the site, however, points clearly to the second half of the ninth century B.C., and it is not improbable that the Phoenician presence at Kition started from this early period (Coldstream 1981, 19–20). Among the Phoenician pottery are a number of Red Slip plates of fine ware (previously known as "Samaria" ware) and particularly a double bowl of ritual character, measuring 34cm. in diameter, 21cm. in height. Similar (but smaller) double bowls have been found elsewhere in the Phoenician world.

The lowest floor of the temple (Floor 3) was covered with ashes and charcoal, which indicate a destruction by fire of the twenty-eight pillars and the beams of the roof. It appears that the first temple was destroyed by fire and was soon rebuilt. In the southwest corner of the courtyard of the temple a large number of miniature bowls and juglets, mostly of Black-on-Red, Black Slip, and Red Slip wares, were found, together with carbonized animal bones, all mixed with ashes. The Black Slip bowls have two handles that are topped by finials in the form of a lotus flower, recalling a bronze version known in Cyprus since the eleventh century B.C. (e.g., at Palaepaphos) and also later at Eleutherna on Crete. There was also an iron skewer and an iron knife. All these were covered by the subsequent floor of the temple, Floor 2A, which means that they were deposited before the inauguration of the new (second) temple. The fact that most of them were found intact suggests that we do not have here an ordinary deposit (as in a bothros) where vases are usually crushed, but a deposit associated with a ceremony. This may have been a foundation ceremony, with foundation deposits and a sacrifice, performed in one of the corners of the temple (not under a wall, since it was only the columns and the roof of the temple that were rebuilt, not the walls). This would assure the goddess that her new temple would not suffer the same fate as the first one, which was destroyed by fire.

This temple has been identified as the temple of Astarte on the basis of the material found in it, namely, an inscribed bowl and a large number of female terra-cotta figurines. The inscribed bowl, of Red Slip ware, may date to the first half of the eighth century B.C. (and not circa 800 B.C., as I proposed earlier). It is fragmentary and bears an incomplete engraved inscription in Phoenician, which has been interpreted variably by scholars. Dupont Sommer (1970) proposed the following decipherment:

(1) In memorial. ML had his hair (herein) shaved and prayed to Lady Astarte and Astarte listened to his prayer (2) And were offered (as a sacrifice): on the part of ML, a sheep and a lamb, together (3) with this hair; on the part of the family of ML, a lamb. This vase (4) ML filled with his hair (herein) … seven in number, because of the prayer made in Tamassos (5) … the gift … which he liked … (6) Tamassos …

It is clear from the above that ML, who may be identified with the well-known Phoenician name Moula, probably a citizen of Tamassos, went as a worshiper together with his family to the temple of Astarte. We shall see later on that there was a temple of Astarte at Kition, which is known from another inscription. The ritual performances described on the bowl recall in a striking manner the ritual ceremonies that are mentioned by Lucian about one thousand years later. Observing the worshipers at Hierapolis in Syria, Lucian mentions that, just before their marriage, boys and girls go to the temple, have their hair cut, put it in vases of gold or silver that are fixed in the temple, and inscribe their names thereon. Lucian adds that he did exactly the same when a young man, and that his own hair was in such a bowl, with his name engraved on it, in the temple.

An inscription, painted in black ink on both sides of a small marble plaque now in the British Museum, was discovered during the British leveling operations at the "Acropolis" of Kition. The inscription, published for the first time by Ernest Renan in 1881, is dated to the fourth century B.C. and refers to the accounts of the temple of Astarte, enumerating several categories of persons who were employed in the temple together with their remuneration (Masson and Sznycer 1972, 21–68). Among them are the "sacred barbers," whose function has now become clear since the discovery of the inscribed bowl. Several different interpretations of the inscription on the Red Slip bowl have been proposed, namely by Teixidor, Liverani, and Amadasi (for a discussion and references see Amadasi and Karageorghis 1977, 149–160; Bonnet 1988, 329).

Some scholars have challenged the identification of this temple as a temple of Astarte and proposed that it may have been dedicated to a male god because of the bucrania found on Floors 3–2a, two bronze male figurines, and numerous figurines of the god Bes (Caubet 1986, 159–160; Bonnet 1988, 323–324; idem 1996, 73–74; Lipiński 1995, 139). They did not take into account that the vast majority of the terra-cotta fig-

310

urines found on *all* floors of the temple represent female figures, namely, of the types kourotrophos, *dea gravida*, nude goddess, etc. (see Karageorghis 1998e; idem forthcoming a and b). There were also a number of figurines of the well known type of "goddess with uplifted arms," introduced to Cyprus from Crete in the eleventh century B.C.; the type survived down to the end of the Cypro-Archaic period. The identification is further strengthened by historical circumstances. The years around the mid-ninth century B.C. coincide with the long and prosperous reign of Ethbaal, king of the Tyrians and the Sidonians, who reigned for 32 years (887–856 B.C.). Prior to becoming king he was a

310. Terra-cotta statuette of an enthroned "Astarte" on horseback. K. Severis Collection, Nicosia. Height: 18.2cm. The "goddess" is mounted sidesaddle on the throne with her feet on a footstool, and she wears a crown. She has red spots on her cheeks, and both the throne and her garments are lavishly decorated with linear ornaments in black and red paint. The horse has short "legs" perforated for four wheels. It was an old custom both in the Near East and the Aegean to carry the image of the divinity in procession. This highly unusual figurine may come from the Paphos region. It may be dated to circa 800 B.C.

high priest of Astarte, and when he ascended the throne he instituted her cult as the official cult of his kingdom. It is natural, then, that in a major Phoenician community like that of Kition, King Ethbaal should dedicate the rebuilt temple to the goddess Astarte.

The fact that figurines and other objects appropriate for the cult of a male divinity were found in the same temple does not negate this suggestion. It is known that the goddess could be worshiped together with a male companion, a baal; this has already been suggested by Bonnet (1996, 74). In Cyprus it is not an unusual phenomenon, either in antiquity (e.g., the cult of Athena together with Hercules at Kakopetria in the classical period) or in the present day, where votives of all kinds, appropriate for both a male and a female saint at the same time, are offered in local chapels or churches by both men and women.

Marguerite Yon, who excavates at Kition-*Bamboula*, shares this view, as is clear from an article that she published in 1984: "Les cultes d'Astarté et de Melqart sont attestés de façon irréfutable pour la période où l'on a des documents explicites (déjà fin du VIe à la fin du IVe s.), et il est probable que cet ensemble abritait les deux; l'inscription des comptes 'du temple d'Astarté' évoque également les 'piliers de Mikal,' qui est une divinité masculine. De la même manière, dans la quartier de Kathari fouillé par V. Karageorghis où se trouve le grand temple construit au IXe s. de façon beaucoup plus monumentale qu'à Bamboula par les Phéniciens, les figurines et les inscriptions attestent tout à la fois la présence divine de la Déesse (c'est-à-dire Astarté), et de Ba'al Melquart ('le Seigneur de la ville'). A Kathari comme à Bamboula, il semble que les deux cultes ne pouvaient être dissociés de façon aussi rationnelle qu'on voudrait le penser; et cette situation n'est peut-être pas étrangère à une tradition chypriote très ancienne où l'on retrouve, au cours du IIe millénaire, l'association de la Grande Déesse (Astarté ou Aphrodite) et du Seigneur, dieu de la fertilité (par la suite identifié pour certains aspects avec un Zeus)" (Yon 1984, 97; see also eadem 1985, 223–224).

We have already discussed elsewhere the importance of the wearing of bulls' masks during ritual ceremonies by priests or worshipers (Karageorghis and Demas 1985, 259–261). At Kition there is evidence for this custom on Floor II of Temple 5 (Late Cypriote IIIB) but it was also retained during the Phoenician period. About a dozen oxen skulls were found on the earliest floor of the temple. They were grouped together, not very far from the table of offerings. When they were restored it became clear that the backs had been purposely cut and cleaned of all projecting bones so that the skulls could be worn as masks, probably by the priests, during ritual ceremonies. Anthropomorphic masks in clay have been found at Kition, dating to the twelfth and eleventh centuries B.C.

Wearing masks, both zoomorphic and anthropomorphic (a fragmentary one was found in Bothros 13A, associated with Floor 3), had a long tradition in Cyprus, from the Bronze Age down to the end of the Archaic period. The skulls of oxen at Kition may have been worn over a piece of cloth or leather, so as to create a real mask. On the clay zoomorphic masks worn by the human figures, as represented by terra-cotta figurines found in sanctuaries at Kourion and Ayia Irini, part of the dewlap is represented; this must have been added to the skull. The purpose was no doubt to enter into direct association with the god by putting on his divine emblem and thereby acquiring some of his qualities and powers. The same idea existed in both the Aegean and the Near East, where for centuries minotaurs and bull-men dominated religious scenes depicted in art. There is literary confirmation of this custom for a later period: the writer Lucian in his treatise *De Dea Syra* (*On the Syrian Goddess*) describes a practice, according to which "when a man goes as a worshipper for the first time to Hierapolis [in Syria], he cuts his hair, then he sacrifices a lamb, he kneels down and puts the animal's head and feet on his own head, and prays to the gods to accept his sacrifice" (Lucian, *De Dea Syra*, 60).

The sacrifice of lambs and sheep in general must have been a very frequent practice in the Phoenician temple of Kition. Large quantities of sheep bones were found in the bothroi outside the great temple. Sheep bones were also found in a carbonized condition among the ashes of altars in the temenos.

East of the great temple of Astarte are the remains of Temple 4, which had more or less the same history as the former. It had a Late Bronze Age predecessor that was abandoned circa 1000 B.C. and was rebuilt by the Phoenicians on the foundations of the earlier temple. The tripartite holy-of-holies of the Late Bronze Age was now reduced to a one-room holy-of-holies in the eastern part. A hearth and table of offerings were constructed more or less in the middle of the courtyard, west of the holy-of-holies. Three stone bases in an east–west line along the north wall supported a roof.

The temple had a lateral entrance at the southwest corner of the courtyard. Female terra-cotta figurines may suggest that Temple 4 was also dedicated to a female divinity.

Temple 5 of the Late Bronze Age period was also rebuilt, but on a completely different plan from its Late Bronze Age predecessor. The Phoenician temple was built with rubble. Its holy-of-holies was on the west side, as during the Late Bronze Age. This Phoenician temple was probably dedicated to a male god, if we are to judge from the profusion of male terra-cotta figurines associated with it. On its earliest floor Greek Middle Geometric I sherds were found, belonging to an oenochoe of an Attic workshop, dating soon after 850 B.C. (Coldstream 1981, 17, 19).

The Great Temple of Astarte was destroyed by fire some time during the first half of the eighth century B.C. The temple that succeeded it was built on the older foundations, but a new floor (Floor 2A) was constructed above the debris of the destruction. The east gate and its porch were retained as the principal entry. The interior space now had two rows of pillars, creating three aisles, of which the central one was the largest and highest. Along the north wall two platforms were constructed for the deposit of offerings. The naïskos at the western extremity of the central nave, which was already present in Floor 3, was retained. A central opening behind the naïskos led to the long narrow corridor, and probably to the terrace above it.

This new temple of Floor 2A survived down to circa 600 B.C., and its life span corresponds to one of the most important periods in the history of Kition. The early part corresponds to the reign of Hiram II of Tyre, who, as we know, paid tribute to King Tiglathpileser III of Assyria (745–727 B.C.). It is also known that the king of Qartihadast (if this is the name of Kition and not of Amathus, as we shall discuss below), paid tribute to Hiram II and declared himself his "servant." In 709 or 707 B.C. Cyprus was occupied by the Assyrian King Sargon II, according to an inscribed stela found at Kition and now in Berlin. Seven kings of Cyprus "kissed" Sargon's feet. Thus, it is quite possible that the kings of Kition now followed a new policy, being more faithful to the Assyrians than to the king of the mother city, Tyre. During this period occurred the campaign of Eloulaios against Kition revolting against Tyrian rule, probably at the instigation of the Greek cities of the island that were on good relations with Sargon II. The latter allowed a certain degree of

311

312

autonomy to the Cypriote kings provided they paid their tribute regularly. Sennacherib of Assyria interpreted the action of Eloulaios as a declaration of war. In 701 B.C. he occupied the Tyrian kingdom except Tyre itself and Eloulaios fled to Kition, where he died in 694 B.C. On the famous prism of Esarhaddon (680–669 B.C.) "ten kings of the land of 'Yatnana [Cyprus] in the middle of the sea" are recorded, among whom is Damasu of Qartihadast (Kition) (for the history of this period see Gjerstad 1948, 436–448; Reyes 1994, 23–26). This means that the governor of the town, who was "servant of Hiram," was appointed as king by the Assyrians, and that Kition could now follow a policy independent of Tyre. This does not mean, however, that the Phoenicians lost control of Kition in any way. On the contrary, they may have collaborated more faithfully with the Assyrian masters of the island than the other kings, whose names, as they appear on the Esarhaddon prism, appear to be Greek. They must have developed their commercial fleet and carried out trade with both East and West. It is not surprising that Cyprus appears in the list of "thalassocracies" mentioned by Eusebius (see Karageorghis 1982, 128–129).

The Iron Age

II. The Cypro-Archaic I Period (750–600 B.C.)

1. The Assyrian "Rule"

Whether the Cypro-Geometric III period started circa 800 B.C. or earlier, it is only toward the end of the ninth century that substantial information about the history of the island becomes available. The Phoenician presence on the island at the end of the century must have considerably enhanced the economy of Cyprus, the renewal of exploitation of the copper mines, and the contacts with the outside world. During this period the kingdoms of Cyprus flourished economically, as we shall see below, and this has induced some scholars to suggest, in my opinion erroneously, that the kingdoms were established as such only in the eighth century B.C. (for discussion see Rupp 1987, 1988, and 1989).

Very little is known about the political structure in Cyprus during the ninth century B.C. We usually refer to phenomena of the eleventh century B.C., with the establishment of monarchical institutions and the exhibition of status and power in funerary dedications. What happened to the local Cypriote population? Was there a clear separation between the Greek element and the autochthonous part of the population? In recent years the notion of the existence of an indigenous Eteocypriote population that gathered at Amathus after the domination of the Greeks elsewhere in the island has tended to be eclipsed (cf. Reyes 1994, 13–16). The "evidence" for such a notion is based on later sources (cf. Reyes 1994, 13–14) and on three inscriptions in the Cypriote syllabary, but in an unknown "Eteocypriote" language, of fourth century B.C. date, found at Amathus (for references see also Reyes 1994, 14–15).

From the beginning of its existence as a town (eleventh century B.C.), Amathus did not differ culturally in any way from the other cities of Cyprus (see above, also Reyes 1994, 15–17; Iacovou 1999b, 152–153). Large numbers of mainly Euboean drinking cups and local imitations have been found in the tombs of Amathus (Coldstream 1987). It is true that already in the eighth century B.C. there was a strong Phoenician element in the population of Amathus, as shown by the large quantity of Phoenician pottery found in tombs. This has even led some scholars to identify Amathus with Qartihadast, an identification that is usually claimed by Kition (Hermary 1987; for further references and the archaeological evidence see Reyes 1994, 14–15, n. 18), and this may have caused some confusion among later writers. But the material culture of Amathus does not differ from that of the

313. Gold bowl, said to have been found in a tomb at Kourion. The Cesnola Collection, the Metropolitan Museum of Art, New York, no. 74.51.4551. Height: 4.9cm.; diam.: 14.2cm. The interior of the bowl is decorated in repoussé with incisions. At the bottom there is an omphalos surrounded by petals of a rosette. In two concentric zones the rest of the body is decorated with stylized papyrus motifs and seven swimming ducks, symmetrically arranged, three bulls, and three fallow deer. This bowl belongs to a class that betrays strong Egyptian influences, probably introduced by the Phoenicians. Circa 700 B.C.

314. Two skyphoi from Amathus (excavations of the Cyprus Department of Antiquities). Tomb 321, no. 182 (left) and no. 286 (right). No. 182 is Euboean Sub-proto-geometric III (circa 800–750 B.C.). Height: 8.7cm.; diam.: 13.6cm. No. 286 is a Cypriote imitation in Bichrome III ware (circa 850–750 B.C.). Height: 13.8cm.; diam.: 21cm. Limassol District Museum. The elite of Amathus became very fond of imported drinking cups from the Aegean, particularly from Euboea, for their dinner parties, as is shown by their frequent discovery in tombs and in the settlement.

314

315. Two Greek imported drinking cups (skyphoi) in the Cesnola Collection, the Metropolitan Museum of Art, New York, nos. 74.51.589 (left) and 74.51.588 (right). The cup on the left, 8.6cm in height, is Euboean from the first half of the eighth century B.C., the cup on the right, 9.4cm in height, is Attic, circa mid-eighth century B.C. The first one is decorated with pendant semi-circles, the second one with birds within rectangular panels.

316. Pedestal crater from Amathus (excavations of the Cyprus Department of Antiquities). Tomb 321, no. 283. Height: 45cm.; mouth diam.: 33cm. Limassol District Museum. The main decoration consists of two birds within rectangular panels on one side between the handles; on the other side is a hatched meander. Euboean, Late Geometric, circa 740–720 B.C. Euboea had close contacts with Cyprus during the eighth century B.C. and even earlier. Euboean vases, especially drinking cups, were not only imported to Cyprus, especially at Amathus, but also imitated locally.

317. Euboean Sub-protogeo-metric III (circa 800–750 B.C.) pottery from the tombs of Amathus (after Coldstream 1995, 201, fig. 1).

315

316

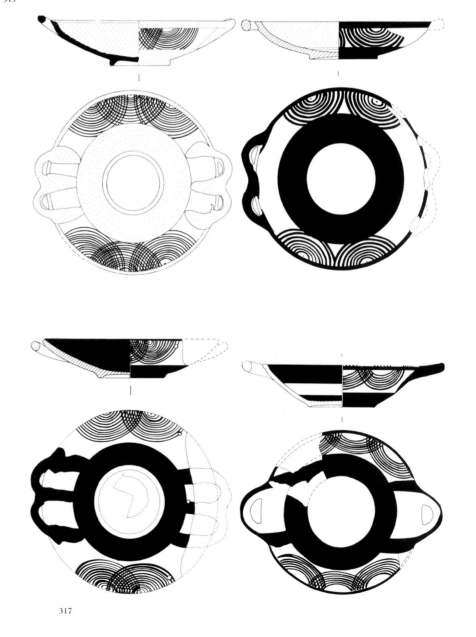

317

318

319

rest of Cyprus. In the eighth century B.C., however, the situation changed, and the presence of the Phoenicians may have caused some cultural separation. This may explain the recent discovery of a Phoenician-type cemetery at Amathus, separated from that of the rest of the population (Christou 1998). This part of the cemetery is situated in the sand at the seashore, at some distance from the much larger main cemetery of the town. It is unfortunate that the excavation of this cemetery was not carried out properly—it was only discovered to be a cemetary after most of it had been bulldozed! Although it did not yield funerary stelae (at least none was reported), it had many characteristics of a Phoenician cemetery: the incinerated remains of infants were found in identical urns placed in superimposed rows in the sand. Those of the lower row were placed in shallow cavities. Skeletal remains of small animals were found in some of the urns, and small objects of metal, bone, and alabaster were found all around the urns. Next to the area that was reserved for the burial of infants another area was excavated that yielded the remains of adults in larger amphorae. Although one cannot call this a tophet, it has all the characteristics of a Phoenician burial ground; it may have been reserved for the important Phoenician community of Amathus (see Karageorghis 1995c, 329–330). The cemetery may date to the Cypro-Archaic period. We hope that the urns and their contents will one day be published, in order to save at least some information from this cemetery, equally as ill-fated as the one recently discovered at Tyre (Seeden 1991).

The first epigraphic reference for the existence of kings and kingdoms in Cyprus is the stone stela with a cuneiform inscription found in 1845 either at Idalion or at Kition (most likely Kition) and now in Berlin. It was erected at the very end of the eighth century B.C.; it mentions Sargon II's third year as a king of Babylon, his fifteenth as king of Assyria. Thus a fixed date of 707 B.C. may be suggested. The stela shows, in low relief, the bearded king in profile, dressed in the long fringed Assyrian robes and wearing a ceremonial headdress. Such stelae were common throughout the Assyrian empire and "presumably substituted for the presence of the Assyrian king, a reminder of the relations with him, and perhaps even a tangible object upon which an oath of loyalty might be sworn" (Reyes 1994, 50–51). The cuneiform inscription, carved on the sides of the stela, reads as follows (ibid., 51).

"'[Seven king]s of the land of Ia,' a district [of Iad]nana, which [is situated] at seven days' journey [in the midst of] the sea of the setting sun, and whose dwellings are distant—[since] far-off days [they had not paid?] the tax (sibtu) of Assyria, for none of the kings, my fathers [who preceded] me [had even hea]rd the name of their land—they heard from the midst of the sea of [the deeds that I had performed] in Chaldaea and the Hatti-land, and their hearts beat fast; their [trib]ute: gold, silver, [vessels of] ebony, boxwood, the treasure of their land, [into] Babylon to my presence, [they brought and] they kissed my feet".

As seen in the inscription, Cyprus was now called Iadnana, identified by some scholars as the land of Danaans (Stylianou 1992, 382–386). This is of con-

318. Skyphos imitating Greek prototypes, probably made in Cyprus by Greek potters. Cyprus Museum, Nicosia, Inv. no. 1979/VI-16/1. Height: 6cm.; diam.: 10.7cm. Similar bowls have been found at Al Mina in south Turkey.

319. Jars for the burial of infants from a burial ground near the beach at Amathus. They may be associated with the burial ground of the Phoenician community of Amathus during the Cypro-Archaic period. Though this burial ground may recall the "tophets" of the Punic world (but also of Phoenicia itself), it should be noted that it has not yielded any stelae that are characteristic of "tophets." The jars were buried in the sand, in superimposed layers.

320. The stela of Sargon II, in the Vorderasiatisches Museum, Berlin, Inv. no. VA 968. Gabbro stone. Height: 2.09m. It shows the bearded king on the front, and along the sides is a carved cuneiform inscription recording that seven kings of Cyprus kissed his feet.

321. Silver bowl with gilding on the interior, said to have belonged to the "Curium Treasure." The Cesnola Collection, the Metropolitan Museum of Art, New York, no. 74.51.4554. Height: 3.1cm.; diam.: 16.8cm. The interior is decorated in repoussé with incisions. The central medallion is filled with a winged deity in Assyrian dress killing a rampant lion. An Egyptian falcon flies above the deity's head. The narrow inner zone contains a frieze of animals, trees, sphinxes, and a lion striding over a fallen human figure; there is also a kneeling archer attacking a lion, etc. The broader outer zone is decorated with a human figure in Assyrian garments killing a griffin, an Egyptian king attacking enemies, large lotus flowers, various monsters, etc. This bowl belonged to a king: in a specially reserved space there is a Cypro syllabic inscription that reads: "I am [the bowl] of Akestor, king of Paphos." This inscription was partly erased and a second inscription replaced it, which reads: "I am [the bowl] of Timokretes." This replacement probably occurred in the fifth century B.C. Gold and silver bowls have been found in "royal" tombs, occasionally bearing the names of kings or simply their owners. This bowl, one of the best preserved, dates to circa 725–675 B.C.

320

siderable importance, because this would mean that the name of Cyprus as a land of the Greeks was quite familiar in Sargon's court (cf. Iacovou 1999b, 154). This identification, however, is still a matter of dispute. It may well be that the Assyrians devised names during this period for the Greeks, "Iamana," and for the Cypriots, "Iadnana." This, according to Boardman, "implies some degree of interest and mutual dealing; perhaps even associating Greeks and Cypriots in Assyrian minds" (Boardman 2001, 18). That Sargon did raise this stela is confirmed by a clay inscribed prism from Nimrud, the capital of the Assyrian empire (Gadd 1954).

For nearly half a century students of Cypriote archaeology and history have followed Gjerstad in accepting an Assyrian occupation of Cyprus circa 709 B.C., which was followed by a period of about one hundred years of "independence," from 669 to 560 B.C. Thus the Assyrians were thought to have occupied Cyprus from 709 B.C. to 669 B.C. (for references see Reyes 1994, 23–24, 49–51). More critical examination of the Assyrian texts and especially the fact that similar declarations of an Assyrian ruling governor collecting taxes were erected in other places of the Near East that did not have Assyrian governors led Reyes to propose convincingly that these declarations "were simply meant to mark geographically strategic points around the Assyrian Empire, or as propagandistic statements of power" (Reyes 1994, 52–53). Reyes explains the reference to the gifts sent by the seven kings of Cyprus as follows: "It does not follow … that the Cypriots were unhappy to pay tribute to the Assyrian king. Indeed, just as other Levantine communities had, the Cypriots probably recognized the commercial and political advantages of participating in an economic system protected by the Assyrians. Since there was a large Phoenician population settled in Cyprus, the kings of the island may well have been kept advised of events in Syria and Palestine through their Phoenician contacts, and then acted in their own interests. It is possible too that the Assyrian rulers also used Phoenician contacts to ensure the continued movement of goods from the island into the Assyrian palaces, but the extent to which they did so, if at all, remains unknown" (Reyes 1994, 54–55).

It is worth mentioning here a novel theory put forward very recently by Boardman regarding the relations between Assyria and Cyprus at the end of the eighth century B.C. (Boardman 2001a, 16–22). In trying to confirm that there was a Greek colony at Al

322

322. Fragmentary silver bowl said to have formed part of the "Curium Treasure." The Cesnola Collection, the Metropolitan Museum of Art, New York, no. 74.51.4557. Diam.: 17.5cm. The interior of the bowl was engraved with pictorial compositions in concentric zones, of which two survive partially. The inner zone was decorated with hunters of animals, flowers, and monsters. The outer one represents a feast in honor of two human figures reclining on couches; above them are engraved inscriptions in the Cypriote syllabary, but in the Greek language. Above the male figure the inscription reads simply "the king." Above the female figure the inscription reads "Kypromedousa," i.e., "she who reigns over Cyprus." This may be either the name of the queen, or, as recently suggested, an epithet for Aphrodite. There are musicians and gift bearers on either side, proceeding toward the reclining human figures. Circa 710–675 B.C.

Mina, at the mouth of the Orontes River, he reexamined the pottery from Al Mina, both Greek and Cypriote. He concluded that a proportion of the Greek pottery was made by Greeks not in Greece, but possibly in Cyprus or in Syria. The shapes of the drinking cups are Greek, but in their decoration there are some features in the Cypriote Bichrome technique. This means, according to Boardman, more than a casual awareness of Cypriote decoration. He goes on to suggest that much of the Cypriote pottery from Al Mina is not normal Cypriote, but probably of local Syrian manufacture. Thus, he suggests, there may have been Cypriots and Greeks alike in Syria at the end of the eighth and the early seventh century B.C., making their own pottery. In order to explain this phenomenon he suggests that during this period the Assyrians, who were tireless movers of populations, may have moved some Cypriots by force and settled them in Syria, beside the other Greek settlers of Al Mina. This happened at the time when Sargon's inscribed stela was erected at Kition, and it should be considered within the framework of the desire of the Assyrians to extend their control over Syria, using also the presence of the Phoenicians in Cyprus. It is now believed that Sargon's stela was erected after Tyre (a vassal to Assyria), reported to Sargon the failure of Cyprus to pay tribute (ibid., 17). By doing so the

Assyrians assured the continued trade by Greeks and Cypriots via Syria, since neither the Assyrians not the Syrians were sailors. Thus the Cypriots, from Iadnana, side by side with other Greek speakers from Iadnana, were playing the role of hostages as much as traders, as part of an Assyrian political requirement. This is an interesting theory, which, however, needs to be investigated further. I personally am not entirely convinced that the Cypriote pottery from Al Mina was made in Syria; the role of the Greeks at Al Mina is still disputed, and the role of the Phoenicians is not entirely clear in the relations between the Aegean and the Levant. If it proves valid, then it will elucidate the phenomenon of the orientalizing revolution in Greek art and Cyprus during this period and the influx of orientalia in both regions (for a further discussion see Boardman 2001b).

There is another reference to Cyprus in an inscription found in the Assyrian palace of Sennacherib. It records that Luli, "King of Sidon," revolted against the king of Assyria but was afraid to fight him; instead he fled to Cyprus to seek refuge. This, as Reyes rightly pointed out, may indicate that Cyprus was not under Sennacherib's direct control (Reyes 1994, 57).

The third reference to Cyprus in an Assyrian inscription is made on the well-known clay prism that commemorates the rebuilding of the royal palace of Nineveh and dates to 673/2 B.C., in the reign of the Assyrian king Esarhaddon. It names ten Cypriote kings who sent raw materials for the rebuilding of his palace (Reyes 1994, 160):

Ekištura, king of Edil (Idalion)
Pilagura, king of Kitrusi (Chytroi)
Kisu, king of Sillua (? Salamis or Soloi)
Ituandar, king of Pappa (Paphos)
Eresu, king of Silli (? Salamis or Soloi)
Damasu, king of Kuri (Kourion)
Admesu (? Girmesu), king of Tamesi (Tamassos)
Damusi, king of Qartihadast (usually equated with Kition)
Unasagusu, king of Lidir (Ledra)
Bušusu (? Pušusu), king of Nûria (uncertain)
(after Reyes 1994, 160)

That Cyprus had seven kings in the eighth century B.C. and ten in the seventh century B.C. is not certain. Gjerstad already pointed out that the number "seven" in Sargon's text is very probably a conventional one, the number seven being a mystic number (cf. Snodgrass 1988, 10). It is interesting and important that out of the ten kings mentioned in the prism of

323

Esarhaddon, at least eight have Greek names. In this respect we should mention a silver bowl that is said to have been found at Kourion and is now in the Metropolitan Museum of Art, New York. The bowl, dated to the late eighth century B.C., is engraved with the Greek name Akestor, king of Paphos (for references see Reyes 1994, 57–58). On another silver bowl, also from Kourion, again in the Metropolitan Museum of Art, there is a banquet scene that is attended by a king and queen. The bowl is dated to the early seventh century B.C. Above the king there is the engraved word "the king"; above the queen is her name engraved as "Kypromedousa" (she who rules over Cyprus) (Karageorghis *et al.* 1999a). Hermary suggests that this is the name not of the queen but of Aphrodite (Hermary 2000) (see further discussion of this bowl below). On a pair of gold bracelets, also from Kourion, the Greek name of another king of Paphos is mentioned: Etewandros (for references see Karageorghis *et al.* 1999a, 18).

Of the ten kingdoms, eight have been identified more or less certainly. Nuria has been identified conjecturally with Amathus, Qartihadast with Kition (for references see Reyes 1994, 24). Three important cities, all of which may possibly have been kingdoms (as they were in the classical period), i.e., Lapithos, Marion, and Golgoi, are not mentioned. Eusebios, a later Greek author, counts Cyprus among the "thalassocracies" of the eighth century B.C. To explain this claim entirely in terms of the presence of the Phoenicians in Cyprus may not be altogether correct. This has been discussed recently by Boardman, who credits the Cypriots for much of the trade with Egypt and the rest of the Mediterranean during this period (Boardman 2001a, 14–15). The presence of merchant marks in the Cypriote syllabary on two Greek vases of about 700 B.C., one found in south Italy and the other in north Greece, offers corroborating evidence for the role of Greek Cypriots in Mediterranean trade. Indeed, the dense forests of Cyprus offered the necessary timber for building up a sizable merchant fleet.

2. The Royal Tombs of Salamis

Before turning to the material culture of Cyprus during the late Cypro-Geometric and the Cypro-Archaic periods (discussed in separate sections below), it is important to examine the tombs of the "royal" necropolis of Salamis, perhaps the foremost of all the island's kingdoms. Not only will they throw light on the material culture and interconnections, but they also have a direct bearing on the status of the king and his position in Cypriote society. This discussion will also provide the opportunity to place Cyprus

323. Salamis Tomb 79 (excavations of the Cyprus Department of Antiquities). General view of the large dromos in front of the stone-built façade of the chamber. The latter was found looted (it was reused in the Roman period). The roof of the chamber was covered by a huge monolith. The tomb was used twice in the Cypro-Archaic I period, circa 700 B.C., the second burial following the first by a few years. On the sloping cemented floor of its spacious dromos were found the remains of two chariots, the bronze trappings of horses, ivory furniture, two bronze cauldrons, and a large quantity of vases, some containing food. Tomb 79 was no doubt a "royal" tomb, the richest found in the necropolis of Salamis.

324

325

324. Bronze tire-disc from the decoration of Chariot B, found in the dromos of Salamis Tomb 79, no. 220.1 (excavations of the Cyprus Department of Antiquities). Height: 31.5cm. Cyprus Museum, Nicosia. Decorated in repoussé with a winged lion striding over a fallen human being. The scene symbolizes the conquest of the Egyptian Pharaoh over his enemies. The influence of Egyptian iconography is obvious (after Karageorghis 1974, pl. CCLXXIX).

325. Salamis Tomb 79 (excavations by the Cyprus Department of Antiquities). The upper part of the decoration of one of the two iron linchpins of Chariot B, no. 188: a bronze warrior wearing a crested helmet and a scale corselet. The scales were inlaid with blue paste, as were his eyes. Under his right arm he holds a long sword, hanging from a strap over his right shoulder. Hollow cast. A short tunic appears below the corselet, decorated with engraved flowers. Total height: 36.5cm.

within the cultural scenario of the whole of the Mediterranean region, illustrated by the "heroic burials" of the Aegean and the princely burials of Etruria. The importance of the city of Salamis during the eleventh century B.C. has already been mentioned. In view of its situation on the east coast of Cyprus, with a natural harbor and a rich hinterland, its king must have dominated a large portion of the fertile Mesaoria plain. No architectural remains dating to the period immediately after the eleventh century B.C. have so far been discovered at the city site, but in the "royal" necropolis there is evidence for a monumental tomb dating to the Cypro-Geometric III period. A built tomb (Tomb 50A), largely destroyed when Tomb 50 was constructed (see below), yielded material that helps to bridge the gap between the eleventh and eighth centuries B.C. (Karageorghis 1978, 11–13; idem 1980b).

It demonstrates that Salamis already had an aristocratic society, the members of which were buried in monumental tombs. This, however, is better demonstrated by a series of impressive built tombs of the eighth century B.C., the most important of which is Tomb 79. Although the chambers of all these tombs had been looted in the past, their large dromoi were found intact. Not only did they yield precious objects, offered to the dead to demonstrate their status, but in the dromoi funerary customs were observed that befitted an elite society of warrior-kings.

i. Tomb 79

Tomb 79 (Karageorghis 1973, 4–122) was found looted, and it had also been reused during the Roman period. The chamber was rectangular, measuring 3.2×2.4m. and had a gabled roof. Its lower part consisted of three large hard limestone rectangular blocks carved and fitted together to form the floor of the chamber and the side walls to a height of 45cm. The upper part of the chamber, including the roof, consisted of a monolith carved so as to form a saddle roof, four vertical side walls, and a rectangular stomion. The total height of the side walls (south and north) is 130cm. The height of the west wall to the roof is 180cm. The stomion was in the east wall of the chamber, north of the central axis; it measured 150cm. in height and 100cm. in width. There was no threshold, the floor of the chamber being on the same level as that of the propylaeum outside.

The façade of the chamber, constructed of well-dressed blocks of hard limestone, formed a rectangular Π-shaped recess, 7m. wide and 3.2m. deep. The original height of the façade, judging from the original thickness of the monolith, must have been 2.8m.; only 1.9m. is preserved since the front of the monolith was cut away by stone robbers. The stomion measures 1m in width and 1.55m. in height. The total width of the façade was 12.8m., and this corresponds also to the maximum width of the dromos, which narrows near the entrance to 9m. The total length of the dromos is 16.8m. The floor was covered with concrete cement and sloped down toward the stomion.

The fill of the dromos, consisting of loose earth, was undisturbed and was carefully excavated. The stratification of the fill showed that there were two burial periods in the tomb. During the first burial, which may be dated by the pottery to the end of the eighth century B.C., two vehicles were placed in the dromos, a chariot and a hearse, one drawn by four, the other by two, quadrupeds (horses?). The skeletal remains of these animals, however, were thoroughly disturbed during the second burial (which, as we shall see below, followed a few years after the first) and were found broken and scattered in the fill of the dromos, which was replaced after the second burial. The vehicles themselves were placed on the south side of the dromos, the chariot with the edge of its two poles touching the south wall of the dromos, and the hearse just behind it to the east. The chariot could still be wheeled away in perfect condition (this is why we assume that there was only a very short interval between the two periods), while the hearse had lost its wheels and pole.

The chariot, registered as Chariot B, had two poles. These, as well as all the wooden parts of the chariot, had left in the soil their distinct impressions, which were carefully measured, photographed, and drawn. Both ends of the poles were protected by bronze caps. At the back of each pole, on the part that was projecting beyond the chariot box, an ovoid bronze disc hung vertically, allowing the bronze cap of the terminal to show through. These discs are decorated in repoussé with a winged lion striding over a conquered, fallen enemy in the well-known Egyptian fashion. The disc is perforated all around its perimeter and was probably sewn on a plaque of another material (leather?), which has perished.

The axle had at each end a bronze cap in the shape of a sphinx head with a broad collar rim around the neck, the eyes inlaid with white paste. Inserted vertically through the neck of the sphinx, and consequently

326

through the axle, was an iron linchpin, bearing at the top a bronze figurine of a fully armed soldier cast hollow with a rattle inside it. This figure, about 37cm. high, with eyes inlaid with blue paste, wears above a short chiton a scaled corselet inlaid with blue paste. The corselet recalls the cuirass that King Kinyras offered to Agamemnon, as described by Homer in the *Iliad* (XI, 19–40), which was also decorated with a blue inlay (kyanos). The figure also wears a helmet with a semi-circular crest terminating above the forehead in a disc, also inlaid with paste. Under his left arm he holds the pommel of a sword that is hanging from a belt across his torso. The glitter of the bronze, the polychromy of the inlaid paste, and the rattle of the linchpins must have added an impressive note to the solemn pomp of the funeral cortège when this vehicle was passing.

The second vehicle, registered as Hearse Γ (gamma), was not as well preserved as the chariot. It had lost its wheels, but enough was left to show that the body was richly decorated with bronze nails. Around the floor of the hearse there were five bronze lions' heads, one at each of the four corners and one in the middle of the front. They are hollow with a socket at the top,

probably for the attachment of a post to support a canopy. Their rendering is very naturalistic and suggests Egyptian prototypes.

Of the two other vehicles associated with the second burial, one is a hearse and the other a war chariot. They were both found in their original positions with the skeletons of the horses still lying *in situ*, though those of the hearse had been damaged by looters, being near the surface by the entrance of the dromos. The chariot, registered as Chariot Δ (delta), was a biga (that is, designed to be pulled by two horses). Its chariot box, 90cm. wide, 72cm. long, and 25cm. deep, was divided into two compartments, one for the charioteer and the other for the warrior, as in Chariot B. On top of the yoke at regular intervals were four bronze rings for the reins, and there were also four bronze decorative flower-shaped standards, about 50cm. high.

The horses associated with such richly decorated vehicles were suitably caparisoned. They had bronze blinders and headbands, the upper part of the latter decorated with prominently curving crests, bronze breastplates decorated in repoussé, and a side pendant

327

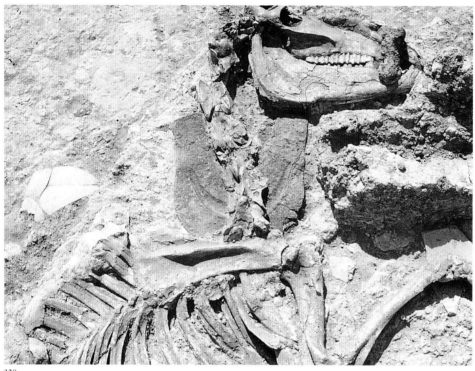

328

327. Salamis, Tomb 79 (excavations of the Cyprus Department of Antiquities). Skeletons of two horses and the impressions of a chariot found *in situ*, on the floor of the dromos. The yoke of the chariot was decorated with flower-shaped bronze standards.

328. Salamis, Tomb 79 (excavations of the Cyprus Department of Antiquities). Skeleton of a chariot horse, with bronze breastplate and iron bits *in situ*, on the floor of the dromos.

ornament, one for each horse (only the outer flanks of the horses being thus protected); these were decorated with large beetles in repoussé. The bits were of iron. All these items were found *in situ* and indicate the original position and function of this gear, which was previously known only from often imperfect representations, such as in reliefs, where three-dimensional rendering was lacking.

The four horses of Chariot B and the two horses of Hearse Γ were presumably also buried wearing all their harness, and this in fact was found, all piled up in a corner of the propylaeum. During the second burial (which followed, as mentioned above, shortly after the first, when vehicles B and Γ were moved aside), the metal gear of the horses was collected and put away, while the skeletal remains were destroyed. The bronze gear of the first burial is all very lavishly decorated in repoussé.

The four breastplates were decorated in repoussé with two registers of oriental monsters, including griffins, sphinxes, winged human figures holding situlae, scorpion-men, etc. In the center there is a winged solar disc above a stylized "tree of life." Below there is a human figure holding a kid in his arms.

Two side pendant ornaments (which protected the upper part of the horses' forelegs) were decorated with a winged nude Ishtar in the center, holding a lion in each hand and standing on the backs of two other lions. The lions above are being attacked by griffins, and those below hold calves in their mouths. There is a winged solar disc and a Hathor head above the head of Ishtar. The borders of the discs are decorated with friezes of animals. The association of Ishtar with horses is well known in the ancient Near East (Leclant 1960; Bonnet 1996).

Nanno Marinatos, in a recently published book (2000, 18–24), put forward an interesting theory, that the naked female figures appearing on weapons and horse ornaments have an apotropaic function, protecting the warrior and rider, and are therefore connected with male, rather than female, worshipers. Commenting on the bronze horse gear from Salamis Tomb 79, particularly the side pendant ornament with the nude female figure holding a lion in each hand and standing on the back of two other lions, she stresses the association of danger and sexuality, the first symbolized by all the animals attacking each other while the nude goddess controls them. She concludes that "the hierarchy of nature, as well as danger and sexuality, form one single coherent complex that is part of the warrior's ideology. The nude deity is his protectress" (ibid., 21). This symbolism bringing danger and sexuality together has a long tradition in Old Babylonian art and must have been transmitted to Cyprus and the Aegean, especially Crete, through north Syria (ibid., 8–9).

There are two kinds of front bands that decorated the foreheads of the horses; they are both crested. One group is decorated with superimposed rows of couchant lions, uraei, nude human figures, and a winged solar disc. The other group is decorated with two figures of the winged god El, a solar disc, and stylized lotus flowers. They all consist of two parts hinged in the middle and have a loop for attachment at the top.

The blinders are decorated either with a lion attacking a kneeling bull or a winged sphinx striding over a prostrate African, representing the Egyptian Pharaoh striding over his enemies.

In addition to these harness ornaments we may also mention bronze bells and belts that were found on the pile of gear and that may also have belonged to the horses of the first burial.

A stylistic analysis of these objects and determination of their origin will not be attempted here. Although similar objects are known from elsewhere in Cyprus, the decoration of these is unique and points to the art of the Near East, probably north Syria. There are also elements in their decoration that recall the art of Urartu, or Mesopotamia, but it is hard to assign to them any specific style. These Near Eastern influences may have constituted a koine of Phoenician art, which borrowed various elements from Egypt, north Syria, and Urartu (cf. Porada in Karageorghis 1973c, 82–86; Reyes 1994, 65).

In any case, there is no doubt that the richly decorated chariots and hearses, combined with the lavishly ornamented horses—let alone their colorful caparisons—must have offered a spectacle of extraordinary pomp and luxury.

Of the warrior's armor the only objects that survived are a large bronze spearhead and the hemispherical silver umbo of a shield, with the outer surface gilded. The rim of the umbo is perforated all around for fixing onto the leather surface of the shield.

Another extraordinary object found in the dromos of Tomb 79, near the north wall of the propylaeum and obviously belonging to the first burial, was a bronze cauldron standing on an iron tripod base. The height of the cauldron including the attachments and tripod is 125cm. The vessel was beaten out of two sheets and

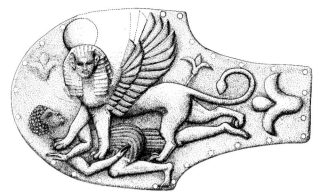

329. Bronze blinder for a horse, from the dromos of Salamis Tomb 79, no. 157 (excavations of the Cyprus Department of Antiquities). Length: 19.5cm. Cyprus Museum, Nicosia. Decoration in repoussé with a winged sphinx striding over a fallen enemy, symbolizing the conquest of the Egyptian Pharaoh over his enemies (after Karageorghis 1973c, pl. CCLXVII).

329

330

331

330. Bronze front band forming part of the horse gear, from Salamis (excavations of the Cyprus Department of Antiquities), Tomb 79, no. 165. Length: 50cm. Cyprus Museum, Nicosia. It consists of two plates joined together with a horizontal hinge. Crest for feathers (?) at the upper part. The decoration, in high repoussé, consists of human figures on the lower plate and couchant lions and uraei on the upper plate; winged solar disc along the top of the lower plate. The Egyptian character of the

decoration is obvious, as on other bronze gear for horses and chariots from Salamis Tomb 79.

331. Bronze side pendant ornament from Salamis (excavations of the Cyprus Department of Antiquities), Tomb 79, no. 135. Length: 45cm.; diam. of disc: 24.5cm. Cyprus Museum, Nicosia. It consists of two plates, joined horizontally with hinges. The upper plate is oblong and narrow, with a hole for suspension. It is decorated in repoussé, with a stylized flower ornament.

The lower part is a disc, decorated in high repoussé with a beetle, a distinctly Egyptian motif. Side pendant ornaments protected (and decorated) the upper part of the forelegs of the horses, as seen on Assyrian reliefs.

161

332

has a very thick rim. All around the cauldron, on the shoulder and just below the rim, are eight griffin protomes, fixed on with rivets, which were cast by the cire perdue (lost-wax) method. There are also four more attachments on the shoulder of the cauldron, each positioned symmetrically between two pairs of griffins. They are made of several parts, some beaten and others cast separately, and represent bearded birdmen or sirens, with broad wings that are attached to the shoulder of the cauldron. Such cauldrons decorated with griffin protomes are known from Etruria and Greece, but they are very rare in the Near East. We know of a number of bronze cauldrons from Altintepe, Toprakkale, Gordion, and elsewhere that are decorated around the rim, usually with bull and siren attachments. The Salamis cauldron is an extraordinary work of art, with more protomes around its rim than any

332. Fragmentary bronze breastplate from Salamis (excavations of the Cyprus Department of Antiquities), Tomb 79, no. 164. Height: 43cm. Cyprus Museum, Nicosia. It is decorated all over in repoussé in two registers, with winged human figures (genies), men with scorpion tails, griffins, etc. The style of the decoration is mixed with Assyrian and Urartian elements of the second half of the eighth century B.C.

333. Bronze front band from Salamis (excavations of the Cyprus Department of Antiquities), Tomb 79, no. 192. Existing height: 44.5cm. Cyprus Museum, Nicosia.

334. Bronze spearhead from Salamis (excavations of the Cyprus Department of Antiquities), Tomb 79, no. 130. Length: 49.5cm. Broad leaf-shaped blade, with four deep grooves along the edge. This is of a unique type and may have been used on ceremonial occasions. Cyprus Museum, Nicosia.

335. Bronze side pendant armament for a horse from Salamis (excavations of the Cyprus Department of Antiquities), Tomb 79, no. 155+162. Length: 58cm. Cyprus Museum, Nicosia. It consists of a long narrow plaque that is hinged on a disk. The central part of the disc is decorated in repoussé, with a winged nude female figure (Astarte) standing on the backs of two seated antithetic lions, which hold in their jaws a calf or a bull. Above the Astarte figure there is a winged Hathor head. Astarte holds in each hand a lion being attacked by a griffin. Astarte is here represented as the mistress of animals. She has a particular relation with horses.

333

334

335

162

other known specimen. Next to this cauldron there was a second one, standing on a high conical foot but much damaged. The rim was decorated with three bulls' heads facing inward; the plates onto which the handles were riveted were decorated in relief with a Hathor head flanked by two palmettes; above the Hathor head there was a winged solar disc.

Finally, among the metal objects found in the dromos of Tomb 79 were a pair of firedogs and a bundle of twelve iron obeloi (skewers). The firedogs, 1.1m. long, terminate in the stern and prow of a ship respectively, not unlike others found at Patriki and Palaepaphos in Cyprus, at Kavousi and Eleutherna in Crete, and at Argos in the Peloponnese. The skewers, 1.5m. long, were bound together with two rings, with a loop between for carrying (cf. Karageorghis 1973c, 118). Skewers and firedogs are known also from the princely tombs of Etruria and must have formed part of the tomb-furniture of "heroic" burials. We know from Homeric descriptions how important the preparation of roasted meat was for a warrior's feast (see below). Skewers of bronze and iron, as already mentioned, are known in tombs of warriors in Palaepaphos and Kition as early as the eleventh century B.C.

The most spectacular objects from the dromos of Tomb 79 are pieces of furniture, comprising one bed and three thrones. We will describe the best pre-served, which are the ivory bed, one ivory throne, and another covered with thin sheets of silver. All three were made of wood, and the entire surface of each was decorated. One throne was covered with plaques of ivory, fixed or inlaid, and thin sheets of gold on the upper part of the backrest. The wood had completely disintegrated, but the ivory and gold were preserved *in situ*. With the help of cloth and wire we were able to remove these parts to the laboratory of the Cyprus Museum, where they were placed in position on a wooden frame that copied the exact dimensions of the original throne. Particularly delicate was the inlaid decoration of the backrest, with vertical guilloche patterns alternating with plain vertical bands; there were also two horizontal friezes of inlaid anthemia. The throne was also decorated on either side, between the arms and the seat, with two openwork plaques of ivory: one represents a composite flower motif and the other a winged sphinx and stylized flowers. Both plaques were also encrusted with blue and brown paste. The sphinx, a symbol of royalty, suggests an Egyptian inspiration for the throne, but this motif is also quite common in Phoenician and Syrian art,

336

336. Bronze cauldron standing on an iron tripod, from Salamis (excavations of the Cyprus Department of Antiquities), Tomb 79, no. 202. Total height: 125cm. Cyprus Museum, Nicosia. It was hammered out of two metal sheets. There are eight cast protomes of griffins and four double-headed "sirens" riveted around the rim of the vessel. The cauldron is supported on an iron tripod decorated with lilies. Such vessels have hitherto been known from Etruria and Greece; this is the first to appear in the East Mediterranean. The ultimate origin of the style may be Urartian with Phoenician influences, circa 700 B.C.

163

337-338. Detail from a large cauldron from Salamis (excavations of the Cyprus Department of Antiquities), Tomb 79, no. 203. The cauldron is supported on a high conical stand. Height: 55cm. Cyprus Museum, Nicosia. The rim was decorated with two antithetic groups of bull protomes, looking toward the inside of the cauldron; they are fixed on a horizontal attachment on which a loop handle is also fixed. Below each handle there is a rectangular plaque decorated in repoussé with a Hathor head flanked by papyrus flowers; above the head is a winged solar disc. This cauldron is in a koine style, with mixed oriental motifs, which prevailed in the Eastern Mediterranean at the early part of the eighth century B.C. It was found next to the griffins-and-sirens cauldron described above.

339-340. Iron firedog (no. 127) and a bundle of twelve iron skewers (oboloi) (nos. 263–274) from Salamis (excavations of the Cyprus Department of Antiquities), Tomb 79. Cyprus Museum, Nicosia. Length of skewers: 153cm.; length of firedog: 110cm.; height: 12cm.

341. Salamis, Tomb 79 (excavations of the Cyprus Department of Antiquities). Among the four thrones found in the dromos of the tomb, one (Throne A), together with a footstool, was made of wood covered with silver plating. The wood disintegrated, but the silver left its stains on the soil. The restored throne is 102.5cm. high, and the stool is 21cm. high. Cyprus Museum, Nicosia. The various parts of the throne were fixed together with rivets of silver with gold-plated heads.

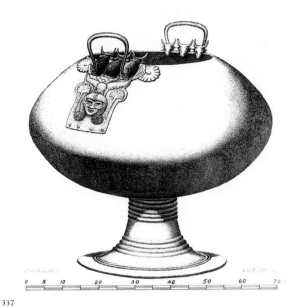

337

338

339

340

especially in the ivory carvings from the palace of Nimrud.

The second throne was covered with thin sheets of silver. It had a footstool, recalling the thrones and footstools mentioned quite often by Homer when describing the reception of guests in palaces. The throne was decorated with silver nails, the heads of which were covered with sheets of gold. A throne of ivory is described by Homer: the throne of Penelope, which is a striking match for the throne from Salamis Tomb 79 (*Odyssey* xix.55–59; Karageorghis 1967b, 168–170; idem 1968, 102). The throne decorated with sheets of silver also corresponds to the Homeric descriptions of "silver-studded" thrones (θρόνος ἀργυρόηλος) (e.g., *Odyssey* vii. 162).

The bed, whose ivory plaques were found scattered on the floor of the dromos and mixed with the bronze gear of the horses of the first burial (circa 700 B.C.), was reconstructed in the same way as the thrones. It recalls the bed of Odysseus, which he made himself (*Odyssey* xxiii. 199–200). The bedstead was tentatively restored to accommodate a frame of ivory plaques.

341

342

343

342-343. Salamis, Tomb 79 (excavations of the Cyprus Department of Antiquities). Throne 5, found on the floor of the dromos, near the façade of the tomb, was made of wood and was covered with ivory plaques. Restored height: 90cm. The backrest of the throne was decorated with vertical panels of inlaid guilloche, its lower part with friezes of inlaid anthemia. Below the handles there were two ajouré plaques of ivory, one representing a winged sphinx and the other a composite lotus flower. At the upper part of the inner curve of the backrest there was a horizontal band of thin gold sheet. This throne recalls the throne of Penelope, described by Homer in the *Odyssey*. It is of Phoenician workmanship, like the ivory bed from the same tomb.

They are decorated in relief with figures: the god Heh holding a branch of a palm tree from which the Egyptian symbol of life, ankh, is hanging. The trousers of Heh are covered with thin sheets of gold. Other plaques were carved with stylized anthemia with interlocked stems, the flowers inlaid with small pieces of blue paste. There were also plaques representing antithetic sphinxes on either side of a "sacred tree" motif, also adorned with thin sheets of gold. Two plaques that probably belonged to the vertical sides of the bedstead were decorated with stylized anthemia and buds inlaid with blue paste, partly covered with thin sheets of gold. There were also lotus flowers and heads of the god Bes carved in the round; this god was a protector of the household and of women in pregnancy. We know from Homer how Odysseus made and decorated his own bed. The Bible tells us that the prophet Amos complained that the rulers of his time were corrupt, using ivory beds (King 1988, 139–149; Campbell 1998, 311–312).

Other ivory objects found in the dromos include an S-shaped leg of a table, of solid ivory. There was also a massive ivory object in the shape of an incense burner. It consists of three superimposed rows of drooping petals surmounted by three horns inserted into a disc and ending in a volute at the top. Such incense burn-

ers, but in bronze, considered Cypriote, have been found in Cyprus and elsewhere in the Mediterranean. Incense burners were probably used during ritual symposia, as is seen on some Assyrian reliefs.

The various customs observed in other tombs, as well as particular objects among the tomb offerings, are mentioned briefly below. In the fill of the dromos of Tomb 2, very near the surface, the skeletons of two humans were found (Karageorghis 1967a, 118–121). Examples of this custom of human sacrifices in honour of the dead have already been noted at Lapithos in the eleventh century B.C. and also in the CG III period (dramatically described by Gjerstad et al. 1934, 243–245). The same custom is observed in the heroic burials of Eleutherna in Crete (cf. Stampolidis 1996, 149–200). This custom is also alluded to in the *Iliad* (XXIII.175–176). Cremation, which, as we have already shown, appeared in the eleventh century B.C. in both Cyprus and the Aegean, reappeared at Salamis in the eighth–seventh centuries B.C., although in only a few cases (Karageorghis 1967a, 119–21).

Particularly characteristic of the Salamis "royal" burials are the sacrifices of horses and chariots in the spacious dromoi of the tombs. Sacrifices of horses are known from Anatolia, Palestine, and the Aegean world, in Cyprus during the Late Bronze Age period

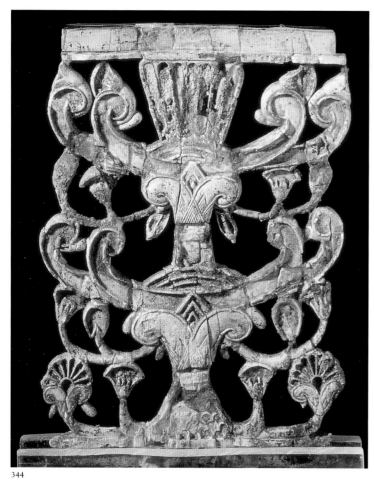

344

345

346

347

348

349

344-346. Salamis, Tomb 79 (excavations of the Cyprus Department of Antiquities), details of Throne 5.

347-349. Salamis, Tomb 79 (excavations of the Cyprus Department of Antiquities). Detail from the bedstead of Bed A. Note the nonsensical inscription in blue paste hieroglyphs at the top. They are simply decorative, as in some cases on Phoenician metal bowls.

350. Salamis, Tomb 79 (excavations of the Cyprus Department of Antiquities). Bed A, restored from fragments found in the dromos. Cyprus Museum, Nicosia. The bed was made of wood covered with ivory plaques decorated in relief with Egyptian motifs. At the upper part there was a frieze of nonsensical hieroglyphs in blue paste. Beds of ivory constituted an extreme luxury in royal palaces, against which the prophet Amos animadverted bitterly. Phoenician workmanship.

350

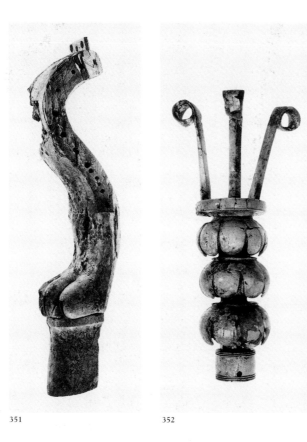

351 352

(cf. Karageorghis 1968b, 5, with bibliography), and at Lefkandi circa 950 B.C. (Popham et al. 1993, 21–22), but the reappearance of this funerary custom in the eighth–seventh centuries in Cyprus is a novelty. Coldstream goes so far as to suggest that "the princely burials of Salamis were influenced in large measure by the circulation of Ionic epic poetry and especially of the *Iliad* in the royal court of Salamis" (Coldstream 1977, 350). The sacrifice of horses is mentioned by Homer in the *Iliad* (XXIII.171–172). It is significant that this also occurred in Crete (for references see Popham *et al.* 1993, 22, no. 9), a place where other characteristics of "heroic" burials are encountered, as mentioned above. But it should also be noted that in a Neo-Assyrian text there is a description of a royal funeral that involves the slaughter of horses and the offering of a bronze bed. There are also chariot sacrifices known from other places in the Eastern Mediterranean (for references see Reyes 1994, 63, nn. 79–80). The sacrifice of chariots and horses in Etruscan tombs formed part of the funerary customs for the Etruscan princes. It is regrettable that most of these tombs were excavated at a time when archaeological methods and possibilities for conservation were poor, and only traces of their original splendor survive. Recent excavations at the Etruscan cemetery at Cerveteri have, however, brought to light a wealth of information

regarding princely burials (for more information see *Principi Etruschi tra Mediterraneo ed Europa*, Venezia 2000; Rizzo and Martelli 1988–89; Emiliozzi 1998). Among the other tombs of the "royal" necropolis at Salamis, the following features are worthy of special mention.

ii. The tumulus above Tomb 3

Tumuli were also common above monumental built tombs in Phrygia and Etruria (Prayon 2000; Bartoloni 2000). In Homer we have frequent reference to a tymbos (a pile of earth) above the tomb of an important warrior (Karageorghis 1967a, 121–124). In addition to impressions and remains of a chariot, a bronze spear, a pharetra (quiver) with iron arrows, and a bronze shield, the same Tomb 3 yielded a silver-studded sword, of a type that is known to Homer (ξίφος ἀργυρόηλον) (Karageorghis 1967b, 167–168), and of which several examples are known from Cyprus (Karageorghis *et al.* 1999, 108–109; Karageorghis *et al.* 2000, 164–165). Among the large storage jars found in the dromos of Tomb 3 there is one of Plain White ware that bears a painted inscription in the Cypriote syllabary. It represents the Greek word for olive oil in the genitive, i.e., "[an amphora] of olive oil." It evokes the Homeric passage in book XXIII of the *Iliad*, where Achilles places amphorae of olive oil or fat on the pyre of his friend Patroclos (Masson 1967). Tomb 3 may date to circa 600 B.C.

iii. Tomb 47

In Tomb 47 the skeletons of two horses were found *in situ* on the floor of the dromos. They had blinders and front bands of thin sheets of gold, which must have been attached to some perishable material, perhaps leather. Gold front bands and blinders were worn by the horses of Iris in the *Iliad* (V. 358, 363). This tomb dates to the Cypro-Archaic I period.

iv. Tomb 1

In Tomb 1, which may be dated to the early part of the Cypro-Archaic I period, the incinerated remains of the dead, probably a woman, were found in a bronze cauldron, together with her necklace with beads of gold and rock crystal. The pottery found in this tomb included a "dinner set" consisting of one footed crater, probably from Attica, twenty skyphoi from Attica, and two skyphoi and ten plates from Euboea. Such plates have been identified as Euboean imitations of a Cypriote shape made for the market in

Cyprus and further east as far as the mainland. This is considered by Boardman to be an indication of the presence in the East Mediterranean of Euboean ships (Boardman 2001a, 15 and n. 19). A similar "dinner set" was found in a tomb at Amathus (for more detailed references see Crielaard 1999, 265–271; Coldstream 1987, 22–26; idem 1995). Gjerstad suggested that the "dinner set" in Salamis Tomb 1 may have been part of the dowry of a Greek princess who married into the royal family of Salamis (Gjerstad 1979); this romantic view, however, may not be valid. Such dinner sets have been found not only in other parts of Cyprus but formed part of the funerary gifts in other regions of the Mediterranean, e.g., in the tombs of the princes of Etruria. They formed part of the lifestyle and ritual banquets that were widespread among the members of the elite society in the ninth–eighth centuries B.C. In Etruria the drinking cups and dinner sets are quite common, and they include cups and bowls of gold, silver, and bronze (see below). They are found side by side with firedogs and obeloi, craters for mixing wine and water, large jars for cooking, etc. (Winther 1997; Malkin 1998, 103, 1067, with bibliography; Ridgway 1997, 338–339; Gras 2000; Ampolo 2000; Karageorghis 2000b; Delpino 2000). In Homer feasts with eating and drinking were the privilege of aristocratic society; they occurred during funerals, weddings and "royal dinners" (Van Wees 1995, 154-177).

v. Tomb 2

Inside the looted chamber of Tomb 2, dating to the Cypro-Archaic I period, a silver bowl was discovered, which was decorated twice. The first decoration consists of an Egyptianizing composition of human figures in a central medallion and four narrow zones encircling the inside of the bowl; three of them are filled with stylized floral motifs, while the fourth contains nonsensical Egyptian hieroglyphs. The later decoration consists of a central medallion containing a winged sphinx and three encircling zones, of which the outer is ornamented with panels filled alternately with stylized floral motifs and winged sphinxes. This bowl may have been in use from the beginning to the end of the Cypro-Archaic I period (cf. Markoe 1985, 185–186, and 156; Matthäus 1985, 175, dates this bowl to his period IV, or 675–625 B.C.).

Finally we mention a clay incense burner from Tomb 23, nos. 4 and 5, supported by three molded "caryatids" and painted with flower motifs in yellow and black

353

354

355

169

356. The façade and part of the dromos of Salamis, Tomb 3 (excavations of the Cyprus Department of Antiquities).

357. Salamis, Tomb 3, no. 95. A silver-studded iron sword (excavations of the Cyprus Department of Antiquities). Length (with restored handle): 92cm. Cyprus Museum, Nicosia. The hilt, probably of wood, was fixed to the tang by five bronze rivets with silver-plated heads. The sword was in its wooden or leather scabbard, which has left traces on the iron blade. Only the ivory toggle of the scabbard has survived. The sword was found inside the chariot box, in the dromos of the tomb. Homer refers to such silver-studded swords.

358. Salamis, Tomb 3, no. 101 (excavations of the Cyprus Department of Antiquities). Amphora of Plain White IV ware. Height: 69cm. Cyprus Museum, Nicosia. Below one of the handles a syllabic inscription painted in black paint, reading "of olive oil," recalling the amphorae of oil deposited on the pyre of Patroclos in the twenty-third book of the *Iliad*.

356

357

358

paint. Similar objects are of Phoenician inspiration (cf. Reyes 1994, 63, n. 83). A limestone incense burner of a similar type was recently found at Idalion.

The results of the excavations of eighth–seventh-century-B.C. tombs in the "royal" necropolis of Salamis have been surveyed in some detail. They illustrate very effectively the cultural atmosphere in Cyprus during a period that is usually identified as "Homeric." The Homeric character of Cypriote society is matched by the conservative character of the Cypriots, who retained elements of a Mycenaean past (cf. their clinging to a syllabic script) but at the same time were exposed to a new, oriental, culture. As early as the eleventh century B.C., as we have seen already, the elite society of Cyprus had a considerable amount in common with the Greek aristocracy.

The heroes and their world that fascinated Homer were never forgotten, and Homer contributed to their survival in perpetuity. Although social and political conditions had changed since the eleventh century B.C., Homer described the heroic world based not only on memory, but also on survivals, admittedly within the elite society of rich and powerful citizens,

359

359. Salamis, Tomb 3 (excavations of the Cyprus Department of Antiquities). On the floor of the dromos are skeletons of horses, bronze ornaments for the chariot pole, and pottery leaning against the mud brick side wall of the dromos.

360. Salamis, Tomb 47 (excavations of the Cyprus Department of Antiquities). Two skeletons of chariot steeds, one with its neck twisted around the pole. This horse was frantically trying to escape as it saw its companion being slaughtered. The horses have gold-plated front bands and blinders.

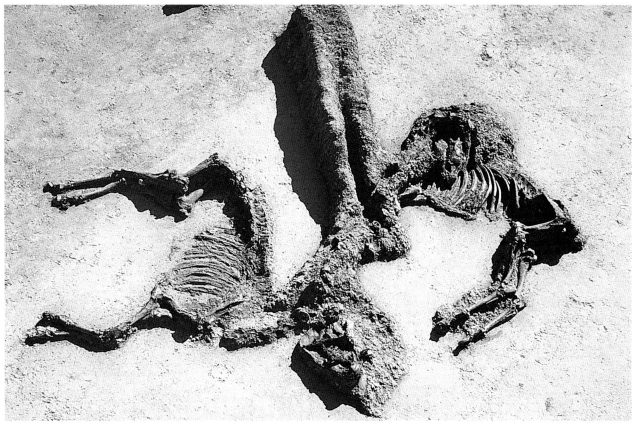

360

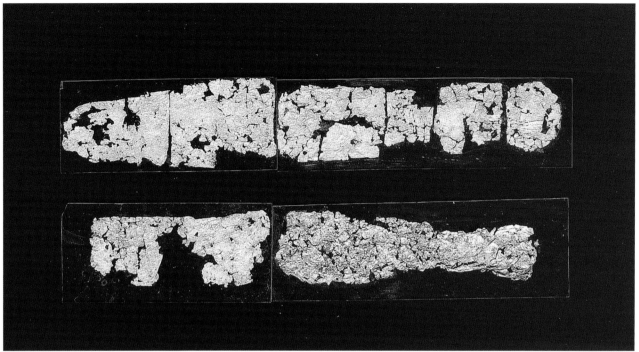

361. Salamis, Tomb 47 (excavations of the Cyprus Department of Antiquities). Gold plating for the front bands of horses nos. 85 and 82. Cyprus Museum, Nicosia. Maximum length: 37cm. They probably covered bands of organic material such as leather. Homer refers to the horses of Hera as having front bands of gold.

362. Salamis, Tomb 1, no. 222. Geometric crater, probably Attic (excavations of the Cyprus Department of Antiquities). Cyprus Museum, Nicosia. Height: 48cm. It has a deep hemispherical body and stirrup handles and stands on a high pedestal. Together with a number of imported plates and bowls of the same period it formed part of a "dinner set" dated to the second quarter of the eighth century B.C. It was no doubt the privilege of the elite society of Salamis (perhaps members of the royal family) to display wealth during symposia, and subsequently these vessels accompanied the dead to his or her tomb.

361

who replaced the earlier warrior elite in the social echelon of the eleventh century but retained a number of their characteristics. The kings or nobles who were buried in the tombs of the "royal" necropolis of Salamis and in some tombs at Palaepaphos in the eighth–seventh centuries B.C. cannot all be regarded as heroes, but they were accompanied by all those luxuries that a hero was due: a chariot, horses, slaves, firedogs, swords, shields, helmets, and luxury goods such as ivory furniture of Levantine origin, bronze vessels of Phoenician workmanship, gold and silver drinking cups, and bowls of Cypro-Phoenician workmanship (cf. Morris, 2000, 178–186).

Whether there is continuity from the eleventh century B.C. onward and the heroic burial customs were maintained within a narrow circle of an aristocratic elite, or whether these customs were revived in the ninth–eighth centuries B.C. as a result of the development of a rich aristocracy or even, as Coldstream suggested, as the consequence of the frequent recital of Homeric epic, as least in the royal court of Salamis, is conjectural. Myths were, no doubt, widespread during this period, as seen in works of art such as pottery. In Cyprus we may find mythical representations even in the eleventh–tenth centuries B.C. In Etruria mythical representations are quite common in pottery, mainly of the seventh centuries B.C., no doubt transmitted through intimate contact with the western Greeks (Ampolo 2000; Rizzo and Martelli 1988–89). By the eighth–seventh centuries B.C., a period that may be

362

considered as contemporary with Homer, there was a widespread knowledge of such Homeric burials in many parts of the Mediterranean world.

The "Homeric" associations of Cyprus have often been discussed by scholars, who refer usually to the epic poem entitled τὰ Κύπρια (ἔπη) (the *Cypria*), which narrates the events leading up to the Trojan War and various incidents in the war previous to the time described in the *Iliad*. The author of this epic was Stasinos, a son-in-law of Homer. Its date may be later than the *Iliad*, and it is said to have been given by Homer as a dowry to his daughter. It has been suggested that various myths in the *Iliad*, the *Odyssey*, and the Homeric *Hymns* relating to Aphrodite, known to Homer as Kypris (the Cyprian), have Near Eastern associations; these have been emphasized by many scholars. "Such tales could well have formed a popular ingredient in the repertoire of a singer or storyteller at the courts of Cyprus" (Richardson 1991, 127). One of the themes of the *Cypria* is Zeus's original plan to relieve the earth of overpopulation by the great wars of Thebes and Troy, the Near Eastern origin of which is universally acknowledged. In the article quoted above Richardson concludes: "If I were asked what songs the poetic forerunners of Stasinos may have sung in the echoing palatial halls of Salamis or Paphos before a mixed audience of Greeks, Phoenicians, and other peoples of the Near East, I should be strongly tempted to reply that these are the kind of themes that are likely to have been among the most popular in this part of the world" (Richardson 1991, 128).

Relations with the Greek world were never interrupted during the Cypro-Archaic I period. Greek traditions were current among citizens of Greek descent, particularly at Salamis, but also in other Cypriote cities. It should be mentioned here that at the end of the seventh century B.C. a Cypriot dedicated a bronze tripod to the temple of Apollo at Delphi. His name, Hermaios, is engraved in the Cypriote syllabary on a leg of the tripod (Masson 1971, 295–304).

As we have shown above, the bronze and ivory work from the Salamis tombs attains an extremely high artistic standard and technical achievement, especially the ivory furniture with plaques made in the ajouré technique and decorated with cloisonné work inset with colored paste. It is comparable to Phoenician ivory furniture from Nimrud and Samaria. Ivory furniture was very much prized by the aristocratic elite of the Near East and the rest of the Mediterranean, as we have seen already. Elaborately decorated pieces of fur-

niture are often depicted on Assyrian reliefs. It has been suggested that the ivories found at Nimrud and other Assyrian cities may have been taken as tribute or booty from Phoenicia itself. We agree, however, with Markoe that we should consider the possibility of Phoenician artists producing these ivories in Syria, in the palaces, as indeed may be the case elsewhere (cf. Markoe 2000, 146–147; cf. recently Buchholz 2000, 218–219).

3. The "Cypro-Phoenician" Bowls

Homer often refers to "the art of the Sidonians," especially their silverwork (cf. Markoe 2000, 148–150). Indeed, there is a group of bowls, used as drinking cups, found mainly in Cyprus and elsewhere in the Mediterranean, all decorated in repoussé and with engravings, that are often referred to as "Cypro-Phoenician" (Markoe 1985; see, however, idem 2000, 148, n. 9, where the bowls are called Phoenician,

363

though "the term should not be taken literally as a geographic designation"). They have been found mainly in "royal" tombs, in Cyprus, Etruria, and the Aegean. A silver example from Salamis Tomb 2 was discussed above.

The earliest such drinking bowls are of bronze. One was found in a datable context at Lefkandi on Euboea; it may be assigned to the tenth century B.C. (for references see Markoe 2000, 149). The style of the decoration does not show any Egyptian influence; this appears only on later examples. The Lefkandi bowl is decorated with human figures holding vases and marching toward an enthroned lady in front of whom there is a table with fruit or cakes. Behind are musicians, and antithetic sphinxes on either side of a stylized tree motif (Popham 1995). These early bowls are usually shallow.

The usual technique for the interior decoration of the bowls is a combination of chasing, engraving, and shallow repoussé work (cf. Hendrix in Karageorghis et al. 1999a). The bowls show considerable homogeneity in the arrangement of the iconographical decoration: there is a central medallion filled with a rosette or a composition with human or animal figures, and one or more concentric zones decorated with a variety of subjects: antithetic animals (mainly sphinxes), heroic combats, processions of human figures, banquet scenes, etc. (A general discussion of these bowls was undertaken by Markoe in 1985. For a review of Markoe's book see Winter 1990, especially p. 241, where she discusses the votive procession toward an enthroned female figure.) A few characteristic examples will be described below.

First let us examine two such bowls, of silver, one gold plated, from Praeneste (Markoe 1985, 1791, E2) in Italy (Villa Giulia Museum in Rome), and the other (fragmentary) from Kourion in Cyprus, now in the Metropolitan Museum of Art, New York (Markoe 1985, 177, Cy7; Karageorghis 1998f, 46–51). They are decorated in shallow repoussé with engraved outlines and details. The decorated interior surface consists of inner and outer registers and a central medallion. The outer register, which is the most important one, is surrounded by a serpent coiled head to tail (cf. Marinatos 2001); it is decorated with what may be interpreted as a mythical representation. The decoration of this register is very similar on the two bowls, that on the Praeneste bowl being better preserved.

Of the thirty or so silver bowls of the Cypro-Phoenician group presently known, only these two are deco-

rated with the same narrative scene, which must have been widely circulating and well known. It is an episodic narrative representing the exploits of a hero or king who leaves a walled city and returns to it at the end. The narrative consists of nine consecutive episodes and is often described as the "Hunter's Day" or the "Ape Hunt" because the hero has been interpreted as a hunter of apes.

These two bowls have been the subject of many discussions, and their narrative has been interpreted in various ways. Some scholars have identified the hero or king with Melqart or Baal, but this interpretation does not correspond to any Near Eastern mythological scenes relating to Melqart or Baal. Güterbock (1957, 69–70) describes the narrative as follows:

"The prince leaves his town in a chariot; he dismounts and shoots a stag; he pursues the bleeding animal; while his charioteer attends to the horses, the prince flays the stag; he makes offerings to a winged deity, while an ape snatches a bone from the sacrifice; the ape attacks the prince, but the winged goddess lifts him up, chariot and all, and so saves him; put down again, the prince, in turn, attacks the ape; he kills him and returns to his city."

This composition has been characterized as a unique example of a fully developed continuous narrative style in the Phoenician artistic corpus. The fact that the story is represented in two almost identical copies, and that in both the element of divine intervention is quite decisive in the narrative, has induced some scholars to accept that this story "is not merely the product of a Phoenician artist's vivid imagination, but does, in fact describe a lost fable or epic" (Markoe 1985, 67ff.). Based on the fact that this representation is unique and that Phoenician and Near Eastern art, as already mentioned above, do not have in their repertoire such a continuous mythological narrative either for a king or for Melqart or Baal, Hermary has recently proposed another interpretation (Hermary 1992, 130–136). Without denying the Phoenician aspect of the representation, and realizing that an argument cannot be based on a lost tale or epic poem, such as those of Ugarit, he suggested an interpretation of the Praeneste bowl in terms of Greek mythology. The period circa 700 B.C. in Cyprus is well known for the diffusion of Homeric epic. Kourion, where one of the two silver bowls was found, was a Greek city whose inhabitants boasted, according to Herodotus, that they were descendants of the Argives (Herodotus v, 113). Other silver bowls found at Kourion bear the

364. Silver bowl, gold plated, from the Bernardini Tomb (Praeneste, Etruria). Museo di Villa Giulia, Rome, Inv. no. 61565. Height: 3.3cm.; diam.: 18.9cm. The entire surface is decorated in repoussé with incised lines. The central medallion is decorated with a composition of three human figures and two dogs. The style is clearly Egyptianizing. The inner zone is decorated with horses and birds. The main, outer zone depicts the "Ape Hunt" legend or the "Hunter's Day," with various episodes from the life of a king. The whole zone below the rim of the bowl is encircled by a snake. An almost identical outer zone appears on a silver bowl from Kourion. Dated circa 710–675 B.C.

364

name of the owner, no doubt a Greek king or noble, engraved in the Greek language but in the Cypriote syllabary (Masson 1961, 193–195; Markoe 1985, 177–180, Cy8 and 11); these names are Epioros, Dieithemis, and Pausandros. In their courts, no doubt, epic poetry must have been recited and was well known in the milieu in which the artist was working. Thus the artist could translate the myths into an artistic language with which he was familiar, hence the oriental appearance of the figures of the narrative.

Before leaving the heroic mythological cycle represented by the silver bowls from Praeneste and Kourion, two other documents should be discussed. They date to the seventh century B.C., both were found in

Cyprus, and both bear mythological scenes. Although they do not refer to any specific heroic event and the heroes are anonymous, they may be directly connected with Homeric epic.

The first is a fragmentary silver bowl from Amathus, now in the British Museum (Markoe 1985, 172–174, Cy4). It is decorated in repoussé, with engraved outlines and details. As in the case of the two bowls discussed above, its interior decoration consists of an inner and an outer register and a central medallion. The inner register is composed of Egyptian divinities; the outer register is the most important and the one that has relevance here.

Stylistically, the bowl has been dated to slightly before

365

the middle of the seventh century B.C. The theme of the decoration is military, with chariots, cavalry, and hoplites attacking a walled city that is defended by archers in towers. Of the chariots only one is partly preserved, with realistically rendered galloping horses and a dog running to the left. The composition of chariots recalls one around the neck of a White Painted III ware amphora from Khrysokhou (ancient Marion), now in the Cyprus Museum, Nicosia (Karageorghis and Des Gagniers 1979, vase SI.1), but the rendering of the figures on the amphora is very stylized, perhaps under the influence of Late Geometric Greek vase painting. Others have seen an Egyptian influence in the rendering of the horses of the chariot and the dog, which may recall pharaonic scenes. (For a general discussion see Karageorghis 1973a.) In front of the chariot group there are two riders on galloping horses, wearing oriental helmets. They are preceded by three archers on foot, wearing Assyrian garments and oriental headdresses. In front of them are four hoplites, dressed and armed in a perfectly Greek fashion. They wear short tasseled tunics and Ionian helmets, and they hold round shields with insignia of various motifs—griffins, radiating discs, etc.—such as those on the shields of warriors on early Greek vases. Ahead of them a soldier tries to place a ladder against the fortification wall. The fortification, naturalistically rendered, has three towers, in each of which there are archers ready to shoot. On the opposite side of the fortification a second soldier tries to place a ladder, and behind him two other soldiers, without helmets but protected by their raised shields with spikes of a Cypriote type, are ready to go up the ladder. Behind them, two men are cutting a palm and other trees. Finally, two horse riders, only partially preserved, arrive on the scene. Thus, the fortress is the central

part of the composition, toward which warriors from both sides, in chariots, on horseback, and on foot, advance ready to attack it. A similar scene is depicted on a bronze bowl from Delphi (Markoe 1985, 205–206, G4), where the oriental influence is quite strong. In a recent reference to this representation Niemeier suggests that it reflects warlike events in the Near East around 700 B.C., in which Greek mercenaries were involved (Niemeier 2001, 21, 24).

Mythological scenes or scenes that would have been inspired from epic poetry appear also in vase painting, as for example on a Bichrome IV ware crater from Tamassos, now in the British Museum, which is decorated with a chariot and a hunting scene on the one side; on the other side there is also a chariot, a hunting scene, and a warrior who decapitates his enemy with an axe and a dagger. Such scenes are often described in Homeric epic. Hermary has identified this figure as a Cypriote aristocrat of Greek descent, whose ideal is the Homeric hero (for a discussion see Karageorghis 1998f, 53–54). Mythological scenes, often inspired from Greek epic, are also depicted in Etruscan art at the same time (e.g., Ampolo 2000; Rizzo and Martelli 1988–89).

A fragmentary silver bowl from Kourion is decorated in the outer register with a banquet scene. In the center of the zone there is a table with fruit, and on either side two human figures, a king (on the left) and a queen (on the right), recline and face each other across the table (Karageorghis *et al.* 1999a). The queen wears an Egyptian wig, and in her left hand she holds what may be a hemispherical bowl shown in section. In his right hand the king holds a round object, possibly a fruit or a drinking cup; he wears an Egyptian crown. Behind the king is a double-flute player. Behind the queen are four female figures: the first three are a double-flute player, a lyre player who is singing, and a tambourine player; the fourth figure holds out two or three shallow bowls in her left hand and carries a jug in her right. A large amphora stands behind her. To its left is a table set with a small amphora flanked by jugs; two ladles hang from the table. To the left of the table is a group of three women, each bearing offerings in both hands: the first holds bowls shown in section; the second carries two legs of a lamb or goat, the third, trussed geese. Behind them a bird faces to the right. Above the queen is an engraved inscription of six signs from the Cypriot syllabary. Some signs above the king are more difficult to read.

366

The two inscriptions above the queen and the king were engraved at the same time as the rest of the decoration (cf. Markoe 1985, 73; Hermary 1986b, 194). It is certain that the inscription above the queen is a proper name with the prefix "Kypro-," common in Cypriote onomastics. A reading by Neumann after the cleaning of the vase (mentioned above), suggests that the name is Κυπρομέδουσα, "she who reigns over Cyprus." He reads the signs above the king as "[?]-[?]-le-se" and suggests that they form the word for king, "pa-si-le-se" (βασιλής) (for a different interpretation see Hermary 2000, where he suggests that Κυπρομέδουσα refers to Aphrodite (see also discussion above). The theme of the outer register is a royal banquet, similar to banquet scenes depicted on other bowls (see Karageorghis 1993c). Because the focal point of the symmetrical composition is a royal couple, not an enthroned divinity, the bowl was not a

366. Fragmentary silver bowl from Amathus, now in the British Museum, London, no. 123053. Height: 3.6cm.; diam.: 18.8cm. The interior is decorated in repoussé with incisions. The outer zone of the bowl is filled with a scene relating to the attack on a walled city, with archers and cavalry.

votive offering in a temple (cf. Markoe 1985, 176–77, n. 19). It is said to have been found in a royal tomb at Kourion. Markoe suggested, on stylistic grounds, that it dates from the first quarter of the seventh century B.C. (1985, 151, 153, 156). Several of the images in the composition have parallels with known objects from the Cypro-Archaic period. The curved legs of the offering table are comparable to ivory furniture legs found at Salamis (Karageorghis 1973c, 36, 96, no. 249). Punctures on the table may represent decorative rivets, like those in the wood of the ivory hearse from Salamis Royal Tomb 79 (Karageorghis 1973c, 61). The second table resembles several clay models of the period (cf. Karageorghis 1996c, 80–81). One woman holds a jug similar to Phoenician vessels of the Cypro-Archaic I period (cf. Bikai 1987, cat. nos. 353, 355, 356, pl. XIV).

The artist was surely familiar with Egyptian art. Several bowls are shown in section to reveal their contents, a representational style with a long tradition in Egyptian art. The offerings are also comparable: grains or small fruits, lambs' or goats' legs, trussed geese. The Cypriote engraver adapted the Egyptian motifs to his own taste; the musicians and offering bearers on this bowl embody the boisterous atmosphere of a banquet, not the static style of Egyptian art.

The griffins flanking a sacred tree in the central register are a well-known motif in Phoenician art, particularly in ivory carving (Markoe 1985, 38, 87). Unlike the outer register, which depicts a specific scene at a given time, the middle register is decorative, with somewhat unrelated figures shown at different scales.

Last let us turn to a bronze bowl from Salamis (Markoe 1985, 174–175, Cy5) dated to the Cypro-Archaic II period (circa 600–500 B.C.). The writer republished this bowl in a recent article, correcting some details of the iconography (Karageorghis 1993c). Inside the bowl, at the top of the decorated zone, a woman sits on a chair facing right, holding a child (probably suckling) on her lap; she wears an Egyptian wig and has an Egyptianizing face. There are other human figures preparing for a banquet or engaged in erotic embraces.

The medallion depicts the Pharaoh smiting enemy captives. Behind him is an attendant dressed in a shenti and wearing a pointed cap; he is equipped with a quiver and bow. A falcon-headed god (Re-Harakhte) stands in front of the Pharaoh.

The erotic scene includes musicians, a dancer, people drinking, and other figures bringing wine. This is certainly not a scene from daily life, nor even of a royal couple (as on Markoe's Cy6), but from a ritual feast, a *hieros gamos* (cf. Dentzer 1982, 76), where many individuals are involved. The central woman and infant represent the culmination of the scene, in a sense, the outcome of the *hieros gamos*.

The style underlines the strong influence of Egyptian art in the rendering of the figures. This influence was already noted by Gjerstad (1946, 14), who also stressed the Cypriote stylistic elements. Egyptian influence may have been direct but it is more likely the Cypriote artist borrowed his theme from the art of neighboring cultures in Syria and Phoenicia and added to it local elements from his own traditions (cf. Dentzer 1982, 74–75).

In his discussion of the theme of the procession toward the seated figure with an infant, Markoe (1985, 56–57) suggested that the figure is probably an enthroned goddess or a priestess enacting the rôle of a deity, in this case Astarte-Aphrodite. Ohnefalsch-Richter (1893, 129) identified the woman and infant as Isis-Osiris, Ishtar-Tammuz, Aphrodite-Adonis. The resemblance of the attitude and hairstyle of the seated figure to Egyptian iconography led some scholars to correctly identify her as Isis with Horus (Dentzer 1982, 74). The ritual feast is in her honor, as already observed by Ohnefalsch-Richter (1893, 128–129) and repeated by Markoe (1985, 66) and Dierichs (1989, 12–13). They all emphasize the fact that this is not just any feast but a particular one. Dierichs (op. cit.) compared the scene with the erotic scenes taking place in a sacred garden, which appear on a large Bichrome V bowl from Achna (see below, no. 373). Her interpretation of these scenes, which seems rather fanciful, is not discussed here. The sense of humor of the Cypriote artists of all periods should not be ignored. Symbolism was surely not their only intent whenever they raised their brush to decorate a vase. Dierichs's interpretation of the three erotic scenes on the Salamis bowl as signifying three specific, successive episodes, i.e., the appearance of the hetaira, her being taken away, and finally the erotic embrace, is no longer valid now that the new drawing of the scene on the Salamis bowl has revealed more information.

In a recent study the scene on this bowl has been associated with the biblical marzeah, a social and religious institution, the members of which met regularly to celebrate with food, drink, and occasionally sacral sexual orgies (Beach Ferris 1992, 132ff.). The suggestion has been made that this and other bowls, also decorated with banquet scenes, may have been used at the banquet occasions they depict (ibid., 134). This is in perfect agreement with the description of the lifestyle of the elite society in various places of the Mediterranean world during the eighth–seventh centuries B.C., as discussed above.

Among the other metal bowls from Cyprus two more, in excellent condition, now in the Metropolitan Museum of Art, New York, are worthy of mention. A gold bowl of about 700 B.C., probably from Kourion, is decorated with two zones of engraved papyrus motifs and seven swimming ducks, symmetrically arranged among the papyri. The Egyptian style is obvious (Karageorghis *et al.* 2000, 184–185, no. 301). We have already referred to the bowl of Akestor, king of Paphos, found at Kourion, dated to the Cypro-Archaic I period (750–600 B.C.). The medallion is decorated with a four-winged deity in Assyrian style. There are also Egyptian falcons in the medallion. The two zones, an outer and an inner, are filled with a series of animals (the narrow inner zone) and human figures. The outer broader zone is decorated with a human figure in Assyrian dress killing a rampant grif-

fin; an Egyptian king striking enemy captives; a human figure dressed in a lion's skin (Melqart?) fighting a lion, etc. (for more details see Karageorghis *et al.* 2000, 182–183, no. 299).

4. Vase Painting

Ceramic art flourished during the eighth century B.C. As well as the White Painted wares (decoration in black paint on a white ground), Bichrome ware (black and red painted decoration on a white ground) was particularly popular. Another ceramic achievement of the Cypriote potter was the Black-on-Red ware, inspired initially from the Levant, but perfected in Cyprus during the Cypro-Geometric III and Cypro-Archaic I periods (Brodie and Steel 1996).

There was much ordinary decoration of vases with concentric circles and other abstract geometric motifs, but here we will discuss some extraordinary compositions with figured motifs (human and animal) that indicate cultural connections both with the Near East and the Aegean.

As mentioned above, there was a serious attempt on the part of the Cypriote vase painter to represent an

367-370. Amphora of Bichrome III ware, from Platani (Famagusta District), known as the Hubbard Amphora, from the name of its previous owner. Cyprus Museum, Nicosia, Inv. no. 1938/XI-2/3. Height: 68cm.; mouth diam.: 38.5cm. On one side of the vase is a seated goddess(?) receiving offerings from a female attendant and drinking through a straw. At one end of the decorated zone a bull protome is hanging on the wall; at the other end a winged sphinx is smelling a flower. On the other side of the vase is a male lyre player and four female figures holding hands and dancing. This is one of the most ambitious representations of Cypro-Geometric III pictorial vase painting. Both scenes depicted on the vase may relate to ritual.

367

369

368

370

179

371

 often stylizing the human and animal figure. Simple human and animal motifs were quite popular, such as armed warriors or men and women holding flowers or other offerings for a divinity, but more ambitious vase painters depicted processions of human figures either performing a dance or carrying gifts. These were probably influenced by similar representations on metal bowls.

One such vase is a large amphora of the Cypro-Geometric III period, probably from Platani in the Famagusta District, now in the Cyprus Museum, known as the "Hubbard Amphora." Both sides of the vase between the handles are decorated with friezes of human figures in action. On one side there is an enthroned female figure; in front of her is a table with various vessels on it, and she is drinking from a jar through a siphon. A striding female figure brings more vessels to place on the table, obviously for the seated woman, and fills the jar from which the seated figure is drinking. Behind the striding figure there is a bucranium hanging on a wall, indicating the sacred character of the composition. Behind the seated figure is also a sphinx smelling a flower that it holds in its raised right(?) foreleg. This scene has been interpreted as a funerary ritual, and its inspiration is oriental (cf. Karageorghis and Des Gagniers 1974, 8–9).

Side B of the same amphora shows a group of female dancers holding hands, led by a male musician, all holding flowers. Such dancers are to be seen also on metal vessels from Cyprus, and they may be of oriental inspiration, but they are equally common on Greek vases of the Late Geometric period, and these may also have influenced the Cypriote vase painter.

Although the style of rendering the human figures is often awkward, lacking the vigor of the Greek Late Geometric vase painting, the composition as a whole is lively but naïve, not following any stylistic rules. This has led some scholars to call it "styleless" (cf. Buchholz 2000, 264–265). There is a comparable scene on a Cypro-Geometric III Black-on-Red jug from Khrysochou, in the Paphos District, now in the Cyprus Museum. It represents a similar female figure seated on a throne and drinking from a jar through a siphon, with another figure behind her bringing a fish on a plate and a flower. Two confronted sphinxes and a lion attacking a bull complete the composition (Karageorghis and Des Gagniers 1979, vase SB.1).

Religious ritual and scenes of festivities that took place in sanctuaries or sacred gardens inspired other Cypriote vase painters of the Cypro-Archaic I–II

371-372. Jug of Bichrome IV ware. Bank of Cyprus Cultural Foundation Museum, Nicosia. Height: 37cm. The shoulder zone is decorated with a group of seven draped female figures holding large flowers. They form three groups of women facing one another; one is isolated. They wear richly decorated robes. On the ground are three birds and lotus flowers. Probably this is a scene related to a procession of worshipers bringing gifts to a divinity. Cypro-Archaic I period, seventh century B.C.

373. Bowl of Bichrome V ware, from Achna. The British Museum, London, Inv. no. 1905.7-12.1. Height: 13.3cm.; diam.: 35cm. The interior is decorated with groups of female figures in a garden and erotic scenes.

ambitious "mythological" scene on the base of a Cypro-Geometric I plate from Palaepaphos-*Skales*. The mythological themes, however, did not continue in later Cypriote vase painting, although motifs from Greek mythology, in particular the centaur, continued to appear sporadically, e.g., on a late-tenth century B.C. Black Slip Painted II ware plate from Larnaca, where the centaur is a direct descendant of the Greek centaur, with a horse's body and a human head and torso, holding a tree or a branch (Karageorghis and Des Gagniers 1974, 42, vase XIII.1; Kourou 1991; Buchholz 2000, 228).

Unlike his Greek contemporary, who produced lively pictorial compositions with human figures (battles, processions, etc.) in Geometric vase painting, the Cypriote vase painter preferred rather static motifs,

periods. A good example is a Bichrome IV ware jug formerly in the G.G. Pierides Collection, now in the Museum of the Cultural Foundation of the Bank of Cyprus (Karageorghis and Des Gagniers 1974, vase VIII.16). It is decorated all around the shoulder with female figures holding flowers, birds, and quadrupeds, no doubt to dedicate to a sanctuary. The interior of a Bichrome V ware plate from Achna (Famagusta District) is decorated with groups of confronted female figures smelling flowers in a garden, and also erotic scenes with two couples, no doubt recalling sacred prostitution in the sanctuary of the Great Goddess in Paphos, as described by Herodotus (ibid., 31–32). Mythological scenes in Cypro-Archaic I–II vase painting are rare. We have already referred to the possibility of interpreting a scene on a Bichrome IV crater from Tamassos as a scene from epic poetry. It may also be suggested that a large bird with a small, ugly human figure next to it, which decorate a Bichrome IV jug in the Cyprus Museum, may represent a pygmy and a crane, the myth of which appears in the *Iliad* (III.6) and which is of oriental origin (Karageorghis and Des Gagniers 1974, vase IX.10). However, stylization of the figures and oversimplification of the composition make this interpretation rather conjectural.

A large number of vases of the Cypro-Geometric III –Cypro-Archaic I–II periods are decorated with metopes containing static, confronted sphinxes or griffins, a motif no doubt borrowed from Egypt, probably via the Levant as a result of Phoenician activity. The sphinx is represented in its role as guardian or symbolizing royal power—the powerful pharaoh defeating his enemies—but in Cypriote art it becomes simply decorative. The original role of this monster, however, is maintained on the bronze horse gear and decorative parts of chariots, as we have seen already when describing the rich "royal" tombs of Salamis.

Although in general the character of Cypriote vase painting at this time was static and "styleless," there are occasional examples of some exceptionally lively compositions in what is known as the "free-field" style of the Cypro-Archaic I period. This style usually appears as the decoration on jugs. Simple, single or occasionally multiple motifs, human or animal, spread over the curved surfaces of jugs. The stylized bull figure smelling a flower on a Bichrome IV jug from Arnadhi in the Famagusta District (Karageorghis and Des Gagniers 1974, vase XVI.b.14), the stylized bird catching a fish (ibid., XXIV.b.45), on a jug of Bichrome IV ware, and the bird in front of a curving bough

372

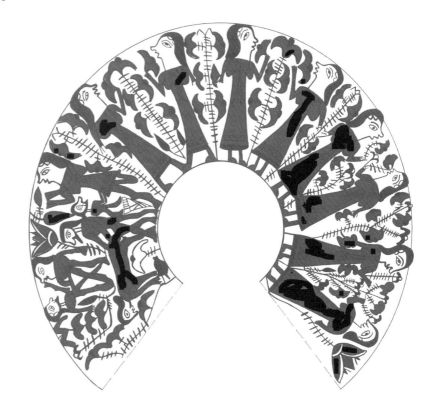

373

374

374. White Painted III crater from Khrysochou (south of Marion). Cyprus Museum, Nicosia, Inv. no. 1973/III-16/2. Height: 59cm.; mouth diam.: 36cm. The neck is decorated on either side between the handles with a chariot scene and a horse rider.

(ibid., vase xxv.f.1) are real works of art, illustrating the ability of the Cypriote vase painter to decorate the curved surface of a vase very satisfactorily, fully conscious of his role as a vase decorator rather than a painter on a flat surface.

Especially successful are the chariot scenes. As early as the Cypro-Geometric III period there is an example of such a scene around the neck of a White Painted III crater from Khrysochou. On Side A a pair of horses gallop to the left, with the rider obviously on the back of one of them. The other horse is led; there is a dog beneath the horse's body. The horses are followed by a chariot group. The rider's quiver and the dog, as well as the two spears at the back of the chariot, indicate that this is either a hunting scene or a battle scene. There is a similar scene on the other side of the crater, but with only one, ridden, horse.

Representations of warlike scenes, especially war chariots and cavalrymen, were very fashionable in the iconography of the Near East and the Aegean during the eighth century B.C. This was the period of the great achievements of the Assyrian army, of which the chariot corps and the cavalry were the principal force. Scenes related to the exploits of the Near Eastern kings were abundant in sculpture, and these influ-

enced other arts and crafts, for example ivory carving and metalwork. Such works of art were easily portable, and indeed quite a number of them reached Cyprus, including the decorated metal bowls; but it should be remembered that art of perishable materials, such as carpets and wall hangings, must also have traveled.

In the Aegean the representation of chariots and cavalrymen is very frequent in late Geometric vase painting. It is known that tapestries decorated with warlike scenes were popular in the Homeric period; and we may cite the passage in the third book of the *Iliad* where Helen, by the method of tapestry weaving, represented the battles of the Trojans and the Achaeans (*Iliad* III. 125–127). The continued popularity of Homeric epic must have been one of the reasons for the revival of such scenes in artistic iconography.

The rendering of details of the horse harness and the figure drawing in general betray how heavily indebted the painters were to Assyrian representations, probably known to them through minor works of art such as ivories and metal bowls. However, some other details, such as the two horses on Side A of the Khrysochou crater, with their high necks and small heads, show influences from late Greek Geometric vase painting. This vase, in fact, epitomizes the stylistic tendencies in Cypriote artistic production during the eighth century B.C., particularly because it shows that, beyond influences and imitations, the Cypriote vase painter retained his own qualities of freedom in rendering pictorial compositions with a highly developed sense of humor.

There are several other examples of compositions with war chariots and scenes of hunting from a chariot in the vase painting of the Cypro-Archaic I period. The most ambitious is on a vase from Nicosia, showing hunters returning from a successful campaign. The style is rather naïve and static, illustrating the inability of the vase painter to show action (Karageorghis and Des Gagniers 1974, vase II.4).

A war chariot in the "free-field" style is represented on the body of a Bichrome IV ware jug, now in the Berlin Museums. At the back of the chariot box hangs a shield, decorated with a large lion's head as a boss; on the chariot pole hang two heads of decapitated enemies, following an oriental custom. The influence of Assyrian art is indisputable (Karageorghis and Des Gagniers 1974, vase II.6).

Ships were no doubt a familiar scene in the busy harbors of Cyprus (for descriptions of depictions see Karageorghis and Des Gagniers 1974, vases XI.1–3). The representation of a merchant ship on a jug (ibid., vase XI.2) of White Painted IV ware, from the Karpass and now in the British Museum, vividly illustrates the Cypriote sense of humor, which is also seen in many other aspects of Cypriote art.

A Black-on-Red I (III) bowl dating to the ninth century B.C., now in Otterlo, Holland (Karageorghis and Des Gagniers 1974, vase VII.1) is decorated all around with seven warriors armed with shields and spears, very clearly inspired by Greek Geometric representations. The Cypriote vase painter obviously wanted to represent the warriors holding large Boeotian shields, but not understanding the particular shape he transformed the lower parts of the shields into kilts for the warriors and showed each of them holding another, small and round, shield. It is quite likely that the warriors were Greek mercenaries, whose presence in the Near East from the eighth century B.C. onward is quite frequent (cf. Niemeier 2001).

It is interesting to compare Cypriote vase painting of the eighth–seventh centuries B.C. with that of mainland Greece (Attica and Corinth) on the one hand, and that of the East Greek world (Ionia) on the other. Narrative and action under the strong influence of myth are characteristics of mainland Greek art. The East Greek vase painters were conscious that they were decorators of the surface of vases, with static representations of animals and friezes of plants or flowers, in exactly the same way as the Cypriote vase painters. The maximum degree of narrative that the Cypriots could attain was the procession of human figures, influences from cultic representations, and occasionally scenes of symposia, as seen also on some fikellura vases and metal bowls. East Greek art and Cypriote art represented a different world from that of mainland Greece, much different in spirit and nearer to the world of the Orient, to which they were both exposed. There may, of course, be a few exceptions to the general rule.

5. Sculpture

The introduction of large-scale sculpture, in both limestone and terra-cotta, was a major development in Cypriote art of the seventh century B.C. Both materials had been used for minor sculptures (figurines) during earlier periods, but now for the first time large, life-size, and occasionally over-life-size sculptures began to be made in the island.

E. Gjerstad (1948, 355) dated the first appearance of large-scale terra-cotta sculptures in Cyprus to circa 650 B.C. Stratified examples from the Heraion on Samos, however, are placed slightly earlier, circa 670/660 B.C., by G. Schmidt (1968, 93–98). Schmidt's dating has been accepted by most scholars and is followed here, in the absence of any firm evidence to support a different chronology. A slightly later chronology has been proposed by B. Lewe (1975, 91ff.), who does not accept the Samian dating as absolutely valid. Gjerstad's stylistic analysis is basically followed here, although the writer does not entirely accept his detailed subdivisions.

What caused the first appearance in Cyprus of large-scale terra-cotta sculpture of Gjerstad's Proto-Cypriote style? He proposed (1948, 355–356) that the inspiration for monumental sculpture in the island, together with "a few isolated traits," was drawn from Egypt, although the actual "sculptural style was developed according to the purely Cypriote disposition of culture with its Syro-Anatolian affinities." The same source was responsible for the transmission of monumental votive sculpture to Greece, though it is not easy to determine whether this transmission was direct or indirect. Gjerstad suggested that there were already interrelations between Egypt and Cyprus in the Cypro-Geometric III period, but these may not have

375

375. Terra-cotta chariot group from the sanctuary of Ayia Irini (Swedish Cyprus Expedition), no. 2000. Length: 20.5cm. Cyprus Museum, Nicosia, sixth century B.C. This is a four-horse chariot, with a charioteer and a fully armed warrior in the chariot box. The horses and human figures are painted with black, red, and blue-green paint. Several other terra-cotta chariot groups have been found in the sanctuary of Ayia Irini and other sanctuaries dedicated to male divinities (e.g., Meniko and Peyia). Real chariots and horses were sacrificed in the dromoi of royal tombs of the Cypro-Archaic I–II period.

precise evidence regarding the male–female distinction is provided by smaller, well-preserved terra-cotta figures holding attributes such as animals and tambourines (for a discussion of this problem regarding the Samian material see Schmidt 1968, 100–103).

The relevant features of Proto-Cypriote sculptures for determining their stylistic class are the head and facial expression. The crude and rustic body merely serves as a simple support for the head. The head is usually carefully rendered with accentuated facial details that give the face the individuality of a portrait (Gjerstad 1948, 95). The artist gave rein to his imagination in the depiction of lively expressions and in this respect was less bound by strict stylistic rules. The stern and severe expressions of Style I faces at Ayia Irini may be due to the temperament of one particular master artist who imposed his taste on apprentices working in his

377

atelier or within the same community. Clay is easy to manipulate, and the expression of the face, especially the mouth, can be changed with a mere touch of the fingers. During modeling the coroplast could easily modify the "style" and facial expression several times by the simple addition or removal of clay, or even unintentionally. Stone sculpture is very different. The use of even a relatively soft rock like limestone presupposed certain stylistic rules that the sculptor learned to follow. He may have had fixed "models" that characterized a certain style. The material dictated not only manufacturing techniques but also the rendering of certain features that would ultimately have affected the style. Although the products of coroplastic art are not considered inferior to stone sculpture, it is generally agreed that stone sculptors, working in established artistic workshops, produced more durable and consequently more expensive works of art.

Stone sculpture from the seventh century B.C. is rare, and at present only works from the region of Golgoi are known. There is also no marble on Cyprus—or any other hard stone suitable for carving large-scale sculpture. The Cypriote artist was confined to soft limestone, abundant in the central and southeastern parts of the island. So it is not surprising that the earliest sculpture appeared in the Golgoi area and gradually spread to other centers, such as Idalion, Arsos, and Kition, in the same limestone-rich region.

Bearded human figures wearing conical headdresses, made in both limestone and terra-cotta, have a long history in Cypriote sculpture, dating from the end of the seventh to the fifth century B.C. (see Markoe 1987; Hermary 1989, 22–33). These sculptures represent priests or dignitaries, although ordinary people wore the same headdress (Hermary 1989, 22), the top of which is often bent toward the back; bands support the two cheekpieces.

The earliest sculptures, from about the end of the seventh century B.C., have accentuated facial characteristics: a large nose, pointed lips, and large ears. Several such examples are preserved in various museums, particularly in the Louvre; an example 39.5cm high (Hermary 1989, no. 3) is illustrated here.

The smaller sculptures, both in limestone and in terra-cotta, especially the latter, are no less interesting. The terra-cotta "idols" or "figurines," representing human and animal figures, follow a long Cypriote tradition that had continued from the Chalcolithic period onward. Such figurines were dedicated both in sanctuaries and in tombs. Among the most significant are

association with a reckless lifestyle. The twisted locks of hair recall female coiffure. The short tunic or band around the waist shows the human association of the monster, but particular care is taken to allow the genitals to appear.

From the seventh century B.C. representations of the three-bodied monster Geryon appear. This monster lived in Erythia, surrounded by the waves, beyond the ocean (Hesiod, *Theogonia*, 287–294), at Cadiz, in the well-known Phoenician settlement of the southernmost part of Spain. The "Greco-Phoenician connection" of this hero must have appealed particularly to the Cypriots of the seventh century B.C., and they often portrayed him in art; such representations could easily be recognized by both the Cypriots and the Phoenicians of the island. It is interesting to note that the myth of Hercules and Geryon was also popular in other lands that had Phoenician connections, namely, Samos, Sicily, and Spain, but this does not mean that the myth itself had its origin in Phoenicia. In Greek myth, Hercules is asked by Eurystheus, king of the Argolid and Tiryns, to kill Geryon. He manages to kill not only Geryon, but also the herdsman Eurytion and his dog Orthros; afterward he flees with Geryon's cattle.

From Cyprus two fragmentary representations of Geryon in terra-cotta are known, medium sized and both dating to the middle of the seventh century B.C. One was found at Pyrga, south of Idalion, and is now in the British Museum; the other was found in a favissa near Peyia, in the Paphos District, and is now in the Paphos District Museum. In both representations Geryon is shown as three-headed and three-bodied, with a shield corresponding to each body. The facial characteristics and garments are similar to those of other Cypriote terra-cotta sculptures. The problem with the earliest Cypriote representations of the myth of Geryon is that they do not tell the whole story but show only the three-bodied monster by itself, without any reference to Hercules. This may either be owing to the fact that it was difficult to represent in the round a composition that involved a number of human and animal figures, or because the Cypriots developed a fascination with the three-bodied monster itself.

In sculpture as well as vase painting, the end of the Cypro-Geometric III and the Cypro-Archaic I periods is characterized by the appearance of mythological scenes and other mythical creatures, obviously as a result of the orientalizing tendencies in both the Cypriote and Greek arts.

382

Although the sphinx was very popular in vase painting, its representations in clay are very rare (cf. Karageorghis 1996c, 9–11). The most popular animal representations in the coroplastic art of the eighth–seventh centuries B.C. are horses, with or without riders, and bulls. The horses are high necked and decorated all over in the same style as the pottery of the period. It should be remembered that during this period the horse was considered a status symbol for the military aristocracy, and, as has been mentioned, real horses were sacrificed in the dromoi of "royal" tombs. They are also found in sanctuaries dedicated to male divinities. The bull figures followed a long tradition in the coroplastic art of Cyprus; the animal's association with fertility was steadfastly maintained. Bull figures appear both in tombs and in sanctuaries. Their religious associations were enhanced even further with the increase in the number of rural sanctuaries during

382. The upper part of a terra-cotta representation of the three-bodied hero Geryon. From Pyrga (Famagusta District). The British Museum, London, Inv. no. 1866.1-1.298 and 299. Preserved height: 24cm. The three bodies adjoin one another. Each held a round shield in the left hand, and the right arm was bent up to brandish a spear, now missing. The heads are molded and wear a pointed helmet with downturned cheekpieces. Each warrior wears a wide collar around the neck and a rectangular plaque at the back. There are traces of red and black paint. There are several representations of Geryon in Cypriote art, both in terra-cotta and limestone. This one dates to the second half of the seventh century B.C.

189

the Cypro-Archaic period. The size and style of the bull figures vary. Some of them are of medium size and hollow, especially those from Ayia Irini and Kourion, where they followed the tradition of the Cypro-Geometric period. In most cases, however, they were small and solid, as they were already during the Cypro-Geometric III period in other regions, e.g., at Palaepaphos. Another quite common type of terra-cotta figurine was the model of a chariot with a human figure without horses. The chariots are wheelmade; they are decorated in the style of Bichrome III and IV ware, indicating that this type of chariot is confined to the eighth–seventh centuries B.C. They have a semicircular body, a tubular socket for an added pole, and separate, solid wheels. The whole chariot gives the impression of a toy rather than an actual model.

We should recall that in the necropolis of Salamis the remains of actual chariots dating to the eighth–seventh centuries B.C. have been found, including both quadrigas (four-horsed chariots) and bigas (two-wheeled, single-poled chariots). Although these were used in funerary ceremonies, their resemblance to the contemporary Assyrian war chariots and to the terra-cotta models of the same period suggests that actual war chariots (rather than hearses) may have been used for funerals, suitably decorated for the purposes of the funerary procession.

Cypriote terra-cotta figurines as well as large-scale sculpture are found not only in Cyprus but also in other parts of the Greek world, mainly the sanctuaries of Hera in Samos and Athena at Lindos (Karageorghis *et al.* 2001, 58–63). At Samos they appear as early as circa 670/660 B.C. (cf. Schmidt 1968, 93–98). They have molded heads; the bodies, unfortunately, have not survived. The figures continued to appear at Samos during the early sixth century B.C. Whether these were produced on the spot from Cypriote molds or exported as complete statues from Cyprus is not easy to say. It is equally difficult to decide whether they were dedicated by Cypriote worshipers or taken as souvenirs by Greek visitors to Cyprus. In the temple of Athena at Lindos it is mainly small terra-cotta Cypriote figurines that appear. A large-scale terra-cotta female statue was found at Old Smyrna, dating to the late seventh century B.C. (Gjerstad 1978).

383

6. The Sanctuaries

The sacred area of Kition has already been described, with its large Phoenician temple and the smaller temples, including the sacred enclosures (temene). These temples are of largely Phoenician character and were associated with the new Phoenician community within the urban center of Kition. They have yielded large quantities of objects, e.g., terra-cottas, bronzes, faiences, etc. (Lagarce and Leclant 1976). However, in the rural areas and smaller towns there were a number of rural sanctuaries that followed an older tradition in their architecture, which is quite different from the sophisticated architecture of the temple of Astarte at Kition.

The simplest form of rural sanctuary is that at Ayia Irini, which succeeded a Late Bronze Age sanctuary. It was first erected at the beginning of the Cypro-Geometric period as a temenos with a peribolos, and it lasted until the Cypro-Geometric III period, with alterations that included a new monolithic altar in the middle of the temenos. In the Cypro-Archaic I period the temenos was renovated and enlarged, and it continued in use until about 500 B.C. It was sur-

rounded by a peribolos wall. The altar was located in the center, and on top of it was placed a cult symbol in the shape of an oval stone (a baetyl). Two small rectangular rooms were erected, which the excavators identified as enclosures for sacred trees. There were also two roofed shelters around the altar. Thus an area was screened off from the rest of the temenos, creating an inner court. A similar but more developed type of sanctuary appeared at Tamassos-*Frangissa* and at Achna, where the inner court was enclosed by a peribolos wall, and more space was provided for the deposit of important votive offerings.

The divinity worshiped in the sanctuary at Ayia Irini was connected with fertility but also responded to other needs of the community. Judging from the large numbers of bull figurines found among the votive offerings, as well as from the presence of bisexual centaurs and minotaurs (demons who accompanied the divinity), we may infer that the main aspect of the cult was connected with fertility. There were also human figurines wearing bulls' masks, probably representing priests performing a ritual. Such figurines have been found also in sanctuaries of other male divini-

384. Terra-cotta figurine of a hermaphrodite centaur, probably from Salamis. Cyprus Museum, Nicosia, Inv. no. 1991/I-21/1. Height: 23.1cm. Early seventh century B.C. The monster wears a helmet and holds a shield and probably a spear. He is decorated in red and black paint. Terra-cotta figurines of centaurs have been found in sanctuaries of the Cypro-Archaic period, e.g., at Ayia Irini.

385. Two bull figurines, one silver (left) and one gold (right), from the Archaic altar of the sanctuary of Apollo Hylates at Kourion (excavations of the American Mission, University of Missouri, 1980). Cyprus Museum, Nicosia. Length of silver figurine: 4.9cm. (tail missing); length of gold figurine: 3.1cm. Apollo was worshiped at Kourion from the eighth century B.C. and was originally a god of cattle, hence these offerings. The technique of the figurines betrays Anatolian influences. Seventh century B.C.

386. Terra-cotta figurine of a priest (?) wearing an anthropomorphic mask, from Amathus, Tomb 557, no. 15. Height: 13.4cm. Limassol District Museum. The body is decorated with bands of black and red paint (after Karageorghis 1995d, 55, fig. 30).

387. Terra-cotta figurine of a priest (?) wearing a bull's mask, from Amathus, Tomb 200, no. 1. Limassol District Museum. Height: 13.2cm. The figure is decorated with red and black painted bands (after Karageorghis 1995d, 56, fig. 31).

385

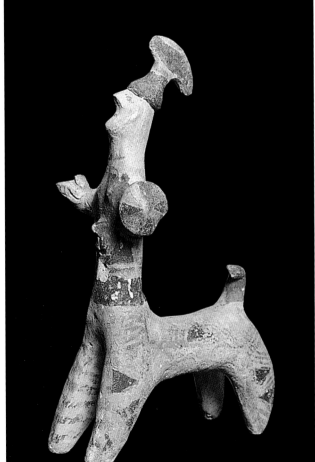

384

386

387

ties, e.g., in the sanctuary of Apollo at Kourion, and also in tombs at Amathus (Karageorghis 1995d, 55–57). This practice, which had a long tradition in Cypriote religion going back to the Early and Middle Bronze Age, must have been widespread during the eighth–seventh centuries B.C., judging from the numbers of small clay votive bulls' masks found in tombs. Clay anthropomorphic masks of a votive character have been found both in tombs and sanctuaries elsewhere in the island (cf. Karageorghis 1993a, 107–122; idem 1995d, 54–55). The male god who was worshiped in the sanctuary of Ayia Irini was also related to war. Armed men, wearing helmets and holding shields and daggers, are to be found among the clay votive figures and figurines. There are also clay mod-

388

els of four-horse war chariots that, as we know from Herodotus, were used in Cyprus in warfare as late as the fifth century B.C. The human figures found in the sanctuary, the vast majority of clay, are of different sizes and were arranged in rows all around the altar. They represent warriors and bearers of gifts. The large ones are hollow. Some of them are over-life-size and were made in several pieces that were assembled and fixed together. The large ones must have been offered by rich members of the community, and the small ones, made in a simple "snowman" technique, were offered by ordinary people. It is interesting that among the clay figurines there is one with African facial characteristics, who holds a large Egyptian ankh symbol. About two thousand clay sculptures and figurines have been found in the sanctuary of Ayia Irini. There must have been one or more local production centers, as was the case in other places where there were sanctuaries, such as Idalion, Kourion, etc. The large numbers of votive offerings may indicate the prosperity but also the piety of the population.

Several other sanctuaries are known to have flourished in the island during the Cypro-Geometric III and the Cypro-Archaic periods. At Kourion there was a sanctuary of Apollo Hylates, who was worshiped there as a god of cattle and fertility, probably a descendant of the Late Bronze Age "Apollo Keraeatas" of Enkomi, whose cult was introduced from Arcadia in the Peloponnese. His cult appeared at Kourion already in the eighth century B.C. It consisted of an open-air temenos with a circular altar built of rubble. Several terra-cotta figurines of bulls were found on it, as well as two small bull figurines of gold and silver, respectively. This sanctuary, like that of Ayia Irini and others elsewhere on the island, continued to function throughout the sixth century B.C.

Every time a sanctuary became filled with votive gifts, those that were not of precious material—usually the terra-cotta figurines—were carefully removed, placed in shallow pits somewhere in the neighborhood of the sanctuary, and covered with soil. These are the bothroi or favissae, which have been found in numbers in various parts of the island, in association with sanctuaries. Several were associated with the temple of Astarte at Kition, and rich bothroi were also found in the vicinity of the temple of Apollo at Kourion. They are extremely useful, not only for the vast amounts of material that they have yielded, but also because they provide very useful material for the various chronological phases in the life of the sanctuaries. One such bothros was found recently in the vicinity of the village of Peyia, near the western coast of Cyprus in the Paphos District. It yielded some large-size terra-cotta sculpture, models of chariots; and a figure of Geryon, mentioned earlier. The divinity worshiped in this sanctuary was obviously male.

7. Funerary Architecture

Some of the finest examples of tomb architecture in the "royal" necropolis of Salamis, dating from the Cypro-Geometric to the Cypro-Archaic II period, have already been discussed. Two tombs at Tamassos, constructed with ashlar blocks, date to the Cypro-Archaic II period. They imitate wooden architecture and recall tombs of Anatolia; it has been suggested that they may have been constructed by itinerant artists from this neighboring country (Karageorghis 1978). They each have a stepped dromos and their stomia are flanked by two pilasters with an "aeolic" capital, betraying Phoenician influence. One tomb has an antechamber and a chamber, the second only one chamber. The first tomb, which is the best preserved, is decorated inside with miniature friezes of lotus flowers in relief. In both tombs the deceased was buried in a large limestone sarcophagus.

Several other built tombs of the late Archaic period have been found at Amathus. They all have a stepped dromos, in one case covered with a vault, and the chamber usually has a saddle roof. Another built tomb was found at Kition-*Phaneromeni*; a second one was excavated recently within the boundaries of ancient Kition (Karageorghis 2000c, 11–12).

This tomb consists of an antechamber and a funerary chamber, each measuring 2.5×2m., communicating with a passage. The tomb is entirely constructed of regularly hewn blocks of stone; its floor is covered with large gypsum slabs. The two chambers had a vaulted roof. The dromos of the tomb, 16.44m. long and more than 2m. wide, was carved in the natural rock, and the sides were dressed with stone. Three skeletons of equids were found buried in the dromos, associated with bronze blinders and iron bits. The ceramic material and the jewelry, as well as the tomb architecture, suggest that this tomb was used for the burial of a distinguished member of the Phoenician community of Kition.

Although the skeletons of "horses" may recall some of the "royal" tombs of Salamis and elsewhere, they differ in that they were not associated with any remains of chariots. Furthermore, it is not certain that these

389

are skeletons of horses rather than of donkeys, as is the case in e.g., Salamis Tombs 19 and 31, where skeletons of unyoked donkeys were found (Karageorghis 1967a, 117–118). It would not be surprising if this custom was adopted by some of the rich Phoenicians of Kition. This tomb, which might be called a "royal" tomb, on analogy with the tombs of Salamis of the Cypro-Archaic period, is of considerable importance and should be taken into account in the discussion of the controversy regarding the identification of Qartihadast.

389. The antechamber of Tamassos built Tomb 5. This is the finest of two "royal" tombs in the necropolis of Tamassos. It has a stepped dromos and its stomion was flanked by two pilasters with "aeolic" capitals, carved in relief, betraying Phoenician influence. The tomb had a chamber and an antechamber, decorated with miniature carved friezes of lotus flowers in relief. The roof seems to imitate wooden architecture; we have suggested that the Tamassos tombs were constructed by itinerant masons from Anatolia in the Cypro-Archaic II period (circa 600–550 B.C.).

The Sixth Century B.C.

The Cypro-Archaic II Period (circa 600–480 B.C.)

There was no clear-cut cultural division between the end of the seventh and the beginning of the sixth century B.C., although the year 600 B.C. is generally considered to be the end of the Cypro-Archaic I period and the beginning of Cypro-Archaic II (cf. Gjerstad 1948, 424–426).

1. Egyptian and Greek Influences

Not only is this period of Cypriote archaeology known from the archaeological material, but for the first time there is historical evidence, namely from Herodotus, who (II.182.2) says that the Pharaoh Amasis of Egypt "seiged Cyprus, the first man to do so, and compelled it to pay tribute." This statement by Herodotus has caused considerable discussion. There is some corroborating evidence supporting a date of about 570 B.C. for this "event." A stela from Elephantine in Egypt, with a hieroglyphic inscription referring to the first four years of the Pharaoh Amasis's reign, reports that in January 570 B.C. Amasis defeated the Pharaoh Apries, who tried to regain power in Egypt with the aid of Cypriote ships. As a result of this action by Apries, according to the inscription, Amasis "cut off" the island (for a general discussion see Reyes 1994, 69–74). Thus Herodotus's statement may be regarded as a historical possibility but there is nothing to show whether Apries's action concerning Cyprus reflects a military domination or simply an alliance (Reyes 1994, 74). What, then, were the political relations between Cyprus and Egypt? Reyes argued, based on the contents of a Neo-Babylonian tablet, to our view convincingly, that the Egyptians did not seize Cyprus, as suggested by Herodotus, but subdued it, and made it tributary (Reyes 1994, 75–78). Furthermore, there is evidence that Amasis adorned many of the Cypriote temples with dedications that are worthy of mention (Reyes 1994, 78). Rather than an Egyptian domination, an alliance with Egypt by 567 B.C. seems more probable. In any case, relations may have been "less hostile than is normally assumed from Herodotos II.182.2" (Reyes 1994, 78).

We have shown above how Cypriote art (sculpture and vase painting) was often influenced by both Greek and Near Eastern artistic styles. It is apparent that the Greek influence became stronger in the Cypro-Archaic I period, perhaps as a result of intensified trade between the two regions. Those frequent contacts are reflected by Herodotus, who mentions the visit to Cyprus of the Greek legislator Solon during the first half of the sixth century B.C. Solon visited the king of Aepeia Philokypros and advised him to transfer his capital to a more suitable place; Philokypros followed this advice, giving to the new town the name Soloi, in honor of his distinguished visitor. It is quite probable, however, that Solon never visited Cyprus and that this was an imaginative story emanating from the fact that Solon and Philokypros were connected by friendship; Solon in fact dedicated an elegiac poem to Philokypros (Reyes 1994, 123–124; see also Stylianou 1992, 400–401).

There were also close contacts with the Greek colony of Naucratis. The story of Herostratos, who bought a statuette of Aphrodite at Paphos and carried it to Naucratis, is very characteristic. On one of his journeys he landed at Palaepaphos and bought a rather Archaic-looking statuette of the goddess. During a storm on the way home, the passengers on the ship prayed to this image of Aphrodite, and the goddess of the seas promptly saved them by a miracle. When he reached Naucratis, Herostratos dedicated the statuette in the local temple of Aphrodite (Maier and Karageorghis 1984, 208–209).

Several scholars have argued that the archaeological record is not a criterion for an Egyptian domination over Cyprus, as Gjerstad (1948, 466–467) suggested. The Egyptianizing character of Cypriote sculpture may have been introduced to Cyprus by the Phoenicians, as had already happened prior to 570 B.C., rather than being the result of Egyptian domination (cf. Markoe 1990; Reyes 1994, 82–84). The Egyptianizing phase of Cypriote sculpture is quite predominant in the artistic production of Cyprus during the last quarter of the sixth and the first quarter of the fifth centuries B.C. It is represented by a series of limestone statues, mainly of large size, wearing the Egyptian *shenti* kilt, with its central pendant flap, plain or deco-

390. A headless limestone statue of the mythical three-bodied monster Geryon, said to have been found at Golgoi. The Cesnola Collection, the Metropolitan Museum of Art, New York, no. 74.51.2591. Preserved height: 52.7cm. The shields and the short kilt of the monster are elaborately decorated in low relief with Greek mythological scenes from the cycles of Hercules and Perseus. Greek myths were widespread in Cyprus during the second half of the sixth century B.C., to which this statue belongs.

rated with uraei (Markoe 1990, 113). The chests of these figures are often decorated with the triple collar, characteristic of the New Kingdom statuary fashionable in sixth-century-B.C. Phoenicia. An impressive number of such statues were found in the sanctuary of Golgoi and are now in the Metropolitan Museum of Art, New York.

It should be noted, however, that side by side with the Egyptian influence on Cypriote sculpture, there was a strong influence from Ionia. It has even been suggested that the style and the workmanship, even of the Egyptianizing statues, essentially reflected Hellenic influence (for references see Reyes 1994, 83).

Apart from the Egyptianizing trends in Cypriote sculpture, a similar trend may be observed in other aspects of art. An important case is that of the painted decoration of the interior of Tomb 80 in the necropolis of Salamis. It is built with ashlar blocks and has a vaulted roof (Karageorghis 1973c, 123–127). The nearest parallels for painted tombs are the tombs of Egypt. In fact, there is a striking similarity between

the motifs used for the ceiling of the Salamis tomb and those used for the ceiling of an earlier Egyptian tomb, dating to the period of Rameses II. The decoration is symmetrically arranged like a grid with stars at the intersections, resembling stars in the sky. The papyrus flowers and lotus buds are motifs of Egyptian art, and they appear in the same arrangements in other Near Eastern arts. As a whole, the painted decoration may recall the painted interior of Egyptian sarcophagi. This tomb may date to the end of the Cypro-Archaic II period and the beginning of Cypro-Classical I. It had been looted, so it is not possible to know exactly when it was first used. The looters left only a few insignificant objects.

Reyes, discussing this tomb, refuted the idea that its Egyptianizing decoration was the result of contacts with Egypt, believing that it provides a glimpse of what was a widespread practice in the Eastern Mediterranean (1994, 80). Although the writer agrees with the suggestion that this tomb dates to a late period, it seems unwise to deny that artistic influences could have come directly from Egypt. It is quite natural that there was a kind of "Egyptomania" in the sixth century B.C. in Cyprus, and even afterward, when Cyprus entered the Persian Empire (cf. Reyes 1994, 84), considering the profound impact of Egyptian art on all the peoples of the Eastern Mediterranean and particularly the Levantine region. Although it is possible that some of the "Aegyptiaca" found in Cyprus, namely scarabs and pendants of faience, reached the island via the Levant, some direct imports cannot be excluded (cf. Reyes 1994, 79). Boardman is probably right when he proposes that there was a direct route to and from Egypt that did not need to hug the Levantine coast (Boardman 2001a, 14–15).

The above argument may be applied concerning the frequent occurrence of the motif of the Hathor head in the art of Cyprus, particularly in the sixth century B.C. It is to be found in vase painting of the Amathus style and also in stone sculpture found at Amathus, as well, in other works of art, e.g., jewelry and terracotta. Is the frequency of this motif at Amathus the result of close trade and contact between Amathus and Egypt, as suggested by Reyes (ibid., 82)? Is it not more plausible to suggest the presence of an Egyptian minority within the population of Amathus, for whom the Hathor head had a religious meaning rather than being simply a decorative motif, and who had some impact on local religious practices? The fact that Amathus is the closest Cypriote urban center to Egypt

may support this suggestion. The cultic scene on a fragment of a vase in the Amathus style now in the Louvre, showing human and animal figures in front of a Hathoric capital mounted on a pedestal, may provide supporting evidence (Karageorghis and Des Gagniers 1974, 510, vase no. 7; cf. also Buchholz 1993).

2. The "Amathus-Style" Pottery

The motif of the Hathor head decorates a number of vases of the so-called Amathus style of the Cypro-Archaic II period. Reyes argued against the association of this Egyptian motif with any political domination of Cyprus in the sixth century B.C. and put forward the suggestion, which the writer had proposed earlier (Karageorghis 1989), that some pictorial motifs and scenes appearing on vases of this style may have been taken from East Greek vase painting; others may have been taken from Phoenician art (Reyes 1994, 80).

The "Amathus style" made a lively contribution to Cypriote vase painting before its degeneration in the fifth century B.C. The vase painters working in this

393

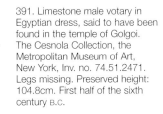

391. Limestone male votary in Egyptian dress, said to have been found in the temple of Golgoi. The Cesnola Collection, the Metropolitan Museum of Art, New York, Inv. no. 74.51.2471. Legs missing. Preserved height: 104.8cm. First half of the sixth century B.C.

392. Limestone statuette of a beardless youth, probably from a tomb at Amathus. The Cesnola Collection, the Metropolitan Museum of Art, New York, no. 74.51.2571. Legs and arms are missing; the right hand is placed on the chest. Preserved height: 12.4cm. It shows strong Egyptian influence: the youth wears a wig, a collar, and the Egyptian shenti. Red and black paint are preserved on the face and body. It dates to the early sixth century B.C. and may have been buried with an Egyptian.

393. Bronze statuette of a male figure from Idalion. The British Museum, London, Inv. no. 1983.3-20.339. Height: 21.3cm. He wears an Egyptian dress and a conical headdress. His left arm is bent against the chest; his right arm is stretched down beside the body. The Egyptian influence is obvious. First half of the sixth century B.C.

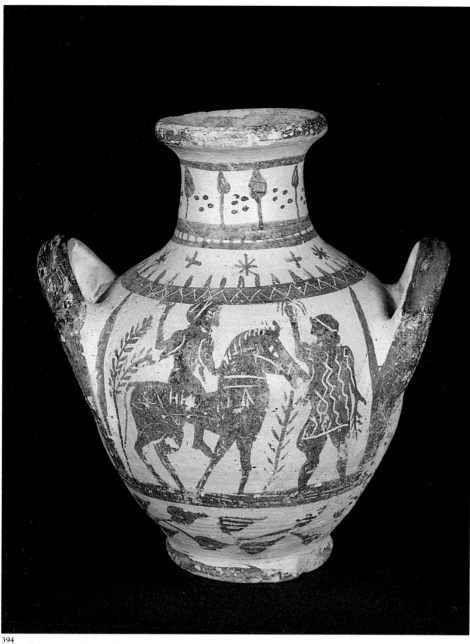

394

394. Jug of White Painted V ware (Amathus style) from Amathus, Tomb 251, no. 8. Limassol District Museum. Height: 13.5cm. One side of the vase is decorated with a horse and a rider, with a second human figure walking in front of the horse. The other side is decorated with two winged sphinxes confronting each other on either side of a "sacred tree." The figures are rendered in silhouette, with details shown by means of incised lines, a technique that imitates Attic Greek vase painting. This style, which also betrays iconographic influences from the Aegean, flourished at Amathus in the sixth century B.C.

ii:29; Karageorghis and Des Gagniers 1974, vases xxv.j.1–20; idem 1979, vases xxv.j.1–10). Apart from its occurrence on juglets, this "bird style" also appears on craters, but only very rarely (Karageorghis and Des Gagniers 1974, vases xxv.h.11–12).

From the second half of the sixth century B.C. trade between the Aegean and the Greek colonies of the Eastern Mediterranean increased considerably, especially with the foundation of Naucratis in Egypt and the prosperity of the Greek cities of Cyprus, which led to the more frequent import of Greek vases to Cyprus. Rhodian vases of the figurative style have been found in fairly large numbers at sites such as Amathus, from the seventh century B.C. onward (Thalmann 1977). We know that this pottery occasionally influenced the iconography of certain Cypriote potters. The appearance of the Black-Figure style in Attic pottery, with its ceramic perfection and wonderful figurative decoration, revived the interest and taste in Greek vases among the Cypriots. At this time when interest in Greek culture in general was revived among the Cypriots, the Greek myths, which were the subjects of the decoration of many Black-Figure vases, must have had a particular appeal.

The local potters at Amathus created the "Amathus style" after about the middle of the sixth century B.C. or even earlier (cf. Hermary 1986a, 170). The vases decorated in this style are usually medium-size amphoriskoi of a traditional Cypriote type (20–25cm. in height, although a few are even smaller). The painted decoration is applied all over the body, but the main decoration is in the main zone of the body between the handles. The rest of the body is decorated with horizontal bands filled with abstract or floral motifs of various kinds. The main decorated zone, usually figurative, is in the White Painted or Bichrome technique. Very often the motifs are rendered in silhouette, with details indicated by incisions made after firing, no doubt an influence from both the Rhodian and Attic Black-Figure vases.

The Cypriote potter had demonstrated in several cases that he could imitate imported Rhodian vases and their decoration very accurately, especially in the case of animals painted in outline. However, he found it particularly difficult to imitate the human figures of the Attic Black-Figure vases, especially when rendered in silhouette with engraved details. Whenever he tried to do so the result was a failure. There is, however, one exception. On one side of a very small amphoriskos discovered recently at Amathus there is a

style were quite ambitious; they produced compositions with human and animal figures and were under the strong influence of Greek art. The style has already been discussed by several scholars (Karageorghis and Des Gagniers 1974, 91–93, vases 1–13; Karageorghis 1989; Hermary 1997). There is also another class of pottery particular to Amathus that is decorated in a simpler style. The most popular motif of this style was the bird, by itself or in a frieze, occasionally associated with stylized tree motifs. This motif usually appears on juglets of the end of the Cypro-Archaic I period (White Painted IV or Bichrome IV), on the body opposite the handle, usually in the "free-field" style. The juglets have a depressed body, short neck, and trefoil mouth (e.g., Gjerstad 1948, fig. XXVI-

composition of a horse rider and a groom decorating the zone between the handles. Although the figure drawing does not attain the perfection of the Black-Figure equivalent, the composition is nevertheless quite convincing and successful. The other side of the vase is decorated with a composition that has deep roots in Near Eastern art, namely, a sphinx on either side of an elaborate flower motif. This composition, however, found its way quite early into the orientalizing art of Greece.

There are other amphoriskoi decorated with a similar motif (Karageorghis 1989, 84; idem 1990b). Some of these compositions may have been taken "secondhand" from the Aegean, where in turn they had been taken from the Near East, the region where they flourished, particularly in the seventh century B.C. (cf. Karageorghis 1990b, 124).

On a recently discovered Bichrome V ware jug from Amathus the decoration in a rectangular panel consists of the bust of a bearded human figure in profile.

He is shown in silhouette, with details such as the hair and the beard rendered by grooves. The influence from East Greek iconography is obvious (Karageorghis 1998a). The Amathus potters must soon have realized that they could not cope adequately with the representation of human figures. Although the most ambitious of them did attempt this, others turned their hand to motifs and compositions that they could illustrate more satisfactorily. Such motifs were the Hathor heads, roosters, floral or tree motifs, etc. (for the introduction of the Hathor head motif in Cypriote art of the sixth century B.C. see also Buchholz 1993).

The most ambitious scene that was ever attempted by an Amathusian painter is the one on an amphoriskos in the British Museum (Karageorghis and Des Gagniers 1974, 516–517). The best-preserved side is decorated with a number of human figures standing or seated under a tree, in a feasting mood, enjoying a *fête champêtre* (see also Des Gagniers 1972). In a recently published article Raptou associated it with a cultic

395-396. Amphoriskos of the "Amathus style," from a private collection, on loan to Princeton University Art Museum. Restored height: circa 23cm. Both sides of the body between the handles are decorated with two antithetic winged sphinxes wearing the crowns of Upper and Lower Egypt, on either side of a composite flower motif. Ample use of incised lines for the rendering of details. The Egyptian influence is obvious. Early sixth century B.C.

395

396

199

397

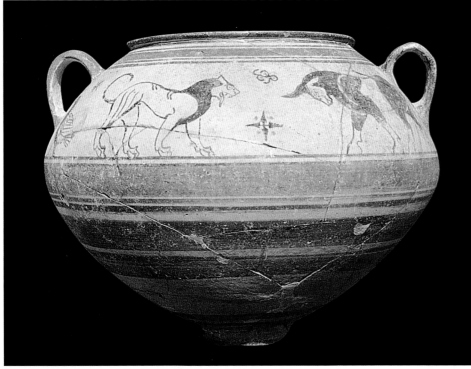

398

397. Fragmentary amphoriskos from Amathus. The British Museum, London, Inv. no. 1894.11-1.475. Restored height: 24.1cm. It is decorated on both sides in the Bichrome V technique. On the preserved side the main zone is decorated with an ambitious composition with human figures seated or standing among trees. The lower zone is decorated with a frieze of lotus flowers.

398. Jar of Bichrome V ware found in a tomb at Goudhi, south of Marion (Paphos District). Height: 29.5cm.; diam.: 22.3cm. Paphos District Museum, no. 2235. It is decorated on both sides between the handles with friezes of animals (lions, bulls, a wild boar, a bird, dogs), resembling very closely the style of Rhodian vase painting of the end of the seventh century B.C.

scene in honor of the Great Goddess of Cyprus, under the inspiration of a cultic scene associated with the corresponding goddess of Samos (Raptou 1999).

In other parts of the island the Cypriote potter imitated the "animals style" of Rhodian painting from the end of the seventh to the beginning of the sixth century B.C. This is particularly clear on a jar of Bichrome V ware from Goudhi in the Paphos District (Karageorghis 1979a). Cypriote vase painters often attempted to depict stags and goats in this style, but they tried to retain the traditional Cypriote composition (e.g. Karageorghis and Des Gagniers 1974, vases XVII.26, XVIII.9, 12; for influences from other regions of the Aegean see ibid., B.3, VII.1). The Goudhi jar provides the first example of a case where the Cypriote vase painter copied everything from Rhodian pottery: the motifs, the composition, even the filling ornaments.

3. Sculpture

The sixth century B.C. may be considered the heyday of Cypriote sculpture, both in stone and in terra-cotta. A dominant figure in stone sculpture is the panhellenic hero Hercules, whose popularity in the iconography of Greek art during this period is well known. In Cyprus the hero was worshiped almost like a god and was often assimilated with the Phoenician god Melqart. In the iconography a genuine Cypriote type developed, combining both Greek and oriental characteristics. Hercules was particularly favored at Kition, where the influence of the Phoenicians was quite strong. There are also some other fine examples of limestone colossal statues dating to the end of the sixth century B.C.

One of the most important among the various representations of Hercules is the colossal limestone statue from Golgoi, now in the Metropolitan Museum of Art, New York; it is 2.17m. high. Hercules is shown standing, holding arrows in his right hand, now missing, and the bow in his left hand, also missing. He wears a lion skin and a kilt that reaches his knees. The more popular type of Hercules shows him wearing a lion skin and brandishing a club with his right arm; in his left hand he often holds a miniature lion by the hind legs, with the animal's head downward and the face turned up. This type of statue, produced at the end of the sixth century B.C., survived down to the period of Alexander the Great. The prototype is obviously oriental. In some cases the god is represented nude, no doubt under the influence of Greek art.

Much has been written about the origin of the myth and the representations of Hercules in the Greek and the Near Eastern worlds. Cyprus, lying between the two, was inevitably influenced by both (for a general discussion and bibliography see Karageorghis 1998f, 68–83).

Of particular interest is the representation of Hercules on a relief limestone slab of the end of the sixth to the beginning of the fifth century B.C. from Golgoi, now in the Metropolitan Museum of Art. It represents the story of Hercules stealing the cattle of Geryon. Whereas in the seventh century B.C. such continuous stories were not attempted by Cypriote sculptors but were known only from representations on metal bowls, as seen above, now the Cypriote sculptor very boldly embarked on the representation of complicated compositions in low relief. The Golgoi relief depicts Hercules, Eurytion, his dog Orthros, and the cattle of Geryon; Geryon himself is not shown. Hercules is almost naked, with the lion skin falling down his back. The herdsman is still alive; he is represented as a Silenus or Bes, and he holds a stone to throw at Hercules. No doubt there must have been a local version of the myth among the Cypriots that referred to the physical appearance of Eurytion and the enemies of Hercules in general as monsters. The cattle are rendered in perspective, as in Greek art. This relief was probably detached from the pedestal of a colossal statue of Hercules.

Geryon, who first appeared in terra-cotta already in the seventh century B.C., reappeared in limestone sculpture in the second half of the sixth century B.C. There are three limestone sculptures found in a temple at Golgoi, now in the Metropolitan Museum of Art, New York. The largest dates to the second half of the sixth century, and the two smaller ones to the early sixth century B.C. The shields and kilt of the larger statue are decorated in relief with scenes from the exploits of Hercules and the slaying of Medusa by Perseus. The style and iconography betray strong Greek influences. The shield on the right of Geryon is decorated with Perseus beheading the Gorgon Medusa in the presence of the goddess Athena, holding a shield and a spear. Perseus, between Athena and the Gorgon, wears a short kilt and points with his sword at the Gorgon, who raises her arms toward her head. On the central shield Hercules carries away one of the Kerkopes on his shoulders and is attacked by another. On the left Hercules is kneeling and is shooting at a centaur. On Geryon's kilt two figures with raised

399

399. Colossal limestone statue of a bearded figure from Pyla, now in the Kunsthistorisches Museum, Vienna, Inv. no. 1341. Preserved height: 20.1cm. Both arms are slightly bent downward, beside the body. The lower part of the legs and feet are missing. He wears a wreath around the head; he is partially draped with a mantle that leaves a large part of the right shoulder, as well as the left side of the body and both legs, uncovered. This statue may date to circa 500 B.C.

401

400

swords combat lions. Athena, Perseus, Hercules, and the Kerkopes wear crested Greek helmets and hold plain round shields. There is red paint on the figures and also on the background.

The shield of one of the smaller statuettes is decorated in low relief with Hercules attacking a crouching lion. There is a rich variety of types in the repertoire of sixth-century limestone sculpture. Some of them still show traces of their polychrome painted decoration, in black, red, and other colors, as in Greek sculpture (for a general discussion of the various types of Cypriote sculpture see Hermary 1989; for sculptures in the Cesnola Collection of the Metropolitan Museum of Art see Karageorghis et al. 2000).

A series of statues represents young beardless male figures, characterized as princes, wearing typical Cypriote short trousers, often decorated with a rosette in relief, and a diadem, also adorned with rosettes. Their stance is rigid, and they are never larger than life-size. Their attitude recalls that of Greek kouroi.

402

One of the most outstanding specimens of Cypriote limestone sculpture is that of a priest from Golgoi, dating to the last quarter of the sixth century B.C. It is now in the Metropolitan Museum, New York. The figure wears a pointed helmet, richly decorated with floral patterns in low relief and a bull protome at the top. He is draped with a *chiton*, decorated at the lower part with a frieze of engraved buds and lotus flowers and a richly folded *himation*. The garments and the helmet decorated with a bull's protome justify the sacerdotal identification, which is also confirmed by an engraved inscription on the left shoulder in the Cypriote syllabary reading: "Of the Paphian goddess," although this is by no means certain.

One of the major types of this period, the Egyptianizing male votaries, of which several examples have been found at Golgoi, has already been discussed above.

One of the best-known examples of Cypriote sculpture of this period is the Zeus Keraunios found at Kition and now in the Cyprus Museum. The god wears a long tunic and mantle (aegis) over his shoulders. In his raised right hand he holds a thunderbolt, while in his left hand he held an eagle, of which only the claws survive. He is bearded and has the expression of Archaic Cypro-Greek sculpture of circa 500 B.C.

It was during the sixth century B.C. that a style in limestone sculpture appeared mainly in the Dodecanese (cf. Di Vita 1991; Sørensen in Karageorghis *et al.* 2001, 77–90), but also in Samos, Knidos, and Naucratis in Egypt. It is represented by small statues around 10–15cm. high, of human figures, but also of animals, mainly lions. These are usually referred to as "of Cypriote type," but it is not certain where they were actually made. Recent research has demonstrated that many of them were made of Cypriote limestone, especially those found on Samos, but some of those found at Naucratis were made of local limestone. Were there Cypriote itinerant artists producing such statuettes in various places of the Greek world, where

402. Limestone slab with a scene of Hercules stealing the cattle of Geryon, said to have been found at Golgoi. The Cesnola Collection, the Metropolitan Museum of Art, New York, Inv. no. 74.51.2853. Height: 52cm.; length: 87.3cm. Decoration in low relief. On the far left a large figure of Hercules stands on a rectangular podium. End of the sixth century B.C.

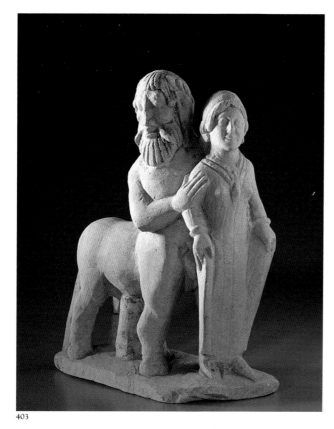

403. Small limestone group representing a centaur carrying away a nymph from Amathus. Musée d'Art et d'Histoire, Geneva, Inv. no. P.620. Height: 18.3cm.; length: 15cm.

404. Plan of a rural sanctuary at Meniko-*Litharkes*. One part is for the god Baal Hamman (right), and the other for his companion Tanit (left). The main divinity who was worshiped in the sanctuary is Baal Hamman, a Phoenician-Punic god.

403

they were in demand as offerings to sanctuaries? Were many of them exported directly from Cyprus? In several cases the influence of East Greek sculpture is obvious. Whatever the case, the involvement of Cyprus in their production is beyond any doubt (for a recent discussion see Kyrieleis 1991, 132, who suggests that "some of these are likely to have been produced at Naucratis by Cypriot or Greek artists working in a distinct Cypro-Egyptian Greek style"; see also Kourou, Karageorghis *et al.* 2002, with bibliography. In a very recent article Jenkins has proposed that these statuettes were produced in Cypriote workshops, which adapted native style and iconography for a Greek market (Jenkins 2001).

There are no known representations of Apollo from the eighth century B.C. In the sixth century B.C., however, the cult of this god, who was previously worshiped as a god of cattle and fertility, spread to other parts of Cyprus, where he was worshiped as the god of music, no doubt under the influence of the Greek god. There are two limestone statues of the god holding a lyre, found in a sanctuary at Potamia, near Idalion, dating to about 500 B.C. (Karageorghis 1979b); one of them shows him wearing a very fine mantle whose delicately indicated folds leave large portions of his body uncovered. Apollo, however, like several other gods of the Greek pantheon, was more widely known in Cyprus during the fifth century B.C.

A small limestone group of a centaur carrying away a nymph is characteristic of the influence that Greek art exercised on Cypriote art of the very end of the sixth century B.C.; it is now in the Musée d'Art et d'Histoire, Geneva. The representation simply shows the Greek myth, but the Cypriote sculptor failed to render the lively action that is characteristic of Greek art. The figures are static and almost unrelated to each other, although typologically they are both inspired by Greek art (Karageorghis 1998, 90).

4. The Sanctuaries

As well as the sanctuaries at Kition, Palaepaphos, and Kourion, to which reference has already been made, there is a rural sanctuary that was excavated by the present writer at Meniko in the central part of Nicosia District, west of Nicosia, that may date to the middle of the sixth century B.C. (Karageorghis 1977a, 17–45). The sanctuary consisted of two architectural units, parallel to each other and separated by a staircase. The first and largest of these units comprised an open-air courtyard, on the floor of which there were patches

404

of burnt soil with ashes, suggesting sacrifices. A staircase led from the courtyard to an inner court with a cella at the far end, the latter probably being roofed. Adjacent to the inner courtyard there was another rectangular room, which also opened onto the outer courtyard. In the cella of this first architectural unit a terra-cotta statuette of the god Baal Hamman was found. He is bearded, with twisted ram's horns, wears a long *chiton*, and is seated on a throne with a stool at his feet. In the same cella two clay and one limestone thymiateria (incense burners) were excavated. Terra-cotta human figures were found scattered in various parts of the sanctuary. In addition there were figurines of bulls, horses, and riders. Noteworthy is a terra-cotta group with a large bull being led to sacrifice by two small human figures, one on either side. A terra-cotta figurine of a ram and a model chariot were also found. The god worshiped at Meniko thus combined many qualities. The cult of this god was also known in Libya and in Carthage, where Baal Hamman was worshiped in association with the goddess Tanit Pene Baal, who had the same attributes as Astarte. There was also a cult of this god in Syria and Phoenicia, from where it may have been introduced to Cyprus.

It is interesting that in the middle of the sixth century B.C. there was a Phoenician cult in central Cyprus. Meniko lies not far from the copper mines, and, as already noted with regard to the Phoenician inscription from the temple of Astarte at Kition, the Phoenicians had found their way to Tamassos in this mining area by the end of the ninth century B.C. The discovery, in the Meniko sanctuary, of clay bull figurines, warriors, and a chariot model demonstrates that the essential elements of the old Cypriote religion and the concept of a god with several attributes had not disappeared.

The second architectural unit of the Meniko sanctuary is situated immediately to the east of the first. It consists of two rectangular rooms, and access to one of them is through a staircase, as for the first unit. This unit may have been dedicated to the companion goddess of Baal, as in Libya, Tanit Pene Baal. The large

405. Terra-cotta group consisting of a large bull standing on a flat rectangular plinth, with small kilted human figures on either side. From a rural sanctuary at Meniko-*Litharkes* (excavations of the Cyprus Department of Antiquities), no. 16. Cyprus Museum, Nicosia. Height: 28.5cm. The bull was obviously being led to the sacrifice, recalling some bronze representations also found in Cyprus from the Late Bronze Age and later periods. Sixth century B.C.

406. Terra-cotta figurine of a bearded Baal Hamman, seated on a throne. From the cella of the rural sanctuary at Meniko-*Litharkes* (excavations of the Cyprus Department of Antiquities). Height: 18.5cm. Cyprus Museum, Nicosia. Decoration in red and black paint. The god has ram's horns and wears a long robe. Limestone representations of the god are also known and may have been introduced to the island by the Phoenicians. He is assimilated with the local god protector of farmers and shepherds.

405

406

407. Two terra-cotta models of "naïskoi" (miniature sanctuaries). Cyprus Museum, Nicosia. Probably from Amathus. On the left: C71. Height: 14.2cm.; on the right: C75. Height: 11.5cm. Inside the cubiculum of C71 there is an aniconic representation of the Great Goddess, a baetyl, decorated with pellets and two painted eyes. Inside the cubiculum of C75 there is a torso of a female figure. The upper part of the façade of both naïskoi is decorated with a disc-and-crescent motif, which is the symbol of the Great Goddess. Both models are richly decorated with black and red paint; the female figure inside the cubiculum of C75 is painted yellow, indicating golden garments.

408. Terra-cotta votive mask of a grimacing male, with grooves on the cheeks. Probably from Kourion. Cyprus Museum, Nicosia, C134. Height: 12.9cm. Small masks were not worn but were deposited as votive offerings in sanctuaries or offered as tomb-gifts. The grimacing masks are characteristic of the Punic world.

409. Terra-cotta anthropomorphic votive mask in the Tornaritis Collection, Nicosia. Height: 12.3cm. Traces of red and black paint. The Phoenician influence is obvious.

407

408

409

limestone symbol resembling "horns of consecration" in the second cella may well be associated with Tanit, rather than representing a survival of the Aegean "horns of consecration" as was originally believed. If this new identification is correct, then the cult of two purely Phoenician divinities was well established in the main mining area of the island by the middle of the sixth century B.C. On the other hand, instead of the worship of Tanit, a Punic deity, one might argue for that of Astarte, whose cult has a long tradition in Cyprus, and indeed the qualities of the old fertility gods of Cyprus are still present.

Numerous bothroi near sanctuaries, containing mainly terra-cotta figurines, have been found in many parts of the island. We mention in particular one found at Patriki, at the beginning of the Karpass peninsula, situated within the cultural sphere of Salamis (Karageorghis 1971). It yielded mainly large-scale terra-cotta statues. One of them represents Bes, the Egyptian god, holding three pairs of snakes in his hands. One pair start from the feet, climb the legs on the outer side, twist around the forearms and over the breast, and turn their heads downward onto the figure's arms. The second pair climb the inner side of the legs and terminate in front of the figure's lower neck. The Egyptian god Bes was known in Cyprus already in the Late Bronze Age but must have been reintroduced to the island under the influence of the Phoenicians (for a discussion and bibliography see Hermary 1989,

410

411

410. Three molded terra-cotta female figurines from Arsos. Cyprus Museum, Nicosia. From left to right: C603, height: 25.2cm.; C608, height: 30.1cm.; C598, height: 30.4cm. They wear a thin transparent garment painted red. The one on the right holds a disc (tambourine?) against her stomach. They are richly adorned with jewelry (earrings and necklaces). They may represent priestesses of the Great Goddess, who had a sanctuary at Arsos. Sixth century B.C.

411. Terra-cotta "wall bracket" decorated with a molded female figure holding her breasts, from Amathus (excavations of the Cyprus Department of Antiquities), Tomb 199, no. 73. Height: 30.7cm.; length of "arm": 18.3cm. Limassol District Museum. This is one of a small group of wall brackets found in Cyprus. One of them has a lotus flower inserted in the clenched fist of the "arm" at its lower part. The wall brackets were probably decorative and had no practical use. The careful modeling of the face and the application of the paint betray an able coroplast of the Cypro-Archaic II period.

412. Terra-cotta molded nude female figurine from Amathus (excavations of the Cyprus Department of Antiquities), Tomb 190, no. 82. Height: 15.1cm. Limassol District Museum. The figurine holds her breasts, the nipples of which appear between the thumb and fingers. Traces of red paint on the body. She wears a necklace and earrings. She is very characteristic of the "Astarte"-type figurines, many of which have been found in tombs at Amathus, where they were placed as symbols of regeneration. At the top of the acropolis of Amathus there was a famous temple of Astarte-Aphrodite.

413. Terra-cotta figurine of a draped female figure holding her breasts. Pierides Foundation Museum, Larnaca. Height: 32cm. Molded, hollow, wearing a hieratic dress. Traces of red, black, and yellow paint. From the village of Achna (between Larnaca and Famagusta). A sanctuary of the Great Goddess was discovered near the village in 1883, which continued in use down to the Hellenistic period.

414. Terra-cotta molded female figurine from Lapithos. Cyprus Museum, Nicosia, C292. Height: 23.5cm. She is draped with a garment that allows the form of her body to appear. She is adorned with elaborate necklaces, earrings, and earcaps. In her right hand she holds a dove against her stomach. Traces of red and black paint. Seventh century B.C. Identical figurines have been found at Arsos and may be considered worshipers of the Great Goddess.

415. Terra-cotta model of a ship, formerly in the Kakoulli Collection, Nicosia, now in the Pierides Foundation Museum, Larnaca. Length: 42.5cm. It has an elaborate prow and stern. The crew of seven includes a seated figure, much larger than the rest, next to which there is a thymiaterion. This model is said to have been found at the bottom of the sea off Amathus, the site which has yielded the vast majority of ship models hitherto known. They have been found in tombs, but some also at the bottom of the sea; it has been suggested that they were votive offerings, purposely thrown into the sea to secure protection from its perils. This model may date to the sixth century B.C.

412

413

414

415

295–298). The same deposit also yielded terra-cotta statues of worshipers holding animal offerings, resembling similar statues found in the sanctuary of Ayia Irini.

Excavation of two sanctuaries at Idalion yielded a large number of terra-cotta statues, of which several heads are now in the British Museum and the Musée du Louvre (Caubet 1992). One of them is supposed to have been dedicated to Apollo and the other to Aphrodite (see Gaber and Morden 1992).

In the copper-producing area of Tamassos a late Archaic sanctuary was found that continued in use until the Classical period; it was dedicated to Astarte-Kybele. It consisted of a courtyard surrounded by a peribolos wall, a vestibule, and a cella. Two altars were found in the sanctuary, one of them a monolith measuring 140 x 125cm., with a large cavity in the center, surrounded by other smaller cavities. It may have been the altar of the "mother of the gods," Kybele, according to epigraphic evidence. In association with the temple there was evidence for metallurgical activity,

an association well known in Cyprus from the Late Bronze Age onward (Buchholz and Umtiedt 1996, 31–32).

A bothros excavated at Salamis, site *Toumba*, yielded some fine terra-cotta statues of colossal size, unfortunately very fragmentary, and others of a medium size. They are now scattered in various museums in England (the British Museum, the Fitzwilliam Museum, and the Ashmolean Museum). The excavators exported mainly heads, but also some exceptional "cuirasses" (corselets) decorated all over with painted motifs, including pictorial and floral ones (Wilson 1980, 61–62). Similar corselets were found in another rich bothros at Kazaphani, in the northern part of Cyprus (Karageorghis 1978b).

Large terra-cotta sculptures were also found at the temenos-type sanctuary of Apollo Reshef at Tamassos-Frangissa, excavated in 1885 (Buchholz 1991). Some of them are of a colossal size. They are dispersed among the Cyprus Museum, the British Museum, and the Royal Ontario Museum, Toronto.

416. Terra-cotta of a female tambourine player from Amathus (excavations of the Cyprus Department of Antiquities), Tomb 276, no. 253. Height: 24.2cm. Limassol District Museum. The body is bell shaped, wheelmade; the face was molded. Black and red paint on face and body. Figurines of the same type were found in Tyre, in Palestine, and on Samos, dating to the ninth–eighth centuries B.C. Musicians were often placed in sanctuaries in Cyprus to provide music for the divinity. The tomb in which this figurine was found yielded pottery dating to the Cypro-Archaic I period and later.

417. Terracotta figurines of female figures. Cypro-Archaic II period. Louvre Museum, Paris. a) Inv. no. AM 1607. Height 12cm. The figure is playing a tambourine. b) Inv. no. AD 1591. Height: 17.5cm. She is playing a lyre. c) Inv. no. AM 1582. Height: 12cm. She is holding a lamb in her arms.

416

417

209

418. Four-sided amulet seal (with impressions) of black jasper (?), from Amathus. Tomb 212, no. 2. 15 x 10 x 6.5cm. All four sides are engraved severally with (a) Athena, wearing a crested helmet, holding a spear and shield; (b) an owl or falcon; (c) a winged goddess (probably Isis); (d) a four-winged goddess. This seal, of Cypro-Greek style, is characteristic of the mixed style of the Cypro-Archaic II period.

418

The statues discovered in these sanctuaries and bothroi date to the Archaic period, more precisely to the period from the mid-seventh century to the end of the sixth century B.C. Some of them preserve part of the torso (e.g., examples from Patriki, Kazaphani, Tamassos, Salamis), but the vast majority comprise only the head. The coroplastic art of Cyprus of the sixth century B.C., however, is best represented by the material from the sanctuary of Ayia Irini. Two types of terra-cottas that are of particular interest are the votive masks and the models of naïskoi, respectively. The masks, both anthropomorphic and zoomorphic, have a long tradition in Cyprus, but the sixth-century types, especially the anthropomorphic, may have been introduced by the Phoenicians (Karageorghis 1993d, 107–122). Numerous terra-cotta figurines, mainly of a female figure in various attitudes, have been found in tombs and sanctuaries.

Important material, consisting of stone sculptures of small size, but also a life-size head of Aphrodite, have been found in a deposit west of Salamis, near the monastery of St. Barnabas. The majority of the statues are of the Greek kore type and date from the sixth to the fifth centuries B.C. The figures hold a flower, a fruit, or a dove and are mostly dressed with a *chiton* and *himation* in the Greek fashion. It has been suggested that the cult with which they were associated was that of Aphrodite, and this is supported by literary evidence. In the Homeric Hymn to Aphrodite there is already a reference to the cult of the goddess at Salamis, although it is impossible to prove that this material comes from the temple mentioned in the hymn (Yon 1974).

Finally, at the top of the acropolis of Amathus, two monumental stone vases were discovered, one complete and the other fragmentary. They may be associated with the cult of Aphrodite that is known from later periods. The style of the carved decoration of one of these vases, now in the Louvre, is of the late Archaic period. Both vases may have been covered by a roof supported by wooden pillars; their function was probably lustral (Hermary and Schmid 1996, 110–120).

Clay models of naïskoi have been found in tombs, except for one fragment from Amathus, which may have belonged to a sanctuary. The naïskoi have a symbolic usage and a magical power, to protect the living who dedicate them through the divinity to which they are offered, and later, after death, when placed in tombs as funerary offerings. The tombs to which the naïskoi belong may be dated to the Cypro-Archaic II period (Karageorghis 1996c, 57–67). Most of them represent a cubiculum with a divine figure inside, usually female. The crescent symbol at the top of most of them indicates their association with Astarte. Several naïskoi enclose an aniconic object, a baetyl, instead of a divinity. They illuminate an aspect of religious architecture that is of importance for Cyprus, especially with regard to the sanctuary of Aphrodite in Paphos. The portable baetyls from the sanctuary of Apollo at Kourion and the temple of the Great Goddess at Amathus, as well as their representations on coins from Phoenicia and Asia Minor, suggest that the aniconic conception of the divinity was a phenomenon that was widespread not only in various parts of Cyprus (Paphos, Amathus, Kourion) but also in other lands, particularly Phoenicia. Although the stone baetyls mentioned above date to the Roman period, like the schematic representations of the sanctuary on coins (gems and sealings date to the Hellenistic and Roman periods), the aniconic representation of the divinity in its central cella must have had a very high antiquity, perhaps deriving from some local or oriental traditions. The naïskoi may help to further the understanding of this aspect of the cult of the Great Goddess of Cyprus (Karageorghis 2000d).

5. Seals

The first floruit of Cypriote glyptics (mainly cylinder seals and conoid stamp seals) occurred during the Late Bronze Age; the second one emerged during the sixth century B.C., mainly with stamp seals, scarabs, and scaraboids. This was preceded by the import from Egypt of scarabs in white steatite or faience, either directly or, probably, indirectly through Phoenicia.

A local production of seals developed during the sixth

419

420

419-420. Scarab of agate (and Impression), most likely from Marion, now in the Collection of the Cultural Foundation of the Bank of Cyprus (formerly the G. G. Pierides Collection, Nicosia). Length: 2cm. The seal represents Theseus with quiver and sword attacking the Minotaur, with Ariadne on the right, looking on. In the field there is a Cypro-syllabic inscription reading "of Dieithemis." End of the sixth century B.C.

century, all cut in hard stone, namely, black serpentine and harder stones like green jasper. These seals are scaraboids or tabloid in shape and are decorated with human and animal figures that may recall Greek geometric stylization, although they were made at a time when the Greeks did not use hard stones in glyptics. Other seals betray Phoenician influences (see Boardman 1989; Reyes 1994, 115–121, with references). Reyes has distinguished several workshops, the most important being that of Pyrga, near Kition, that favor cubical seals in black serpentine and also scarabs with simply carved backs (Reyes 1994, 115–116). Seals from this workshop were exported to other parts of the island, e.g., Ayia Irini and Salamis. There were other workshops that specialized in the device of the scorpion, in geometric warrior figures, and also in seals that were in the shape of heads, often with African features.

421. Impression of a carnelian
scarab in the Kammitsis
Collection, Nicosia. Length:
1.6cm. It represents Hercules
kneeling to shoot at Nessos, who
is trying to pull an arrow from his
back. Deianeira is shown between
them running toward Hercules
and looking back to Nessos. An
Egyptian ankh sign and a flying
falcon in the field above. Cross-
hatched exergue.

422. Silver obol of the king
of Salamis Evelthon (circa
560–525 B.C.). Bank of Cyprus
Cultural Foundation Numismatic
Collection. On the obverse a ram's
head to left. The reverse is blank.

Perhaps the most important series is the one with narrative theme, usually mythological. Although, as Boardman has repeatedly suggested, they include several Phoenician elements, they do not copy Phoenician subjects (Boardman 2001a, 25). Boardman goes on to suggest that they may have been made by Phoenician artists working in Cyprus, who mastered the technique of carving hard stones; the shapes (scarabs or scaraboids) may also betray Phoenician hands, but they were created in a Cypro-Greek environment. Several of them bear engraved inscriptions in the Cypriote syllabary, with Greek names that were placed at the time of the engraving and not later. Their iconography is Greek, though with several local and Phoenician peculiarities. Boardman suggests that "this was also the genesis of hard-stone scarab manu-

421

422

facture in the East Greek world itself, the start of one of the most impressive series of engraved gems to be found anywhere in antiquity" (Boardman 2001a, 25). One of the finest examples of engraved gems with a mythological representation is a carnelian scarab from Marion, formerly in the Kammitsis Collection, Nicosia (Karageorghis 1998f, 85–86). It represents Hercules in a kneeling position, wearing a lion's skin, ready to shoot Nessos, who has already been wounded by one of Hercules's poisoned arrows and is trying to pull it from his back. Deianeira, with an Egyptian-looking face, runs toward Hercules, looking back toward her dying attacker. With her right hand she holds her skirt to be able to run faster, while with her extended left arm she points to the monstrous centaur. In the upper part of the field, on either side of Deianeira's head, there are an Egyptian ankh symbol and a hovering Egyptian falcon. The style of the execution is certainly Cypro-Phoenician, dating to the late sixth century B.C., but the scene is purely Greek, as known from other island gems and other works of Greek art.

Another gem of the same style, from near Marion, formerly in the G. G. Pierides Collection, Nicosia, and now in the Bank of Cyprus Cultural Foundation, is also engraved with an ambitious scene: in the middle is Theseus, who is bearded, muscular, wearing a short tunic on which can be distinguished the tail of a lion's skin, and holding a bow, thus recalling the representation of Hercules. It is not uncommon in Cypriote art, as seen above, to confuse the attributes of the various heroes and to represent them like Hercules, in view of the great popularity of this hero on the island. The hero advances to the left toward the Minotaur, striking him with a sword. The Minotaur has a human body but a bull's head and is retreating backward. Behind Theseus a long-robed veiled woman advances toward the hero; no doubt she is Ariadne. In the field, carefully engraved around the upper perimeter of the gem, is the name Dieithemis (in the genitive), in the Cypriote syllabary, obviously the name of the owner. The engraver seems deliberately to have left room for the syllabic inscription and this indicates that he was working for a Cypriote client on the island (Boardman 1968, 47).

In spite of the proximity of Cyprus to Anatolia, contacts with this northern neighbor seem to have been less close than expected during the Cypro-Archaic period. Some influences from Cilicia or North Syria have been noted in a group of seals found at Ayia

Irini, but also in other areas of the Mediterranean (Reyes 1994, 126, with bibliography). Other Anatolian influences may be observed in sculpture and metalworking, but these are of no particular importance (ibid., 126–127).

6. Persian Rule

Cyprus joined the Persian Empire some time around 525 B.C. (for references see Reyes 1994, 85). The Persians must have maintained the existing kingdoms, most of which had Greek kings, as we learn from Herodotus's account of the events related to the revolt of Ionia and Cyprus against the Persians in 499 B.C. (for references see Reyes 1994, 86–90 and 162, table 4). Cyprus became part of the fifth satrapy, which also included Syria and Palestine (but cf. Stylianou 1992,

414–415). The fifth satrapy paid a tribute of 350 talents to the Great King (Herodotus III.91.1). It is not certain how the Persians maintained control of the island, but it is very likely that they made an alliance with the Phoenicians of Cyprus, who might have served as mercenaries or administrators, thus controlling the Greek kings.

The kingdoms of Cyprus must have enjoyed not only a degree of political independence but also prosperity. As already mentioned, there were strong trade relations with the Aegean during the seventh and sixth centuries B.C., and also with the Levant and Egypt, especially with the Greek colonies of Al Mina in southern Turkey and Naucratis in Egypt (see Boardman 1999, 50–54). A fragment of Hecataeus lists a number of islands in the Nile bearing the names of

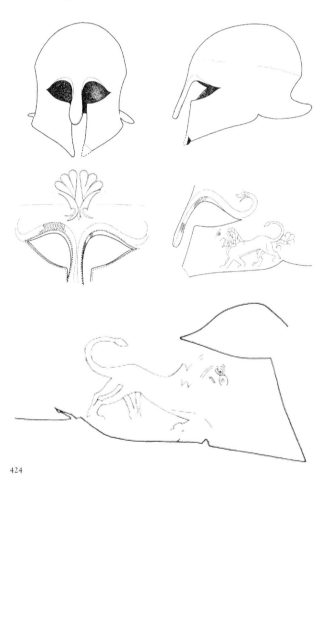

423-424. Bronze Corinthian helmet from the Persian siege-ramp at Palaepaphos (Swiss–German Excavations). Cyprus Museum, Nicosia. Engraved decoration. The helmet belonged to a soldier who fell during the siege of Palaepaphos by the Persians in 498 B.C. It must have been manufactured on the Greek mainland before 530 B.C. (after Maier 1985, 46, figs. 23–24).

423

424

Greek cities or islands; one of these is Cyprus (Stylianou 1992, 400). The Cypriote economy must have also benefited from the trading activities of the Phoenicians, and their exploitation of the copper mines. New settlements appeared at this time, as well as sanctuaries. The magnificence of the tombs, for example at Tamassos, as well as the artistic development of Cyprus during the period bear eloquent testimony to this prosperity (for references see Stylianou 1992, 399–440). Unfortunately, none of the palaces of the Cypriote kings of the sixth century B.C. or the houses of the rich merchants of the period have yet been found.

We learn more from Herodotus about Salamis during the last part of the sixth century B.C., when the city was the champion of the Hellenes of Cyprus in their effort to liberate themselves from the Persian yoke. The first king of Salamis who is mentioned by Herodotus, and of whom coins have survived, is Evelthon, who may have reigned circa 518 B.C. (Reyes 1994, 86, 162). It was during the reign of Evelthon that Pheretima, queen of Libya, paid a visit to the Salaminian king to ask for military assistance in order to reestablish her son on the throne (Herodotus IV. 162). Evelthon, according to Herodotus, gave her a golden spindle and a distaff with wool but no military assistance: "such were the gifts that he gave to women," Herodotus remarks. This shows that the Salaminian king was not only known for his prosperity, but could also exercise foreign policy independent from that of Persia. According to Herodotus again (IV. 162), it was Evelthon who dedicated a marvelous incense burner in the treasury of the Corinthians at Delphi. Another Cypriote, Helicon, son of Akesas of Salamis, dedicated at Delphi a peplos woven by himself (see references in Gjerstad 1948, 460–461).

King Evelthon was the first Cypriote king to issue his own coinage in silver. The idea of coinage came from the Greek world, with which relations became closer, since Ionia was suffering the same Persian oppression. The minting of coins signals the important fact that the social and economic framework of Cypriote society, as indeed of the wider Aegean world to which Cyprus belonged culturally and with which she had particularly strong economic links at this time, was now very different from what it had been at the beginning of the Archaic period. The issue of coinage was meant to serve the needs of a far more complex society, one no longer based entirely on the land (Stylianou 1992, 401). Greek coins must have circu-

lated widely within parts of the Persian Empire and thence to Cyprus. The designs are Greek in style, and it has been suggested that those who made the dies were artists from Ionia (Buchholz 2000, 217). The earliest coins of Evelthon have on the obverse a ram or a ram's head lying to the left; the reverse is blank. Above the ram there is the name of Evelthon inscribed in the Cypriote syllabary. His later coins bear the Egyptian symbol of life, ankh, on the reverse with a sign *ku* (= Kyprion = of the Cypriots) within its ring, which may denote that Evelthon was recognized as superior to the other Cypriote kings (Karageorghis 1982, 154, with references). Evelthon's name was also retained on the coins of his successors.

The date of the revolt of the Cypriote kings against Persia (except the king of Amathus) is a turning point in the history of the island. Although the revolt failed and the Cypriots remained under Persian rule, this event fostered their nationalistic feelings and made them conscious of their Hellenic descent. This had far-reaching effects, both cultural and political. Herodotus describes the dramatic events of the revolt of the Cypriote kings (Herodotus v.104, 108–116). The leader of the Cypriots in this revolt was Onesilos, king of Salamis, who dethroned his pro-Persian brother Gorgos, who subsequently fled to Persia. This demonstrates once more the leading role of the kingdom of Salamis, which was maintained throughout the fifth century B.C.

The names of the kings who participated in the Ionian revolt are listed by Herodotus as follows, all bearing Greek names: Onesilos of Salamis, Aristokypros of Soloi, and Stasanor of Kourion. Although it is generally agreed that the Cypriote kings sided with the rest of the Ionians in a common struggle for political equality and freedom—and this is quite clear from Herodotus's accounts, as we shall see below—Reyes suggests that there may also be other reasons, namely, that "individual kingdoms became entangled in the domestic politics of Salamis" (Reyes 1994, 97). He argues that Onesilos deposed his older brother Gorgos, king of Salamis, by using the Ionian revolt as a pretext for his action and then persuaded the other kingdoms to join. Considering, however, the dominant role of Salamis in Cypriote politics during this period, the action of Onesilos is not surprising. Already Hill supposed that the cause of the participation of Cyprus in the Ionian revolt was a considerable anti-Persian faction in at least some of the Cypriote cities, and that this feeling was "doubtless partly democratic and therefore opposed to the power that upheld the local tyrants, but also partly just racial" (Hill 1940, 117). Stylianou endorses Hill's opinion, adding an extra reason, namely, the fear of the Phoenicians, who had the support of Persia, who for obvious reasons were more loyal to the Great King, which would tend to reinforce the disloyal feelings of the Greeks (Stylianou 1992, 409). These sentiments must have become even stronger, considering that the Cypriots must have been aware of how other Greek states managed their own affairs, whereas they had to pay a tribute to the Persians and support the Persian wars with ships and men whenever called upon to do so.

The hostility of the Phoenicians toward the Greek population of Cyprus is also attested in a later period (fourth century B.C.), when the Phoenicians erected a naval trophy at Kition after a victory of King Milkyaton against his enemies (the Salaminians) and their allies (the Paphians) (Yon and Sznycer 1991). This hostility, we believe, had deeper roots and may date to a much earlier period, when the Greeks and the Phoenicians had conflicting commercial interests in the Mediterranean. The reason, then, was not nationalism but commercial antagonism, which gradually developed into an ethnic antagonism. This view has been seriously questioned by Boardman, who believes in collaboration and even joint enterprises between Greeks and Phoenicians (Boardman 2001b, 39–40).

The Phoenicians of Kition must have sided with the Persians during the revolt. It has in fact been argued by Stylianou that the war between the Idalians and the Kitians, mentioned in the bronze tablet of Idalion, may date to 498 B.C. and not to 470 B.C. and may have been part of the Cypriote revolt against the Persians (Stylianou 1992, 403–405, 425).

The revolt of the Cypriots started in the spring or early summer of 498 B.C. (Herodotus v.106–115, translation by Enoch Powell). Onesilos's task, after having dethroned Gorgos, was to persuade all the other kings to follow his example and join the revolt, which he did, except the Amathusians, who resisted. Was this because the population of Amathus was mixed, with a substantial Phoenician minority? The possibility that part of the population may have been "Eteocypriot" was discussed above. Whatever the reason, Onesilos besieged Amathus, but while doing so he learned that the Persian Artybius had arrived in Cyprus from Cilicia at the head of a powerful army and navy. The Persian army landed somewhere in the northern part of Cyprus, on the Karpass peninsula,

and marched against Salamis, while the Phoenician ships rounded the Karpass peninsula (v.108.2). The Greeks of Salamis, and the Ionian Greeks who came to help them at the invitation of Onesilos, made ready for battle. Herodotus reports a dialogue between the Cypriots and the Ionians that may be purely imaginary and, as Stylianou rightly observes, may befit the style of Homer in the *Iliad* (Stylianou 1992, 426). Nevertheless, it is of importance, and we will quote it here, because it demonstrates how the Greeks, and Herodotus in particular, considered the participation of the Cypriots in the revolt of all the Hellenes against the tyranny of Persia: "Men of Ionia, we Cyprians offer you the choice, which of our two enemies ye will face; for if ye will be arrayed on land and make trial of the Persians, now is the hour for you to get you down out of the ships and array you on land, and for us to enter into your ships to contend with the Phoenicians; but peradventure ye will rather make trial of the Phoenicians. Howbeit, whichsoever ye choose, it behooveth you so to do that for your part Ionia and Cyprus may be free" (Herodotus v. 109, translated by J. Enoch Powell).

The main Cypriote force consisted of the heavy infantry of the Salaminians under Onesilos and the Solians under their king, Aristokypros. The Kourians were taking part in the battle with their war chariots under their king, Stasanor. (Here it is important to note the use of war chariots in Cyprus as late as early fifth century B.C., at a time when they were no longer used in Greece, having been replaced by the phalanx.) The Kourians deserted to the Persians in the initial stages of the battle, and they were followed by the Salaminian chariots. Onesilos and Aristokypros were killed on the battlefield.

There is much archaeological evidence concerning the siege of Palaepaphos, especially at the Northeast Gate of the walls of the city (see Maier and Karageorghis 1984, 192–203). This gate was remodeled just before the attack so as to make entry into the city difficult for the attackers. The Persians erected a siege ramp outside the gate, a technique that they also employed for the siege of other cities, as we learn from Herodotus, already in 545 B.C. (Herodotus I.162, 168). The purpose of such a ramp was to enable the besiegers to move wooden siege-towers to the top so that the defenders could easily be attacked, a type of warfare clearly illustrated by Assyrian reliefs. The collapse of the ramp, which was attempted by the defenders, aimed at destroying the wooden siege-towers. This ramp had a height of 4.5m. above the edge of the counterscarp and more than 7m. above the bottom of the fosse. For the construction of the ramp the Persians accumulated stones of various sizes, earth, and many fragments of sculptures and inscribed stones, having looted a nearby Archaic sanctuary. There were also numerous weapons of bronze and iron, e.g., javelin points, spearheads, and arrowheads. One of the most important finds was a bronze Corinthian helmet with engraved decoration. There were also numerous roughly shaped spherical stones, probably missiles for a stone-throwing engine, the earliest known so far in association with a battle.

The defenders tried to undermine the ramp by digging a passage and four tunnels cut through the rock underneath the wall. The finds inside the mound date to about 500 B.C., thus leaving no doubt concerning the identity of the defenders and the besiegers. The missiles found in the ramp show that heavy fighting occurred during the building of the ramp. Part of the ramp subsided when the timber that supported the roof of the tunnels was burned with the help of inflammable material in bronze cauldrons, and thus the loose fill of rubble above the tunnels collapsed.

In spite of their ingenuity the Greek defenders of Palaepaphos were defeated, and, like all the other cities in the island, they succumbed to the Persians. There is also archaeological evidence for destruction at Tamassos (Buchholz 1977, 303).

The causes for the failure of the revolt will not be examined here. One of them may have been internal antagonisms among the various kings, though this may not be the main reason (cf. Stylianou 1992, 411–412). Herodotus describes the end of the revolt as follows: "But when the Ionians of the sea-fight off Cyprus learnt that Onesilos' cause was come to naught, and that the cities of Cyprus were besieged, all except Salamis, which the men of Salamis delivered unto the former king Gorgus, they straightway sailed back to Ionia. And Soloi withstood the siege for the longest time of all the cities of Cyprus; but the Persians took it in the fifth month, by digging under the wall. Thus were the Cyprians brought into bondage afresh, after they had been free for a year" (Herodotus v.115, translated by J. Enoch Powell).

The participation of Cyprus in the Ionian revolt had far-reaching consequences for the island and its future political development. The Cypriots became even more conscious of their ethnic identity and their common fate with the rest of the Greeks. The pro-Hellenic policy of King Evagoras I of Salamis (411–373 B.C.) was the direct consequence of the events that the Cypriots experienced during their revolt against the Persians. The art of Cyprus and her culture in general were now directly influenced by what was Greek. This may have fostered even further nationalistic feelings, but at the same time it meant the end of originality and freshness in Cypriote artistic production.

The whole of the fifth and a large portion of the fourth century B.C. constituted a period of antagonism and war against the Persians, but at the same time it was a period of strife among the various kingdoms of Cyprus, a phenomenon that was not uncommon in the history of the Greek world. The Phoenician minority of the island did not fail to take advantage of the disunity among the Greek kingdoms of the island and gained considerable political power by siding with the Persians. These, however, are matters that fall outside the chronological limits of this book; we simply mention them as they are directly connected with what happened on the island circa 500 B.C.

7. Epilogue

It is hoped that this survey of one thousand one hundred years in the archaeology and history of Cyprus has demonstrated the important role that this small island played in the development of Mediterranean culture, a remarkably important role when compared with her small size. The wealth of the island in copper contributed decisively to her prosperity and her commercial and, inevitably, cultural relations with the countries of the Eastern Mediterranean, the Aegean, and even beyond.

The period that our survey has covered is one of the most crucial in the political and cultural history of the Mediterranean, with lively interconnections but also antagonisms, emanating from the emergence of powerful "empires" whose ambition was economic and political domination over as wide an area as possible. Cyprus, situated at a crossroads of trade and between several great political powers (Egypt, the Near East, Anatolia, the Aegean), often found herself in the midst of these antagonisms and became the victim of their expansionist ambitions. This was particularly the case during the first half of the first millennium B.C., when the Assyrians and the Egyptians were playing a dominant role in East Mediterranean politics. The generally accepted view about the political role that these two powers played in Cyprus has changed considerably during recent years, and we no longer speak about domination but rather of alliances, although the interpretation of the relevant written sources and the archaeological evidence is still very much discussed. The role of the Phoenicians during much of the first half of the first millennium B.C. is now better understood, and their influence on the economic and artistic life of the island is no longer viewed with prejudice, as it was in the past. The discovery of a large variety of objects of prestige and status symbols in the "royal" tombs at Salamis and elsewhere in Cyprus, as well as the funerary customs observed in these "heroic" burials, have opened new horizons for the understanding of the cultural koine that prevailed during the eighth–sixth centuries B.C. in the Eastern Mediterranean, the Aegean, and the Central Mediterranean. The recent new impetus in the study of the Etruscan civilization provides ample evidence for close interrelations among these regions and the emergence of the "orientalizing" style in Mediterranean culture.

Looking back at the earlier part of the first millennium and the end of the second millennium B.C., we can now appreciate that what was previously considered the "Dark Ages" in the Aegean and elsewhere was not really a dark period, but one of continuity and interrelations. The twelfth and eleventh centuries B.C. for Cyprus may now be studied against their true historical background, namely, the emigration of Aegean refugees to the Eastern Mediterranean some time after 1200 B.C., and the beginning of the Hellenization of Cyprus from the eleventh century B.C. There is corroborating evidence from the study of those periods both from the Aegean and the Syro-Palestinian coast, which helps to explain parallel phenomena in Cyprus. The creation of ten independent kingdoms in Cyprus from the eleventh century B.C. resulted in the firm establishment of Greek culture on the island, which developed with a variety of differences from the Greek culture in the Aegean. We are now thus able to understand the peculiarities of the Greek Cypriote civilization (linguistic, artistic, social, and political), which remained faithful to its Mycenaean origin but at the same time was not unaffected by contacts with the great civilizations of the East. Furthermore, elements of the Bronze Age indigenous Cypriote culture were never forgotten, thus giving a conservative and idiosyncratic character to Cypriote culture in general.

The study of the period from 1500 to 1200 B.C. has benefited considerably from the achievements of underwater archaeology. The excavation of shipwrecks carrying cargoes related to Cyprus has demonstrated the crucial part played by the island's copper production in the economic affairs of the whole of the Mediterranean and the trade relations among the various parts of the Old World. This period is still in the spotlight of archaeological research: new sites have been excavated in Cyprus, the Levant, and the Aegean that throw light on the material culture but also on interconnections in specific areas, including religion, art, architecture, social and political structures, etc.

The change in the attitudes of archaeologists and the broad targets of modern archaeology (not to be confused with theoretical archaeology), assisted by technological progress, have enhanced interest in the study of the past and contributed considerably to the better understanding of everyday life in all its aspects. The study of the ancient world is no longer focused on the study of artistic developments but has become more global, including all aspects of human activity and life. In spite of this optimistic evaluation, there remain areas in the study of the civilization of Cyprus from 1600 to 500 B.C. where further illumination is still needed. The Cypro-Minoan texts still keep their secrets; no satisfactory decipherment of the Cypro-Minoan script has yet been proposed. There are still aspects of the island's culture of the twelfth–eleventh centuries B.C. that have not received a general consensus of scholarly opinion. There are some who do not accept the eleventh century as the initial period for the establishment of the ten kingdoms in Cyprus and prefer a later (eighth century B.C.) date. There is still some confusion among a few scholars as to how and when the Hellenization process of Cyprus began. Although there is a vast amount of material available to illustrate the art and funerary architecture of Cyprus circa 500 B.C., no public or domestic buildings have been discovered, and very few architectural remains of sanctuaries. The palaces of the rich kings of Salamis and the other kingdoms of the island have not yet been revealed.

We do not envisage that all these problems will be solved within the next few years. But as excavations and research in Cyprus and the neighboring countries continue with the same vigor we will have a clearer idea, especially now that new scientific technologies are mobilized to help the archaeologists. The present survey may be used as a *point de repère* for future endeavors.

Bibliography

AA — Archäologischer Anzeiger

AJA — American Journal of Archaeology

BAR — British Archaeological Reports

BASOR — Bulletin of the American Schools of Oriental Research

BCH — Bulletin de Correspondance Hellénique

BSA — Annual of the British School at Athens

CRAI — Comptes Rendues de l'Académie des Inscriptions et Belles-Lettres

RDAC — Report of the Department of Antiquities, Cyprus

SCE — Swedish Cyprus Expedition

SIMA — Studies in Mediterranean Archaeology

Allen, S.H. 1994: 'Trojan Grey Ware at Tell Miqne-Ekron', BASOR 293, 39-51.

Amadasi, M.G.G. and Karageorghis, V. 1977: Fouilles de Kition III. Inscriptions Phéniciennes. Nicosia.

Ampolo, C. 2000: 'Il mondo omerico e la cultura Orientalizzante mediterranea', 27-35 in Principi Etruschi tra Mediterraneo ed Europa.

Andreadaki-Vlasaki, M. 1997: 'La nécropole du Minoen Récent III de la Ville de la Canée', 487-509 in Driessen and Farnoux (eds) 1997.

Åström, P. 1972: The Swedish Cyprus Expedition. Vol. IV, Parts IC and ID. The Late Cypriote Bronze Age. Lund.

Åström, P. 1979: 'The find contexts of some Minoan objects in Cyprus', 56-62 in Karageorghis (ed.) 1979.

Åström, P. 1989: 'Early connections between Anatolia and Cyprus', 15-17 in K. Emre et al. (eds), Anatolia and the Ancient Near East. Studies in Honour of Tahsin Özgüç. Ankara.

Åström, P. and Masson, E. 1982: 'A silver bowl with Canaanite inscription from Hala Sultan Tekke', RDAC, 72-76.

Åström, P. et al. 1976: Hala Sultan Tekke 1. Excavations 1887-1971 (SIMA XLV.1). Göteborg.

Åström, P. et al. 1977: Hala Sultan Tekke 3. Excavations 1972 (SIMA XLV.3). Göteborg.

Aupert, P. 2001: 'Amathousiens et Étéochypriotes', 161-168 in V. Fromentin and S. Gotteland (eds), Origines Gentium (Ausonius-Publications, Études 7). Bordeaux.

Aupert, P. et al. 1996: Guide d'Amathonte. Paris.

Barako, T. J. 2000: 'The Philistine settlement as mercantile phenomenon?' AJA 104, 513-530.

Baramki, D.C. 1958: 'A Late Bronze Age tomb at Sarafand, ancient Sarepta', Berytus XII, 129-142.

Baramki, D.C. 1973: 'The impact of the Mycenaeans on ancient Phoenicia', 193-197 in Karageorghis (ed.) 1973.

Bartoloni, G. 2000: 'La tomba', 163-171 in Principi Etruschi tra Mediterraneo ed Europa.

Basch, L. 1987: Le musée imaginaire de la marine antique. Athens.

Basch, L. and Artzy, M. 1985: 'Appendix II. Ship graffiti at Kition', 322-336 in Karageorghis and Demas 1985, Part I.

Bass, G.F. 1967: Cape Gelidonya: a Bronze Age Shipwreck (Transactions of the American Philosophical Society, N.S., Vol. 57 Part 8). Philadelphia.

Bass, G.F. et al. 1989: 'The Bronze Age shipwreck at Ulu Burun: 1986 Campaign', AJA 93, 1-29.

Baurain, C. 1984: Chypre et la Méditerranée centrale au Bronze Récent (Études Chypriotes VI). Paris.

Beach Ferris E. 1992: 'The Samaria ivories, Marzeah and Biblical texts', Biblical Archaeologist 55, 130-139.

Benson, J.L. 1961: 'Coarse ware stirrup jars of the Aegean', Berytus XIV, 37-51.

Benson, J.L. 1973: The Necropolis of Kaloriziki (SIMA XXXVI). Göteborg.

Betancourt, P. et al. (eds) 1999: Meletemata. Studies in Aegean Archaeology presented to Malcolm H. Wiener as he enters his 65th year (Aegaeum 20). Liège-Austin.

Bietak, M. 2000: 'Rich beyond the dreams of Avaris: Tell el-Dab'a and the Aegean world - a guide for the perplexed'. A response to Eric H. Cline', BSA 95, 185-205.

Bietak, M. and Marinatos, N. 2000: 'Avaris (Tell el-Dab'a) and the Minoan world', 40-44 in A. Karetsou (ed.), Κρήτη-Αἴγυπτος, πολιστικοί δεσμοί τριῶν χιλιετιῶν. Athens.

Buchholz, H-G. 1977: 'Bemerkungen zu einigen neuen C-14 Analysen Zyperns und Griechenlands', RDAC, 290-308.

Buchholz, H-G. 1986: 'Spätbronzezeitliche Ohrringe Zyperns in Gestalt von Rinderköpfen und ihr Auftreten in Griechenland', Acta Praehistorica et Archaeologica 18, 117-155.

Buchholz, H-G. 1991: 'Tamassos-Phrangissa (1885)', Centre d'Études Chypriotes, Cahier 16, 3-15.

Bikai, P.M. in press: 'Statistical observations on the Phoenician pottery of Kition', Appendix I in Karageorghis in press b.

Bikai, P.M. 1983: 'Appendix II. The imports from the East', 396-406 in Karageorghis 1983.

Bikai, P.M. 1987: The Phoenician Pottery of Cyprus. Nicosia.

Bikai, P.M. 1992: 'The Phoenicians', 132-141 in Ward and Joukowsky (eds) 1992.

Bikai, P.M. 1994: 'The Phoenicians and Cyprus', 31-37 in Karageorghis (ed.) 1994.

Boardman, J. 1968: Archaic Greek Gems. Schools and Artists in the Sixth and Early Fifth Centuries B.C. London.

Boardman, J. 1970: Greek Gems and Finger Rings, Early Bronze Age to Late Classical. London.

Boardman, J. 1991: 'Cypriot, Phoenician and Greek seals and amulets', 159-163 in V. Karageorghis, O. Picard and C. Tytgat (eds), La nécropole d'Amathonte, Tombes 110-385, vol. V (Études Chypriotes XIII). Nicosia.

Boardman, J. 1999: The Greeks Overseas, their Early Colonies and Trade (4th ed.). London.

Boardman, J. 2001a: Cyprus between East and West (16th Annual Lecture on the History and Archaeology of Cyprus, Bank of Cyprus Cultural Foundation). Nicosia.

Boardman, J. 2001b: 'Aspects of "colonization"', BASOR 322, 33-42.

Bonnet, C. 1988: Melqart. Cultes et mythes de l'Héraclès Tyrien en Méditerranée (Studia Phoenicia VIII). Leuven.

Bonnet, C. 1996: Astarte. Dossier documentaire et perspectives historiques. Rome.

Bonnet, C. and Jourdain-Annequin, C. (eds) 1992: Héraclès. D'une rive à l'autre de la Mediterranée. Bilan et perspectives. Brussels-Rome.

Brodie, N. and Steel, L. 1996: 'Cypriot Black-on-Red ware: towards a characterisation', Archaeometry 38, 263-278.

Buchholz, H-G. 1993: 'Ägyptisierendes aus Tamassos', RDAC, 195-206.

Buchholz, H-G. 2000: 'Kyprische Bildkunst zwischen 1100 und 500 v. Chr.', 215-266 in C. Vehlinger, Images as Media. Sources for the cultural history of the Near East and the Eastern Mediterranean (1st Millennium BCE). Göttingen.

Buchholz, H-G. and Karageorghis, V. 1973: Prehistoric Greece and Cyprus. London.

Buchholz, H-G. and Untiedt, K. 1996: Tamassos. Ein antikes Königreich auf Zypern (SIMA Pocket-book 136). Jonsered.

Buitron-Oliver, D. 1999: 'Kourion: the elusive Argive settlement and its burial grounds from the 11th to the 8th century B.C.', 69-77 in Iacovou and Michaelides (eds) 1999.

Cadogan, G. 1988: 'Maroni IV', RDAC, 229-231.

Cadogan, G. 1992: 'Maroni VI', RDAC (Part 1), 51-58.

Campbell, E.F. 1998: 'A land divided. Judah and Israel from the death of Solomon to the fall of Samaria', 273-319 in M.D. Coogan (ed.), The Oxford Dictionary of the Biblical World. Oxford.

Carpenter, J.R. 1981: 'Excavations at Phaneromeni: 1975-1978', 59-78 in J.C. Biers and D. Soren (eds), Studies in Cypriote Archaeology (Institute of Archaeology, University of California, Los Angeles, Monograph XVIII). Los Angeles.

Carter, J.B. and Morris, S.P. (eds) 1995: The Ages of Homer. A Tribute to Emily Townsend Vermeule. Austin.

Castellana, G. 2000: La cultura del Medio Bronzo nell'agrigentino ed i rapporti con il mondo miceneo. Regione Siciliana.

Catling, E.A. and Catling, H.W. 1973: 'A shield of Warrior Vase type from Kaloriziki Tomb 40', 130-132 in Benson 1973.

Catling, H.W. 1955: 'A bronze greave from a 13th century B.C. tomb at Enkomi', Opuscula Atheniensia 2, 21-36.

Catling, H.W. 1964: Cypriot Bronzework in the Mycenaean World. Oxford.

Catling, H.W. 1968: 'Kouklia-Evreti Tomb 8', *BCH* 92, 162-169.

Catling, H.W. 1971: 'A Cypriot bronze statuette in the Bomford Collection', 15-32 in C.F.A. Schaeffer, *Alasia* I. Paris.

Catling, H.W. 1974: 'The Bomford horse-and-rider', *RDAC*, 95-111.

Catling, H.W. 1975: 'Cyprus in the Late Bronze Age', 188-216 in I.E.S. Edwards *et al.* (eds), *The Cambridge Ancient History*, Third Edition, Vol. II:2. Cambridge.

Catling, H.W. 1980: 'Cyprus and the West 1600-1050 B.C.', *Ian Sandars Memorial Lecture*. Sheffield.

Catling, H.W. 1984: 'Workshop and heirloom: prehistoric bronze stands in the East Mediterranean', *RDAC*, 69-91.

Catling, H.W. 1986: 'Cypriot bronzework - East or West?' 91-103 in Karageorghis (ed.) 1986.

Catling, H.W. 1994: 'Cyprus in the 11th century B.C. - an end or a beginning?' 133-141 in Karageorghis (ed.) 1994.

Catling, H.W. 1995: 'Heroes returned? Subminoan burials from Crete', 123-136 in Carter and Morris (eds) 1995.

Catling, H.W. 1997: 'Κύπρος, Κρήτη και Αιγαίο κατά την εποχή του Ορειχάλκου' 371-430 in Papadopoulos (ed.) 1997.

Caubet, A. 1982: 'Ras Shamra et la Crète', 17-22 in M.Yon (ed.) *La Syrie au Bronze Récent*. Paris.

Caubet, A. 1986: 'Les sanctuaries de Kition à l'époque de la dynastie Phénicienne', 153-168 in C. Bonnet *et al.* (eds), *Religio Phoenicia* (*Studia Phoenicia* IV). Namur.

Caubet, A. 1987: 'La musique à Ougarit', *CRAI*, 731-754.

Caubet, A. 1992: 'The terracotta workshop of Idalion during the Cypro-Archaic period', 128-151 in P. Åström (ed.), *Acta Cypria* Part 3. Jonsered.

Caubet, A. and Poplin, F. 1987: 'Les objets de matière dure animale: étude du matériau', 273-306 in M. Yon (ed.), *Ras-Shamra Ougarit* III. *Le centre de la ville*. Paris.

Caubet, A. and Yon, M. 1974: 'Deux appliques murales chypro-géometriques au Louvre', *RDAC*, 112-131.

Cesnola, A. Palma di 1882: *Salaminia*. London.

Chavane, M.-J. and Yon, M. 1978: *Salamine de Chypre* X: *Testimonia Salaminia*, Fasc. 1. Paris.

Childs, W.A.P. 1997: 'The Iron Age kingdom of Marion', *BASOR* 308, 37-48.

Christou, D. 1994: 'Kourion in the 11th century B.C.', 177-188 in Karageorghis (ed.) 1994.

Christou, D. 1998: 'Cremations in the Western Necropolis of Amathus', 207-215 in Karageorghis and Stampolidis (eds) 1998.

Cifola, B. 1994: 'The role of the Sea Peoples and the end of the Late Bronze Age: a reassessment of textual and archaeological evidence', *Orientis Antiqui Miscellanea* I, 1-23.

Clerc, G. 1983: 'Appendix I. Aegytiaca de Palaepaphos-Skales', 375-395 in Karageorghis 1983.

Clerc, G. 1990: 'Appendix I. Un fragment de vase au nom d'Ahmosis(?) à Palaepaphos-Teratsoudhia', 95-103 in Karageorghis 1990a.

Cline, E.H. 1994: *Sailing the Wine-Dark Sea: International trade and the Late Bronze Age Aegean* (BAR International Series 591). Oxford.

Cline, E.H. and Cline, D. Harris (eds) 1998: *The Aegean and the Orient in the Second Millennium B.C.* (*Aegaeum* 18). Liège.

Coldstream, J.N. 1977: *Geometric Greece*. London

Coldstream, J.N. 1981: 'The Greek Geometric and plain Archaic imports', 17-22 in Karageorghis *et al.* 1981.

Coldstream, J.N. 1987: 'The Greek Geometric and Archaic imports', 21-31 in V. Karageorghis, O. Picard and C. Tytgat (eds), *La Nécropole d'Amathonte Tombes 113-367* II. *Céramiques non Chypriotes* (Études Chypriotes VIII). Nicosia.

Coldstream, J.N. 1989: 'Status symbols in Cyprus in the eleventh century BC', 325-335 in Peltenburg (ed.) 1989.

Coldstream, J.N. 1995: 'Amathus Tomb NW 194: the Greek pottery imports', *RDAC*, 187-198.

Coldstream, J.N. 1995a: 'Greek Geometric and Archaic imports from the tombs at Amathus – II', *RDAC*, 199-214.

Coldstream, J.N. 1999: 'On Chronology: the CG II mystery and its sequel', 109-118 in Iacovou and Michaelides (eds) 1999.

Courtois, J-C. 1983: 'Le trésor de poids de Kalavassos-*Ayios Dhimitrios* 1982', *RDAC*, 117-130.

Courtois, J-C. 1992: 'Une baignoire monolithe en calcaire du Bronze Récent à Enkomi', 151-154 in Ioannides (ed.) 1992.

Courtois, J-C., Largarce, J. and Lagarce, E. 1986: *Enkomi et le Bronze Récent à Chypre*. Nicosia.

Crielaard, J.P. 1995: 'Homer, history and archaeology. Some remarks on the date of the Homeric world', 201-268 in Crielaard (ed.) 1995

Crielaard, J.P. 1999: 'Early Iron Age Greek pottery in Cyprus and North Syria: a consumption-oriented approach', 261-290 in J.P. Crielaard, V. Stissi and G.J. van Wijngaarden (eds), *The Complex Past of pottery. Production, Circulation and Consumption of Mycenaean and Greek Pottery (sixteenth to early fifth centuries BC)*. Amsterdam.

Crielaard, J.P. (ed.) 1995: *Homeric Questions. Essays in philology, ancient history and archaeology, including the papers of a conference organized by the Netherlands Institute at Athens (15 may 1993)*. Amsterdam.

Csornay-Caprez, B. 2000: *Cypriote Antiquities* (Bibliotheca Archaeologica 30). Rome.

Cuteri, F.A. 1999: 'Risorse minerarie ed attività metallurgica nella Sila Piccola meridionale e nella Pre-Sila del versante tirrenico. Prime osservazioni', 293-320 in De Sensi Sestito (ed.) 1999.

D'Agata, A-L. 1997: 'The shrines on the Piazzale dei Sacelli at Ayia Triadha. The LM IIIC and SM material: a summary', 85-100 in Driessen and Farnoux (eds) 1997.

D'Agata, A-L. 1999: *Haghia Triada* II. *Statuine Minoiche e post-Minoiche dai vecchi scavi di Haghia Triada (Creta)*. Padua.

Deger-Jalkotzy, S. 1994: 'The post-palatial period of Greece: an Aegean prelude to the 11th century B.C. in Cyprus', 11-30 in Karageorghis (ed.) 1994.

Delpino, F. 2000: 'Il Principe e la cerimonia del banchetto', 191-195 in *Principi Etruschi tra Mediterraneo de Europa*.

De Miro, E. 1996: 'Recenti ritrovamenti micenei nell'agrigentino e il villagio di Cannatello', 995-1011 in De Miro *et al.* (eds) 1996, Vol. III.

De Miro, E. *et al.* (eds) 1996: E. De Miro, L. Godart and A. Sacconi (eds), *Atti e memorie del Secondo Congresso Internazionale di Micenologia, Roma-Napoli 14-20 ottobre 1991*, Vols I-III. Rome.

De Sensi Sestito, G. (ed.) 1999: *Tra l'Amato e il Savuto*, Vol. I. Rubbettino Editore, Calabria.

Des Gagniers, J. 1972: 'Une fête champêtre sur une amphore d'Amathonte', *Revue Archéologique*, 53-56.

Dentzer, J-M. 1982: *Le motif du banquet couché dans le Proche-Orient et le monde grec du VII au IV siècle avant J-C*. Rome.

Dierichs, A. 1989: 'Zu einer zyprischen Schale', *Boreas* 12, 9-14.

Dikaios, P. 1969-1971: *Enkomi Excavations 1948-1958*, Vols I-III. Mainz.

Di Vita, A. 1991: 'Chypre dans les dépôts votifs de Athana Ialisia', 89-92 in Karageorghis (ed.) 1991.

Dothan, T. and Ben-Tor, A. 1983: *Excavations at Athienou, Cyprus, 1971-1972* (Qedem 16). Jerusalem.

Driessen, J. 1994: 'La Crète Mycénienne', 66-83 in *Les Mycéniens. Des Grecs du IIe millénaire* (*Les Dossiers d'Archéologie* 195, juillet-août).

Driessen, J. and Farnoux, A. (eds) 1997: *La Crète Mycénienne* (*BCH* Supplément 30).

Dupont Sommer, A. 1970: 'Une inscription phénicienne archaïque récemment trouvée à Kition (Chypre)', *Mémoires de l'Académie des Inscriptions et Belles-Lettres* 44, 1-28.

Emiliozzi, A. 1998: *Carri da guerra e principi Etruschi*. Rome.

Eriksson, K. 1993: *Red Lustrous Wheel-made Ware* (*SIMA* CII). Jonsered.

Eriksson, K. 2001: 'A preliminary synthesis of recent chronological observations on the relations between Cyprus and other eastern Mediterranean societies during the late 'Middle' Bronze - early Late Bronze II periods', 1-40 in *Special Research Programme 'Synchronisation of Civilisations in the Eastern Mediterranean in the Second Millennium B.C.' of the Austrian Academy of Sciences at the Austrian Science Fund*. Vienna.

Evans, A.J. 1906: 'The prehistoric tombs of Knossos', *Archaeologia* 59. London.

Finkelstein, I. 1995: 'The date of the settlement of the Philistines in Canaan', *Tel Aviv* 22, 213-239.

Flourentzos, P. 1997: 'The Early Geometric Tomb no. 132 from Palaepaphos', *RDAC*, 205-218.

Flourentzos, P. 2000: 'A unique bronze thymiaterion from Palaepaphos', 453-462 in Ioannides and Hadjistylli (eds) 2000.

Fortin, M. 1978: 'The fortification wall at Lara', *RDAC*, 58-67.

Frost, H. 1985: 'Appendix I. The Kition anchors', 281-321 in Karageorghis and Demas 1985, Part I.

Furumark, A. 1965: 'The excavations at Sinda. Some historical results', *Opuscula Atheniensia* 6, 99-113.

Furumark, A. 1972: *Mycenaean Pottery I. Analysis and Classification*. Stockholm.

Furumark, A. 1992: *Mycenaean Pottery III. Plates*. Stockholm.

Gaber, P. and Morden, M. 1992: 'University of Arizona Expedition to Idalion, Cyprus, 1992', *Centre d'Études Chypriotes, Cahier* 18, 21-26.

Gadd, C.J. 1954: 'Inscribed prisms of Sargon II from Nimrud', *Iraq* 16, 191-193.

Gale, N.H. (ed.) 1991: *Bronze Age trade in the Mediterranean* (SIMA XC). Jonsered.

Giesen, K. 2001: *Zyprische Fibeln. Typologie und Chronologie* (SIMA Pocket-book 161). Jonsered.

Gilboa, A. 1999: 'The view from the East - Tel Dor and the earliest Cypro-Geometric exports to the Levant', 119-139 in Iacovou and Michaelides (eds) 1999.

Gitin, S. *et al.* (eds) 1998: *Mediterranean Peoples in Transition. Thirteenth to Early Tenth Centuries BCE. In Honor of Professor Trude Dothan.* Jerusalem.

Gjerstad, E. 1926: *Studies on Prehistoric Cyprus.* Uppsala.

Gjerstad, E. 1946: 'Decorated metal bowls from Cyprus', *Opuscula Archaeologica* 4, 1-18.

Gjerstad, E. 1948: *The Swedish Cyprus Expedition Vol. IV, Part 2. The Cypro-Geometric, Cypro-Archaic and Cypro-Classical Periods.* Stockholm.

Gjerstad, E. 1978: 'The Cypro-Archaic life-size terracotta statue found in Old Smyrna', *Proceedings of the Xth International Congress of Classical Archaeology* II, 709-713.

Gjerstad, E. 1979: 'A Cypro-Greek royal marriage in the 8th cent. B.C.', 89-93 in V. Karageorghis *et al.* (eds), *Studies Presented in Memory of Porphyrios Dikaios.* Nicosia.

Gjerstad, E. *et al.* 1934: *The Swedish Cyprus Expedition. Finds and Results of the Excavations in Cyprus 1927-1931.* Vol. I. Stockholm.

Graham, J.W. 1987: *The Palaces of Crete.* Princeton.

Gras, M. 2000: 'Il Mediterraneo in età Orientalizzante: merci, approdi, circolazione', 15-26 in *Principi Etruschi tra Mediterraneo ed Europa.*

Güterbock, H.G. 1957: 'Narration in Anatolian, Syrian and Assyrian art', *AJA* 61, 62-71.

Guy, P.L.O. and Engberg, R.M. 1938: *Megiddo Tombs.* Chicago.

Hadjicosti, M. 1999: 'Idalion before the Phoenicians: the archaeological evidence and its topographical distribution', 35-54 in Iacovou and Michaelides (eds) 1999.

Hadjioannou, K. 1971: 'On the identification of the Horned God of Engomi-Alasia', 33-42 in C.F.A. Schaeffer, *Alasia* I. Paris.

Hadjisavvas, S. 1994: 'Alassa Archaeological Project, 1991-1993', *RDAC*, 107-114.

Hadjisavvas, S. and Hadjisavva, I. 1997: 'Aegean influence at Alassa', 143-148 in D. Christou, *et al.* (eds): *Proceedings of the International Archaeological Conference Cyprus and the Aegean in Antiquity from the Prehistoric Period to the 7th Century A.D., Nicosia 8-10 December 1995.* Nicosia.

Haldane, C. 1990: 'Shipwrecked plant remains', *Biblical Archaeologist* 53.1, 55-60.

Haldane, C. 1991: 'Organic goods from the Ulu Burun shipwreck', *Institute for Nautical Archaeology Newsletter* 18.4, 11.

Haldane, C. 1993: 'Direct evidence for organic cargoes in the Late Bronze Age', 348-360 in J. Oates (ed.), *Ancient trade: new perspectives (World Archaeology* 24.3).

Hall, J.M. 1997: *Ethnic Identity in Greek Antiquity.* Cambridge.

Hallager, E. and Hallager, B.P. (eds) 1997: *Late Minoan III Pottery. Chronology and Terminology. Acts of a Meeting held at the Danish Institute at Athens, August 12-14 1994.* Athens.

Hallager, B.P. and McGeorge, P.J.P. 1992: *Late Minoan III Burials at Khania. The Tombs, Finds and Deceased in Odos Palama* (SIMA 93). Göteborg.

Heltzer, M. 1989: 'The trade of Crete and Cyprus with Syria and Mesopotamia and their eastern tin-sources in the XVIII-XVII century B.C.', *Minos* N.S. XXIV, 7-28.

Hermary, A. 1986a: 'Divinités Chypriotes, II', *RDAC*, 164-172.

Hermary, A. 1986b: 'La coupe en argent du British Museum ('the Amathus Bowl')', 179-194 in R. Laffineur, *Amathonte* III. *Testimonia* 3: *L'orfèvrerie.* Paris.

Hermary, A. 1987: 'Amathonte de Chypre et les Phéniciens', *Studia Phoenicia* V, 375-388.

Hermary, A. 1989: *Musée du Louvre. Département des Antiquités orientales. Catalogue des Antiquités de Chypre. Sculptures.* Paris.

Hermary, A. 1991: 'Les débuts de la grande plastique chypriote en terre cuite', 139-147 in F. Vandenabeele and R. Laffineur (eds), *Cypriote Terracottas. Proceedings of the First International Conference of Cypriote Studies, Brussels-Liège-Amsterdam, 29 May - 1 June 1989.* Brussels-Liège.

Hermary, A. 1992: 'Quelques remarques sur les origines proche-orientales de l'iconographie d'Héraclès', 129-143 in Bonnet and Jourdain-Annequin (eds) 1992.

Hermary, A. 1997: 'Le 'style d'Amathonte'', 157-161 in V. Karageorghis, R. Laffineur and F. Vandenabeele (eds), *Four Thousand Years of Images on Cypriote Pottery. Proceedings of the Third International Conference of Cypriote Studies, Nicosia, 3-4 May 1996.* Brussels-Liège-Nicosia.

Hermary, A. 1999: 'Amathus before the 8th century B.C.', 55-67 in Iacovou and Michaelides (eds), 1999.

Hermary, A. 2000: 'Déesse plutôt que reine? A propos d'une coupe en argent de la Collection Cesnola', *Centre d'Études Chypriotes, Cahier* 30, 67-78.

Hermary, A. and Iacovou, M. 1999: 'Amathous-Diplostrati Tomb 109', *RDAC*, 151-162.

Hermary, A. and Schmid, M. 1996: 'Le sanctuaire d'Aphrodite', 110-132 in Aupert *et al.* 1996.

Hill, G. 1940: *A History of Cyprus I. To the Conquest by Richard Lion Heart.* Cambridge.

Hirschfeld, N. 1993: 'Incised marks (post-firing) on Aegean wares', 311-318 in Zerner (ed) 1993.

Hirschfeld, N. 1996: 'Cypriots in the Mycenaean Aegean', 289-297 in De Miro *et al.* (eds) 1996.

Hirschfeld, N. 2000: 'Marked Late Bronze Age Pottery from the Kingdom of Ugarit', 163-200 in Yon *et al.* 2000.

Iacovou, M. 1988: *The Pictorial Pottery of Eleventh century B.C. Cyprus* (SIMA LXXIX). Göteborg.

Iacovou, M. 1989: 'Society and settlements in Late Cypriot III', 52-59 in Peltenburg (ed.) 1989.

Iacovou, M. 1994: 'The topography of eleventh century B.C. Cyprus', 145-165 in Karageorghis (ed.) 1994.

Iacovou, M. 1999a: 'The Greek exodus to Cyprus: the antiquity of Hellenism', *Mediterranean Historical Review* 14.2, 1-28.

Iacovou, M. 1999b: '*Excerpta Cypria Geometrica.* Materials for a history of Geometric Cyprus', 141-166 in Iacovou and Michaelides (eds) 1999.

Iacovou, M. and Michaelides, D. (eds) 1999: *Cyprus, the Historicity of the Geometric Horizon.* Nicosia.

Iakovides, S. 1970: Περατή. Τό Νεκροταφείο Β'. Γενικαί Παρατηρήσεις. Athens.

Ioannides, G. (ed.) 1992: *Studies in Honour of Vassos Karageorghis* (Κυπριακαι Σπουδαι ND'-NE'), Nicosia.

Ioannides, G.K. and Hadjistylli, S.A. (eds), Πρακτικά του Γ' διεθνούς Κυπρολογικού Συνεδρίου (Λευκωσία, 16-20 Απριλίου 1996). Nicosia.

Jacobsson, I. 1994: *Aegyptiaca from Late Bronze Age Cyprus* (SIMA CXII). Jonsered.

Jenkins, I. 2001: 'Archaic kouroi in Naukratis: the case for Cypriot origin', *AJA* 105, 163-179.

Jones, R.F. and Vagnetti, L. 1991: 'Traders and craftsmen in the Central Mediterranean: archaeological evidence and archaeometric research', 127-147 in Gale (ed.) 1991.

Kanta, A. 1998: 'Introduction. 16th-11th cent. B.C.', 30-66 in N. Stampolidis, A. Karetsou and A. Kanta (eds), *Eastern Mediterranean. Cyprus-Dodecanese-Crete. 16th-6th cent. B.C.* Heraklion.

Karageorghis, J. 1977: *La grande déesse de Chypre et son culte.* Lyon.

Karageorghis, V. 1965: *Nouveaux documents pour l'Étude du Bronze Récent à Chypre (Études Chypriotes* III). Paris.

Karageorghis, V. 1967a: *Excavations in the Necropolis of Salamis* I. Nicosia.

Karageorghis, V. 1967b: 'Homerica from Salamis (Cyprus)', 167-171 in W.C. Brice (ed.), *Europa. Studien zur Geschichte und Epigraphik der frühen Aegaeis. Festschrift für Ernst Grumach.* Berlin.

Karageorghis, V. 1967c: 'An early XIth century B.C. tomb from Palaepaphos', *RDAC*, 1-24.

Karageorghis, V. 1968a: 'Die Elfenbein-Throne von Salamis, Zypern', 99-103 in *Archaeologia Homerica* Band III. Göttingen.

Karageorghis, V. 1968b: 'Notes on a Late Cypriote settlement and necropolis site near the Larnaca Salt Lake', *RDAC*, 1-11.

Karageorghis, V. 1971: 'A deposit of Archaic terracotta figures from Patriki, Cyprus', *RDAC*, 27-36.

Karageorghis, V. 1973a: 'A Cypro-Geometric III chariot crater', *RDAC*, 167-178.

Karageorghis, V. 1973b: 'A Late Cypriote hoard of bronzes from Sinda', *RDAC*, 72-82.

Karageorghis, V. 1973c: *Excavations in the Necropolis of Salamis* III. Nicosia.

Karageorghis, V. 1974: *Excavations at Kition* I. *The Tombs.* Nicosia.

Karageorghis, V. 1975: *Alaas. A Proto-Geometric Necropolis in Cyprus.* Nicosia.

Karageorghis, V. 1976: *Kition. Mycenaean and Phoenician Discoveries in Cyprus.* London.

Karageorghis, V. 1977a: *Two Cypriote Sanctuaries of the End of the Cypro-Archaic Period.* Rome.

Karageorghis, V. 1977b: 'More material from the Protogeometric necropolis of 'Alaas'', *RDAC*, 141-149.

Karageorghis, V. 1977c: *The Goddess with Uplifted Arms* (Scripta Minora 1977-1978). Lund.

Karageorghis, V. 1978a: *Excavations in the Necropolis of Salamis.* Vol. IV. Nicosia.

Karageorghis, V. 1978b: 'A 'favissa' at Kazaphani', *RDAC*, 156-193.

Karageorghis, V. 1979a: 'Two

pictorially decorated vases of the Cypro-Archaic period', 123-128 in V. Karageorghis et al. (eds), *Studies Presented in Memory of Porphyrios Dikaios*. Nicosia.

Karageorghis, V. 1979b: 'Material from a sanctuary at Potamia', *RDAC*, 289-315.

Karageorghis, V. 1979c: 'Some reflections on the relations between Cyprus and Crete during the Late Minoan IIIB period', 199-203 in Karageorghis (ed.) 1979.

Karageorghis, V. 1980a: 'Kypriaka V', *RDAC*, 128-135.

Karageorghis, V. 1980b: 'Nouveaux documents pour l'étude de la nécropole de Salamine', 153-159 in *Salamine de Chypre, histoire et archéologie. État des recherches* (*Colloques Internationaux du CNRS no. 578*). Paris.

Karageorghis, V. 1982: *Cyprus, from the Stone Age to the Romans*. London.

Karageorghis, V. 1983: *Palaepaphos-Skales. An Iron Age Cemetery in Cyprus (Ausgrabungen in Alt-Paphos auf Cypern. Band 3)*. Konstanz.

Karageorghis, V. 1986: 'Kypriaka IX', *RDAC*, 45-54.

Karageorghis, V. 1989: 'Some remarks on the 'Amathus Style' in Cypriote vase-painting', 83-86 in H-U. Cain, H. Gabelmann and D. Salzmann (eds), *Festschrift für Nikolaus Himmelmann*. Mainz.

Karageorghis, V. 1990a: *Tombs at Palaepaphos. 1. Teratsoudhia, 2. Eliomylia*. Nicosia.

Karageorghis, V. 1990b: 'The Princeton amphoriskos of the Amathus style', *RDAC*, 121-125.

Karageorghis, V. 1992: 'The crisis years: Cyprus', 79-86 in Ward and Joukowski (eds) 1992.

Karageorghis, V. 1993a: *The Coroplastic Art of Ancient Cyprus. II. Late Cypriote II - Cypro-Geometric III*. Nicosia.

Karageorghis, V. 1993b: 'Le commerce Chypriote avec l'Occident au Bronze Récent: quelques nouvelles découvertes', *CRAI*, 577-588.

Karageorghis, V. 1993c: 'Erotica from Salamis', *Revista di Studi Fenici XXI*, Supplemento, 7-13.

Karageorghis, V. 1993d: *The Coroplastic Art of Ancient Cyprus III. The Cypro-Archaic Period. Large and Medium size Sculpture*. Nicosia.

Karageorghis, V. 1994: 'The prehistory of an ethnogenesis', 1-10 in Karageorghis (ed.) 1994.

Karageorghis, V. 1995a: 'Cyprus and the western Mediterranean: some new evidence for interrelations', 93-97 in Carter and Morris (eds) 1995.

Karageorghis, V. 1995b: 'Relations between Cyprus and Egypt. Second Intermediate Period and XVIIIth Dynasty, 73-79 in M. Bietak (ed.), *Egypt and the Levant V*. Vienna.

Karageorghis, V. 1995c: 'Cyprus and the Phoenicians. Achievements and perspectives', 327-34 in *I Fenici: Ieri Oggi Domani*. Rome.

Karageorghis, V. 1995d: *The Coroplastic Art of Ancient Cyprus IV. The Cypro-Archaic Period. Small male figurines*. Nicosia.

Karageorghis, V. 1996a: 'Aegean influences on the coroplastic art of Late Bronze Age Cyprus', 1051-1061 in E. De Miro et al. (eds) 1996.

Karageorghis, V. 1996b: 'Some aspects of the maritime trade of Cyprus during the Late Bronze Age', 61-70 in Karageorghis and Michaelides (eds) 1996.

Karageorghis, V. 1996c: *The Coroplastic Art of Ancient Cyprus. VI. The Cypro-Archaic Period. Monsters, Animals and Miscellanea*. Nicosia.

Karageorghis, V. 1997a: 'The Pictorial Style in vase-Painting of the early Cypro-Geometric period', 73-80 in Karageorghis et al. (eds) 1997.

Karageorghis, V. 1997b: 'An enthroned Astarte on horseback(?)', *RDAC*, 195-203.

Karageorghis, V. 1997c: 'Η Ύστερη Χαλκοκρατία', 237-285 in T. Papadopoulos (ed.), Ιστορια της Κύπρου, Vol. I, Nicosia.

Karageorghis, V. 1998a: 'Two pictorially decorated vases from Amathus', *RDAC*, 107-110.

Karageorghis, V. 1998b: 'Myce-

naean 'acropoleis' in the Aegean and Cyprus: some comparisons', 127-136 in Cline and Harris Cline (eds) 1998.

Karageorghis, V. 1998c: 'Hearths and bathtubs in Cyprus. A 'Sea Peoples' innovation?' 276-282 in Gitin et al. (eds) 1998.

Karageorghis, V. 1998d: *Cypriote Archaeology Today. Achievements and Perspectives*. Glasgow.

Karageorghis, V. 1998e: 'Astarte at Kition', 105-108 in R. Rolle and K. Schmidt (eds), *Archäologische Studien in Kontaktzonen der antiken Welt* (*Veröffentlichungen der Joachim Jungins-Gesellschaft 87*). Hamburg.

Karageorghis, V. 1998f: *Greek Gods and Heroes in Ancient Cyprus*. Athens.

Karageorghis, V. 1999a: 'An Anatolian terracotta bull's head from the Late Cypriote necropolis of Agia Paraskevi', *RDAC*, 147-150.

Karageorghis, V. 1999b: 'A Mycenaean pilgrim flask reexamined', 395-402 in Betancourt et al. (eds) 1999.

Karageorghis, V. 1999c: 'The art of Cyprus at the end of the Late Bronze Age', 47-69 in J. Koumoulides (ed.), *Cyprus: the Legacy. Historic Landmarks that influenced the art of Cyprus. Late Bronze Age to A.D. 1600*. Bethesda.

Karageorghis, V. 1999d: 'Aspects of trade between Cyprus and the west during the 14th-13th centuries B.C.', 121-130 in Phelps et al. (eds) 1999.

Karageorghis, V. 1999e: *Ancient Cypriote Art in the Severis Collection*. Athens.

Karageorghis, V. 1999f: 'Notes on some 'enigmatic' objects from the prehistoric Aegean and East Mediterranean regions', *AA*, 501-514.

Karageorghis, V. 2000a: 'Cultural innovations in Cyprus relating to the Sea Peoples', 255-279 in E.D. Oren (ed.), *The Sea Peoples and their World: a Reassessment* (*University Museum Monograph 108*). Philadelphia.

Karageorghis, V. 2000b: 'Cipro 'omerica'', 37-42 in *Principi Etruschi tra Mediterraneo ed Europa*.

Karageorghis, V. 2000c: 'Phoenician News from Cyprus', *National Museum News* (Beirut) Spring 2000, 10-14.

Karageorghis, V. 2000d: 'Aniconic representations of divinities in Cypriote 'Naïskoi'', 51-62 in *Actas del IV Congreso Internacional de Estudios Fenicios y Púnicos. Cadiz, 2 al 6 de Octubre de 1995*, I. Cadiz.

Karageorghis, V. 2001a: 'Why White Slip?', 9-13 in Karageorghis (ed.) 2001.

Karageorghis, V. 2001b: 'Bichrome Wheelmade ware: still a problem?', in P. Åström (ed.) *Proceedings of a conference on Chronology of Bichrome Wheel-made ware and Base-ring ware, Stockholm, May 2000*.

Karageorghis, V. 2001c: 'Patterns of fortified settlements in the Aegean and Cyprus c. 1200 B.C.', 1-12 in Karageorghis and Morris (eds) 2001.

Karageorghis, V. 2001d: 'Notes on the origin of Cypriot wheelmade terracotta figurines', 78-83 in S. Böhm and K.-V. von Eickstedt (eds), *IΘAKH. Festschrift für Jörg Schäfer zum 75. Geburtstag am 25. April 2001*. Würzburg.

Karageorghis, V. in press a: *Excavations at Kition VI. The Phoenician and Later Levels. Part I*. Nicosia.

Karageorghis, V. in press b: *Excavations at Kition VI. The Phoenician and Later Levels. Part II*. Nicosia.

Karageorghis, V. and Demas, M. 1984: *Pyla-Kokkinokremos. A Late 13th-Century B.C. Fortified Settlement in Cyprus*. Nicosia.

Karageorghis, V. and Demas, M. 1985: *Excavations at Kition V. The Pre-Phoenician Levels*. Nicosia.

Karageorghis, V. and Demas, M. 1988: *Excavations at Maa-Palaeokastro 1979-1986*. Nicosia.

Karageorghis, V. and Des Gagniers, J. 1974: *La céramique Chypriote de style figuré. Age du Fer (1050-500 av. J.-C.)*.

Karageorghis, V. and Des Gagniers, J. 1979: *La céramique Chypriote de style figuré. Age du Fer (1050-500 av. J.-C.). Supplément*. Rome.

Karageorghis, V. and Iacovou, M. 1990: 'Amathus Tomb 521: A Cypro-Geometric I group', *RDAC*, 75-100.

Karageorghis, V. and Karageorghis, J. in press: 'The genesis of Aphrodite in Cyprus', in S. Parpola (ed.), Proceedings of the 47° Rencontre Assyriologique Internationale: Sex and Gender, Helsinki 2nd-6th July 2001.

Karageorghis, V. and Kassianidou, V. 1998: 'Metalwork and recycling in Late Bronze Age Cyprus - the evidence from Kition', *Oxford Journal of Archaeology 18*, 171-188.

Karageorghis, V. and Papasavvas, G. 2001: 'A Bronze ingotbearer from Cyprus', *Oxford Journal of Archaeology 20*, 339-354.

Karageorghis, V. et al. 1981: *Excavations at Kition IV. The non-Cypriote Pottery*. Nicosia.

Karageorghis, V. et al. 1999a: V. Karageorghis, E. Hendrix and G. Neumann, 'A Cypriot silver bowl reconsidered', *Metropolitan Museum Journal 34*, 13-35.

Karageorghis, V. et al. 1999b: V. Karageorghis, E. Vassilika and P. Wilson, *The Art of Ancient Cyprus in the Fitzwilliam Museum, Cambridge*. Nicosia.

Karageorghis, V. et al. 2000: V. Karageorghis, J.R. Mertens and M.E. Rose, *Ancient Art from Cyprus. The Cesnola Collection in the Metropolitan Museum of Art*. New York.

Karageorghis, V. et al. 2001: *Ancient Cypriote Art in Copenhagen. The Collections of the National Museum of Denmark and the Ny Carlsberg Glyptotek*. Nicosia.

Karageorghis, V. (ed.) 1973: *Acts of the International Archaeological Symposium 'The Mycenaeans in the Eastern Mediterranean'*, Nicosia 27th March- 2nd April 1972. Nicosia.

Karageorghis, V. (ed.) 1979: *Acts of the International Archaeological Symposium 'The Relations between Cyprus and Crete, ca. 2000-500 B.C.'*, Nicosia 16th-22nd April 1978. Nicosia.

Karageorghis, V. (ed.) 1986: *Acts of the International Archaeological Symposium 'Cyprus between the Orient and the Occident'*

Nicosia, 8-14 September 1985. Nicosia.

Karageorghis, V. (ed.) 1991: *Proceedings of an International Symposium 'The Civilizations of the Aegean and their diffusion in Cyprus and the Eastern Mediterranean, 2000-600 B.C.' (18-24 September 1989).* Larnaca.

Karageorghis, V. (ed.) 1994: *Proceedings of the International Symposium 'Cyprus in the 11th Century B.C.'.* Nicosia.

Karageorghis, V. (ed.) 2001: *The White Slip Ware of Late Bronze Age Cyprus. Proceedings of an International Conference Organized by the Anastasios G. Leventis Foundation, Nicosia, in Honour of Malcolm Wiener, Nicosia 29th-30th October 1998.* Vienna.

Karageorghis, V. and Michaelides, D. (eds) 1995: *Proceedings of the International Symposium 'Cyprus and the Sea'.* Nicosia.

Karageorghis, V. and Michaelides, D. (eds) 1996: *The Development of the Cypriot Economy, from the Prehistoric Period to the Present Day.* Nicosia.

Karageorghis, V. and Morris, C. (eds) 2001: *Defensive Settlements of the Aegean and the Eastern Mediterranean after c. 1200 B.C. Proceedings of an International Workshop held at Trinity College Dublin, 7th-9th May, 1999.* Nicosia.

Karageorghis, V. and Stampolidis, N. (eds) 1998: *Proceedings of the International Symposium Eastern Mediterranean: Cyprus-Dodecanese-Crete, 16th – 6th cent. B.C.* Athens.

Karageorghis, V. *et al.* (eds) 1997: V. Karageorghis, R. Laffineur and F. Vandenabeele (eds), *Four Thousand Years of Images on Cypriote Pottery. Proceedings of the Third International Conference of Cypriote Studies, Nicosia 3-4 May 1996.* Brussels-Liège-Nicosia.

Kassianidou, V. 1999: 'Bronze age copper smelting technology in Cyprus - the evidence from Politico-Phorades', 91-97 in S.M.M. Young *et al.* (eds), *Metals in Antiquity* (BAR International Series 792). Oxford.

King, P.J. 1988: *Amos, Hosea, Micah. An archaeological commentary.* Philadelphia.

Knapp, A.B. 1986: *Copper Production and Divine Protection: Archaeology, Ideology and Social Complexity on Bronze Age Cyprus* (SIMA Pocketbook 42). Göteborg.

Knapp, A.B. 1991: 'Spice, drugs, grain and grog: organic goods in Bronze Age East Mediterranean trade', 21-68 in Gale (ed.) 1991.

Knapp, A.B. *et al.* 1999: A.B. Knapp, V. Kassianidou and M. Donnelly, 'Excavations at Politiko-Phorades 1998', *RDAC*, 125-146.

Knapp, A.B. (ed.) 1996: *Sources for the History of Cyprus. Vol. II. Near Eastern and Aegean Texts from the Third to the First Millennia B.C.* Altamont, NY.

Knappett, C. 2000: 'The provenance of Red Lustrous Wheelmade Ware: Cyprus, Syria or Anatolia?', *Internet Archaeology* 9, 1363-1387.

Kopcke, G. 2001: 'Das schöne Gerät – Eine betrachtung Mykenischer Vasen', 239-248 in S. Buzzi *et al.*, *Zona Archeologica. Festschrift für Hans Peter Isler zum 60. Geburtstag.* Bonn.

Kourou, N. 1991: 'Aegean Orientalizing versus Oriental art: the evidence of monsters', 111-123 in Karageorghis (ed.) 1991.

Kourou, N. 1994: 'Sceptres and maces in Cyprus before, during and immediately after the 11th century', 203-227 in Karageorghis (ed.) 1994.

Kourou, N. 1997: 'Cypriot zoomorphic askoi of the Early Iron Age. A Cypro-Aegean interplay', 89-106 in Karageorghis *et al.* (eds) 1997.

Kourou, N. 2000: 'Τα ειδώλια της Σίφνου από την Μεγάλη Θεά στην Πότνια Θηρῶν και την Αρτέμιδα', 351-370 στα *Πρακτικά Α' Διεθνούς Σιφναϊκού Συμποσίου, Σίφνος 25-28 Ιουνίου 1998.*

Kourou, N., Karageorghis, V. *et al.* 2002: *Limestone Statuettes of Cypriote Type found in the Aegean. Provenance Studies.* Nicosia.

Kyrieleis, H. 1991: 'The relations between Samos and the Eastern Mediterranean. Some aspects', 129-132 in Karageorghis (ed.) 1991.

Lagarce, E. and Leclant, J.

1976: 'Vase plastique en faïence Kit. 1747: une fiole pour eau de jouvence', 183-289 in G. Clerc *et al.*, *Fouilles de Kition* II. *Objets Égyptiens et Égyptisants.* Nicosia.

La Torre, G.F. 1999: 'La questione *Temesa*: nuovi documenti e prospettive di ricerca', 237-252 in De Sensi Sestito (ed.) 1999.

Leclant, J. 1960: 'Astarté à cheval d'après les representations égyptiennes', *Syria* 37, 1-67.

Lemos, I. 1994: "Birds Revisited", 229-237 in Karageorghis (ed.) 1994.

Leonard, A. 1994: *An Index of the Late Bronze Age Pottery from Syria-Palestine* (SIMA CXIV). Jonsered.

Lewe, B. 1975: *Studien zur archaischen Kyprischen Plastik.* Ph.D. dissertation, Johann Wolfgang Goethe-Universität. Frankfurt am Main.

Lipinski, E. 1995: *Dieux et déesses de l'Univers Phénicien et Punique* (Studia Phoenicia XIV). Leuven.

Lolos, Y.G. 1999: 'The cargo of pottery from the Point Iria wreck: character and implications', 43-58 in Phelps *et al.* (eds) 1999.

Lo Schiavo, F. 1995: 'Cyprus and Sardinia in the Mediterranean trade routes toward the west', 45-60 in Karageorghis and Michaelides (eds) 1995.

McFadden, G.H. 1954: 'A Late Cypriote III tomb from Kourion: Kaloriziki no. 40', *AJA* 40, 131-142.

Maier, F.G. 1985: *Alt-Paphos auf Cypern. Ausgrabungen zur Geschichte von Stadt und Heiligtum 1966-1986.* Mainz am Rhein.

Maier, F.G. 1999: 'Palaipaphos and the transition to the Early Iron Age: continuities, discontinuities and location shifts', 79-93 in Iacovou and Michaelides (eds) 1999.

Maier, F.G. and Karageorghis, V. 1984: *Paphos. History and Archaeology.* Nicosia.

Malbran-Labat, F. 1999: 'Nouvelles données épigraphiques sur Chypre et Ougarit', *RDAC*, 121-123.

Malkin, I. 1998: *The Returns of*

Odysseus. Colonization and Ethnicity. Berkeley-Los Angeles-London.

Manning, S.W. 1999: *A Test of Time. The Volcano of Thera and the Chronology and History of the Aegean and East Mediterranean in the mid Second Millennium B.C.* Oxford.

Manning, S.W. *et al.* 2001: 'Absolute age range of the Late Cypriot IIC period on Cyprus', *Antiquity* 75, 328-340.

Marinatos, N. 2000: *The Goddess and the Warrior. The Naked Goddess and Mistress of Animals in Early Greek Religion.* London-New York.

Marinatos, N. 2001: 'The adventures of Odysseus and the East Mediterranean tradition', 105-125 in A. Kyriatsoulis (ed.), *Kreta + Zypern. Religion und Schrift. Von der Frühgeschichte bis zum Ende der archäischen Zeit.* Ohlstatt, Bayern.

Markoe, G.E. 1985: *Phoenician Bronze and Silver Bowls from Cyprus and the Mediterranean.* Berkeley-Los Angeles-London.

Markoe, G.E. 1987: 'A bearded head with conical cap from Lefkoniko: an examination of a Cypro-Archaic votary', *RDAC*, 119-125.

Markoe, G.E. 1988: 'An Egyptianizing votive statuette from Kourion', *RDAC* (Part 2), 17-18.

Markoe, G.E. 1990: 'Egyptianizing male votive statuary from Cyprus: a reexamination', *Levant* XXII, 111-122.

Markoe, G.E. 2000: *The Phoenicians.* Berkeley-Los Angeles.

Masson, E. 1974: *Cyprominoica* (SIMA XXXI.2). Göteborg.

Masson, E. 1983: 'Premiers documents Chypro-minoens du site Kalavassos-*Ayios Dhimitrios*', *RDAC*, 131-141.

Masson, E. 1988: 'Les plus Anciennes Crémations à Chypre: Témoignages d'une Croyance Spécifique', *RDAC* (Part 1), 321-324.

Masson, E. and Masson, O. 1983: 'Les objets inscrits de Palaepaphos-Skales', 411-415 in Karageorghis 1983.

Masson, O. 1961: *Les inscriptions syllabiques. Receuil critique et commenté* (Études Chypriotes I). Paris.

Masson, O. 1967: 'Appendice IV. Les inscriptions syllabiques', 132-142 in Karageorghis 1967a.

Masson, O. 1971: 'Un bronze de Delphes à inscription Chypriote syllabique', *BCH* 95, 295-304.

Masson, O. and Sznycer, M. 1972: *Recherches sur les Phéniciens à Chypre.* Paris.

Matthäus, H. 1985: *Metalgefäße und Gefäßuntersätze der Bronzezeit, der geometrischen und archaischen Periode auf Cypern.* München.

Matthäus, H. 1999: '... ἀγνὴν ὀδμὴν λιβανωτὸς ἵησιν. Zu Thymiateria und Räucherritus als Zeugnissen des Orientalisierungsprozesses im Mittelmeergebiet während des frühen 1. Jahrtausends v. Chr.', *Centre d'Études Chypriotes, Cahier* 29, 9-31.

Mazar, A. 1994: 'The 11th century B.C. in the land of Israel', 39-58 in Karageorghis (ed.) 1994.

Merrillees, R.S. 1968: *The Cypriote Bronze Age Pottery found in Egypt* (SIMA XVIII). Lund.

Merrillees, R.S. 1971: 'The early history of Late Cypriote I', *Levant* 3, 56-79.

Merrillees, R.S. 1989: 'Highs and lows in the Holy Land. Opium in Biblical times', *Eretz-Israel* 20, 148-154.

Morhange, C. *et al.* 2000: 'Recent Holocene paleo-environmental evolution and coastline changes of Kition, Larnaca, Cyprus, Mediterranean Sea', *Marine Geology* 170, 205-230.

Morris, I. 2000: *Archaeology as Cultural History. Words and Things in Iron Age Greece.* Oxford

Muhly, J.D. 1980: 'Bronze figurines and Near Eastern metalwork', *Israel Exploration Journal* 30, 148-161.

Muhly, J.D. 1999: 'The Phoenicians in the Aegean', 517-526 in Betancourt *et al.* (eds) 1999.

Muhly, J.D., Maddin, R. and Stech, T. 1988: 'Cyprus, Crete and Sardinia: copper ox-hide ingots and the Bronze Age metals trade', *RDAC* (Part 1), 281-298.

Negbi, O. and Negbi, M. 1983: 'Stirrup jars versus Canaanite jars: their contents and reciprocal trade', 319-329 in Zerner (ed) 1993.

Nicolaou, I. and Nicolaou, K. 1989: *Kazaphani. A Middle/Late Cypriot tomb at Kazaphani-Ayios Andronikos: T.2A*, B. Nicosia.

Niemeier, W.-D. 2001: 'Archaic Greeks in the Orient: textual and archaeological evidence', *BASOR* 322, 10-32.

Nowicki, K. 2000: *Defensible sites in Crete c. 1200-800 B.C. (LM IIIB/IIIC through Early Geometric) (Aegaeum* 21). Liège-Austin.

Ohnefalsch-Richter, M. 1893: *Kypros, die Bibel und Homer*. Berlin.

Oren, E.D. (ed.) 2000: *The Sea Peoples and their World: a Reassessment* (University Museum Monograph 108). Philadelphia.

Papadopoulos, T. (ed.) 1997: Ἱστορία τῆς Κύπρου, Vol. Αʹ, Ἀρχαία Κύπρος, Μέρος Αʹ. Nicosia.

Pecorella, P.E. 1977: *Le tombe dell'età del Bronzo Tardo della necropoli a mare di Ayia Irini 'Paleokastro'*. Rome.

Pelon, O. 1976: *Tholoi, tumuli et cercles funéraires*. Paris.

Peltenburg, E.J. 1974: 'Appendix I. The glazed vases', 105-144 in Karageorghis 1974.

Peltenburg, E.J. 1991: 'Greeting gifts and luxury faience: a context for orientalising trends in late Mycenaean Greece', 162-179 in Gale (ed.) 1991.

Peltenburg, E.J. (ed.) 1989: *Early Society in Cyprus*. Edinburgh.

Petit, T. 1991-92: 'L'origine des cités-royaumes Chypriotes à l'Âge du Fer. Le cas d'Amathonte', *Université de Saint-Etienne, Études d'Histoire*, 5-17.

Petit, T. 2001: 'The first palace of Amathus and the Cypriot progenesis', 53-75 in *The Royal Palace Institution in the First Millennium BC* (Monographs of the Danish Institute at Athens 4). Athens.

Phelps, W. *et al.* (eds) 1999: *The Point Iria Wreck. Interconnections in the Mediterranean ca. 1200 B.C. (Proceedings of the International Conference, Island of Spetses, 19th September 1998)*. Athens.

Pieridou, A. 1964: 'A Cypro-Geometric cemetery at 'Vathyrkakas' Karavas', *RDAC*, 114-129.

Pilides, D.M. 1992: 'Handmade burnished ware in Cyprus: an attempt at its interpretation', 179-189 in Ioannides (ed.) 1992.

Pilides, D.M. 1994: *Handmade Burnished Wares of the Late Bronze Age in Cyprus (SIMA* CV). Jonsered.

Pini, I. 1979: 'Cypro-Aegean cylinder seals. On the definition and origin of the class', 121-127 in Karageorghis (ed.) 1979.

Pope, M.H. 1981: 'The cult of the dead at Ugarit', 159-179 in G.D. Young (ed.), *Ugarit in Retrospect. Fifty years of Ugarit and Ugaritic*. Winona Lake.

Popham, M. 1979: 'Connections between Crete and Cyprus between 1300-1100 B.C.', 178-191 in Karageorghis (ed.) 1979.

Popham, M. 1995: 'An engraved Near Eastern bronze bowl from Lefkandi', *Oxford Journal of Archaeology* 14, 103-106.

Popham, M. *et al.* 1993: M.R. Popham, P.G. Calligas and L.H. Sackett, *Lefkandi* II. *The Proto-Geometric Building at Toumba*. Oxford.

Porada, E. 1971: 'Appendix I. Seals', 783-810 in Dikaios 1969-71.

Porada, E. 1983: 'Appendix II. A seal ring and two cylinder seals from Hala Sultan Tekke', 219-220 in P. Åström *et al.*, *Hala Sultan Tekke 8. Excavations 1971-79*. Göteborg.

Prayon, F. 2000: 'Tomb architecture', 335-343 in M. Torelli (ed.), *The Etruscans*. Milan.

Principi Etruschi tra Mediterraneo ed Europa. Marsilio pub. Bologna, 2000.

Pulak, C. 1991: 'The Late Bronze Age shipwreck at Ulu Burun, 1991 field season: 'ingot summer'', *Institute for Nautical Archaeology Newsletter* 18.4, 4-10.

Pulak, C. 1998: 'The Ulu Burun shipwreck: an overview', *The International Journal of Nautical Archaeology* 27.3, 188-224.

Pulak, C. 2001: 'The cargo of the Uluburun ship and evidence for trade with the Aegean and beyond', 13-60 in L. Bonfante and V. Karageorghis (eds), *Italy and Cyprus in Antiquity: 1500-450 BC*. Nicosia.

Quilici, L. 1990: *La tomba dell'età del Bronzo Tardo dall'abitate di Paleokastro presso Ayia Irini*. Rome.

Raptou, E. 1999: 'Une 'fête champêtre' à Amathonte et le culte d'Héra à Chypre', *RDAC*, 207-222.

Rethemiotakis, G. 1997a: 'A chest-shaped vessel and other LM IIIC pottery from Kastelli-Pediada', 407-421 in Driessen and Farnoux (eds) 1997.

Rethemiotakis, G. 1997b: 'Late Minoan III pottery from Kastelli Pediada', 305-336 in Hallager and Hallager (eds) 1997.

Reyes, A.T. 1994: *Archaic Cyprus. A Study of the Textual and Archaeological Evidence*. Oxford.

Richardson, N.J. 1991: 'Homer and Cyprus', 125-128 in Karageorghis (ed.) 1991.

Ridgway, D. 1997: 'Nestor's cup and the Etruscans', *Oxford Journal of Archaeology* 16, 325-344.

Rizzo, M.A. and Martelli, M. 1988-89: 'Un incunabolo del mito greco in Etruria', *Annuario della Scuola Archeologica di Atene* LXVI-LXVII, 7-56.

Ross Holloway, R. 1981: *Italy and the Aegean, 3000-700 B.C. (Archaeologia Transatlantica* I). Louvain-la-Neuve.

Ross Holloway, R. 2000: *The Archaeology of Ancient Sicily*. London-New York.

Rupp, D.W. 1987: 'Vive le Roi: the emergence of the state in Iron Age Cyprus', 147-168 in D.W. Rupp (ed.), *Western Cyprus: Connections (SIMA* LXXVII). Göteborg.

Rupp, D.W. 1988: 'The 'Royal Tombs' at Salamis (Cyprus): ideological messages of power and authority', *Journal of Mediterranean Archaeology* 1, 111-139.

Rupp, D.W. 1989: 'Puttin' on the Ritz: manifestations of high status in Iron Age Cyprus', 336-362 in Peltenburg (ed.) 1989

Rutter, J. 1992: 'Cultural novelties in the post-palatial Aegean world: indices of vitality or decline?' 61-78 in Ward and Joukowski (eds) 1992.

Rystedt, E. 1987: 'Oxhide ingots or campstools? Notes on a motif in Mycenaean pictorial vase painting', *RDAC*, 49-53.

Schaeffer, C.F.A. 1952: *Enkomi-Alasia*. Paris.

Schaeffer, C.F.A. 1971: *Alasia* I. Paris.

Schilardi, D.U. 1984: 'The LH IIIC period at the Koukounaries acropolis, Paros', 184-206 in J.A. MacGillivray and R.L.N. Barber (eds), *The Prehistoric Cyclades. Contributions to a workshop on Cycladic chronology*. Edinburgh.

Schilardi, D.U. 1992: 'Paros and the Cyclades after the fall of the Mycenaean palaces', 621-639 in J-P. Olivier (ed), *Mykenaïka, Actes du IXe Colloque international sur les textes mycéniens et égéens (BCH* Supplément XXV). Paris.

Schilardi, D.U. 1995: Παρατηρήσεις γιά τήν Ἀκρόπολη τῶν Κουκουναριῶν καί τῆ Μυκηναϊκή Πάρο κατά τόν 12ο αἰ. π.Χ.', Ἐπετηρίδα τῆς Ἑταιρείας Κυκλαδικῶν Μελετῶν IB, 481-506.

Schmidt, G. 1968: *Kyprische Bildwerke aus dem heraion von Samos (Samos* VII). Bonn.

Seeden, H. 1991: 'A tophet in Tyre?', *Berytus* 39, 39-87.

Settis, S. and Ampolo, C. (eds) 1996: *I Greci*. Turin.

Sherratt, E.S. 1992: 'Immigration and archaeology: some indirect reflections', 316-347 in P. Åström (ed.), *Acta Cypria. Acts of an International Congress on Cypriote Archaeology Held in Göteborg on 22-24 August 1991*, Part 2. Jonsered.

Sherratt, E.S. 1994: 'Commerce, iron and ideology: metallurgical innovation in 12th-11th century Cyprus', 59-106 in Karageorghis (ed.) 1994.

Sherratt, E.S. 1998: 'Sea Peoples' and the economic structure of the late second millennium in the eastern Mediterranean', 292-313 in S. Gitin *et al.* (eds) 1998.

Sjöqvist, E. 1940: *Reports on Excavations in Cyprus*. Stockholm.

Snodgrass, A.M. 1980: 'Iron and early metallurgy in the Mediterranean', 335-374 in T.A. Wertime and J.D. Muhly (eds), *The Coming of the Age of Iron*. New Haven - London.

Snodgrass, A.M. 1988: *Cyprus and Early Greek History* (The Bank of Cyprus Cultural Foundation Fourth Annual Lecture). Nicosia.

Snodgrass, A.M. 1994: 'Gains, losses and survivals: what we can infer for the eleventh century B.C.', 167-175 in Karageorghis (ed.) 1994.

South, A.K. 1982: 'Kalavasos-Ayios Dhimitrios 1980-81', *RDAC*, 60-68.

South, A.K. 1988: 'Kalavasos-Ayios Dhimitrios 1987: an important ceramic group from Building X', *RDAC*, 223-228.

South, A.K. 1991: 'Kalavasos-Ayios Dhimitrios 1990', *RDAC*, 131-139.

South, A.K. 1994: 'Urbanism and trade in the Vasilikos Valley in the Late Bronze Age', 187-197 in S. Bourke and J-P. Descoeudres, *Trade, Contact and the Movement of Peoples in the Eastern Mediterranean*. Sydney.

South, A.K. 1997: 'Kalavasos-Ayios Dhimitrios 1992-1996', *RDAC*, 151-175.

South, A.K. 2000: 'Late Bronze Age burials at Kalavasos-Ayios Dhimitrios', 345-364 in Ioannides and Hadjistylli (eds) 2000.

Stager, L. 1991: 'When did the Philistines arrive in Canaan? Multiple clues help unravel the mystery', *Biblical Archaeology Review* XVII, 10-19.

Stager, L. 1995: 'The impact of the Sea Peoples in Canaan (1185-1050 BCE)', 332-348 in T. Levy (ed.), *Archaeology of Society in the Holy Land*. New York.

Stampolidis, N.C. 1995: 'Homer and the cremation burials of Eleutherna', 289-338 in Crielaard (ed.) 1995.

Stampolidis, N.C. 1996: *Eleutherna. Antipoina*. Rethymno.

Steel, L. 1993: 'The establishment of the city kingdoms

in Iron Age Cyprus: an archaeological commentary', *RDAC*, 147-156.

Steel, L. 1994: 'Representations of a shrine on a Mycenaean chariot crater from Kalavasos-Ayios Dhimitrios, Cyprus', *BSA* 89, 201-211.

Steel, L. 1997: 'Pictorial White Slip: the discovery of a new ceramic style in Cyprus', 37-47 in Karageorghis *et al.* (eds) 1997.

Steel, L. 1998: 'The social impact of Mycenaean imported pottery in Cyprus', *BSA* 93, **285**-296.

Stylianou, P.J. 1992: *The Age of the Kingdoms. A political History of Cyprus in the Archaic and Classical Periods* (Ίδρυμα Άρχιεπισκόπου Μακαρίου Γ΄, Μελέται καί Υπομνήματα). Nicosia.

Swiny, S. 1997: 'Ή Πρώιμη Έποχή τού Χαλκού', 213-236 in Papadopoulos (ed.) 1997.

Swiny, S., Hohlfelder, R.L. and Swiny, H.W. (eds) 1998: *Res Maritimae. Cyprus and the Eastern Mediterranean from Prehistory to Late Antiquity* (*CAARI Monograph* 1). Atlanta.

Taylor, J. du P. 1952: 'A Late Bronze Age settlement at Apliki, Cyprus', *Antiquaries Journal* 32, 133-167.

Taylor, J. 1957: *Myrtou-Pigadhes. A Late Bronze Age Sanctuary in Cyprus*. Oxford.

Tegou, E. in prep.: 'Θολωτός τάφος τῆς πρώϊμης Έποχης του Σιδήρου στήν Παντάνασσα Άμαρίου Ν. Ρεθύμνης'.

Thalmann, J.P. 1977: 'Céramique trouvée à Amathonte', 65-86 in E. Gjerstad (ed.), *Greek Geometric and Archaic Pottery found in Cyprus* (*Acta Instituti Atheniensis Regni Sueciae* XXVI). Stockholm.

Todd, I.A. 2001: 'Early connections of Cyprus with Anatolia', 203-213 in Karageorghis (ed.) 2001.

Vagnetti, L. 1986: 'Cypriot elements beyond the Aegean in the Bronze Age', 201-216 in Karageorghis (ed.) 1986.

Vagnetti, L. 1996: 'Espansione e diffusione dei Micenei', 133-172 in Settis and Ampolo (eds) 1996.

Vagnetti, L. 1999: 'Mycenaeans and Cypriots in the Central Mediterranean before and after 1200 B.C.', 187-208 in Phelps *et al.* (eds) 1999.

Vagnetti, L. and Lo Schiavo, F. 1989: 'Late Bronze Age long distance trade in the Mediterranean: the role of the Cypriots', 217-243 in Peltenburg (ed.) 1989.

Van Wees, H. 1995: 'Social event and social structure in Homer', 146-182 in Crielaard (ed.) 1995.

Vermeule, E. and Karageorghis, V. 1982: *Mycenaean Pictorial Vase Painting*. Cabridge(Mass.) - London.

Vermeule, E. and Wolsky, F. 1990: *Toumba tou Skourou. A Bronze Age Potters' Quarter on Morphou Bay in Cyprus*. Cambridge, Mass.

Vichos, Y. 1999: 'The Point Iria wreck: the nautical dimension', 77-98 in Phelps *et al.* (eds) 1999.

Vichos, Y. and Lolos, Y. 1997: 'The Cypro-Mycenaean wreck at Point Iria in the Argolic Gulf: first thoughts on the origin and nature of the vessel', 321-337 in Swiny, Hohlfelder and Swiny (eds) 1997.

Wachsmann, S. 1997: 'Were the Sea Peoples Mycenaeans? The evidence of ship iconography', 339-356 in Swiny, Hohlfelder and Swiny (eds) 1997.

Ward, W.A. and Joukowski, M.S. (eds) 1992: *The Crisis Years: the 12th Century B.C. From Beyond the Danube to the Tigris*. Dubuque.

Watrous, L.V. 1992: *Kommos III. The Late Bronze Age Pottery*. Princeton.

White, D. 1985: 'Excavations on Bates' Island, Marsa Matruh', *Journal of the American Research Center in Egypt* XXIII, 75-84.

Wilson, V. 1980: 'The Tubbs-Munro excavations at Salamis 1890', 59-70 in Yon (ed.) 1980.

Winter, I.J. 1990: Review of Markoe 1985, *Gnomon* 62, 236-241.

Winther, H.C. 1997: 'Princely tombs of the Orientalizing period in Etruria and *Latium Vetus*', 423-446 in H.D. Anderson *et al.* (eds), *Urbanization in the Mediterranean in the 9th to 6th centuries BC* (*Acta Hyperborea* 7). Copenhagen.

Wright, G.R.H. 1992: *Ancient Building in Cyprus*. Leiden-New York-Cologne.

Yon, M. 1971: *La tombe T.I du XIe s. av. J.-C.* (*Salamine de Chypre* II). Paris.

Yon, M. 1974: *Un dépôt de sculpture archaïque* (*Salamine de Chypre* V). Paris.

Yon, M. 1980a: 'La fondation de Salamine', 71-80 in Yon (ed.) 1980.

Yon, M. 1980b: 'Rhytons chypriotes à Ougarit', *RDAC*, 79-83.

Yon, M. 1984: 'Fouilles françaises à Kition-Bamboula (Chypre) 1976-1982', *CRAI*, 80-97.

Yon, M. 1985: 'Mission Archéologique Française de Kition-Bamboula 1976-1985', 219-226 in V. Karageorghis (ed.), *Archaeology in Cyprus 1960-1985*. Nicosia.

Yon, M. 1997: *La cité d'Ougarit sur le tell de Ras Shamra*. Paris.

Yon, M. 1999a: 'Salamis and Kition in the 11th-9th century B.C.: cultural homogeneity or divergence', 17-33 in Iacovou and Michaelides (eds) 1999.

Yon, M. 1999b: 'Chypre et Ougarit à la fin du Bronze Récent', *RDAC*, 113-119.

Yon, M., Bordreuil, M.P. and Malbran-Labat, F. 1995: 'La Maison d'Outenou dans le quartier sud d'Ougarit (fouilles 1994). Les archives de la Maison d'Ourtenou', *CRAI*, 427-456.

Yon, M. and Sznycer, M. 1991: 'Une inscription phénicienne royale de Kition', *CRAI*, 791-823.

Yon, M. *et al.* 2000: M. Yon, V. Karageorghis and N. Hirschfeld, *Céramiques mycéniennes. Ras Shamra Ougarit* XIII. Paris-Nicosia.

Yon, M. (ed.) 1980: *Salamine de Chypre, Histoire et Archéologie. État des recherches* (*Colloques Internationaux du Centre National de la Recherche Scientifique, no. 578. Lyon 13-17 mars 1978*). Paris.

Zerner, C. (ed.) 1993: *Wace and Blegen. Pottery as Evidence for Trade in the Aegean Bronze Age, 1939-1989*. Amsterdam.

Index

Photographic Credits

The main source of the photographs and drawings in this book is the archive of the author, except for the following:

Archaeological Museum, Sassari, Sardinia: 59

Art Museum, Princeton: 395-396

Ashmolean Museum, Oxford: 193, 255

Paul Åström: 182, 190, 225-226, 228, 231

Bank of Cyprus Cultural Foundation: 70, 77-84, 93-94, 371-372, 419-420, 422

Bible Lands Museum, Jerusalem: 203

Sir John Boardman: 102

Trustees of The British Museum: 9, 201-202, 204-205, 365-366, 382, 393, 397

Gerald Cadogan: 129, 131-132

Cyprus Museum, Nicosia: 24, 30-32, 38, 49, 64-66, 68-69, 71, 89, 95, 173, 175, 177, 206, 229-230, 233, 238-240, 289-290, 292, 304-305, 375-376

Franz Maier: 232

E. Di Miro: 58

Sophocles Hadjisavvas: 104-105, 178-179

Hebrew University of Jerusalem, Institute of Archaeology: 227

Kunsthistorisches Museum, Vienna: 389

J. and E. Lagarce: 114, 119-120, 183

Yannos Lolos: 116, 134-135

Medelhavsmuseet, Stockholm: 11, 111, 174, 377, 388

Trustees of The Metropolitan Museum of Art, New York: 16, 73-74, 76, 109, 198-199, 286, 303, 313, 321-322, 390-392, 400, 402

Musée d'Art et d'Histoire, Geneva: 403

National Museum of Denmark, Copenhagen: 106

Pierides Foundation Museum, Larnaca: 379

Cemal Pulak, Institute of Nautical Archaeology, Texas A and M: 44, 51-55

Réunion des musées nationaux and the Département des Antiquités, Musée du Louvre: 45, 48, 90, 112, 189, 191, 378

Royal Ontario Museum, Canada: 197

Costakis and Leto Severis Foundation, Nicosia: 8, 21-22, 39

Alison South: 46, 47, 56, 60-63, 110, 126-128, 130

Vorderasiatisches Museum, Berlin: 320

Marguerite Yon: 234, 248, 251.

Figs. 15 and 41 are after Vermeule and Wolsky 1990, figs. 2 and 30, pls 182-183.

This book was printed for Mondadori Electa S.p.A.
by Martellago Mondadori Printing S.p.A.
Via Castellana 98, Martellago (Venice) in the year 2002